A HUNTER'S WANDERINGS

IN AFRICA

BEING

A NARRATIVE OF NINE YEARS SPENT AMONGST THE GAME OF THE FAR INTERIOR OF SOUTH AFRICA

CONTAINING ACCOUNTS OF EXPLORATIONS BEYOND THE ZAMBESI, ON THE RIVER CHOBE AND IN THE MATABELE AND MASHUNA COUNTRIES, WITH FULL NOTES UPON THE NATURAL HISTORY AND PRESENT DISTRIBUTION OF ALL THE LARGE MAMMALIA

BY

FREDERICK COURTENEY SELOUS

WITH INTRODUCTION BY
MIKE RESNICK, SERIES EDITOR

A NARROW ESCAPE; MASHUNA LAND, SEPTEMBER 17, 1878.

See page 365.

A HUNTER'S WANDERINGS
IN AFRICA

BEING

A NARRATIVE OF NINE YEARS SPENT AMONGST THE GAME OF THE FAR INTERIOR OF SOUTH AFRICA

CONTAINING ACCOUNTS OF EXPLORATIONS BEYOND THE ZAMBESI, ON THE RIVER CHOBE AND IN THE MATABELE AND MASHUNA COUNTRIES, WITH FULL NOTES UPON THE NATURAL HISTORY AND PRESENT DISTRIBUTION OF ALL THE LARGE MAMMALIA

BY

FREDERICK COURTENEY SELOUS

WITH INTRODUCTION BY
MIKE RESNICK, SERIES EDITOR

THE RESNICK LIBRARY
OF AFRICAN ADVENTURE

No. 6 in the series

Publisher: Ralph Roberts
Vice-President/Operations: Pat Roberts

Resnick Library of African Adventure
Series Editor: Mike Resnick

Editor: Ralph Roberts

Cover Design: Ralph Roberts
Interior Design & Electronic Page Assembly: **WorldComm**®
Photographs as indicated

Originally published in 1881.

ISBN 1-57090-141-4   trade paper
ISBN 1-57090-142-2 limited edition hardback

Alexander Books—a division of Creativity, Inc.—is a full–service publisher located at 65 Macedonia Road, Alexander NC 28701. Phone (828) 252–9515, Fax (828) 255–8719. For orders only: 1-800-472-0438. Visa and MasterCard accepted.

Alexander Books is distributed to the trade by Midpoint Trade Books, Inc., 27 West 20th Street, New York NY 10011, (212) 727-0190, (212) 727-0195 fax.

This book is also available on the internet in the **Publishers CyberMall.** Set your browser to **http://abooks.com** and enjoy the many fine values available there.

INTRODUCTION

Frederick Courteney Selous is generally acknowledged as the greatest African hunter of all time. I personally would argue that that particular honor goes to W.D.M. "Karamojo" Bell, but I hasten to add that I'm in a minority. Be that as it may, while Selous was first and foremost a hunter, he was also a man of many other accomplishments as well. He was a trusted lieutenant of Cecil Rhodes, who gave him full credit for opening Rhodesia and winning the Second Matebele War. He was a close personal friend of President Theodore Roosevelt. He was a naturalist whose careful observations and succinct writings were read by layman and scholar alike. The African wing of the British Museum of Natural History is named after him, and a bust of him is prominently displayed. The largest nature reserve in the world, Tanzania's Selous Reserve, bears his name. The crack special forces unit in the Zimbabwe War of Independence was the Selous Scouts. There was even a stakes-winning American racehorse who carried his name not too many years ago.

He has also been a constant source of inspiration to those who write about the exotic lands where he spent most of his life. He was the model for H. Rider

Haggard's Allan Quatermain, the first of whose adventures were published in 1885, and more than a century later he was still appearing in such diverse places as an Indiana Jones television adventure and my own science fiction novelette, "Every Man a God," as well as my novel *Purgatory* (Tor, 1993) where he appears, thinly disguised, as "T.J. Fuentes."

What kind of a man makes such a lasting impression, reaching over the generations to people who were born decades after he himself died?

Well, he was born in London on New Year's Eve of 1851. We don't know much about his youth except that he was continually in trouble with his headmaster for cutting classes and collecting birds' eggs from private land (his passion for birds' eggs remained with him throughout his life, and his collection, while not the largest, was considered to have some of the finest specimens in the world). We also know that he read Baldwin's *African Hunting From the Natal to the Zambezi*, and that it shaped his life, for from that day forth he had only one desire: to become a big game hunter in Africa.

Success did not readily come to Selous upon his arrival in the Dark Continent. His rifle was stolen before he had a chance to fire it, and his first trip inland in search of game was a dismal failure. Undaunted, he went deeper into the unexplored interior, and became one of the first hunters to reach the capital of the mighty Lobengula, king of the Matabele. When he asked Lobengula's permission to hunt elephant on Matabele land, the king found the notion of such a young boy facing such huge creatures uproariously funny. He asked Selous if he had ever so much as seen an elephant, and Selous answered truthfully that he hadn't. That struck the king's funnybone again, and he gave his permission, doubtless sure that the young Londoner would die beneath the feet and tusks of the first elephant he encountered.

It was all the encouragement Selous needed. He promptly collected 450 pounds of ivory from bulls he shot, traded with the Matabele for another 1,200 pounds, and made a quick profit of some three hundred pounds sterling, a sum which enabled a man to live like royalty in Africa in 1870.

He continued hunting for his livelihood through 1888, spending most of his time in Southern Africa (and especially those areas now known as Botswana and Zimbabwe), but then became closely involved with Cecil Rhodes' efforts to occupy Mashonaland, shortly to become known as Southern Rhodesia (and, still later, Zimbabwe).

Rhodes initially felt he could overrun Logenbula's army with a small force of hardened veterans, but Selous, who knew both Logenbula and the territory far better, convinced him that this would be suicidal, and talked Rhodes into building a road *around* the Matabele territory and then going north to the Portugese frontier.

The scheme worked, and Mashonaland soon came peacefully under British rule. (Actually, it *officially* came under the rule of the British South Africa Company, but in practice they were one and the same.)

It was entirely due to Selous' innovative suggestion, and his willingness to implement it, treating with the various tribes while the road was under construction, that Rhodes was able to annex Mashonaland, but although Rhodes himself called Selous "the man above all others to whom we owe Rhodesia to the British Crown," he actually treated Selous rather shabbily, breaking a number of promises to him and finally refusing to see him at all, now that his usefulness was seemingly at an end.

"Seemingly" was the key word, for in 1893 the Matabele, known for their warlike nature and inhospitability toward intruders, took up arms against the colonists. Selous acted as Chief of Scouts, heading a column of 700 white irregulars and a handful of disenchanted Matabele, and within a year had put down the insurrection, getting wounded in the process. Again, once the perceived need for him was no longer there, he became the invisible man to Rhodes.

Selous returned to England in 1894, where, because of the book you now hold in your hands and his part in the Matabele war, he found himself a hero and a celebrity. He took time off to court and marry Marie Maddy and write up his experiences in the service of Cecil Rhodes, *Sunshine and Storm in Rhodesia*, then went on an Asian hunting expedition.

Shortly thereafter, he linked up with Rowland Ward, the taxidermist-turned-publisher, and for the first time in his life he no longer had to hunt for a living; from this point forward, his writing generated enough income for him to go where he wanted and do what pleased him. Which meant that he still hunted, but now it was for trophies, for museums, and for pleasure.

(One of the great disappointments facing the visitor to the Selous section of the British Museum of Natural History is the absence of the many excellent trophies Selous' widow turned over to them. The last time I was there they were all stored away — still in excellent condition — in a sub-basement, near the record tusks of the fabled Kilimanjaro Elephant. When I asked why they were not on display, the answer seemed ridiculous: Selous did not kill these animals on license, and therefore they were illegally poached. The argument would hold a lot more water if they had *had* hunting licenses back then.)

By the time his *Sport and Travel East and West* appeared, he had struck up a correspondence with Theodore Roosevelt, one that would last throughout the rest of his life. He paid a number of visits to the White House, exchanged observations about wildlife with the enthusiastic President, and finally wrote *African Nature Notes and Reminiscences* at Roosevelt's behest.

"Mr. Selous," wrote the President, "is much more than a mere big-game hunter, however; he is by instinct a keen field naturalist, an observer with a power of seeing, and remembering what he has seen; and finally he is a writer who possesses to a very marked and unusual degree the power vividly and accurately to put on paper his observations...His book is a genuine contribution alike to hunting lore and to natural history." Fine praise indeed, coming from literally the most popular man in the world at the time.

It is commonly believed that Selous acted as Roosevelt's white hunter during the ex-President's 1909-1910 safari — the famous photo of Roosevelt and Selous sitting on the front of the engine, just above the cow-catcher, on the train ride from Mombasa to Nairobi has done nothing to dispel the notion — but this is not the case. Selous is the one who talked him into it, and outfitted it, making all the necessary arrangements for the first major safari in history, including the hiring of 500 porters, but his domain was Southern Africa, and he felt that Roosevelt needed men around him who knew East Africa. To that end, he wisely engaged William Judd and R.J. Cunninghame as Roosevelt's guides and hunters.

Selous continued hunting all over the world and collecting his birds' eggs until World War I broke out in 1914. Though 63 years old, he immediately volunteered for service, and was sent to East Africa as a Lieutenant, where he found himself serving with Richard Meinertzhagen, another old-time hunter (and the author of *Kenya Diary*).

The Fusiliers were as idiosyncratic in personnel as Roosevelt's Rough Riders, and they were sent out after the brilliant German commander, Paul von Lettow-Vorbeck, chasing him fruitlessly all over Tanganyika. Within half a year they had lost more than a third of their 1,100 men, more to disease than to battle, and within another six months they were down to less than 450 men. Selous, the hardened old Africa hand, withstood every disease that knocked out his younger, stronger comrades. He shrugged off malaria, avoided dysentary, seemed immune to bilharzia — but there was one physical problem he couldn't ignore, though he did his best: hemorrhoids. He held out for more than a year, saddling up every morning, treating them with ointment in the evenings, but finally he could stand the excruciating pain no longer, and in June of 1916 he was sent home for hemorrhoid surgery, hardly a common procedure back then. It proved successful and, amazingly, he was back in Africa again in August.

This time he had a battalion of 1,400 men, but once again, disease and von Lettow-Vorbeck took a tremendous toll, and by December he was down to under 600 men, more than 200 of them unfit for duty. The British finally caught up with the Germans just after New Year's Day of 1917, and engaged in a number of hand-to-hand, bayonet-wielding encounters.

Then came the fateful morning of January 4. Let us turn to Captain R. J. Haines of the South African Forces for an account of it:

> *"Captain Selous...was literally adored by the men. From a boy he had always been a hero of mine.*
>
> *"The day he was killed, I passed him in the morning with his company. I was driving an armoured machine-gun, as the driver was ill. As I passed him, I shouted out, 'I shall be back and have tea with you today, sir,' for we used to joke him about his habit of drinking tea with every meal.*
>
> *"That was the last I saw of him. There was some fighting in the bush, and when I came back in the afternoon I was greeted with news of his death. I was just in time*

to see him buried. He was sewn up in a blanket, and buried with five other men of the Royal Fusiliers. I was told he was wounded in the right arm, which was bandaged up, and he remained with the company.

"A little later he was again hit in the mouth and was killed instantaneously and apparently painlessly."

He was buried at approximately Latitude 7 degrees South, Longitude 38 degrees East, in the heart of what is now the Selous Reserve.

Selous left a lot of legacies. Not the least was his trophy collection, which his widow turned over to the Natural History Museum. More important was his writing, which always strove for accuracy, and disdained heroic description (though many of the events, no matter how much he tried to downplay them, came across as heroic for the very simple reason that they *were* heroic.)

Most important of all, I think, was the sense of proportion and rationality he brought to hunting through both his example and his writings. Given his status as the most famous of African hunters, and his access to the public through his arrangement with Rowland Ward, he could have perpetuated many of the myths of both Africa and hunting. Instead he described the life of the African hunter as it really was, debunking the braggarts, meticulously observing the intricate patterns of Nature, examining the native populace with an understanding not often seen before, and relating his adventures with a combination of honesty and modesty.

He was quick to dispute what he considered inaccuracies in the works of others. For example, where David Livingstone had written that one feels no pain while being mauled by a lion, Selous, who had undergone maulings himself, pointed out that it hurt like hell. (Though it may be that Livingstone was in shock, while the more self-reliant Selous was struggling to free himself.)

He also judged men by their merits and not their color, which was rarer than you might think for a man of his era and in his situation, and his observations and experiences led him to conclude that the Zulus were far more admirable and courageous than the Boers, a statement that might have gotten him jailed in 1879 (or in 1979, come to think of it.)

When other hunters and writers claimed that there were distinct subspecies of lion and black rhinoceros, Selous refused to take their word for it, and set out to learn the truth for himself. He shot samples of each, measured them, weighed them, had the pelts and horns analyzed, meticulously drew pictures of each, and concluded that neither animal possessed any subspecies — a conclusion that science has since verified.

He was dubious of all unsubstantiated claims to world-record status by hunters, remarking wryly that "Animals shrink before the tape measure."

One would think that he ranked among the leading killers of African fauna, but in fact that is far from the case. He was extremely selective (his lifetime total of lions, for example, was 31, most killed for pelts, a few for meat (of which he was inordinately fond) and, in his own words, "I never killed an animal for mere sport."

But while he didn't kill for sport, he was a sportsman to the core, a man of whom Roosevelt later said, "There was never a more welcome guest at the White House than Frederick Selous." He not only encouraged the President to come to Africa on safari, but used to delight the Roosevelt children by acting out the parts of all the animals he had encountered.

His friend and biographer, John G. Millais, summed up his character thus:

"Perhaps Selous' chief success as a hunter lay in his untiring energy and fearless intention to gain some desired object. He brought the same force into play in pursuit of a bull elephant as of a small butterfly, and allowed nothing to stand in his way to achieve success. Time, distance, difficulty, or danger were all things that could be conquered by a man of strong will, and his bodily strength was such that even to the end he almost achieved the virility of perfect youth."

Roosevelt added that "It is well for any country to produce men of such a type; and if there are enough of them the nation need fear no decadence."

When Selous left England as a young man, he wrote, "If I can't get good shooting and fishing in this world, I'll get it in the next."

Well, he certainly got it here... and given his determination, one suspects that he is currently stalking a herd of elephants across some heavenly savannah.

— Mike Resnick

PREFACE

SINCE Baldwin's book upon African hunting appeared, now nearly twenty years ago, no work has been published which can be considered in any way as a guide for men who are about to visit the interior of South Africa in search of sport, and would wish to know the state of the country at the present day from a sportsman's point of view.

This want I hope that the present volume may to some extent supply, for as during eight years I have led the life of a professional elephant-hunter, my pages are naturally chiefly devoted to the *feræ naturæ*, amongst which I have been constantly living. Some of my conclusions with regard to lions, rhinoceroses, or other animal, may differ from those arrived at by other men equally competent to give an opinion ; but, at all events, they are the result of a long personal experience of the beasts themselves, and have not been influenced in any way by the often unreliable stories of " old hunters."

The seven plates of antelopes' heads form a

complete series, representing every species, from the
smallest to the largest, that is to be met with north
of the Limpopo river up to 12° south latitude.
They have all of them been most carefully drawn
by Mr. J. Smit, to whom my best thanks are due,
from actual specimens now in my possession, which
have been mounted by the well-known taxidermist
Mr. Rowland Ward of Piccadilly, and are therefore
faithful representations as regards markings and
length of horn of the animals themselves.

At the end of the book I have appended some
game lists kept during my last two hunting expeditions.   This has not been done out of any wish to
show what a large bag I have made ; but as it has
been copied from my game book, kept carefully from
day to day, I think it will give any one intending to
visit the interior of South Africa a better idea of the
sort of sport and the different species of game he is
likely to fall in with at the present day in different
parts of the country, than any detailed description.
Sometimes it certainly represents all the game I was
able to shoot, with an immense amount of hard
work ; at others it does not record one-fourth part
of what I might have killed had I wished to make a
bag.   Some people may consider it a dreadful record
of slaughter, but it must be remembered by these,
that I was often accompanied by a crowd of hungry
savages, exclusive of the men in my employ, all of

whom were entirely dependent upon me for their daily food, whilst in some of my expeditions my rifle supplied me almost entirely with the means of obtaining from the natives corn, guides, porters, etc., which better-equipped parties would have paid for with calico, beads, or other merchandise. In some of my journeys I have penetrated into regions hitherto unvisited by Europeans, and in such cases have always made rough sketch-maps, two of which have been published by the Royal Geographical Society. As these expeditions were, however, undertaken in search of elephants and not with any scientific objects, I do not claim any credit to myself for their results.

Some portions of the present volume have already been printed from time to time in the columns of *The Field* newspaper. As the articles in question recounted some of the most interesting of my hunting adventures experienced some years ago when elephants were still plentiful, I make no apology for again reproducing them. My thanks are also due to my sister, Miss A. B. Selous, for the time, trouble, and patience expended by her upon the ten illustrations representing the hunting-scenes which embellish my pages, all of which were drawn under my own supervision, and from my oral descriptions; and also to Mr. Edward Whymper for the careful and painstaking way in which he has diminished these draw-

ings and reproduced them upon the wood.   In conclusion, I have only to add that in the following
pages I have done my best to express myself in
plain, intelligible English ; and if I have not succeeded in this respect as well as I could wish, I trust
that my shortcomings will be leniently judged when
it is remembered that the last nine years of my life
have been passed amongst savages, during which
time I have not undergone the best training for a
literary effort.

THE AUTHOR.

BARRYMORE HOUSE,
   WARGRAVE-ON-THAMES,
     June 1881.

CONTENTS

PART I

CHAPTER I

CHAPTER II

CHAPTER III

CHAPTER IV

CHAPTER V

CHAPTER VI

CHAPTER VII

CHAPTER VIII

CONTENTS

PART II

CONTENTS

CHAPTER XVIII

CHAPTER XIX

CHAPTER XX

CHAPTER XXI

CHAPTER XXII

ILLUSTRATIONS

ILLUSTRATIONS xix

PART I

CHAPTER I

Land at Algoa Bay—Diamond Fields—Trading trip through Griqua-
land—The Chief Manchuran—Batlapin Village—Griqua Town—
Bushman's Lair—Klas Lucas, the Koranna Chief—Bechuanas at
Lange Berg—Appearance of Country—Return to Diamond Fields
—Preparations for Second Expedition.

On the 4th of September 1871, I set foot for the
first time upon the sandy shores of Algoa Bay, with
£400 in my pocket, and the weight of only nineteen
years upon my shoulders. Having carefully read
all the works that had been written on sport and
travel in South Africa, I had long ago determined to
make my way to the interior of that country as soon
as ever circumstances would enable me to do so ; for
the free-and-easy gipsy sort of life described by
Gordon Cumming, Baldwin, and other authors, had
quite captivated my imagination, and done much to
determine me to adopt the life of ever-varying scenes
and constant excitement, which I have never since
regretted, and for which an inborn love of all
branches of Natural History, and that desire so
common amongst our countrymen of penetrating to
regions where no one else has been, in some degree
fitted me.

As I knew no one in Port Elizabeth who might
have given me advice, I determined first of all to

B

make my way to the Diamond Fields, from which place I rightly judged it would be easier to make a final start for the interior than from the coast. Accordingly, as I had too much baggage to allow me to travel by Cobb and Co.'s coach, which was then running, I looked out for a waggon bound for the New El Dorado, which there was little difficulty in finding, and after striking a bargain with a young transport rider [1] named Reuben Thomas, who undertook to convey me and my 300 lbs. of baggage to the Diamond Fields for the sum of £8, I finally left Port Elizabeth two days later on, September 6th.

The journey between the coast and the Diamond Fields is so uninteresting that I will not weary my readers with any account of it, as I wish to devote my pages to narratives of my experiences in those parts of the far interior at present but very imperfectly or not at all known to the general public.

After a very slow journey of nearly two months, we at last, early on the morning of the 28th of October, reached our destination. As we had only travelled at night, allowing the bullocks to rest during the heat of the day, I had been able to do a good deal of shooting in a small way, and in return for an immense amount of hard walking, had managed to bag one bushbuck ram, one duiker, one springbuck, one klipspringer, and eight grey and red rhebucks, all of which I had carried on my own shoulders to the waggons.

On the evening of the day on which I reached the Diamond Fields, a great misfortune befell me, for a small double breech-loading rifle by Reilly, with which I had been shooting along the road, was stolen

[1] In the Cape Colony, carriers who convey goods from one part of the country to another are called "transport riders."

from the waggon, and no endeavours to trace it were of any avail. My armoury was now reduced to a double ten muzzle-loading rifle by Vaughan, a very inferior weapon, as it threw its bullets across one another, and a little double gun that shot well with both shot and bullet.

On the market next morning I bought a horse for £8, and rode over to Pniel. Here I met a fellow-passenger, Mr. Arthur Laing, who had left the ship at Cape Town and gone up to the Fields direct by passenger cart. He told me that he was tired of digging, and was thinking of making a trading trip through Griqualand, and down the Orange river, taking with him as guide and interpreter a man named Crossley, who knew the country and the people, and who, indeed, had been private secretary to Adam Kok, the Griqua chief, and once held a very good position, from which a passionate devotion to the flowing bowl had dragged him down step by step, till he now did not own so much as the shoes he stood in. He was, however, in his sober moments, which, when within ten miles of a canteen, were both short and infrequent, an intelligent and well-informed man. My friend was very anxious that I should join him, and as I had found that the commencement of winter, viz. April or May, was the best season to start for the far interior, I soon made up my mind to do so, thinking the trip would just about occupy the intervening time. Our arrangements were soon made, and on October 31st we loaded up a small wooden-axled waggon which we had bought for £80, and managed to make a start that same evening.

We at first followed the course of the Vaal river, and on the evening of November 2nd, were out-

spanned upon its banks, when a Kafir chief rode up,
accompanied by about twenty followers. He proved
to be Manchuran, one of the most influential chiefs
among the Batlapins; but for all this, after we had
given him and his brother a good dinner, he was not
above begging for sugar, tea, coffee, or anything else
he could think of. A Kafir will seldom miss a thing
for want of asking for it.

Early on the next morning we reached a large
Batlapin village, where we found the houses very
clean, nice, and comfortable. They are divided into
two compartments, whilst outside there is a sort of
verandah, and round the front of the house a yard
very neatly enclosed, and plastered with cow-dung.
Inside, these houses are large and roomy, being at
least eight feet high, and most of them having a
recess in the wall with shelves for pots, etc. At this
village we tried our 'prentice hands at trading. It
was very tedious work, as the natives wanted to look
at everything, and talked a great deal about every
article they inspected before buying anything. Greatly
to my surprise, they paid for what they bought in
hard cash. The following day we left the banks of
the Vaal river, and trekked through a country
covered with wait-a-bit thorn-bushes towards
Campbell's-dorp, an old mission station; on the way
I saw two hartebeests, but could not get a shot at
them. Campbell's-dorp had evidently known better
days, for there were many deserted gardens and
ruined cottages about the place; still, although most
of the people seemed a lazy, poverty-stricken lot,
some of the better class of Griquas were living in
houses quite as comfortable as those of the lower
class of Transvaal Boers.

On November 9th we trekked, and reached Griqua

Town the following day. This place, like Campbell's-dorp, must have seen better days, but was now almost deserted. During the subsequent five weeks we trekked about from one Griqua farm to another all over the country, buying sheep, goats, oxen, and ostrich feathers, but finding no game except a few springbucks and steinbucks.

On the 21st of December we found ourselves on the banks of the Orange river, at a place called Sea-cow's-bath, where dwelt a very decent old Kafir, Hendrick Kieviet by name. The next day I started early to look for rhebuck amongst the hills bordering the river, but never saw a living thing. One might almost as well look for game in Hyde Park as in Griqualand.

The weather was now intensely hot ; every day the thermometer rose to over 100° in the shade ; and at about midnight, with the moon shining gloriously, it still marked 91°.

Christmas Day.—Made a wonderful pudding of meal and eggs, flavoured with chocolate; we also made a sauce of meal, milk, honey, and chocolate. Both pudding and sauce turned out a glorious success, and, considering the paucity of materials at our disposal, I think we had reason to be proud of it. We invited old Hendrick to dinner, and he was enchanted with the pudding, declaring he had never tasted anything like it, and, judging from the amount he stowed away, evidently thinking he never would again.

January 1st found us still trekking westwards along the northern bank of the Orange river. This day we met two Griqua waggons returning from Damaraland, where they had been on an embassy from Waterboer to the Damara king, in reference to allowing the Griquas to settle in his country.

They had, however, been unsuccessful in their negotiations.

January 4th.—Whilst poking about along the river, looking for guinea-fowls, I came upon a Bushman's lair amongst the trees by the water's edge. A few boughs woven together and forming a sort of canopy was all they had in the way of a habitation; the only weapons they possessed were rude-looking bows and neatly-made poisoned arrows, some about two and a half feet in length, fashioned from reeds, whilst others were only a foot long. Their language seemed even fuller of clicks and clucks than the Koranna, and altogether to a casual observer they appeared to be very few steps removed from the brute creation. The following day three more Bushmen came to the waggon begging for tobacco; they were taller and better-looking than those I had first seen.

January 6th.—Reached Klas Lucas's town, a Koranna chief living (in the dry season) at a ford of the Orange river called Olivenhout's drift. While there a hut was struck by lightning, and of the seven Korannas within, two were killed. Here we turned back, and travelling on the same road by which we had come, reached Keis again on the 19th of the month.

From Keis we trekked north to Lange Berg for two days through very heavy sand, and without a drop of water till we reached the farm of Anthony Potgieter, a coloured man from the Cape Colony. Our cattle, sheep, and goats were terribly thirsty, and it was a sight to see how they all rushed into the water. Old Anthony Potgieter turned out to be a very good old fellow, sending us down lots of milk and some bread, which latter was a great treat, for,

having been unable to obtain either corn or maize
from the wretched Korannas, we had tasted nothing
but mutton for twenty-three days. I saw here a
herd of about thirty hartebeests, but as they were on
the side of a hill, and the ground beneath them was
perfectly open, I could not manage to get a shot at
them.

January 27th.—Left Anthony Potgieter's hospitable hut with regret, and trekked northwards amongst
the Lange Berg Kafirs, reaching Michonya's kraal in
the evening. This old fellow was stingy, even for a
Bechuana, which is saying a good deal. These
people, however, seemed industrious, as at every
kraal they had many acres of ground under cultiva-
tion, and they make a great many karosses, which
they sew with great neatness. They seem, too, to
take kindly to the outward signs of civilisation, and
all who can afford it wear European clothing ; but
they are the stingiest, most begging, grasping, and
altogether disagreeable set of people that it is possible
to imagine. Although possessing large herds of
cows and goats, they will not give a stranger a drop
of milk until he pays for it ; but, on the other hand,
they expect him to give them coffee, tobacco, and,
indeed, everything in his waggon, gratis.

February 5th.—Reached Kobetsi's town, where
we found an Englishman named Funnell had established a store, and from him we were enabled to buy
in a stock of meal and other of the almost necessaries
of life, which we had so long been without. From
this place we could see the Kuruman downs, the
mission station being about fifty miles due east.

The country about here was then in fine order,
for, as rain had just fallen, everything looked green.
The whole landscape was thickly wooded, and the

grass very luxuriant. Altogether, it was a glorious
change after the desert country along the Orange
river to which we had been lately accustomed. The
great drawback was, that there was no game whatever,
not even springbucks, the Kafirs having hunted
everything into the far interior, so that now there
is more game within five miles of Cape Town than
here where we were, more than six hundred miles up
country.

We now turned south again, and on the evening
of February 7th once more reached Potgieter's farm.
The two following days I spent in search of hartebeest,
but though I worked hard, I saw none. The next
morning two Bushmen came in and reported that
gemsbuck were common near the Scurfde Berg, a
chain of hills two days westwards from here ; so I
borrowed Potgieter's cart, and started with the Bushmen to try my luck amongst them.

February 15th.—Reached Witte Sand, a large hill
of pure white sand. This white sandhill, surrounded
as it is on all sides by the dark-red sand of the
neighbouring country, is certainly a very remarkable
phenomenon. Weather intensely hot. Passed the
night at a Bushman town.

February 16th.—Started from Scurfde Berg. Saw
gemsbuck and blue wildebeest spoor, but could not
come up with the animals themselves.

February 17th.—Reached Scurfde Berg, where
with great difficulty we gave the oxen water at two
deep rents in the solid rock. These rents were half-
way up the side of a steep craggy hill, and were
filled with rain-water. Saw no gemsbuck. Weather
intensely hot and sultry ; altogether terribly unpropitious for hunting on foot in the deep sand.

February 19th.—The meat we started with from

Potgieter's being consumed, we had to go back at once, as there seemed but small likelihood of our shooting anything here. Eventually, after travelling almost continuously for two days and a night, during all which time we were without food, we once more reached the farm, where I found my friend tired of waiting for me, and anxious to make a start at once for the Diamond Fields.

March 2nd.—Reached Griqua Town. For some days past Laing had been unwell, and he now fell seriously ill. As it was necessary that one of us should remain for some time yet in Griqua Town, in order to get together some cattle, and collect a few debts at some of the neighbouring farms, I hired a waggon, in which my friend travelled at once by forced marches to the Diamond Fields, where good food and attendance quickly pulled him round.

By the 12th I was myself ready to start, and six days later rejoined Laing at Klip Drift, and was rejoiced to find him already convalescent.

Upon reaching the Diamond Fields we sold off the produce of our trading trip—cattle, goats, and ostrich feathers—and found we had made a profit of about £100. My friend then returned to England, whilst I at once set about making preparations for a journey into the far interior. Buying a strong Scotch cart and four oxen, I first trekked back to Griqua Town, where I had already arranged with a trader, one Van Druten, to purchase his waggon, a span of young oxen, and five horses. For the waggon I gave £145, for the oxen £6 : 10s. per head, and for the horses £11 apiece. At the same time I bought for cash some fat oxen and a lot of sheep and goats, which, after trekking back to Klip Drift, where I left my waggon, I drove over to Kimberley, and

sold at a fair profit on the price I had given for
them.

Whilst in Kimberley I met a fellow-passenger, a
young fellow about my own age, named Dorehill, a
son of General Dorehill, with whom I had contracted
a great friendship on board ship.   He was then living
with a Mr. Sadlier, who hailed from the same town
as himself at home, and whom he had met accidentally
at the Diamond Fields.   On my telling him that I
was off in a few days for the interior, he said he
would very much like to come with me, but scarcely
liked to leave his friend.   However, thinking that on
a long expedition such as that I was about to under-
take, it would be better to travel in company with
friends than entirely alone, I proposed to Dorehill to
come, and get Sadlier to come too, and this was
finally agreed upon.   We now prepared for an immediate start, but not having very much money left
to dispose of, and not being able to get anything on
credit, as we had hoped to do, we had to content
ourselves with a supply of Boer meal, sugar, tea,
coffee, and a small quantity of ammunition, which,
with a few beads, completed our outfit.   In the
matter of arms we were not very well off : Sadlier
had an Enfield rifle, Dorehill a Martini-Henry
carbine, and I myself a short Snider, besides the
muzzle-loading double ten, which I had already
found shot so badly as to be almost useless, and my
little shot-gun.

PLATE I

1. ELAND BULL (Oreas Canna).

    Shot in the Mashuna country, Nov. 5, 1878.
    Length of horns, 2 feet 5 inches.

2. GEMSBUCK ♀ (Oryx Gazella).

    Shot near the Botletlie river, May 15, 1879.
    Length of horns, 3 feet 6½ inches.

3. ELAND BULL (Oreas Canna).

    Shot in the Mashuna country, Oct. 5, 1880.
    Length of horns, 2 feet 3 inches.

PLATE I

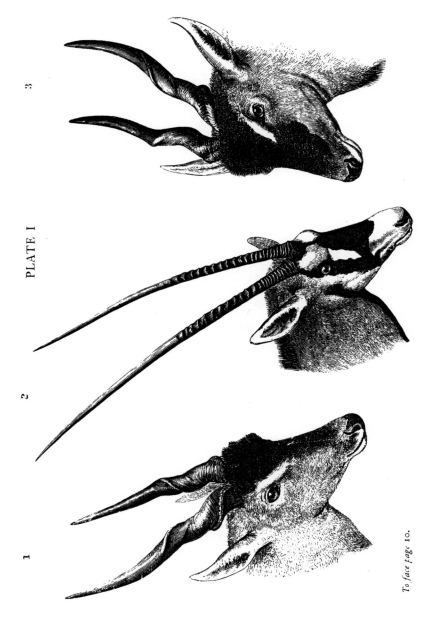

To face page 10.

CHAPTER II

AT length we had everything ready, and in the end
of April 1872, Sadlier, Dorehill, and I crossed the
Vaal river and trekked away towards Kuruman,
where we knew we should strike the main waggon
track to the interior. It was not until the 26th of
May that we reached Kuruman, although it is in
reality only a few days' journey from the Diamond
Fields ; this was chiefly owing to my horses running
away from a place called Daniel's Kuil back to
Griqua Town, and then scattering over the country,
causing a delay of a fortnight before I could recover
them.

Kuruman was by far the prettiest spot I had yet
seen in Africa. In the first place, the eye was delighted by a splendid spring of beautifully clear water,
and, what is most rare in the desert wastes of South-
Western Africa, delightfully shaded by fine trees,
and the magnificent fruit garden originally made by
the Rev. Mr. Moffat was rendered most pleasing by
the large groves of dark-foliaged orange trees, covered

with fruit, unfortunately not quite ripe. We were
most kindly treated by Mr. William Williams, a
trader, who had only the preceding year returned
from a hunting and trading trip in the Matabele
country. He gave me much information about
Matabele Land, and showed me the large-bore
elephant guns which are universally used by the
professional Dutch and native elephant-hunters. I
eventually bought two of these very unprepossessing-
looking weapons, which I will here describe. They
were smooth-bore duck guns of the very commonest
description, taking a round bullet of four ounces, the
guns themselves weighing only $12\frac{1}{2}$ lbs. They were
made by Isaac Hollis of Birmingham, and what they
must have cost originally I am afraid to say, for I
bought them from Mr. Williams after they had been
transported by bullock waggons over 600 miles up
country from Cape Town for £6 apiece. With these
two guns, and another similar but weighing 2 lbs.
heavier, which I bought the following year from a
Dutch hunter for £7 : 10s., and using nothing but
the common trade powder that is sold to the Kafirs
in 5-lb. bags, I killed in three seasons seventy-eight
elephants, all but one of which I shot on foot. Since
then I have shot with very expensive large-bore
breech-loaders and Curtis and Harvey's best powder,
but I have never used or seen used a rifle which drove
better than these common-made old muzzle-loaders.
However, they were so light that, when loaded as
they were by the hand from a leather bag of powder
slung at my side (I find that an ordinary handful of
powder is over twenty drachms), they kicked most
frightfully, and in my case the punishment I received
from these guns has affected my nerves to such an
extent as to have materially influenced my shooting

ever since, and I am heartily sorry that I ever had anything to do with them.

The journey between Kuruman and Secheli's took us some twenty days. The distance was about 260 miles, but a great part of the road lay through a very sandy country, with but little water, and was terribly trying for the oxen. After leaving Kuruman the appearance of the country presented a marked and very agreeable change from anything I had as yet seen ; for whereas, with the exception of the coast-line, there is scarcely a tree to be seen throughout the western portion of the Cape Colony, Griqualand, or the Free State, the country now became thickly wooded with trees of a good size, and in many parts greatly resembled an English park ; the more so as the camel-thorn trees, which were most numerous, looked at a distance something like the oak. The great drawback to this portion of the country is the scarcity of water and the heavy, sandy roads. We passed but few kraals, but at most of the waters there were some Bakalahari tending the cattle of their Bechuana masters. A day's journey before reaching Secheli's we came to a large kraal under the old chief Montsua, a good-looking, portly old man, dressed, like every Bechuana of any standing, from top to toe in European costume, with collar and necktie complete.

Just after leaving Montsua's, Dorehill and I met with an accident. I was taking some cartridges from amongst about a pound of loose powder contained in a small box in the side case of the waggon, when Dorehill came up, and looking over my shoulder with a pipe in his mouth, some lighted tobacco fell into the powder, which immediately exploded. We were rather badly burnt all over our necks and faces,

and the insides of our lips and nostrils ; our eyes,
too, were badly burnt, and one of mine, indeed, did
not get well for a considerable time.   Sadlier, who
had been through the American war, and there learnt
some things useful in such an emergency, at once
rubbed a mixture of oil and salt into our skinless
faces ; it was not a pleasant process, but I have no
doubt it did what he said it would do, *i.e.* prevent
the powder from leaving any mark, as it so often
does.   Upon reaching Secheli's we were very kindly
treated by one and all the traders stationed there,
and as soon as our eyes were a little better we paid
a visit to Secheli, who is a celebrity amongst the
Kafir chiefs of the interior.   Like Montsua, he is
a tall, portly old Kafir, and to me, a stranger, he
appeared to be a very pleasant old fellow.   He was
living in a large well-built house, over the dining-
room mantelpiece of which stood a handsome good-
sized mirror ; above the doorway was a large clock,
while in the bedroom I caught a glimpse of a fine
iron bedstead.   We had tea with him, and I was
surprised to see it served in a silver tea-pot and a
handsome set of china tea-things.   Altogether, judging only from outward and visible signs, old Secheli
appeared to me to be the most completely civilised
Kafir that I had yet seen.   I have since heard that
although a most diligent student of the Old Testament
(for he can read the Sechuana translation), he is not
thought, by those who consider themselves capable
of judging, to be a particularly good and sound
Christian.   He was very anxious about Queen
Victoria's health, and seemed much concerned to
hear of the recent illness of the Prince of Wales.
There I met for the first time a Mr. Frank Mandy,
of Graham's Town, a gentleman with whom I soon

formed a strong friendship, which I hope may never be broken. As he was just starting upon a trading trip to the Matabele country, where he had been before, I was only too glad to be able to travel in company with him, and to benefit by his experience.

We left Secheli's on the 28th of June, before which time our burnt faces would not bear exposure to the sun. The delay, however, enabled our oxen to get a thorough rest before starting on the severe piece of road between Secheli's and Bamangwato. Starting in the evening and travelling all night, we reached Kopong early the following morning, but we were not able to get water for our oxen until late on the afternoon of the second day. As soon as they had drunk, we inspanned and pushed on again, knowing they would drink no more before arriving at Boatlanarma. We had even more trouble getting through the heavy, sandy roads than I had expected, for Mandy's heavily-laden waggon had a knack of sticking fast, when I had to unyoke my bullocks and pull it on a bit. Thus we were three days and nights trekking continuously before we reached water, and our poor oxen were in a terrible state from thirst. At Selinya, a fine roadside vley, about twenty miles beyond Boatlanarma, we first saw the spoor of a lion in the soft mud at the water's edge. That same evening, sitting by our fire, we heard a splashing, then a sort of groan, and running down with fire-brands to the vley, discovered first blood, then entrails, then a dead impala antelope. It had been killed by wild dogs, and although we were upon them almost immediately, they had found time to tear away the greater part of their victim's hind-quarters. We were much obliged to the wild dogs

for this timely supply of meat, for though we had
worked hard and ridden far and wide, we had seen
no game, and consequently eaten no meat, since
leaving Secheli's.   The next day, however, Sadlier
fell in with a troop of hartebeests, and killed two,
whilst I knocked over a little duiker antelope, with
a very fine pair of horns.   Two days and nights'
hard trekking through heavy, sandy country, brought
us to Bamangwato, then governed by Matchin.

As Bamangwato and its present chief, Khama,
and his people have been fully described by recent
writers, I will only say that it is the largest native
town I have seen in South Africa.   It lies at the
entrance of a gorge through a precipitous but not
very lofty range of hills.   Portions of this gorge are
very picturesque, and in one place I was strongly
reminded of the Creux du Vent in the Val de
Travers, near the Lake of Neuchâtel.   At the time
I first visited Bamangwato, both its ruler, Matchin,
and his people had a very bad name—which they
fully deserved—among European traders in the
interior.   Since then things have changed for the
better, and in no other native town in the interior
of South Africa will a traveller now meet with so
little petty annoyance from the inhabitants, or so
much courtesy from the ruler—a state of things for
which the able teaching, both by precept and example,
of the hard-working and indefatigable missionaries,
Messrs. Hepburn and Mackenzie, must have all the
honour due ; indeed, of the natives I have known,
savage or pseudo-Christianised, the only ones for
whom I ever felt either admiration or respect, were
some young fellows I met when hunting in the
Mababe in 1879, and they proved to be mostly
the sons of some of Khama's principal men, brought

up from boyhood under the guidance of the two able missionaries above mentioned.

As all my horses were " unsalted " (*i.e.* had not had the distemper), and were therefore liable to die at any moment, Mandy advised me to try and obtain a " salted " animal.   This I managed by exchanging my fine new waggon for a smaller second-hand one, a common trade rifle, and a salted horse, valued at £75.   This " swop " I made with Peter Skinner, a shrewd but uneducated Scotchman, who had made a considerable sum of money in the interior, but whose bones, poor fellow, now lie beneath the sod on the distant shores of Lake Ngami.

At length, about the middle of August, we left Bamangwato.   We followed the well-defined waggon track leading to the Matabele country, and travelling through a thickly-wooded district, and crossing three small rivers, the Mahalapsi, Metle, and Tauwani, arrived on the third day at two pretty vleys, called Shakani.   At the last river, Tauwani, we found a few families of Bushmen herding a flock of goats belonging to Matchin, whose slaves they themselves were.   From Shakani my salted horse ran back to Bamangwato, and we were delayed a week waiting for the Kafirs I sent to bring him up.   During this time I rode out daily with one or other of my companions in search of game, and we always guided ourselves back by a low range of hills that ran parallel with the road, behind the vleys, and particularly by one single hill that stood by itself.   This I mention, because, as will be seen later on, it is to the fact of having had the position of these hills well impressed upon my mind that I probably owe my life.

At last one evening we again made a start northwards, and after a four hours' trek reached Lemouni

c

pan, a large open piece of ground, in the centre of which lies a large pan or hollow, in the rainy season a veritable lake, but then, in the middle of winter, as dry as a bone. The country was covered in all directions with thick forest or scrubby bush, and, as all know who have travelled there during the dry season, was almost destitute of water, which was only found in odd pools and at long intervals along the waggon road. Except at Pelatsi (nearly twenty-five miles by road from Shakani), where, at the time of which I am writing, there was a Bechuana town, all this desert country, extending from the northern bank of the Limpopo north-west to Lake Ngami, and due north to the far-off Chobe river, is utterly uninhabited except by a few miserable wandering Masaras.

As I have said before, it was August, and mid-winter in these latitudes. Though the sun was very powerful during the day, being fully as hot as in summer in England, yet the nights were intensely cold, and tea left in the kettle was often frozen—a thing one would hardly expect so far in the interior of Africa (over one thousand miles to the north-east of Cape Town). As the oxen and horses would not get any water before reaching Pelatsi—though of course we carried some with us for our own use—we again inspanned after midnight, and trekked on by moonlight till just before day-dawn. Being out of meat, Dorehill, Mandy, and myself then resolved to let the waggons trek on in the charge of Sadlier, whilst we made a round on horseback in search of game, intending to rejoin him in the evening. So, hastily drinking a cup of hot coffee, we saddled up our horses and started.

In the early part of the day we came across a troop

of hartebeests, and, wounding one, had a long chase
after it, but eventually lost it in the thick wood, which
was very awkward to ride through.   After this we
took a course that we imagined to be parallel to the
waggon track, and rode steadily forward till about
two hours after mid-day, when, not having seen any
more game, we turned our horses' heads eastwards
and made for the road, which we hoped to reach in a
couple of hours or so.

We had ridden in this direction for perhaps ten
minutes, when suddenly we descried in the distance,
their heads appearing amongst the tops of the trees, a
fine herd of giraffes, the first Dorehill and I had ever
seen in a wild state.   We at once started in eager
pursuit, hoping to secure some fine fat steaks for
supper, as giraffes are splendid eating and usually in
good condition, and fat is a luxury that no one can
properly appreciate till he has lived for a time on
nothing but the dry meat of the smaller antelopes.

The giraffes, about twenty in number, came up
wind, looking splendid, with their tails twisted up
over their backs like corkscrews, and we at once
galloped obliquely towards them, and managed to
make up a good deal of ground.   They have a most
peculiar gait—a sort of gallop, their hind legs being
straddled out at each step and coming (one on each
side) in front of the fore legs.   If you only look at
their bodies and necks from behind, they appear to be
sailing or gliding along without making any movement
at all.   They get over the ground, however, at a great
rate, and it requires a good horse to run one down.
The great thing is to press them to their utmost speed
at first, when, if fat, they soon get blown and can be
ridden into, and, if the wind is favourable, driven for
miles right up to one's waggons just like an ox or an

eland. At a hard gallop, however, they can spin along for miles, and so we found to-day. After a time the giraffes separated, and suffice it to say that, at the end of an hour or so, I found myself lying on my back, with my right leg nearly broken, by coming violently into contact with the trunk of a tree ; and, on getting up and remounting my horse, not only were the giraffes out of sight, but nowhere could I see either of my two companions. Though, of course, my inexperience contributed much to the unsuccessful issue of this, my first giraffe hunt, yet I cannot help thinking that my horse also had a good deal to do with it, for, having been bred in the open plains of the Transvaal Republic, he was quite at sea in the thick forests of the interior ; and if, when going at full gallop through a thick wood, you intend to pass on one side of a tree, but your horse, being of a different opinion, swerves suddenly and goes to the other, it is awkward, to say the least of it.

My first object was to rejoin my companions ; so, not having heard a shot, and imagining they must by this time have given up chasing the giraffes, I fired as a signal, and at once heard a shot in answer far to my right, and rode in that direction. After riding some distance I again pulled up, and shouted with all my might, and then, not hearing anything, fired another signal shot, but without effect. As my horse was very tired, I now saddled off for a short time and then fired a third shot, and listened intently for an answer, but all was silent as the grave ; so, as the sun was now low, I saddled up again and struck a line for the waggon road, thinking my friends had already done the same thing. In this way I rode on at a slow pace, for my horse was tired and thirsty, keeping steadily in one direction, till the sun, sinking lower and lower, at last disappeared altogether. I expected I should have reached the road before this, and, attributing my not doing so to the fact of the path having taken a turn to the right, still kept on till twilight had given place to moonlight—a fine bright moonlight, indeed, for it wanted but two nights to the full, but, under the circumstances, perhaps a trifle cold and cheerless. Still, thinking I must be close to the road, I kept on for another couple of hours or so, when, it being intensely cold, I resolved to try and light a fire, and pass the night where I was, and ride on again early the following morning. Having no matches, in endeavouring to get a light I had to make use of my cartridges, of which I had only three remaining. Breaking one of these open, I rubbed some of the powder well into a bit of linen torn from my shirt, slightly wetted, and, putting it into the muzzle of the rifle, ignited it with the cap and a little powder left in the bottom of the cartridge. So far well and good, but this was, unfortunately, almost as far as I could get; for, though I managed to induce some grass to smoulder, I could not for the life of me make it flare, and soon had the mortification of finding myself, after two more unsuccessful attempts, just as cold and hungry as before, and minus my three cartridges to boot. Were the same circumstances to occur again, no doubt everything would be very different; but at that time I was quite a tyro in all forest lore. It was now piercingly cold, though during the day the sun had been as hot as at midsummer in England—regular South African fashion. Still, I thought it better to pass the night where I was; so, tying my horse to a tree, I cut a little grass with my pocket-knife to lie upon, and turned in. My entire clothing consisted of a hat, shirt, pair of trousers, and veldt shoes, as I had ridden away from the waggon without my coat. However, lying on my back, with my felt hat for a pillow, I put the saddle over my chest and closed my eyes in vain hope that I should soon fall asleep and forget my cares ; vain indeed, for the bitter cold crept in gradually and stealthily from my feet upwards, till I was soon shivering from head to foot as if my very life depended on it. After having worked hard at this unpleasant exercise for a couple of hours or more, watching the moon all the time, and cursing its tardy pace, I could stand it no longer ; so, getting up with difficulty—for I was regularly stiffened by the cold—I ran backwards and forwards to a tree at a short distance until I was again warm, when I once more lay down ; and in this manner the weary hours wore away till day dawned. During the night a couple of hyænas passed close to me, enlivening the silence with their dismal howlings. I have often thought since that they must have been on their way to drink, perhaps at some pit or spring not far off ; how I wished that I had known where ! I will take this opportunity of saying that the howl of the African hyæna is about the most mournful and weird-like sound in nature, being a sort of prolonged groan, rising in cadence till it ends in a shriek ; they only laugh when enjoying a good feed.

At first dawn of day I once more saddled up and rode in the same direction as before. My poor horse was so tired and thirsty that he would only go at a very slow pace ; so I did not make much progress. On coming to a high tree I stopped and climbed up it, and looked about me to try and recognise some landmark. On every side the country was covered with forest, and in the distance were several low ranges of hills, yet nothing seemed familiar to my eye. Right ahead, in the direction in which I had been riding, appeared a line of densely wooded hills, with one single kopje standing alone just in front of them, and thither I determined to ride. On the way I passed three beautiful gemsbuck, which allowed me to come quite close to them, though they are usually very wild; but they had nothing to fear from me, as I had no cartridges, and so could do nothing more than admire them. Thus I rode on and on, until the idea occurred to me that I must have ridden across the road (a mere narrow track) without noticing it in the moonlight, as I had constantly been star-gazing after the sun went down, so as to guide my course by the position of the Southern Cross. After a time, I at last felt so sure that this was the case, that I turned my horse's head to the right-about, and rode back again in the direction from which I had just come. About mid-day, finding no road, I began to think that I was in stern reality lost in the veldt, without even a bullet to obtain food for myself, and no water within heaven knew what distance away, except the far-apart drinking-places along the road. And where was that road—was it behind me or in front?

Presently, coming in sight of a small stone " kopje," rising like a heap of rocks from the level ground, I rode to it, and tying my horse to a tree at its foot, climbed up to take a look round. A most bewildering prospect it was—a vast ocean of forest on all sides, as far as the eye could reach, here and there bounded by low ranges of wooded hills, that were not visible from the level ground; but nowhere could I make out any landmark to guide me in the least. As I looked steadily in the direction from

which I had just come, I saw a thin wreath of blue
smoke curling up amongst the trees, which evidently
proceeded from a wood fire, not a grass one, and
which I argued must have been kindled by human
beings, in all probability Masaras, who would be able
to guide me to Pelatsi ; so I promptly determined
to retrace my steps once more, and make for the
fire.   After a time I got to about where I thought
the fire ought to be, but, on climbing a high tree, no
smoke was visible, as it had no doubt died out ; so,
coming to the conclusion that the road was really
behind me, and cursing my folly for having wasted
so much time in following such a " will-o'-the-wisp,"
I again turned my jaded horse towards the setting
sun, hoping, by keeping steadily at it, to recross the
road before sundown.   I may here say that, as I
afterwards found out, I never had crossed the road
in the night, as I imagined, but must twice have
turned and ridden away from it when within but a
short distance ; for, believing that it held a north-
easterly direction, instead of turning suddenly due
east, as it does, a few miles beyond Lemouni, I could
not but imagine (after riding such a distance almost
parallel to it, as it turned out) that I had crossed it.
It was by this time tolerably late in the afternoon ;
but I still hoped to reach the waggons before nightfall, and kept my spirits up by thinking how I should
enjoy a cup of tea and a damper with my companions
round the camp fire.   But, as the sun dipped lower
and lower in the western sky, my spirits sank with
it, and at last, when it finally disappeared, I had to
prepare for a second night on the bare ground,
without food, water, fire, or blanket.   Cutting a
little dry grass, I laid it down behind a bush, and
my bed was made.   Although I had twice off-saddled

my horse during the day, he had not eaten a morsel of grass, being too thirsty, poor beast ; so, instead of tying him up to a tree, I hobbled him, thinking he might graze a bit in the cool of the night, and thereby gain a little strength to carry me on the morrow.   It was full moon, and fearfully cold, from which, in addition to hunger and thirst, I suffered intensely, almost shivering myself to pieces ; but everything has an end in this world, and so had this, for me, most intolerably long winter's night.

At the first streak of dawn I endeavoured to rise, but could not stand up, my legs being utterly benumbed with the cold ; at last, however, I got the circulation restored, and began to look about me for my horse.   But nowhere was he to be seen ; and I found by looking at the spoor that he had made off during the night (though fast hobbled) in search of water.   The ground being rather hard, and the spoor (to my inexperienced eyes) difficult to make out, I soon came to the conclusion that it was useless to follow him, and so returned to where I had passed the night.   I now considered what was best to be done. Far away in a south-westerly direction I could see a large high range of hills, which I thought might be the Bamangwato range, and thither, not knowing what else to do, I determined to direct my steps ; so, hanging my saddle in a tree, and shouldering my rifle, off I started.   As it was now forty-eight hours since a morsel of food or a drop of water had passed my lips, I felt, as may be imagined, quite ready for breakfast ; but breakfast not being ready for me, I had to go without it.   All that day I walked as I have seldom walked since, only resting at long intervals for a few minutes at a time, devoured by a burning thirst, and growing sensibly weaker

from hunger. I had started at sunrise, and when
the moon was about an hour high, at last reached
the foot of the mountains I had been making for,
having crossed, I am sure, an enormous extent of
country.   I had been able to get over the even
ground all right, walking along mechanically ; but,
weakened as I was by want of food and water, it
was all I could do to climb up the steep, rocky hill,
and I was forced to sit down and rest at every
few yards.   At last, however, I reached the top,
expecting to see the maize - fields of Bamangwato
beneath me on the other side, and bitter indeed was
my disappointment when I saw nothing but range
upon range of rugged, stony hills.   As, however, I
now needed rest, and nothing more could be done
till the following day, I established myself behind a
large rock and prepared to pass another cold and
hungry night, in no very happy frame of mind, for
I thought I was doomed to die of starvation and
thirst in the wilderness, my fate remaining a mystery
to all my friends ; but mingled with this came a
feeling that it was too hard to die thus like a rat in a
hole, and, though things certainly looked desperate
at present, I still felt some gleam of hope that they
would eventually come right.

I did not suffer so much from the cold on the top
of this range of hills as I had done on the two preceding nights down on the plain, nor did I feel the pangs
of hunger to any great degree ; but, on the other
hand, my thirst was now intolerable, my throat,
tongue, and lips being quite dry and swollen, so that
it was very painful to swallow.   Before sunrise the
next morning I left my stony couch, and went to the
edge of the hill to take a look round.   Being on a
considerable elevation, I commanded a view over a

vast extent of country. Suddenly, whilst gazing ruefully over this wilderness of forest, I fancied I recognised a certain detached "kopje" as one with which I was well acquainted, close to Shakani "vleys," as well as a low range of hills on the other side, and one or two other detached hills. After carefully comparing their relative positions, I felt certain of their identity, and that if I could only manage to hold out till I reached them I was saved; but, as they seemed a long way off, and only loomed blue in the distance, no time was to be lost, so I at once descended from the hill, and started. When on the plain I could see nothing of the hills I was making for, and in order to keep my line I had, from time to time, to climb trees—a most difficult undertaking in my exhausted condition. So eager was I to get forward, that, when forced sometimes to rest through sheer weakness, I could not sit still for more than two or three minutes at a time, as something seemed to impel me to get up and push on again. During this day I saw three ostriches, two hens and a cock. At last, just before sundown, I got close to the kopjes of Shakani, and was making for the water, distant about half a mile, when I saw two Kafirs, no doubt returning from hunting. This was lucky, as, although I knew there were a few Bushmen herding some goats here, I might not have been able to find the two or three miserable huts where they lived (for the bush was rather thick round about), and should thus only have allayed my intense thirst, and once more gone supperless to a cold bed, which might have finished me. Calling to the Kafirs as well as my parched throat would allow, and giving one my rifle to carry, I followed them to their kraal (if three half huts, made of interwoven boughs, can be called one).

Here I sat down, and instantly asked an old Bushman
for water ; but, would you believe it ? the accursed
old heathen, the ingenuous child of nature, would not
give me any, but, holding a giraffe's intestine full of the
precious fluid under his arm, said, " *Buy the water* " !
The " vley " was only about 200 yards off, but when
a man has been four days and three nights without
anything to eat or drink, he does not care to go even
200 yards farther than he can help ; yet, sooner than
be thus taken advantage of, I would have done so,
and was just getting up when a little boy came in
from milking the goats, with a large calabash full of
milk.   On seeing this I changed my mind, and pulling out a large clasp-knife, the only marketable
article I possessed, I said, " Reka marsi " (I'll buy
the milk), and soon got not only it, but a large
gourd of water besides.   Was it not a treat ! and,
I daresay, about the very best thing I could have
taken in my state.

Thinking that I should be too weak to do much
walking on the following day, I tried to make them
understand that if one of them would go to the
waggons and tell my friends where I was, so that
they could bring a horse for me to ride, I would
pay him handsomely.   However, the few words of
Sechuana I knew were quite insufficient to explain my
meaning ; so there was nothing for it but to make
up my mind to walk to Pelatsi, which, according to
Mr. Baines's observations, is twenty-five miles distant
from Shakani.   One man offered to go with me (for
a consideration) and carry my rifle, and also, on my
promising to pay him an exorbitant price for it in
powder on my arrival at the waggons, gave me a
very small piece of steinbuck meat ; after eating
which, and drinking unheard-of quantities of water,

I laid myself close alongside a large fire, and slept soundly till daylight.

The next morning, as soon as it was light, accompanied by the Kafir who carried my rifle, I made a start, and, though very tired and worn out from privation, managed to reach the waggons late in the afternoon, after an absence of five days and four nights. How I enjoyed the meal that was hastily prepared for me, and how delightful it was to keep out the bitter cold with a couple of good blankets, I will leave the reader to conjecture. It was really almost worth all the hardship I had endured. Mandy and my other friends had of course been in a great state of anxiety about my non-appearance, and had done everything they could to recover me. On the night of the giraffe hunt they had gone to the Kafir town at Pelatsi, and, on promising the exorbitant payment of one blanket per man, induced four Bechuana Kafirs and two Masaras from there to go in search of me. With these men Mandy, on the following morning, started back to the place where we had originally diverged from the waggon road the day after trekking away from Shakani, and then showed them my horse's spoor, which was easy to distinguish, being larger than that of either of the other two. He then went with them a considerable distance farther, and, finding that the two Bushmen ran along the spoor at a quick trot, and were able to follow it with the greatest ease, he finally left them and returned to the waggons. These Kafirs, of course, carried each a large calabash of water, and had the meat of an entire duiker antelope and the shoulder of a koodoo, so that they had a moderate supply of provisions for at least three days. On the evening of the next day these scoundrels returned with a very lying and elaborate story, saying they had followed my spoor to a pit with a little water in it, where I had dismounted and drunk, and from there to the road on the other side of Shakani, along which I had ridden at a gallop towards Bamangwato. With this intelligence they came back to the waggons, relieving my friends of all anxiety (except that they wondered what on earth I wanted at Bamangwato), but kindly leaving me to die of hunger and thirst, or find my way back to the road as I best could. The fact is, they just ate up the meat Mandy had given them, and then, returning with their abominable lying story, got their payment and were happy !

My poor horse, which had been worth £80 only three weeks previously, I thought no more about, believing that if he had not died of thirst he must have fallen a prey to lions or hyænas ; but when I reached Tati, a Mr. Elstob, a trader there, thought the animal might have found his way back to Bamangwato, and offered me £10 for the chance, which I accepted. Several months later I heard this had actually happened, but the raw hide thongs with which he had been hobbled had so cut into his legs as greatly to reduce his value. Thus terminated an adventure which, had it not been for a sound constitution, might have terminated me ; as it was, I was never a bit the worse for my sufferings, except that during the next two or three days I experienced a soreness in the throat and a difficulty in swallowing ; but for all that I should be very sorry to go nearly ninety hours without food or water again, or to spend three winter nights without fire or blanket on the bare ground.

The day after I reached the waggons we inspanned, and got to the Serule the following day, where

(though this river is now dry down to the bed rock)
plenty of water could then be obtained by digging.
This being a noted place for giraffes, Mandy and I
rode out to try for one, and soon came upon a solitary
old bull, but as the meat of these old males is so
rank as to be unfit for human food, we let him gallop
away in peace, and went on in search of cows, a fine
herd of which we soon came across.   We at once gave
chase, but unluckily Mandy's horse, at the very outset,
trod in a hole, threw him heavily, and then galloped
away at full speed ; so, as we had agreed not to get
separated again upon any account, I let the giraffes
alone, and pursued my friend's runaway steed, which I
at last managed to catch ; by this time, of course, the
giraffes were far out of sight, so we returned to the
waggons and at once inspanned.   Late in the afternoon of the following day we reached the river Goqui,
where at that time there was a permanent water-hole,
just where the waggon track crossed the river.[1]

It was here I first saw a lion out of a cage.   As
soon as we outspanned, I had my horse saddled up,
and taking one of my men with me, went out to try
and shoot something for supper.   We were returning home by the river and were quite near to the
waggons, when my man suddenly said, " There's a
lion ; I saw him put up his head."   I looked where
he pointed, but, seeing nothing, got off my horse and
advanced to the river bank, when up jumped two
lionesses that had been lying in the long grass, and
trotted away.   I fired, and at the sound a male lion
stood up at the place where the lionesses had been
lying ; he appeared a magnificent old fellow, with a
fine dark-coloured mane.   For some seconds he stood

---

[1] This hole is now dry, though water can usually be obtained by
digging about half a mile farther up the river.

looking at me, only about eighty yards off, and offering a magnificent shot, but before I could make ready, he was off after the others. As the sun was now down, and I had no dogs, I did not like to follow them into the thick bush, and so gave them up, a good deal disappointed with the result of my first encounter with lions.

As I had seen a great deal of lion spoor at the water, I took my blanket when it got dark and lay by the river close to the drinking-place, but though, during the night, I heard some distant roaring, none came near the water ; this was perhaps lucky for me, for, with the foolhardiness of inexperience, I had made no shelter of any kind, but just sat with my back against a small thorn tree. Near the Goqui we first saw a large baobab tree. On our way from here to the Tati gold-fields, we saw nothing remarkable ; we crossed the rivers Macloutsi and Shashi, and at the former first saw rhinoceros spoor, but failed to get a view of the animals themselves. At length we reached Tati, where, at the time of my first visit, there were six or seven Englishmen, only two of whom had anything to do with the mine. A small engine about a mile down the river was driving a crushing-machine belonging to Sir John Swinburne. The shaft from which the quartz was being extracted is called the Blue Jacket, and was an old native digging (probably Mashuna). This shaft must be very old. It was accidentally discovered by some men while prospecting, who, after having dug away about a foot of the surface soil, came upon a large stone which they found was fitted into the entrance of what is now the Blue Jacket shaft, about 100 feet in depth : a wonderful work for the Mashuna, but there is no one else to whom to attribute it.

PLATE II

1. KOODOO BULL (Strepsiceros Kudu).

   Shot in the Mashuna country, Sept. 1, 1880.
   Length of horns, in a straight line from point to base, 3 feet
   5 inches ; measured over the curve, 5 feet 4 inches.

2. KOODOO BULL (Strepsiceros Kudu).

   Shot near the Victoria Falls, July 1, 1874.
   Length of horns, in a straight line from point to base, 3 feet
   7 inches.

3. HORNS OF SITUTUNGA ANTELOPE ♂ (Tragelaphus Spekii).

   Obtained from the natives on the river Chobe, August 1879.
   Length of horns, in a straight line from point to base, 2 feet
   1 inch.

4. SITUTUNGA ANTELOPE ♂ (Tragelaphus Spekii).

   Found dead on the Chobe river near Linyanti, August 5, 1879
   Length of horns, in a straight line from point to base, 1 foot
   10 inches.

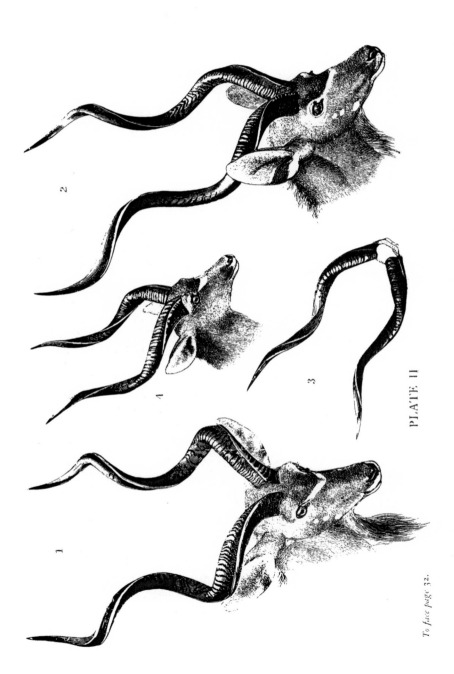

PLATE II

To face page 32.

CHAPTER III

TOWARDS the end of August we left the Tati, passing the Ramaqueban river the following day ; here
I first saw a sable antelope, one of the handsomest
animals in the world. At this river is the grave of
an Englishman named Firmin, who was killed here
by an elephant, the first he had ever seen. This
tract of country had very recently been one of the
best hunting-grounds for elephants to be found in
South Africa ; but these animals, when much
persecuted, soon shift their quarters, and now both
elephants and hunters have left these parts. By the
river Impakwe is an old native furnace for smelting
the gold out of quartz, and a little farther, by the
Inkwesi, only a few years ago, Makobi, a Bechuana
chief, and his whole tribe—men, women, and children
—were exterminated by an army of Umziligazi's
warriors ; to this day skulls may be found on the
hill-tops, where the old towns were situated. At the
time of my first visit there were no Kafirs living
near the Inkwesi river, but in 1875 Lobengula
established several large towns, where strangers on

first entering the country are now detained, while
messengers are sent to the king to give notice of their
arrival.   A day later we reached the Mangwe, where
John Lee, a man of mixed Dutch and English
parentage, has established himself ; he was away in
the hunting veldt, but on the many subsequent
occasions when I have found him at home, he has
invariably treated me with the greatest kindness and
hospitality.   We saw by the spoor that a large white
rhinoceros had crossed the road within one hundred
yards of Lee's house.   Another twelve miles brought
us to Minyama's kraal, the then frontier outpost of
the Matabele country ; here we were delayed while
messengers were sent on to Lobengula, asking his
permission to enter the country, and here for the
first time I realised being among savages, for it was
the first place where I saw no European clothes, and
I must say the people in their own dress, or rather
want of dress, looked infinitely better than the
greasy-shirted, ragged-trousered men to whom I had
been accustomed among the Bechuana tribes.

The greatest part of the inhabitants about here
are Makalakas, whose native dress for both men and
women is almost identical with that of the Bechuanas,
than whom I think them, especially the women, a
better-looking race.   The few real Matabele girls
we saw were very pleasant to the eye, having most
good-tempered-looking faces, and fine, upright, well-
developed, dark chocolate-coloured figures, the naked
beauty of which was but little hidden by their very
scanty attire, which in some cases consisted of a
small flap of goat or antelope skin in front and
another behind, and in others of a little fringe of
"umbentla" (a soft fibre extracted from a kind of
grass) in front, and nothing at all behind.   The

scenery of the whole country between John Lee's and the Shashani river is very remarkable, and exceedingly picturesque. In many parts the country is covered with small hills composed entirely of huge stones, piled one upon another in the most fantastic manner, many of which present a very strong resemblance, especially by moonlight, to old ruined castles. Amongst these wonderfully picturesque hills the waggon road winds for many miles, until, shortly after crossing the Shashani river, it emerges upon the open park-like plateau of the Matabele country, which extends to beyond [1] Gubulawayo.

We found that, owing to the scarcity of grass for cattle near the chief town, Lobengula had trekked away and built a temporary kraal near Amachee Maschlopay (white stones); so we too trekked straight across the country to where he was, getting there towards evening. Here we found Mr. G. A. Phillips, who had already been eight years in the country, trading and hunting, and he kindly gave us a goat to slaughter. The following morning Lobengula, king of the powerful tribe of the Matabele, came down to our waggons. He is a man standing about 5 feet 10 or 11, strongly and stoutly built, and even at that date was growing very stout ; he was then dressed in a greasy shirt and dirty pair of trousers, but I am happy to say that during the last few years I have known him, he has discarded European clothing, and now always appears in his own native dress, in which he looks what he is—the chief of a savage and barbarous people. After saying a few

[1] This town was founded by Lobengula in 1870, and its name implies "the place of him whom they wanted to kill," being derived from the verb "Bulala," to kill, and referring to the revolt against his authority by a portion of his subjects who favoured the pretensions of his rival "Kuruman."

words to Mandy, whom he knew and seemed pleased
to see again, he asked who was the owner of the
other waggon and the cart, and being told by Mr.
Phillips, who acted as interpreter, that I was, he
asked me what I had come to do ; I said I had come
to hunt elephants, upon which he burst out laughing,
and said, "Was it not steinbucks" (a diminutive
species of antelope) "that you came to hunt ?   Why,
you're only a boy."   I replied that, although a boy,
I nevertheless wished to hunt elephants, and asked
his permission to do so, upon which he made some
further disparaging remarks regarding my youthful
appearance, and then rose to go without giving me
any answer.   He was attended by about fifty
natives who had all been squatting in a semicircle
during the interview, but all of whom, immediately
he rose to go, cried out, "How ! how !" in a tone
of intense surprise, as if some lovely apparition
had burst upon their view ; then, as he passed,
they followed, crouching down and crying out,
"O thou prince of princes ! thou black one ! thou
calf of the black cow ! thou black elephant !" etc.
etc.   The Matabele huts are not as good as those
of the Bechuanas, being built on the Zulu plan, with
doors only about two feet broad and under two feet
in height, so that it is a matter of difficulty for a man
of the king's dimensions to get through.   A day or
two later I again went and asked the king for leave
to hunt elephants in his country ; this time he asked
me whether I had ever seen an elephant, and upon
my saying No, answered, "Oh ! they will soon drive
you out of the country, but you may go and see what
you can do !"   On my then saying that I had heard
that he only allowed people to hunt in certain parts
of the country, and asking where I might go, he

replied, "Oh ! you may go wherever you like ; you are only a boy." My friend Dorehill now accepted a situation with Mr. Kisch (a gentleman lately auditor-general of the Transvaal, and at that time trading in the Matabele country), and Sadlier and I prepared to go in hunting alone. It happened that just at this time two Boers, Mynheer Jan Viljoen and one of his sons, had come out of the hunting veldt on horseback, to lay complaints against some Kafirs in their employ before the king, and as they were on the point of returning, they said that if I would wait a day they would travel with me to where their waggons were encamped on the river Gwenia, and then take Sadlier and myself in hunting with them. As Jan Viljoen was one of the oldest and most experienced hunters in South Africa, of course I jumped at the proposal. Although even then over sixty years of age, Jan Viljoen was still, when I last saw him, in 1879, as strong and active as a young man, and has doubtless been taking an active part in the recent troubles in the Transvaal. For a Boer, he is of small stature, though very tough and wiry, with a quick vivacious manner, and keen dark eyes, which betray his French descent. Although hating the British Government with a bitterness that can only be understood by those who know the cruel, mean, and unmanly policy pursued by many of our Cape Colonial Governors towards the Boers, he is noted for the warm hospitality which he is ever ready to extend to any stranger, British or otherwise. He told me he was among the foremost of the " voer trekkers " who, out of detestation of the British rule, left their homes and fled into the wilderness rather than submit to uncongenial laws ; he took part in the fight at Boomplaats, and, having been caught by Sir Harry

Smith, very narrowly escaped hanging. When
things were again quiet, he established himself in the
fertile district of Marico, in the north-west of the
Transvaal, giving his farm the significant name
of " Fär-genog " (Far enough).

On the third day from Gubulawayo we reached
Inyati, the most advanced station of the London
Missionary Society. There I made the acquaintance
of the resident missionary, the Rev. W. Sykes. He
told me that when he first came here, in 1859, game
of every kind abounded, that he had often been
called by the natives to drive elephants out of their
cornfields, that he constantly saw buffaloes and
rhinoceroses going down to the river to drink in
the afternoon, and that lions roared nightly round
his house, and frequently quenched their thirst at
the little reedy pool not more than two hundred
yards from his doorstep. However, times have
changed indeed since then, and game of every
description has now been driven far beyond the
inhabited portion of the Matabele country.

Between Gubulawayo and Inyati the road passes
two places of interest in Matabele history : the first
is " Intaba Izenduna," or the mountain of the headmen, a low flat-topped hill, which gained its name
from the following circumstance. When Umziligazi
first reached what is now the Matabele country, he
passed right through it, intending to journey still
farther northwards and settle beyond the Zambesi ;
some of his indunas, however, seeing that the land
was fair, with plenty of water and good pasturage,
deserted their king and stopped behind. Umziligazi
proceeded on his journey, but before long got into
the country infested by the tsetse-fly, and, finding
that his numerous herds of cattle were being

decimated by these insect pests, retraced his steps
to the elevated, fertile, and healthy country in which
his indunas had already settled themselves. These
men, who little expected to see their king again,
paid dearly for their desertion; the inexorable
monarch surrounded them with his warriors, and,
driving them on to the top of the aforesaid mountain,
slaughtered them to a man. The second place of
interest is the deserted town of " Zwang Indaba,"
situated on the Bembees river. It was here that a
bloody battle was fought in 1870 between Lobengula's
faction and the adherents of Kuruman, the rival
claimant to the throne. Lobengula's force was
numerically much superior to that of his opponent,
which was, in fact, composed solely of the warriors
belonging to the two kraals of Induba and Zwang
Indaba, led by Umbigo, the induna of the latter
town. These men, however, represented the flower
of Umziligazi's warriors, and had they but been
joined by the fierce regiment of Inyama Inghlovo,
according to agreement, the day might have gone
hard with Lobengula. As it was, after a desperate
fight, he dispersed the rebels with much slaughter,
burning down the town of Zwang Indaba and killing
Umbigo; he acted, however, very leniently towards
the vanquished, permitting all who escaped from the
fight to return home and become his subjects. Mr.
Phillips, who with Mr. Sykes attended the wounded
after the battle, told me that, although the king's
people had many guns, nearly all the killed had been
stabbed at close quarters with assegais. In many
instances he found two men lying dead together,
each with the other's assegai through his heart.

On the fifth day from Inyati we reached Viljoen's
encampment on the little river Gwenia, having

crossed the Longwe, Sangwe, Shangani, Vungo, and
Gwelo on our way. With the exception of a few
tsessebe antelope, we saw no game during the journey.
At Gwenia we found the wives and children of the
Viljoens all well. It seemed curious to find white
women and children so far in the interior, but the
Boer elephant-hunters, many of whom have been
obliged to leave Marico on account of debt, always
take their wives, children, cows, sheep, goats, indeed
everything that they have, with them. The way in
which they live is this :—In the commencement of the
hunting season, which lasts from May to December
(the rest of the year being too unhealthy to do
anything), they trek with all their goods and chattels
to a " stand-place," where they build a rough-and-
ready sort of hut of wattle and daub, thatched with
dry grass, and here their women and children live
while the men go elephant-hunting, stopping away
from a week to a month at a time. During the
unhealthy season they live at such places as Inyati,
Gubulawayo, or Tati, buying with ivory and ostrich
feathers the absolute necessaries of life, such as
clothing, tea, coffee, and sugar, which they obtain
from English traders established at those places.

Some of my oxen were now in a fearful state of
emaciation, as may be imagined when I tell you that
for three or four mornings after our arrival at Gwenia,
two of them had to be lifted on to their legs by
means of poles passed under their bellies. When
once up they went off and fed with the rest, but they
were so weak and stiffened with the cold at night that
at first they were unable to get up without assistance.
Being young animals, however, they all pulled through
eventually, and, as soon as the rains fell and the
young grass sprouted, became fat and sleek.

As in three days the Viljoens were going in hunting on foot in the " fly "- infested country to the north-east of their encampment, Sadlier and I employed our time in casting hardened bullets, and making all other requisite preparations ; but, the day before starting, I cut my foot in a way that made walking impossible ; my friends of course could not wait for me, and my feelings of chagrin and disappointment may be imagined. However, there was nothing for it but to make the best of a bad job. Old Viljoen kindly offered to send some Kafirs to the waggons in ten days, by which time he thought my foot would be well again, who would guide me to the hunting encampment ; and asked me in the meantime to take a span of his oxen, and one of his boys as guide, and go to the Mashuna towns of Musigagufa and Indaima to buy some Kafir corn and rice. This I engaged to do, saying that after having bought some corn, I would leave the waggon to follow, and ride back myself, in order to reach Gwenia without fail by the tenth day.

The following morning the Viljoens and Sadlier started on foot for the " fly " country, whilst I, with a heavy heart, inspanned, and followed the waggon track leading to the north-east. In the afternoon we reached a little river called Jomani,[1] where we found an encampment of Griqua and Hottentot hunters. They had a lot of ivory, and I did a little trade with them.

The following night, whilst outspanned near the river Se-whoi-whoi, we were troubled by lions ; I had drawn the waggon against a large clump of bushes, and made a semicircular fence enclosing the

---

1 The " tsetse " fly has now come up to the Jomani, so that hunters of late years have had to travel by another road more to the south.

oxen, which were all made fast to the yokes, whilst on the other side of them I had lighted two large fires.   Hearing a disturbance in the night I got out of the waggon, and, sitting on the fore-case, called out to my driver to know what was the matter. "It's a lion," he answered, and came up to tell me about it.   He had just reached the disselboom when, with a growl, a lion sprang up from close to the wheel and jumped over the low hedge, followed by a puppy I had, barking vigorously.   We soon heard the lion chasing the dog and growling savagely, and the next instant my cur came rushing back with his tail between his legs.   I fired shots after the lion, and that night we were no more troubled.   Next morning we found by the spoor that our visitor had crept from behind the waggon up to the fore wheel, where he was doubtless lying, looking for a fat ox, when I got on to the fore-case.

Two days later, at the river Sebakwe, we found a large encampment of Boer hunters, and among them old Petrus Jacobs, the most experienced elephant-hunter in South Africa.   Eight days before, this old Nimrod, who has probably shot more lions than any man that ever lived, had been terribly mauled by one of these animals, and was lying in a very precarious state.   It appears that, being away hunting on the other side of the Umniati river, he was sitting in the shade of his waggon, when his daughter-in-law, the only other person there, called out " Kek, om Piet, kek, daar kom en vark af naar de water to " (Look, uncle Peter, look, there comes a pig down to the water).   Uncle Peter jumped up, and saying, " That's no pig, my child; it's a lion stalking the horses," seized his rifle, and, followed by three splendid dogs, ran down to drive the

marauder away. On seeing him the lion at once
decamped ; old Piet fired a shot after it, but missed ;
the dogs at once rushed forward, and were soon
heard baying in a little hill composed of large blocks
of stone, which was only a few hundred yards from
the waggon. Reloading quickly, the old man,
accompanied by a small Kafir boy, approached the
hill where the dogs were holding the lion at bay,
and soon saw the tawny monster lying flat and
motionless on the top of a great stone, its head
couched on its outstretched paws, whilst the dogs
were barking furiously below, and endeavouring to
jump on to the rock. As soon as the lion saw his
new adversary, it sprang from the stone, and, hotly
pursued by the dogs, charged straight for him at
full speed. While still at some distance, Piet Jacobs
fired, and must have missed, for the furious brute,
with open mouth and glaring eyes, rushed upon him
and seizing him by the thigh, threw him to the
ground and bit him fearfully. He was also bitten
in the left arm and hand, whilst the left thigh,
though fortunately not broken, was, as he expressed
it, " chewed." All this time the three dogs were
worrying the lion's hind-quarters, and soon made it
so rough for him that he left his human foe to attack
them. Fearfully mangled as he was, the old man
struggled to his feet and staggered to the waggon,
replying to his daughter's startled exclamation, " The
damned lion has done for me." The animal got off,
and the wounded man was taken back as quickly as
possible to the Boer encampment at Sebakwe. I
found his wounds were being dressed with fresh
milk and castor oil, which seemed to act very
effectually, for within two months the sturdy old
fellow was again able to ride on horseback. Years

afterwards he told me that the wounds often gave him great pain, especially in damp weather. Remembering Dr. Livingstone's statement that when he was bitten by a lion he felt no sensation of pain, I asked Jacobs whether this was his case ; but he emphatically denied it, saying that each scrunch gave him the most acute anguish.   I believe, however, that most people who have been bitten by a lion or a tiger, agree with Dr. Livingstone, and imagine that the shock to the nervous system caused by the bite of one of these powerful animals is usually sufficient to deaden all sensation of pain for the time being.

From Sebakwe drift it is about forty miles due south to the Mashuna kraals, situated among the curious rocky hills I have before mentioned, and near the sources of the river Bembees.   Their huts were often perched high up on the crags in the most precarious situations, their corn-bins being often built on round blocks of stone at the very summit of the hill.   The Mashunas live in small towns under many petty chiefs, and as, when attacked by the Matabele, they never combine and help one another, but allow themselves to be overcome piece-meal, they fall an easy prey to these fierce marauders, who have now depopulated an immense extent of country.   The Mashunas are a peaceful and very industrious people, growing large quantities of different kinds of grain, including most excellent rice, and are good workers in iron, making very good assegais, battle-axes, etc.   They also have a musical instrument very similar to the " Marimba " of the natives of Angola, made of about twenty pieces of flat iron fastened in a row on a small board, which, being of varying lengths, produce different notes.

This instrument is played inside a calabash, and, when unaccompanied by vocal music, is not at all unpleasant to listen to. All the domestic animals among the Mashunas are ridiculously small; their cattle smaller than Alderneys, their goats about a meal for two, and their fowls no bigger than partridges. The Mashunas of whom I am speaking are living under the protection of Lobengula, to whom they pay an annual tribute.

After buying corn and rice I left my waggon to be brought on by the driver, and saddling up my horse started alone for Gwenia, in order to reach Viljoen's camp within ten days as agreed upon. I slept the same evening at the Boer encampment at Sebakwe, where old Petrus Jacobs, finding I intended the next night to sleep in the bush entirely alone, would not hear of it. Remarking to his wife, "Allemagtig, de leevws will de arme dome Englesman opfret" (By the Almighty, the lions will eat up the poor stupid Englishman), he called up two of his Kafirs, whom he ordered to go with me, and carry axes with them in order to make a proper camp. The next night we slept, after having built a good fence round the horse, on the farther side of the Se-whoi-whoi river. On the way I saw a splendid herd of elands, one of which I shot, and a good deal of smaller game. Though we heard many lions roaring during the night, none troubled us, and the following day I once more reached Viljoen's encampment.

On passing the Griqua waggons at Jomani, I saw for the first time a Hottentot named Cigar, with whom I before long became much better acquainted. He had just returned from the "fly" country to the north, and brought with him a nice lot of ivory

He told me that if I had not agreed to go with the Viljoens, he would have been glad to have taken me in with him, and shown me how to shoot elephants. Upon reaching Viljoen's encampment, I found that no Kafirs had yet returned from the "fly." Here I remained for a week, expecting news, but getting none. On the seventh day Mandy arrived from Gubulawayo, having come on with some goods to do a little trade with the Boer and Griqua hunters. I was rejoiced to see him, and as he wanted to go on at once to Sebakwe, I resolved to trek with him as far as Jomani, and then go in hunting with Cigar the Hottentot, rather than wait any longer for the Viljoens, who, I thought, must have forgotten me altogether. Upon our arrival at Jomani we found that Cigar had just returned from another short trip, and I soon arranged to accompany him on his next hunt, leaving my waggons and oxen under the charge of his wife. At last, just about the commencement of October, I bade good-bye to Mandy, and at length made a start in elephant-hunting with the Hottentot Cigar.

As but few Englishmen, I fancy, have hunted in so rough-and-ready a fashion as I was compelled to do during this my first hunting season, I may as well say a few words concerning my outfit.

Having now run through all my supplies of coffee, tea, sugar, and meal, we had nothing in the provision line but Kafir corn, and the meat of the animals we shot, washed down by cold water.

Cigar, besides two Kafirs who were shooting for him, and carried their own guns and a supply of ammunition, had only three spare boys, who carried his blankets, powder, Kafir corn, and a supply of fresh meat. He himself carried his own rifle, a heavy

PLATE III

1. Sable Antelope ♂ (Hippotragus Niger).

    Shot on the Chobe river, July 15, 1879.
    Length of horns measured over curve, 3 feet 8 inches.

2. Sable Antelope ♂ (Hippotragus Niger).

    Shot in the Mashuna country, Sept. 22, 1880.
    Length of horns measured over curve, 3 feet 7 inches.

3. Sable Antelope ♀ (Hippotragus Niger).

    Shot in the Mashuna country, Sept. 8, 1878.
    Length of horns measured over curve, 2 feet 8 inches.

4. Roan Antelope ♂ (Hippotragus Leucophæus).

    Shot near the Impaqui river, Sept. 20, 1876.
    Length of horns measured over curve, 2 feet 5 inches.

5. Roan Antelope ♂ (Hippotragus Leucophæus).

    Shot in the Mashuna country, July 10, 1880.
    Length of horns measured over curve, 2 feet 5 inches.

6. Roan Antelope ♀ (Hippotragus Leucophæus).

    Shot near the river Tati, April 22, 1877.
    Length of horns measured over curve, 2 feet 1 inch.

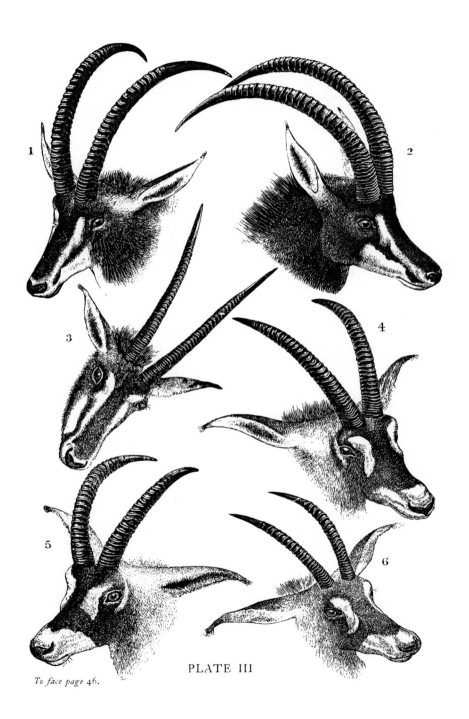

1   2   3   4   5   6

PLATE III

To face page 46.

old six-bore muzzle-loader. As for me, having had to leave two of my Kafirs to look after my horses and oxen, I had but one youngster with me, who carried my blanket and spare ammunition, whilst I shouldered my own old four-bore muzzle-loader (the same before mentioned), and carried besides a leather bag filled with powder, and a pouch containing twenty four-ounce round bullets. Though this was hardly doing the thing *en grand seigneur*, I was young and enthusiastic in those days, and trudged along under the now intense heat with a light heart.

CHAPTER IV

Eland shot—My First Elephant—"Cigar's" Skill in hunting Elephants
—Abundance of Game—Successful Bags—Drought— Rain—Hard-
ship—Maiming Elephants—Stabbing from Trees—A Murder and
Execution—" Bill" and the Crocodile.

On the first day of our hastily organised venture, we
shot a magnificent old eland bull; and made a most
excellent dinner on slices of fat meat from his breast,
and a potful of boiled Kafir corn. Whilst our repast
was preparing, Cigar whiled away the time with many
a story about his elephant-hunting experiences, which
he described most graphically. In South Central
Africa, at the hunter's camp fire, the elephant takes
the place of the grisly "bar" in North America, or
the chamois in the châlets of the Alps in Europe;
and there are more yarns spun concerning him than
about any other animal. As soon as supper was over,
I stretched myself on my bed of dry grass, and, rather
tired with my first day's tramp, soon fell asleep. On
the following morning we were up before the sun,
and, travelling in a northerly direction, soon became
aware that we were in a district frequented by
elephants, for wherever we looked, trees were broken
down, large branches snapped off, and bark and
leaves strewn about in all directions, whilst the
impress of their huge feet was to be seen in every
piece of sandy ground.

About mid-day, while crossing an open place in the forest, we came upon the fresh spoor of an old bull, which of course we followed. From the condition of the bruised leaves scattered along his track we soon found that he was not far ahead of us, and my heart beat hard with joy at the near prospect of at last beholding an African bull elephant, and perhaps managing to shoot him. Well, we had been following on his spoor for about an hour, when, all at once, I, who was walking behind Cigar, was the first to see him, standing in pretty thick bush, like an enormous ant-heap, fanning himself with his gigantic ears. The mighty beast was quite unconscious of our near proximity.

We then went to the foot of a large tree, and taking off our trousers, stood just in cotton shirts, hats, and shoes—nice light running order. Then we advanced quietly upon our victim, who stood, broadside to us, perfectly still, until we were within sixty yards of him, when he must have noticed us, for he wheeled round, spread his huge ears, and then, with raised head, advanced a few paces towards us. We stood motionless, and the suspicious brute, after staring hard for a few seconds, was just in the act of turning, when Cigar whispered to me to fire, so, aiming for his shoulder, I pressed the trigger. He gave a sort of loud roar, and rushed off, we following at our best pace, I myself with an empty gun, for I was afraid of losing sight of him if I stopped to load.

Upon Cigar giving him a shot, he turned and came walking towards us, with his ears up and the end of his trunk raised. I now loaded with all expedition, and, advancing stealthily to within twenty yards of him, again fired, and striking him upon the point of the shoulder, brought him down with a crash.

E

He tried to get up again, but could not manage it.
He was now in a kneeling position, and evidently
dying, and one more bullet in the back of the head
from Cigar's rifle snapped the cord by which he still
clung to life. He was a grand old bull that, for
many a decade before this, to him, fatal day, must
have wandered "monarch of all he surveyed" through
these pathless forests. His tusks were long, white,
and perfect, and proved to weigh 61 lbs. and 58 lbs.
respectively. As it was still early, we chopped out
the tusks and buried them the same day, intending
to pick them up on our return to the waggons.
That evening, for the first time, I tasted elephant's
heart, roasted on a forked stick over the ashes, which
I thought then, and still consider, to be one of the
greatest delicacies that an African hunter is likely to
enjoy. The meat from the thick part of the trunk
and from the cavity above the eye is also very well
tasted, but needs much stewing to make it tender ;
the foot I consider tasteless and insipid.

Early the next day (Wednesday) we struck the
spoor of a herd of elephants, and after following it
for many hours under a burning sun, at last came up
with them fanning themselves with their ears under
a clump of trees. Cigar again gave me the first
shot, and, approaching pretty close, I fired with good
effect, hitting a young bull, with tusks weighing about
20 lbs. apiece, right through the heart. He ran off
with the herd, but fell when he had gone about a
hundred yards. Loading as I ran, I got up to the
elephants again, and with my second bullet brought
down a fine cow that fell to the shot as if struck by
lightning. Never doubting for a moment that she
was dead, I ran past her, and once more getting
pretty close behind the herd, I gave a young bull a

shot that brought him on to his hind-quarters. He regained his legs, and walked off slowly, and I managed, though now very tired, to keep up with him until I had the satisfaction of seeing him fall to the earth with a crash. I could still hear Cigar firing, but I was so thoroughly exhausted that I did not attempt to stir from where I lay panting in the shade cast by my last elephant's carcase.

Presently Cigar returned. He had killed four elephants, and his boys two more. I may here say that Cigar was a slight-built, active Hottentot, possessed of wonderful powers of endurance, and a very good game shot, though a bad marksman at a target. These qualities, added to lots of pluck, made him a most successful elephant-hunter; and for foot hunting in the " fly " country I do not think I could have had a more skilful or a kinder preceptor; for although only an uneducated Hottentot—once a jockey at Graham's Town—he continually allowed me to have the first shot, whilst the elephants were still standing—a great advantage to give me—and never tried in any way to overreach me or claim that he had first wounded any animal that I killed. Strangely enough, Cigar told me that, when the celebrated hunter, Mr. William Finaughty, first took him after elephants on horseback, he had such dreadful fear of the huge beasts that, after getting nearly caught by one, and never being able to kill any, he begged his master to let him remain at the waggons. When I knew him this fear must have long worn off, and I have never since seen his equal as a foot hunter.

We now went back to look at the cow I had shot with my second bullet, and were disgusted to find nothing of her but a piece of the tusk broken off in her fall. She must have been struck too high, and only paralysed for a short time ; at any rate she made good her escape, leaving about 6 lbs. of ivory as a souvenir. On Thursday, after many hours' tracking, we again came up with a herd of elephants. This was an unlucky day with me, for although the elephant I attacked left the herd after receiving my first bullet, he yet ran clean away and got off.

It is fearfully hard work walking for many hours on elephant spoor under a burning sun, carrying one's own gun and heavy ammunition, and having to end with a run. Cigar killed three elephants, all young bulls ; at night two parties of lions came down to the carcases, near which we were sleeping, and together with the hyænas made night hideous with their noisy revels.

On Friday, after chopping out the tusks, we walked back to our camp near the eight animals shot on Wednesday, where Cigar had left two of his Kafirs to chop out the tusks, all sixteen of which we found lying in a row on the ground. About this part of the country there were (at that time) many rhinoceroses, both of the square-mouthed and pre-hensile-lipped species. The day before I had counted eight of them, which we passed during our walk from camp to camp. Many kinds of smaller game were also plentiful, the noble-looking sable antelope being particularly abundant. Elands, roan antelopes, koo-doos, water-bucks, reed-bucks, impalas, tsessebes, zebras, buffaloes, duikers, and steinbucks, were also met with daily ; and in the river Umniati, only a few miles from where we were hunting, Cigar said there were a good many hippopotami. On Saturday we again took a round in search of elephants, and having found no fresh spoor by mid-day, we lay down

in the shade of some large trees—Kafirs and all—
and slept till late in the afternoon. Towards evening
we were returning to camp, when coming to a little
hill we climbed up it to get a view of the surrounding country. We had not yet reached the top
when one of the Kafirs said suddenly, "Look at the
elephants," or words to that effect. Turning my
eyes to where he pointed, I saw at once a string of
elephants walking quickly along in single file, not
more than a quarter of a mile off. As soon as Cigar
saw the direction in which they were going he called
out, "Come on, come on quickly, they'll smell our
spoor and run." We soon clambered down the little
hill and ran to intercept them. We were just in
time, for as the foremost elephant, a huge cow, came
upon our track we emerged from the bush not two
hundred yards away. The keen-scented brute did
not cross our spoor, but stopped dead the instant
her outstretched trunk had caught the taint left by
our footsteps. In this position she stood for a few
seconds, moving the tip of her trunk about close to
the ground, and then, wheeling round, made off at a
run, followed by all the rest. From this incident,
which I myself witnessed, some idea may be formed
of the keenness of scent possessed by the African
elephant. Out of the herd I managed to kill two,
the second one after a very hard run, and Cigar
disposed of three more. It was then dark, so we
made a large fire and slept where we were, without
blankets, alongside one of the carcases. The following Monday we started for the waggons, which we
reached on the third day, taking as much ivory with
us as the Kafirs could carry, and leaving the rest
buried. On our way we shot a white rhinoceros
cow with a fine long horn measuring 3 feet 7 inches.

I need hardly say that I was intensely delighted with the result of this my first elephant-hunting expedition, and was eager to start on a second trip as soon as possible.

Finding on my return to the camp at Jomani that the Griquas and Hottentots were out of ammunition and many other things, I decided to make a quick run back to Gubulawayo with the cart, and procure a supply of what was wanted from Mr. Kisch. Accordingly, having borrowed four fat oxen, I inspanned and started the following day. On reaching Gwenia I found that the Viljoens had returned from the Veldt, bringing with them a fine lot of ivory. Sadlier was very much dissatisfied, saying that the Boers had claimed an elephant which he had shot first, and, as he did not care about hunting any more, he returned to Gubulawayo.

There being a splendid moon, I travelled day and night, and on the fifth night reached Gubulawayo, and loading up all I required except provisions, none of which were to be had, I started back again the same evening, and reached Jomani once more after an absence of only ten days. The country was now getting fearfully parched up and the heat very great, as the rains were due, and the most oppressive weather is always just before the rainy season commences.

On the 2nd of November Cigar and I again went in on foot after the elephants, and in the afternoon of the very first day, after following some distance on their spoor, we came up with a herd of eight or ten bulls, four of which we killed, two of them falling to my rifle.

Two days later, as we were resting late in the afternoon under a shady tree, and when not far from

a small river for which we were making, a large herd
of elephant cows walked out of the forest into a
narrow open glade, about half-a-mile distant, which
they quickly crossed, disappearing in the bush on
the farther side. Though we had been walking for
many hours in the heat of the sun without water,
having found that a rivulet where we expected to
obtain some had dried up, and were very thirsty, we
at once ran to intercept the elephants, and soon came
up with them as they were walking through an open
patch of forest. I fired first, and a large cow which
I had aimed at fell with a crash to the shot as if
struck by lightning. I was loading and running
after the herd when Cigar called out to me, "Look
out, your elephant is getting up again," and, glancing
round, I was just in time to see my supposed victim
regaining her feet. As she only walked off rather
slowly, I soon ran alongside of and gave her another
shot, on which she came to a halt under a large tree.
I then approached her cautiously, but she caught
sight of or winded me, for, raising her head and
extending her ears, she gave a scream and came
towards me at a great rate. I stood where I was
and gave her a shot in the front of the head as she
came on. This shot was too high for the brain, but
it stopped her at once, and she wheeled right round
and went back to the same tree again, where I killed
her with another bullet behind the shoulder. As all
the Kafirs were with Cigar, I now walked back in
the direction of the last shots I had heard, and
threading my way through the bush, came suddenly
upon a young bull elephant—one that Cigar had
wounded. He had evidently heard me, but neither
seeing nor smelling anything, could not make out
my whereabouts. He looked very vicious as he

stood with his head raised and huge ears spread, testing the wind in all directions with the end of his upturned trunk.   He was standing exactly facing me, and in an awkward position for a shot, so I waited for him to turn, which he at length did, when I gave him a good shot behind the shoulder, to which he succumbed, after running at a sharp pace for about 200 yards.   Immediately afterwards Cigar and the Kafirs came up.   We were all excessively thirsty before we saw the elephants, and the run we had had after them had made us thirstier still, so we at once started for the little river not far distant, where we expected to find water.   Just at dusk we reached it almost at the same instant as a black rhinoceros that was approaching from the other side. Ten minutes' walk down the river's bed brought us to the water-hole we were making for, which, to our chagrin, we found to be as dry as a bone.   In this strait there was nothing for it but to follow down the course of the rivulet until we came to water.   For several hours we trudged silently on, sometimes finding a little mud but not a drop of water, which had all been sucked up by the blistering sun.   At last, about midnight, we came to a deep hole in which there was still a little water.   The Kafirs soon dug it out with their assegais, and in another hour we had all quenched our thirst.   It was a warm night, and so done were we, that, without making a fire, or undoing anything, we just stretched ourselves on the sand and were soon fast asleep.   Early the following morning, hearing some of our Kafirs exclaiming, How! how! holding their hands over their mouths and looking down at something, I went to them and asked what it was, when they pointed me out the spoor of a large lion plainly visible in the

soft sand.   He had come to within fifteen paces of
where we had been lying, and then walked silently
away ; I have no doubt that he had come to drink,
and was very much disgusted to find us all round
the water.

At the end of another week we again, having
found no more elephants, returned to the waggons,
the more so as the long-wished-for rain had come at
last, and we ourselves and our blankets had been wet
through for two days past.   The river, where only a
few nights previously we had searched so long for a
drop of water, was transformed into a torrent several
feet in depth.   The whole face of the country was
changed, and where, a week before, we might have
sought in vain, there were now ponds, lakes, rivers,
and brooks enough.

Near our waggons there was a grove of " Macunas,"
the handsomest species of tree in this part of the
country, its wide-spreading branches being covered
with dark-green foliage, and in some years with a
profusion of yellow fruit about the size of a pigeon's
egg.   This tree does not bear every year ; its fruit is
rather nice when perfectly ripe, having something the
taste of a dried date ; the stone, however, is so large
that there is not much edible matter to be got.   It is
a favourite food of the elephants, and they will come
long distances to feed upon it.

We reached the waggons on a Friday, and on the
following Monday again went into the " fly " country
after elephants, this time remaining away for a month,
and penetrating as far as the thickly-wooded hills in
the neighbourhood of the Umniati river, known by
the name of " Mafungabuzi."   On this trip we had
rather a rough time of it, for, as all my Kafir corn
was finished, we had to live entirely upon meat,

without even salt, and upon three several occasions went two whole days without food, for the game, which had been very plentiful before the rains commenced, seemed now to have left this part of the country. The rainy season too had set in in real earnest, and we were constantly exposed to heavy downpours of rain. Every evening we made a rough sort of shed, but the heavy tropical rain came through our hastily-constructed shelter, and flooded the ground beneath us in such a way that we usually got wet completely through. During this trip I shot three more elephants, one of them a fine bull with tusks weighing 50 lbs. apiece. The day I shot this elephant Cigar had killed two others. We had followed their spoor nearly all day, and it was late when we came up with them. I had a very long tiring run after mine, and almost lost him. He made one very determined charge, trumpeting loudly, but I dodged round a bush and he lost sight of me, and at last went through the Umniati river, which was running like a mill-race. This was my last chance. I was some way behind him and very fagged when he went down the bank, but I managed to make a spurt and reached the river's edge just as he was getting out on the opposite side. The bank was here several feet high; the tired and wounded beast had got his front feet on to the top, his hind legs being still in the water, so that his back was on a slope of 45 degrees, when, steadying myself, I fired into his burly carcase; he sank on to his hind-quarters, then heeled right over backwards, and falling with a tremendous splash right into the river, never stirred again. Only a small piece of his rounded side, and the point of one tusk, were visible above the water, so that the next day we had to cut

off his head, and roll it down to a place where the
bank shelved, before we could chop out his tusks.
By the time Cigar joined me the sun had been down
some time.   Having no blankets with us, we made a
good fire, chopped a few bushes which we placed in a
semicircle behind us, and cutting a little grass to lie
upon, at once went to bed.   I was tired to death,
and soon sank into a dreamless slumber.   My sleep
had lasted about an hour when I was awakened by
heavy drops of rain falling on my face.   Getting up,
I saw that the sky looked inky black, and that a
thunderstorm was fast coming up.   Ten minutes
later it burst upon us, and to a fine accompaniment
of thunder and lightning a perfect deluge of rain
came pouring down, and soon extinguished our fire.

As we were on the slope of a hill the water came
rushing down the incline and added to our discomfort.
Cold, wet, and miserable, we sat there until day
broke.   Sometimes I cursed our luck aloud in English,
and one of the Kafirs echoed the sentiment in his own
language.   Otherwise none of us spoke, but endured
with silent resignation what we could not avoid.

During the trip we killed a young elephant bull
that the Mashunas or the Banyai had attempted to
hamstring by severing the tendo Achillis.   Before
the introduction of fire-arms, this method of maiming
elephants and then killing them with assegais must,
I think, have been general in this part of Africa,
though it is now but seldom practised.   The *modus
operandi* has been described to me as follows :—A
cool and skilful man, armed with a very broad-bladed
axe, made for the purpose, with a sharp rough edge,
creeps up behind a sleeping elephant and delivers a
blow with all his force on the back of the hind foot,
about a foot above the ground, endeavouring to sever

the tendo Achillis.   If this is accomplished the poor
animal remains where he stands, almost incapable of
movement, a touching illustration of the triumph of
mind over matter ; whilst if the blow is not delivered
with sufficient force to immediately incapacitate him,
the elephant receives such a fright that he dashes
away in terror, without stopping to inquire into the
cause of his mishap.   All these tribes also kill
elephants by stabbing them from trees with large
heavy assegais made for the purpose.   When a herd
of elephants has been observed feeding quietly along,
several men will take up positions in trees on the
line of march pursued by the unsuspecting brutes.
Presently an elephant will walk immediately beneath
a tree in which one of the wily savages is seated, on
which, raising the heavy-shafted weapon with both
hands above his head, he plunges it with all his strength
between the animal's shoulder-blades.   Away rushes
the wounded beast with the assegai deep in his back ;
the heavy shaft swaying backwards and forwards
forcing the iron ever deeper into his vitals, till at last,
weakened by internal hæmorrhage, he either falls
dead, or is stabbed to death by the pursuers, who
have followed on his bloody tracks.   The blades of
these elephant assegais are often two and a half feet
long by two and a half inches broad, and the shafts
though short are very heavy, being from two to
three inches in diameter.

On my return to Jomani I found Mandy had
arrived there from Sebakwe.   My friend Dorehill
had also come in from Gubulawayo with some goods
to trade with the Griqua and Boer hunters, so we
were once more together again, and had a good talk
over our several experiences since we had last
met.   Mandy had been in with an English elephant-

hunter, Mr. George Wood, to buy corn and rice
from the Mashunas, to the east of the river Hanyane.
They had also bought a few quills of gold-dust that
had evidently been washed out of the sand of a
river's bed. A few days later, George Wood, who was
standing with his waggon on the Se-whoi-whoi river,
only a few miles distant, came over to our camp,
where we regaled him upon rather high eland and
Kafir corn. This day a little tragedy was enacted
at the Griqua waggons. It appeared that a Hottentot
in the employ of a Bastard man named Lucas, had,
a few days before, murdered a Kafir boy in cold
blood, having calmly blown out his brains because
he did not immediately bring him some water when
called. That same night Lucas caught and bound
the young murderer, and brought him into the encampment. All the Kafirs at once assembled and
demanded his life in expiation of that of their
comrade, and upon Lucas giving him up, at once
knocked his brains out with their knobkerries. I
did not know anything about it until the execution
was over. From what Lucas told me there was
little doubt that the ruffian deserved his fate, but I
was glad I did not see him killed. His body was
dragged just over a little ridge not three hundred
yards from the waggons. In the night hyænas came
and laughed and howled round the corpse for hours,
but never touched it. The second night the same
thing happened, but on the third they ate him up.
Now, as these hyænas were beasts belonging to an
uninhabited country, they were unused to human
remains, and had not, I think, lost their instinctive
dread of the smell of man ; for in the Matabele
country, where the bodies of people killed for
witchcraft are always "given to the hyænas," a

corpse is invariably dragged off even from the very gates of a kraal before the first night is many hours old.

About the 20th of December, Mandy, Dorehill, and I, as well as the Hottentots, broke up our camp and started southward for the Matabele country, leaving George Wood still encamped at Se-whoi-whoi. On reaching Gwenia we found that the Boers had already trekked out. Here occurred rather a curious incident. We were strolling along the river in the evening, looking for francolins, when my dog Bill, as he ran along the water's edge, was seized from behind by a smallish crocodile, and pulled under water. The river just here was not more than two yards broad, but deep, and running at the bottom of a steep, high bank. Seeing what had happened, I at once jumped down the bank and stood close to the water; the next instant poor Bill's head came above the surface, only to be dragged again out of sight. Seeing the white belly of the crocodile as he turned with the dog apparently only just under water, I fired both barrels at him, thinking the report alone would make him loose his hold; but it didn't. After a few seconds the poor dog's jaws again reappeared. Reaching out the gun by the barrels, I put the stock near his mouth, and he immediately seized upon it and held on with the grip of a drowning creature (the stock of this gun bears the teeth-marks to this day). I then got hold of the dog's ears, and pulling with all my strength, got the crocodile—the creature still holding fast to the dog's hind-quarters—out of the water to beyond the eyes. Dorehill, who was standing just above, on the top of the bank, then fired into the reptile's head with a charge of shot, when he at once let go and we saw

him no more.   The dog had three bad flesh wounds,
but soon recovered.   I think that the narrowness of
the stream prevented the crocodile from making
much use of his strength.   From here another four
days' trekking brought us to the mission station
of Inyati, and we finally reached Gubulawayo on the
28th of December.   I have not mentioned my horses
during this narrative, and suffice it to say that they
had been dying of the fatal sickness ever since
October, so that I only brought one back with me,
which I gave to Lobengula, as the price of the
hunting country.   Besides the 450 lbs. of ivory which
I had shot myself, I had traded nearly 1200 lbs.
besides ; and altogether, after paying my debt to Mr.
Kisch, found I had made a clear profit during the
three months of nearly £300.   Let no one think,
however, that this may be done at the present day,
for things have changed terribly for the worse since
that time—there being few successful hunters to
trade with, and fewer elephants still to shoot.
When I told the king that his elephants had not
driven me out of the country, but that, on the contrary, I had killed several, he said laughingly, " Why,
you're a man ; when are you going to take a wife?"
Shortly after this my friends Mandy and Dorehill
started for the Diamond Fields, Sadlier having
already left for Bamangwato before our arrival ;
whilst I elected to remain in the country and try and
go in hunting again the following year with George
Wood.

CHAPTER V

About the middle of January George Wood reached Gubulawayo very much knocked out of time by fever ; indeed he was so bad that upon reaching Hope Fountain, the residence of the hospitable missionary Mr. Thomson, he had to be lifted out of his waggon and carried into the house. Once there his troubles were almost over, and, thanks to the untiring kindness and attention of Mrs. Thomson and her husband, he was soon on a fair way to recovery.

George Wood, with whom I became associated for more than two years, had the reputation of being a skilful and experienced hunter, and, besides this, I afterwards found him to be a very cool and courageous man, one whose pulse beat as calmly when face to face with a wounded and angry lion or a charging elephant, as it did when quietly eating his breakfast. He was the last of the English professional elephant-hunters in this part of the country, having hunted for many years in company with the veteran Hartley

and his sons, the Jennings family, and Messrs. W.
Finaughty, J. Giffard, T. Leask, and H. Biles, all of
whom had thrown up the game some two years
previously when they found that the elephants were
retreating into the " fly "-infested districts, whither
they could not be followed on horseback ; for to
hunt these animals on foot was generally considered
to be too fatiguing a pursuit to be followed with
much chance of success by Europeans.

I very soon entered into arrangements to hunt in
company with Wood during the following winter,
and to spend the meantime in trekking about the
Matabele country, visiting the outside kraals and
doing a little trade with the natives. This we at
once set about, and, during the next four months
visited all the chief towns in the country, trading
here and there, and making the acquaintance of all
the chief indunas. In the beginning of February
we rode to Gubulawayo on horseback, leaving our
waggon at Inyati, in order to witness the grand
dance of the " Inxwāla," which is celebrated by the
Matabele every year when the first-fruits of the earth
ripen. About four thousand warriors assembled,
besides a great many women and young girls. The
men were all clothed in their splendid war dress of
black ostrich feathers, which consists of a sort of
cape of black feathers closely sewn together, covering
their chests and shoulders, and built up over their
heads in the form of a Highlander's bonnet, leaving
only their faces exposed. From their waists hung
quantities of leopard and tiger-cat tails or monkey
skins, which with the indunas form such a thick skirt
that you cannot see their legs at all. Some of the
indunas, instead of the bonnet of feathers, wear a roll
of otter skin across their foreheads, in which is stuck

F

a crane's feather, which waves gracefully in the air.
This feather war-dress is most becoming, and makes
even an undersized, ugly savage look well, and as
the greater part of the Matabele are physically a fine
tall race of men, they look magnificent, and when
standing in a semicircle round their king, with their
large ox-hide shields in front of them, must present,
I should think, as imposing a spectacle as any race of
savages in the world.

The young girls wear round their hips the
brightest-coloured calicoes that they can manage to
get hold of, which never, however, reach to their
knees, the rest of their persons being nude. With
their merry, pleasant faces, and upright shapely
figures, they formed the prettiest, if not the most
imposing, portion of the spectacle.

The dancing lasted three days, during which time
a great many oxen were slaughtered for the assembled
people, and immense quantities of beer were drunk.
The third day was the most interesting. In the large
outer kraal the four thousand beplumed warriors
stood in a large semicircle about six deep, all of them
continually humming a low chant, and every now
and then bringing their right feet in unison to the
ground with a stamp. At intervals, amidst applaud-
ing shouts, some well-known brave, after being
called upon by name, would rush out of the ranks
and show how he had killed his enemies, going
through a pantomime of how he warded off the hostile
blows with his shield, and at last delivered the death-
stab with his fatal assegai. Every downward thrust
made with the assegai represented a life taken, and
at every stab the warriors all hummed out with one
accord the word "Jee." One man I watched had seventeen lives to account for, another fifteen, and so on.

At last the king came from the inner kraal, and, advancing into the circle, stood in the midst of his warriors, dancing quietly by himself. He was dressed in monkey skins and black ostrich feathers, and really looked a king. His favourite sister, Ningengnee,[1] was also within the circle, splendidly got up for the occasion, being covered with a profusion of beads, coloured calicoes, brass amulets, and silver chains. As she was immensely fat her gambols were more grotesque than graceful, and she was so short-winded that she was continually obliged to stand and rest with her hands on her thighs. Presently the king walked in the midst of his plumed army to the open ground outside the kraal, and performed a portion of the ceremony which consists in throwing an assegai and then running forward and picking it up again. As he did this all the warriors ran forward as well, striking the inside of their shields at the same time with the butt end of their assegais, and producing a noise literally like thunder. Since then I have thrice again been present at the Inxwala dance, but have never again heard the men beat their shields as upon the first occasion.

Although we commenced to importune Lobengula to allow us to go in hunting in the middle of April, it was not until the 15th of June that he at last gave us permission to make a start. Even then, he would not let us go to the Mashuna country, but told us that we must hunt to the westward of the river Gwai. Shortly before leaving Gubulawayo, the Honourable Guy Dawney arrived from the south, accompanied by Mr. Moore of Natal, and soon afterwards left

---

[1] Ningengnee, more commonly known to white men by the name of "Ni-Ni," was put to death in December 1879 by order of her brother Lobengula, for reasons not very clearly known to any one but himself.

with an escort from Lobengula to visit the Victoria
Falls on the Zambesi. This gentleman gained a
great reputation amongst the Kafirs as a successful
hunter, and is, I believe, considered by them to be
the best runner that has ever visited the country.
He himself was, I think, much pleased with his trip,
and delighted with the beauty and grandeur of the
Falls.

After leaving Gubulawayo, we struck across
country to the north-west, passing Bukwela's kraal,
where we hired Kafirs for the trip, and crossing the
river Gwai (tobacco) soon afterwards. The bed of the
river was here composed of fine white sand, with very
little water apparent above the surface, and was about
150 yards in breadth. After holding the same course
for three days, we cut on to the hunting road leading
from John Lee's farm at Mengwe to the valley of
Linquāsi, which for several years past has been a
regular camping place for hunters during the winter
season. The following day we caught up to a party of
Dutch hunters from Mengwe, consisting of two sons
and a son-in-law of John Lee's, and the Potgieter
family, whom I had met a few months before at
Sebakwe.

About a fortnight from our start we reached
Linquāsi, a long narrow valley, presenting the appearance of an ancient river bed, with several fine deep
holes of water along its course, which, being fed by
springs, never dry up. On the evening of our
arrival, as, riding in front of the waggons, we emerged
from the forest into the open valley, we came in sight
of a black rhinoceros coming down to the water,
which we shot. Two days later we killed two fine
bull elephants within ten miles of our camp. The
Linquāsi valley, which was as far as we dared venture

with our waggons, owing to that scourge of the
African hunter, the tsetse-fly, is situated about sixty
miles as the crow flies nearly due south of the confluence of the Gwai and Shangani rivers.   Here we
made our permanent encampment, building strong
lion-proof enclosures for our cattle, and erecting a
small hut under the shade of a wide-branching goussy
tree, and from here we made raids on foot in search
of elephants into the "fly"-infested country to the
north-west, our stay varying from a fortnight to ten
weeks in duration.

In order to cover more ground, and that the one or
other of us might the oftener be at the waggons, to
see that everything was going on as it should, Wood
and myself deemed it advisable to hunt separately ;
and thus, in the beginning of July, I left the waggons
alone with eleven Kafir servants.   My battery consisted of two four-bore muzzle-loading elephant guns,
and nothing else, weapons which, however suitable
for killing elephants, are altogether unfitted for the
destruction of smaller game.   Thus, although I shot
this season a goodly number of elephants, rhinoceros,
and buffaloes, I seldom fired at anything smaller.

In the course of four months I killed to my own
gun 42 elephants, 11 of which were big bulls, whose
tusks averaged 44 lbs. apiece ; I also shot several
very fine cows, whose tusks weighed from 15 lbs. to
16 lbs.   The tusks of the largest bull I killed, when
thoroughly dried out, weighed 74 lbs. each.   During
the same time, George Wood shot about 50 elephants,
whose tusks, however, did not weigh quite as much
as mine, and our Kafir hunters also shot nearly 40
more, so that altogether we made a very profitable
hunt.   At the beginning of the season I could hardly
speak a word of Matabele, but, after having lived for

four months with Kafirs for my only companions, I
found I could converse tolerably well with them.

The tract of country in which I was principally
hunting was a wild, hilly region, situated in the angle
formed with the Zambesi by the river Gwai, which
empties itself into the Zambesi about eighty miles
to the east of the Victoria Falls.   These hills are for
the most part thickly wooded, though some are very
rocky and precipitous, and nearly all of them rough
and thorny.   In some parts they open out into broad
grassy valleys, which, dotted with clumps of trees and
bush, present quite a park-like appearance.   Most
of these dales are intersected by small rivers, in which,
during the dry season, water is usually to be found
either in occasional pools or by digging in the sand,
whilst after heavy rains they become veritable
torrents.   In other parts, again, narrow steep-sided
ravines, or "kloofs" as they are called in South
African parlance, are met with, the sides and bottoms
of which are often covered with dense jungle, and
such places form during the heat of the day a
favourite resort of elephants and buffaloes.

There is also another curious feature presented
amongst these hills, which is, that some of them,
although steep and rocky on all sides, are perfectly
level on the top, like a table, and covered with very
thick bush, to which large game are also extremely
partial.

All this tract of country, though claimed by the
king of the Matabele, whose father, Umziligazi,
drove out its former possessors, is at present uninhabited; but some forty years ago, before these all-
conquering Zulus invaded it, murdering or driving
away the inhabitants, it must have supported a large
population, as the frequent traces of maize-fields, and

the clearings, once the site of large villages, prove beyond a doubt.

These people belonged to various sections of the Makalaka tribe, and on being driven from their towns and corn-fields, fled across the Zambesi; whither their ruthless destroyers, being without canoes, were unable to follow them. The different species of animals that I noticed in this district, were elephant, black and white rhinoceros, buffalo, zebra, sable and roan antelope, koodoo, impala, reedbuck, wild boars (both the wart-hog and the bush-pig), klipspringer, and grys steinbuck, whilst near the Gwai are found many water-buck, and a beautifully striped and spotted variety of the bush-buck. Between the borders of the hills and Linquāsi, a great part of the country is covered with dense thickets of wait-a-bit thorn, called by the natives "Isinanga," alternating with open goussy forests. Here, in addition to most of the game enumerated above, elands and giraffes are also found.

In illustration of the kind of hunting in which I was engaged during the season, I think I cannot do better than make a few extracts from my journal concerning some of the most interesting of my experiences, parts of which were published a few years ago in the columns of the *Field* newspaper :—

Having made a trial trip of a fortnight's duration into the "fly," during which I had shot seven elephants, amongst them two fine bulls, I found myself, in the commencement of August, in the hilly country near the confluence of the Gwai and Shangani rivers, where I had been hunting during the past ten days with but slight success, having only come across one troop of elephant cows, four of which I had brought to bag. So I now determined to try the

country to the north-west, in the direction of the
Victoria Falls. As none of my " boys " (all native
servants in the interior of South Africa are called
" boys," no matter what their age may be) had any
knowledge of the country in which we were about to
hunt, I had all the calabashes filled with water early
in the morning before starting, though from the lie
of the land I hardly anticipated our suffering much
from want of that thrice-blessed element.   However,
it is always best to be on the safe side, and as it
turned out we did not reach water till late in the
afternoon, when coming upon a large elephant path,
we knew there must be some at no great distance,
and following the path, soon came out upon a fine
valley, running through which was a sand river with
pools of water at intervals along its course.

At some distance up the valley some zebras and
impala were quietly feeding down towards the river,
and nearer to us, just on the edge of the bush, stood
a small herd of sable antelope—amongst them one
particularly fine old bull, with a magnificent pair of
horns curling over almost to his haunches.

Although we still had some buffalo meat left, and
by firing with a heavy gun in the still of the evening
I risked disturbing elephants, if there were any in
the neighbourhood, still, as the wind was favourable,
and we were as yet unperceived, I could not resist the
desire to possess myself of those long sweeping horns ;
so, bidding my Kafirs lie down, I took the most
carefully sighted of the two elephant guns, which
were the only weapons I had with me, and, stalking
carefully from bush to bush, at length arrived within
about 120 yards of the herd.   At this moment the
old fellow, being nearer than the others, must have
caught an indistinct glimpse of me behind the bush ;

for, with head erect and ears cocked, he now gazed intently at the spot where I crouched concealed. Seeing that it was useless to attempt to get any nearer, I noiselessly raised myself to a kneeling position, and, taking a careful aim at his chest, fired. At the shot he fell on his knees, but, recovering, sprang up and bounded off at full gallop after the retreating herd ; but his race was short, for, after rushing along at full speed for about 100 yards, he staggered and fell, and in a few moments the remorseless assegais of my Kafirs had quenched the last sparks of vitality that still remained.

On coming up I found that I had made a very creditable shot, considering my weapon (a smoothbore elephant gun, carrying a four-ounce round bullet, backed by fifteen drachms of coarse powder), the ball, after entering the chest rather low, and passing through the whole length of the body, having made its exit by the left thigh, grazing the heart on its passage.

As it was now late, and we had both fresh meat and water, I determined to sleep here ; so, after cutting off the grand-looking head, and leaving some of the Kafirs to look after the meat, I went with the rest to try and find a suitable place to make a " skerm." But perhaps I ought to explain first of all what a " skerm " is. In the first place, to make one, a lot of bushes and branches of trees are cut, and a semicircular hedge made, after which, the ground enclosed by this hedge having been smoothed to some extent with an axe, stumps chopped out, stones removed, etc., a lot of dry grass is cut and laid down in the centre in the form of a bed, at the foot of which a pole is placed, to keep the grass from getting down into the fire, which is lighted some two or three feet off. On this primitive but comfortable bed the hunter spreads his blanket, his Kafir servants sleeping within the hedge on each side of him, with fires at their feet also.

During the dry season, which lasts, as a rule, in these latitudes, from May till October, nothing can be pleasanter than thus sleeping out in the open air. The atmosphere is dry and bracing—in the winter time very cold ; no dew falls, and the tired hunter on his bed of grass, with nought to shut out the clear starry heavens from his view, envies not the sybarite on his bed of down.

By sunset the "skerm" was made, the meat all cut up and hung on poles, and I had finished skinning the sable antelope's head, and was just thinking about attacking my supper of stewed meat and rice, washed down with a cup of bitter tea, when one of my boys attracted my attention by remarking, "There's a rhinoceros." And looking up I saw a white rhinoceros cow, with an almost full-grown calf, coming down a footpath to the water on the opposite side of the valley. My boys were very anxious that I should go and shoot one, as the white species at this season of the year are always very fat and excellent eating. However, as I wished to get on the next day, and they had as much meat, both sable antelope and buffalo, as they could carry, I would not do so, as I consider it a grievous sin to shoot these lumbering, stupid animals, unless having really need of the meat, or when tempted by a particularly fine horn. About an hour after sundown a large troop of buffaloes came down to a pool a little way up the river, and we could hear them grunting and splashing about for a long time ; a troop of lions also awoke the echoes of the night with their grand music, but at

some distance off; and a couple of hyænas, giving
vent at intervals to their weird, melancholy howls,
testified, I suppose, to their appreciation of the
remains of the sable antelope. At last, lulled by
these voices of the wilderness, and tired by a long
day's march, I fell asleep, nor awoke before the light
in the eastern sky proclaimed the advent of another
day.

This day's walk led us through an undulating
country, bordering on the rough, rugged hills which
stretch from here to the Zambesi. We crossed a
good deal of elephant spoor during the forenoon,
some not more than a day or two old, but saw none
absolutely fresh until late in the afternoon, when we
crossed the spoor of a troop of bulls that had passed
during the preceding night. The "veldt" about
here seemed admirably suited for elephants, as there
were great quantities of the "machabel" tree, of
which they are particularly fond.

As the sun was now fast sinking towards the
horizon, it behoved us to look for water and arrange
our camp for the night. From the game spoor
about—zebra, impala, rhinoceros, buffalo, etc., all of
which are animals that drink regularly every day—we
knew there must be either a vley or river at no great
distance; and soon afterwards, at the foot of a long
low hill, we came to a deep watercourse, and, following
it down for about a mile, discovered a small water
hole under a high bank, which had evidently been
dug out in the sand by elephants or other game.
However, from the broad footpaths which continued
down the river, trampled deep into the ground by
generations of their huge feet, and with quite recent
spoor upon them, it was plain to me that there was
a larger pool at no great distance; so, as there was

sufficient water for drinking purposes at the small hole, and it being already late, I directed my boys to make a skerm on the slope of a hill close by, and then, taking one of my gun-carriers with me, went down the river to see if it was anywhere near. I had not gone a hundred yards before a large herd of buffaloes and zebras feeding on the bank, and some in the river bed about three hundred yards off, showed me that there was water near.

Having still some fresh meat, and not wishing to fire for fear of disturbing elephants, I walked straight down towards the buffaloes, who, after taking a good look at the intruder, turned, and, headed by the zebras, went off at a lumbering gallop for about a hundred yards, then collected into a dense mass, turned again, took another look, and finally disappeared over a piece of rising ground.

I now went down to look at the water, and found not one, but a succession of large pools. At one place there was a little basin under a steep bank, as clear and cool as crystal, as it was so sheltered by the overhanging ledge that the sun never shone upon it. Running down to these pools, at right angles to the course of the river, were two valleys between low ranges of hills, down each of which, and along both banks of the river, came innumerable elephant paths, all converging to the water holes. By the spoor, the broken trees round about, etc., this seemed to be an old time-honoured drinking-place of theirs, and, moreover, as if only the males resorted to it, for —although up and down the river, along the paths, and all around, lay the spoor, some old, some quite fresh, of what my imagination pictured to be gigantic tusked bulls—not a single cow spoor was to be seen. The tracks of game, too, of almost every sort, but especially rhinoceros (both white and black) and buffalo, proclaimed it a favourite resort of these animals also ; indeed, it seemed to me that I had reached a hunter's paradise at last, and so, with joyful expectations for the morrow, I returned with a light heart to the skerm, and determined to stop where I was, at the small pool, which was about a quarter of a mile from the drinking-place, as we should not then be likely to disturb elephants coming down to drink at night.

It was just dark when I reached the skerm ; so, after discussing a frugal but hearty supper, and telling the Kafirs not to make a noise, I was soon dreaming of elephants with abnormal tusks, rhinoceroses with horns five feet long, and other equally pleasant fictions. About midnight I awoke with a start, with the idea that an elephant had " run me in," and was about to work its wicked will upon me ; but, looking up, found one of my boys shaking me by the shoulder, who, with eyes gleaming through the darkness with excitement, informed me that elephants were drinking down at the water, as he had just heard one trumpet. The boys were all up now, and we sat round the smouldering fires, listening with painful intensity for the wished-for sound. " Nansia ! " (There it is) burst from the Kafirs like one man, and the trumpeting of an elephant, evidently down at the water, rang out once more shrill and clear on the still night air. We sat up listening for perhaps an hour, but heard nothing further—nothing at least but the snorting of a black rhinoceros, also on his way to drink—and so once more lay down to recruit ourselves with sleep for the anticipated struggle on the morrow.

Early next morning, as soon as it began to grow

light, we were up and stirring, and after looking at
the priming of the guns, filling the powder bags
(when elephant-hunting on foot, we load with the
hand from a leather powder bag hung at the side),
and putting ten four-ounce bullets into each pouch,
I hastily drank a cup of strong coffee, ate a few
mouthfuls of grilled meat, and started for the water,
leaving my two youngest Kafir boys to look after my
blankets and all the traps at the skerm.

Arrived at the nearest pool, the first glance convinced us that our ears had not played us false in
the night ; for there, deeply impressed in the soft
mud, lay the giant footprints of several splendid bulls.

A careful survey round about soon showed us
that they had come down by the valley to the right,
and after drinking and splashing about at all the
pools, had gone out into the low hills on the left ;
so putting Minyama, my best spooring Kafir, on the
track, we lost no time in starting in pursuit. The
troop, as well as could be judged, consisted of about
ten or twelve bulls, amongst them three or four
regular old teasers, with footprints nearly two feet
in diameter. The spoor led us in a north-easterly
direction, across low undulating hills, and they had
evidently taken it easy here, feeding about on the
succulent "machabel" trees, which were very
numerous ; such havoc, indeed, had they committed,
that it was easy to follow them without looking for
the footprints, just by glancing on ahead at the
trees stripped of their bark, and the clusters of fresh
leaves and chewed bark left along their track. After
following their spoor for about a couple of hours
across this sort of country, it led us to some much
higher and more rugged hills, and here they had
ceased to feed and taken to an old path, stepping it

out at a brisk pace in single file. After following
the spoor for about another hour along this path, it
once more left it, and struck off again in the old
direction across the hills, and, just here getting
amongst a lot of yesterday's tracks, we had great
difficulty in following it; but at length Minyama,
with the sagacity and perseverance of a bloodhound,
ferreted it out, and away we went again. About
eleven o'clock we got into a patch of very thick
scrubby bush (what the Kafirs call "idoro" bush),
in a deep kloof between the hills, and here we went
along with great care and caution, expecting every
instant to see the elephants, as I made sure they
would not pass a place so favourable for their mid-day
siesta; however, they went clean out of here, and up
the steep hill on the other side. Arrived at the top,
we looked down upon a large kloof, enclosed on all
sides with steep hills, and covered with dense bush,
thicker a good deal than that we had just come
through, and as I looked I felt sure my friends were
standing sleeping not many hundred yards off (it
being now about mid-day, and the sun very hot).

The Kafirs here took off their raw-hide sandals,
that they might walk more quietly, and following
the spoor carefully, we descended cautiously into the
depths of the kloof, and near the centre of it came
to a place from which they had evidently not long
moved on, as the dung was still warm. Before we
had proceeded a hundred yards farther, Minyama
suddenly came to a halt, and crouching down, with
his arm pointing forwards and his head turned
towards me, whispered, "Nansia incubu" (There are
the elephants). Ah, how those two words thrill
through the hunter's breast, making his heart leap
again with concentrated excitement!

Stooping down, I now saw them not more than thirty yards off, for the bush was very dense. They were standing huddled together in a mass under the shade of a large tree, gently flapping their huge ears in a sleepy, contented sort of way, all unconscious of the deadly enemy that lurked so near. Judging that when they were started they would make for the steep banks of the kloof, either on the one side or the other, and as what little wind there was was blowing from them towards where we were standing, I sent two of my boys up each side to drive them towards me if they came in their direction (it is usually an easy matter to turn elephants by shouting in front of them, though of course it sometimes happens that, instead of turning, they charge in the direction of the noise). Having made these arrangements, and after taking a gulp of water from the calabash and giving a hitch to my belt, I beckoned to my two gun-carriers, and then taking my first gun, crept quietly to within about twenty yards of the still unconscious elephants, to look for the finest pair of ivories. Owing to the way in which they were crowded together, I could not get a very good view of most of them; one, however, standing to the left of the rest, and turned half away from me, showed a fine long tusk on the right-hand side, offering at the same time a good shot behind the shoulder; and so, not seeing a better chance, I fired. I had hoped to get another shot with the second gun, but the bush was so thick, and the elephants broke away in their panic with such despatch, that I could not get a chance; so calling to my second gun-carrier to keep close, I ran as hard as I could after them. At their first set-off, running all close together, they had cleared a path like a waggon road; but on reaching the steep side of the hill they had to slacken their speed (elephants can only go very steadily up-hill, but down, no matter how rough be the ground, they run at a tremendous pace).

At about 150 yards from the starting-place, the one I had fired at as they stood fell dead, having been shot through the heart, and I dashed past him after the others. Luckily, they ran right on to the two Kafir boys that I had sent up the hill on the right-hand side of the kloof before firing, and on their shouting lustily, immediately turned and came rushing down again, carrying trees, bushes, stones, and everything before them, right past me. As they went by I gave one a shot somewhere about the shoulder ; but the bush being so thick, it was little more than a snap shot, and, although my first gun was loaded again, I had no time for another. However, a four-ounce round bullet, hardened with zinc and quick-silver, is no trifle, even to such a mighty beast as an African bull elephant, and immediately on getting it he slackened his pace, and, not being able to keep up with the rest, turned out and took along the side of the hill. I did my best to keep up with him ; but, although he now only went at a sort of long half walk, half trot, I had to put my best foot foremost to maintain my position in the thick bush, as an elephant, though so large an animal, is a thing easily lost sight of. I was careful to keep under the wind, as a wounded elephant is apt to make himself dis-agreeable, and trusts more to his scent than his eyesight in charging. Three several times did I range alongside, and take the gun from my Kafir's hands to fire ; but the bush was so thick that, though at very close quarters, I could not get a chance, and had to run on again, hoping the ground would get a

G

little more open presently. At last, having crossed
the bottom of the kloof, he either heard something
or got a whiff of tainted air, and turning suddenly
round, with his huge ears extended, his trunk stretched
straight out, and his wicked, vicious-looking eyes
gazing in our direction, stood ready to charge, no
doubt, if he could but ascertain our exact whereabouts. But small time was allowed him for consideration, for to get the gun to my shoulder and
plant a bullet in his exposed chest was the work of
but few seconds. On receiving the ball he fell on
his knees, but recovering, picked himself slowly up,
turned, and resumed his retreat, but now only at a
slow walk.

At this instant, glancing to the right, I perceived
four more elephants coming down the side of the
hill a little on ahead (my boy Minyama afterwards
claimed to have headed these and turned them back
towards the bottom of the valley) ; so, believing that
the one to which I had been paying attention was all
but done for, and wishing to secure another if
possible, I sent my second gun-carrier and two more
boys after him, telling them to finish him, or at any
rate keep him in sight, and then ran to intercept the
other four. I was just in time, and as they passed
in front of me, at not more than forty yards' distance,
in single file, I gave the last one (he having the finest
ivory) a shot in the middle of the shoulder, but a few
inches too high ; however, it slackened his speed
considerably, and he left the others. Quickly reloading, I followed, and getting to where the bush was a
little more open, shouted behind him, "Hi there !
Woho, old man !" and, fatal curiosity, or perhaps a
wish for vengeance, inducing him to turn, planted
another four-ounce ball in his chest. He wheeled

round immediately, but, his strength failing him, only walked a few yards, and stood under a tree, and, after receiving another bullet square in the shoulder, gave a fierce shake of the head, making his huge ears flap again, and, sinking slowly down with his hind legs doubled out, surrendered up his tough old spirit —looking, for all the world, though dead, like a tame elephant when kneeling for people to ascend to the howdah.

Having heard some shots fired by my gun-carrier at the one first wounded, I now made all haste in the direction where the last shot fell; when suddenly, not far to my left, the silent forest rang again with short piercing trumpetings, repeated so quickly one after another, and continuing for such a time, that I made sure one of my boys was caught—as when an elephant is either very near on to his persecutor, or has actually overtaken him, he emits scream upon scream in quick succession, all the time stamping upon and ventilating his enemy with his tusks, and only ceasing to scream when he has done with him; and persons thus operated upon are seldom known to complain of their treatment after it is over.

Before I could reach the scene of action the trumpeting had ceased; so, calling to my gun-carrier by name, I listened anxiously, and in another instant was much relieved to see him, still alive, but looking very crestfallen. There he was, without gun or assegais, all scratched and bleeding from violent contact with the bushes, and his eyes almost starting out of his head with fright, which was scarcely to be wondered at considering the trying ordeal he had just gone through. He said that, having given the elephant two shots, it just walked slowly on without appearing to take any notice, and that then, having

stopped to reload, he had lost sight of him for a
moment, and so running on the spoor with eyes bent
on the ground, had got almost under the brute's very
tusks before he saw him, as the elephant, having
turned and waited behind a bush, let him come quite
close, and then rushing out, had kept him literally
under his trunk for about a hundred yards, and would
no doubt have eventually caught him if he had not
been so weakened by his previous wounds.   In his
flight he had thrown the gun and assegais away, and
he must indeed have had a miraculous escape, for his
back and the calves of his legs had drops of blood
upon them, that could only have come from the trunk
of the elephant.   The two other Kafirs who were
near him, and had bolted on seeing the elephant
charge, now coming up, I told them to take the spoor,
that we might get the gun and then despatch him, as
I was sure he was not far off.   After picking up the
gun and the assegais (one of which had been trodden
on and smashed by the elephant), we took up the
spoor, and, as I had predicted, had not gone far before
we saw him walking slowly along, the blood dripping
from his trunk, looking very sick—though he would
very likely have tried another charge if he had got
the chance, as sometimes they are game to the very
last, and have been known to fall dead whilst in the
act of charging.   I now ran a little wide of him, in a
half-circle, and getting in front waited for him, and
as he passed gave him a ball, at about twenty yards'
distance, through the heart.   Directly the bullet
struck him he broke into a run, and, after going for
about a hundred yards, fell with a crash stone dead,
bringing a small tree down in his fall.

On examination this proved to be the finest of
the three, his teeth weighing 55 lbs. and 57 lbs.

respectively.   Those of the one that fell on his knees, though long, were thinner, and weighed 42 lbs. each ; whilst, on examination, the one I shot first proved to have but one tusk (not a very uncommon thing in South Africa, though more often met with amongst the cows than the bulls), which I did not know when I fired at him.   This single tusk weighed 53 lbs.

As there was not time to chop out the teeth of all three elephants and get back to the skerm before nightfall, I resolved to chop out those of the largest, and send my boys back the next day for those of the remaining two.   After about an hour and a half's hard work the tusks were laid on the grass, and after cutting out the heart (the tit-bit in my opinion, though some people prefer the foot or trunk), all the inside fat—which, when rendered down, is nearly as good as butter—and some meat from the thick part of the trunk, we proceeded to make tracks home-wards, reaching the skerm just about sundown ; and I soon had a piece of elephant's heart, nicely salted and peppered, roasting on a forked stick over the coals ; and if I had but had a white companion with whom to talk over the day's sport and fight the battle o'er again, my happiness would have been complete.

My boys, however, went in for a night of it ; for, after having gorged themselves with fat meat, they commenced dancing, sometimes all at once, some-times one or the other of them performing a *pas seul*, the rest clapping their hands in time to the measure ; then the whole day's sport was gone through in pantomime ; and all the while they sang wild songs, some extemporaneously in praise of their own and my prowess as hunters, while others were the old standard songs of their country, of which there is a large stock.   Altogether it was a wild and interesting

scene, and their naked figures and wild gestures, now
brought into strong relief against the dark back-
ground, and anon but dimly seen in the uncertain
light of the large log fires, recalled vividly to my
mind the pictures, in an old book at home of Captain
Cook's voyages, of the South Sea Islanders dancing
round the fire during the preparation of a savoury
meal of human flesh.

As we were a long way from the elephants'
drinking-place, and a little license must always be
allowed after a successful day's hunt, I let them have
their fling, and they kept it up, eating, dancing, and
singing at intervals, till after midnight ; at length,
however, tired nature asserted her sway, and we all
slept soundly till daylight.

PLATE IV

1. DUIKER ANTELOPE ♂ (Cephalophus Mergens).

   Shot near the river Tati, Sept. 1876.

2. DUIKER ANTELOPE ♀ (Cephalophus Mergens).

   Shot near the Limpopo river, May 1880.

3. ORIBI ANTELOPE ♂ (Nanotragus Scoparius).

   Shot on the Manica plateau, north of the Zambesi river, Dec. 24, 1877.

4. KLIPSPRINGER ANTELOPE ♂ (Nanotragus Oreotragus).

   Shot in the Mashuna country, Sept. 1880.

5. DUIKER ANTELOPE ♂ (Cephalophus Mergens).

   Shot on the borders of the Kalahari desert, July 1872.
   Length of horns, 5 inches.

6. STEINBUCK ♂ (Nanotragus Tragulus).

   Shot in Griqualand, Nov. 1871.

7. STEINBUCK ♂ (Nanotragus Tragulus).

   Shot in the Mashuna country, Dec. 3, 1878.

8. STEINBUCK ♂ (Nanotragus Tragulus).

   Shot near the river Tati, April 1874.

9. GRYSBUCK ♂ (Nanotragus Melanotis).

   Caught by a dog in the Mashuna country, Sept. 11, 1878.

PLATE IV

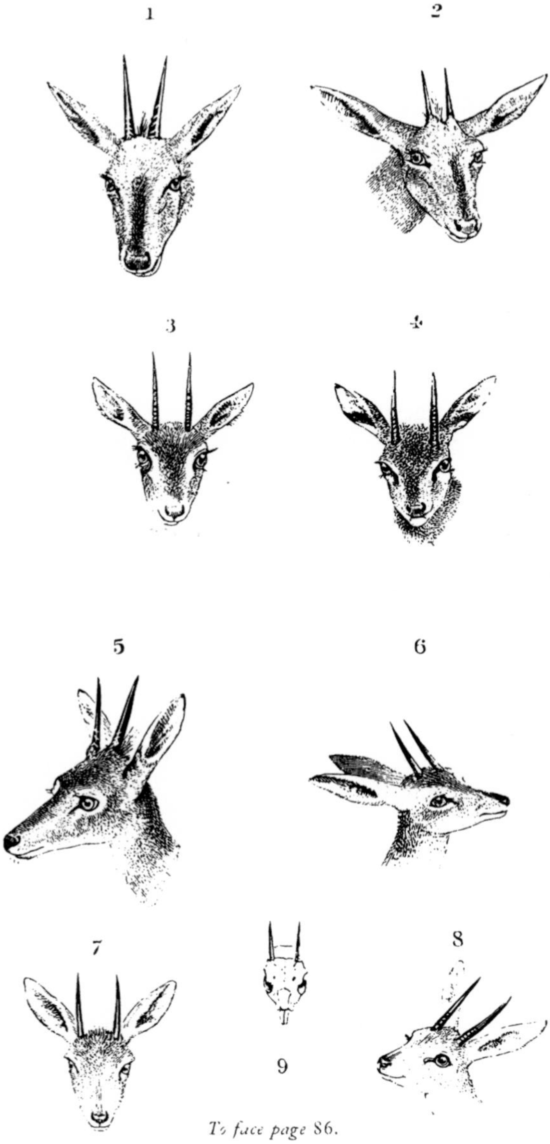

1
2
3
4
5
6
7
9
8

T; face page 86.

CHAPTER VI

NEXT morning I sent a boy down early to see if
elephants had drunk at the water during the night.
As they had not done so, and it being Sunday, I
determined to have a day's rest ; so, keeping a couple
of Kafirs with me at the skerm, I sent the others to
chop out the teeth of the two remaining elephants,
and then taking my blankets and a copy of Byron's
poems, and establishing myself under a shady tree, I
prepared to pass a lazy morning. During the day a
honeybird came to the skerm, chirping and fluttering
about from tree to tree, and doing its utmost to
attract our attention ; and so, reflecting that a little
fresh honey is always a welcome addition to one's
larder in the veldt, I told my two boys to take the
small axe and a firebrand (to smoke the bees) and
follow the noisy little fellow, and soon the faint sound
of chopping announced that he was not hoaxing, as
is sometimes the case, but had guided them to a nest
hard by. In about an hour they returned with a large
piece of mopani bark, bent up at both ends, full of

delicious fresh honey, to which I proceeded to do
ample justice.   Late in the afternoon the boys came
back with the three tusks, and loaded with fat and
meat.   They reported having crossed fresh spoor,
about half-way between the skerm and the dead
elephants; so, there being evidently several herds of
those animals about, I resolved to remain at least a
week here, and hunt the country thoroughly all round.
During the night we heard nothing at the water, but on
going down early the next morning were rejoiced to
find that, nevertheless, a fine troop of bulls had drunk
there, and gone out in the same direction as those
we had followed on Saturday.   Filling the calabashes,
we were soon following at a brisk pace.   For the
first hour they took nearly the same course as those
we had last shot ; but after a time, turning in a more
northerly direction, the spoor took us on to one of
the large elephant footpaths, which are so common in
this part of the country.   Here they had evidently
stepped out at a great pace, as if something had
frightened them.   Hour after hour we trudged along
the path, until I began to think we stood but a small
chance of coming up with them ; but, as elephant
bulls are not to be seen every day, I determined not
to give it up yet awhile, although, as I rested under
a tree for the first time for a few minutes, my boys
tried to dissuade me from following the spoor any
farther—for, said they, the elephants are evidently
trekking, and do not intend standing during the heat
of the day, and we shall only have to sleep without
blankets, food, and water, for nothing.   It was a
sweltering hot day, and our water was indeed very
nearly out ; but, still hoping for the best, I bade them
be quiet and take the spoor again, which they sulkily
did.   After another hour's walking the spoor again

left the path and took across the veldt, the elephants
having commenced feeding again here and there,
tempted by the soft leaves of the machabel, which
grew in great profusion.   About four o'clock I once
more sat down for a few minutes' rest ; but I now
had better hopes of coming up with the elephants, for
they had been feeding quietly along for some time,
though always moving forwards, and I knew we must
have gained greatly on them during the last few
hours.   However, the sun was fast sinking towards the
western hills, and I feared that darkness might come
on before we could overtake them.

My Kafirs now, knowing that even if we turned
back it would be impossible to reach the skerm that
night, and that our only chance of getting meat and
water was by pushing forwards and catching the
elephants, once more took the spoor with renewed
ardour, and we had not gone far before coming to
where they had separated into three parties.   Two
only had continued in the old course, and, as the
spoor of these two was the biggest of the lot, I
resolved to follow them.

The country here became more barren and rugged,
though the valleys were sparsely wooded with the now
almost leafless mopani trees ; but, as the elephants
had been feeding, breaking off a branch here and a
strip of bark there, the spoor was easy to follow, and
we got along at a good pace.   From the appearance
of the dung and the freshness of the leaves and
chewed bark, we were evidently fast overhauling
them, though, as there was scarcely an hour's sun
left, and there is but a scant allowance of twilight in
these latitudes, I began to fear that darkness would
intervene before we caught them.   At last, after
another half-hour's spooring, the foremost Kafir,

turning over some dung with his naked foot, pronounced it to be warm, and I knew we might now
expect to see our game every instant.   Indeed, not
ten minutes afterwards my boy Minyama, who was in
front on the spoor, suddenly bobbed down as if he
had been shot, and I knew he had seen the elephants
so, creeping forwards, I peered cautiously over the
ridge, and there beheld two magnificent old bulls
standing under a large mopani tree about seventy
yards down the side of the hill.   The largest was
standing broadside on, and was truly a splendid beast,
with a pair of remarkably long, white, perfect tusks,
protruding far beyond the lip—the largest, in fact, I
have ever seen before or since in the flesh ; the other
was standing head on to us, but, though his tusks
were foreshortened, owing to his position, I could
see they were also both long and thick.   They were
evidently enjoying a little rest, their large ears flapping listlessly against their sides like two enormous
fans, and little thinking of the persevering enemy
who had followed them like an avenging Fate
through all their turnings, and now at last stood so
near them as they slept in fancied security.   There
was, however, no time to be lost, as the sun had
already disappeared behind the hills, and I knew I
had, at the outside, but a short half-hour of daylight
left.

About half-way down the slope of the hill, between
where we stood and the elephants, lay a fallen mopani
tree, which had been no doubt uprooted by one of
these beasts during the last rainy season ; so, taking
my gun, and followed closely by my second carrier,
I crept, step by step, very cautiously down towards
them.   Though an elephant is very bad of sight, and
one can walk almost up to one if the wind is right

and if there is any bush about, yet here, there being
only the few dead branches of the mopani tree to
screen me from their sight, I was afraid they might
see me, and run before I could get there ; however,
I reached the tree safely enough without disturbing
them, and was just climbing over some of the
prostrate branches to get to the farther side, when,
unfortunately, I trod upon a dry stick, which broke
with a loud crack, and the larger elephant hearing it
immediately walked a few steps forward, and stood
with his head up and ears extended, listening intently.
I was now not more than thirty yards off, and he was
standing broadside on, offering a splendid shot, but,
unfortunately, with his shoulder partially covered by
a small mopani tree against which he stood.   That
hindered me from getting a chance at his heart ; but
there was no time to be lost, as he might imagine
danger was near, and run at any moment ; so, taking
an aim for his lungs (which, if in the right spot, is
almost a better shot for large game than through the
heart), I touched the hair trigger, I myself being
nearly knocked down by the recoil of the heavily
charged gun.   On receiving the bullet the huge beast
uttered a loud roar, half bellow, half groan, and,
followed by his companion, tore down the gently
sloping hill at a tremendous rate.   Throwing down
the gun to be loaded and brought on by my attendant,
I, closely followed by my second gun-carrier and remaining Kafirs (whose work it was to get ahead of
the elephants and turn them back towards me), dashed
after them in eager pursuit.   At the bottom of the
hill, about two hundred yards distant, was a deep
watercourse, and whilst the elephants were getting
through this we gained on them considerably.   The
wounded one, on reaching the top of the opposite

bank, came to a stand, and, turning round, faced his
pursuers, throwing the blood in streams from his
upraised trunk.   Being now close to him, I seized
my second gun from the Kafir's hands, and was just
about to fire, when with a crash this true monarch of
the African forest fell, slain by the only living thing
that could work him harm—ruthless man.   I did not
stop a second to contemplate my prize, but kept on
at my best pace after the other, who was disappearing
over the next ridge, about a hundred and fifty yards
in advance.   The country being pretty open, we were
enabled to keep him in view, although a good distance
off ; but the ground was excessively rough under
foot, great boulders and stones lying about in every
direction, and the way in which the huge beast
scrambled over them was truly marvellous.   At last
he reached a broad dry sand river, with a steep high
bank on the farther side, and as he entered it we were
still some three hundred yards behind.   Now was
my chance, and probably my last, for I knew he
would lose time in climbing out the other side, but
when once up would make the running again, and as
it was in the cool of the evening, the Kafirs would
stand little chance of getting up and turning him ;
so, though terribly blown, I gathered my exhausted
energies together for a last effort, and, closely attended
by my gun-carrier, made a spurt.   As the elephant
neared the top, toiling painfully and slowly up, I got
to within about one hundred and twenty yards of
him, and taking a quick aim, just behind the big ribs
as he turned half sideways, fired.   " Ingenile ! " (It's
gone into him) said the Kafir, and we ran on again,
jumping into the bed of the river just as he disappeared over the opposite bank.   Tired and panting,
we toiled across the deep sand of the river bed, and

on scrambling up to the level ground beyond were
very much surprised and rejoiced to see the object of
our pursuit not a hundred yards off on his fore knees,
with his tusks resting on the ground ; and before we
could get up to him he rolled over on his side, never
to rise again.   The bullet having entered just behind
the ribs and driven well forwards, must have divided
some of the large arteries just above the heart, for on
cutting out that organ the next morning we found it
had not been actually struck, as I had at first imagined.
Thus with two bullets had I laid low two splendid
elephant bulls, and I felt well satisfied with my success.
But it was time to think of other things.   Our last
gourd of water had been emptied at about two
o'clock, and as the day had been excessively hot,
both the Kafirs and myself were much in need of a
drink, even before we came up with the elephants ;
and now, after our hard run, were suffering greatly
from thirst.   However, from the appearance of the·
deep holes dug in the sand of the river bed by
elephants, we imagined that we should find water
close to ; and on those of my boys coming up who,
as they carried the water calabashes and axes, had not
been able to keep up with us during the chase, I told
all the Kafirs to cut some meat from the trunk, that
we might take it with us, and then go and sleep near
the first water hole we came to.   They, however,
protested that " thirst was killing them," and that it
would be better to go and get water first (thinking
there was some close at hand), then fill the calabashes
and come back and sleep at the elephant ; so, not
thinking it would make much difference, I assented,
and we immediately started down the river.   It was
now nearly dark, and we walked along the soft sandy
bed, expecting to find water in one of the holes at

every instant; but we went on and on, scraping at the bottom of one after another without success, till at last we had got so far away that I determined to go to bed hungry when we did find some rather than tramp back again to the elephant.

Having been walking incessantly since the first dawn of day, and having had a most severe chase after the one last killed, I was excessively fatigued, and nothing would have induced me to stir a yard farther but thirst—not even the prospect of a good dinner, although, with the exception of the merest mouthful of grilled meat early in the morning before starting, I had eaten nothing since the preceding evening. However, water one must have: hunger only comes on in pangs, and can be tolerated, but thirst tortures one without cessation until relieved. In this manner I fancy we must have groped our way along for an hour and a half or more, and were beginning to despair, when, just where the river narrowed and ran in between two high hills, we perceived in the gloom of the overhanging cliff the outlines of some native huts. On going up to them (crossing an old corn-field on the way), we found they had been long deserted. They must have been occupied by natives from the Zambesi, who had returned to their own country (probably from fear of the Matabele) after cutting their corn. This discovery put new hope into our hearts, as we felt sure there must be water near at hand; and in fact, after walking a short distance and climbing over a few large boulders in the bed of the river, we discovered a pool under an immense rock, and soon relieved our thirst. On either side of us the hills rose precipitously, and though it was a brilliant starry night, but little light reached the bottom of this ravine, which was dark and gloomy to a degree. However, but little light is needed to enable a thirsty man to drink. After well satisfying ourselves and filling the calabashes, we commenced climbing the hill to look for a place where we might pass the night, and finding a tolerably flat ledge about half-way up, I resolved to go no farther. We were too tired to think of making a skerm; so, lighting a fire, I lay down on the bare ground, without a blanket, placing my felt hat on the top of a stone for a pillow, the Kafirs disposing themselves round two or three other fires; and although I reflected that there were many other things in this world more acceptable for supper after a hard day's work than cold water, yet in spite of hunger, fatigue, and a bed on the cold ground, I felt elated and joyful at the thought of the successful issue of the day's sport. After a time the extreme feeling of hunger passed off, and I slept pretty well, though awakened at intervals by the cold. At about midnight two or three lions came to the little pool below us to drink, and made the narrow ravine resound again with their grand deep voices. At any other time I should have lain and listened with pleasure to this magnificent serenade; but just now, being very tired and wanting to sleep, I was glad when they took their departure, which was doubtless hastened by a few big stones which I directed the Kafirs to roll down the hill towards them, when I once more fell asleep, only to be awakened by the cold which always precedes early dawn.

As soon as it was light enough we refilled the calabashes, and started for the dead elephants, as we had a hard day's work before us if we were to chop out the tusks and get back to the skerm that evening. Not having now to follow the bends of the river, we soon reached our nearest prize, and, leaving half the Kafirs here, I told them to be quick and chop out the tusks and satisfy their hunger, and then come on to me and the rest of the boys at the other elephant.

On reaching the carcase of the latter, I found he had indeed a splendid pair of tusks—the upper one, as he lay on his side, protruding 4 feet beyond the lip, measuring (after being chopped out) 6½ feet in length, and weighing 84 lbs.,[1] the lower tusk being almost exactly similar, but weighing 2 lbs. less; the other had also a very fine pair of tusks, weighing 59 lbs. each; and after I had put a few square inches of elephant's heart out of sight (I am afraid to say how many), I felt at peace with all mankind, and well repaid for all the little inconveniences I had gone through on the previous day.

In about an hour and a half the boys came up with the first pair of tusks, and as much fat and meat as they could carry. As our two were also ready, we soon had the meat tied up, and, after telling off two boys to carry each of the big tusks by turns, once more turned our faces homewards, striking a bee-line straight across country. On our way we came across a great deal of game, including several rhinoceroses, both of the black and white species, two large herds of buffalo, and many zebras, impalas, wild pigs, etc.; we saw, however, no fresh elephant spoor.

At length, just at sundown, we reached the large drinking-place near our skerm, and while walking along the path leading from it to our camp, met two black rhinoceroses, which, however, luckily for themselves I think (for I had my old elephant gun in my

---

[1] These tusks afterwards lost 10 lbs. each in weight in drying out.

hands), did not think proper to molest us, but after eyeing us intently for a few seconds, and giving vent to a few snorts, wheeled round, and took themselves off at a quick trot. In a few minutes I once more reached my headquarters, and as the two boys I had left behind had cooked me a very nice stew of elephant's heart and rice, and had a kettle of tea ready, it need scarcely be added that it was not long before I was enjoying a delicious meal, bringing an appetite to bear upon it that none but a hunter can appreciate. The boys being too much knocked up with the last two days' work to care to dance, though their appetites were unimpaired, I was soon fast asleep beneath my kaross, dreaming of sport, such as one never meets with save in the happy hunting-grounds of the imagination.

For another fortnight, I remained in the same skerm or camp already described, hunting through the surrounding country in every direction with good success, and bagging three more fine bull elephants and five cows, two of the latter carrying remarkably fine tusks. As I then had more ivory than my eleven Kafirs could carry at once, I determined to get it to the waggons at Linquāsi as quickly as possible, and so set to work to transport it thither by instalments. Towards the end of the month I got the whole lot as far as Dett, a long open valley in the midst of thick goussy forests, with a spongy, marshy bottom, which is distant from two to three days' walk from Linquāsi. Here I met my Hottentot waggon-driver John, and two Kafirs, who were on their way from our headquarters with powder and lead to W.,[1] my partner, of whom I had heard nothing for more than two months. They told me

1 George Wood.

H

that W.'s skerm was two days' hard walk from here, in the hills, and a little to the west of where I had been hunting.   On hearing this news I at once gave up all idea of returning to the waggons, and so, after burying the ivory in a large hole dug in the soft sand to a depth which I thought would impede any hyænas from smelling it out, and, by scratching up the sand, exposing it to view, I started back for the hills with my guides.

On the morning of the third day, we reached W.'s skerm, perched like a crow's nest on the top of a hill, past the foot of which ran a broad sand river, with a thin stream of water meandering down it like a silver wire.   The day after leaving Dett, we met a large party of Matabele on their way from their own country, near the sources of the Gwai, to collect salt in a pan amongst the hills ; they all carried war shields, and woe betide any unfortunate Amachankas they might happen to come across ; if they escaped being murdered, they would be infallibly stripped of all their possessions by these unscrupulous marauders. Some of these men knew me, and were very civil. After half an hour's conversation, I continued my journey, several of them following me in the hope that before long I might shoot them some large animal ; and, as luck would have it, before we had proceeded a mile we came upon a black rhinoceros lying asleep, which John and I disposed of without much trouble.   I only took the meat from the ribs for myself, leaving the remainder of the carcase for the Matabele, who, I think I may safely say, did not leave much of it for the vultures and hyænas.

On my arrival at the skerm, I found that W. was away hunting, but late in the evening he returned, and was very much surprised to find me awaiting

him.   We had both been lucky since our last
meeting, and, over a substantial meal of rhinoceros
liver and rice and a kettle of coffee, we sat till far
into the night recounting to one another our various
hunting experiences during the past two months.
W.'s plan of procedure was a little different from
mine ; he had given ten of his Kafirs guns, and they
all hunted with him, firing away at the elephants
indiscriminately.   As a natural consequence, after
every successful hunt there were several claimants for
some of the elephants shot, and it was often difficult
to decide who amongst them had really given the
disputed animal the first bullet.   Three of my Kafirs
also carried guns, but I usually sent them out
hunting alone ; not that I cared much about their
disputing among themselves, but I very much object
to any of my servants claiming an elephant which I
think I have killed myself.   W., however, having
probably shot more elephants than any Englishman
living, was past this vanity, and only thought of how
to secure the greatest quantity of ivory.

The day following my arrival, we left the skerm,
and went away to the north-west, leaving two Kafirs
behind to look after the ivory and baggage.   We
remained away five days, but only shot two elephant
cows.   The hills here (close to the Zambesi) were
higher and more rugged and precipitous than those I
had been hunting amongst farther to the eastward,
and in many of the deep narrow ravines the scenery
was most striking.   Though the sides of these kloofs
in some cases were almost perpendicular, several trees
had nevertheless found a hold for their roots in the
interstices of the rocks, and amongst them the
fantastic-shaped baobabs, with their long leafless limbs,
looked particularly strange.

At first sight, many of these cliffs appeared in-
accessible to any animal but a baboon ; but we found
that the elephants had made regular paths up and
down many of them, which paths zigzagged backwards
and forwards like a road down a Swiss mountain, and
in some places great blocks of stone had been forced
aside by the efforts of these bulky engineers, in order
to render their footing the more secure.

That elephants can climb up and down very steep
places is, however, well known ; but it may be new
to some readers to hear that rhinoceroses are almost
equally active. I have seen many of the black and
one of the white species scramble with marvellous
activity and sureness of foot up and down the
most steep and stony hills that it is possible to
imagine.

One evening, as W. and I were sitting on the
summit of one of these steep hills, our attention was
directed by the Kafirs to a grey shapeless mass lying
amongst some large blocks of stone, near the top of
a high ridge just opposite to us. Opinions differed
as to whether it was an old buffalo bull, a rhinoceros,
or a rock ; but, as we watched, the last idea was
quickly dispelled, for the hitherto motionless mass
raised itself slowly, and, gaining a standing position,
displayed to our view the well-known contour of a
black rhinoceros. Being out of meat, this was just
the thing we were looking for ; so we at once made
preparations to circumvent him. But, although the
wind was favourable, the hill-side was bare and stony,
and, despite our utmost pains to tread softly, he
heard us coming, and made off before we were well
within range. We both fired at once, W.'s six-to-
the-pound bullet catching the animal low down in
the fore-leg, and mine hitting him in the ribs, but

too far back.   At first he kept along the ridge, and
W.'s ball having slightly crippled him, we managed
to get right above him with our second guns ; on
seeing which he turned, and went at a gallop down
the almost precipitous face of the hill, picking his
steps amongst the great blocks of stone in an extraordinary manner.   Before he had got far, however,
W. fired from above, when, the animal's fore-legs
seeming to give way, he pitched on his head, and
turned the fairest and most astonishing somersault I
ever saw.   He was up again in a second, but I was
close behind, and when on reaching the level ground
he turned along the face of the hill and offered me a
good chance, I fired at his shoulder, making a bad
but very lucky shot, as I broke his neck, and of
course killed him on the spot.   We found that the
bullet W. had fired from above had caught him in
the neck, about a foot behind the head ; it must have
just grazed the vertebral column, paralysing the
animal for an instant, which accounted for the
wonderful manner in which he had rolled head over
heels down the hill.

On reaching W.'s skerm once more, we held a
council of war, and determined that, as the elephants
seemed to have left this part of the country, and
neither of us had been to the waggons to see how
our property was being looked after for more than
two months, we ought to go thither at once.   Accordingly, the next morning we started eastwards, and
late in the afternoon reached the skerm which had
been my headquarters during the best part of August,
and which we had no difficulty in finding, as it was
situated at the foot of a peculiarly-shaped hill.
Strange, we had been hunting within a day's journey
of one another for so long, and yet neither of us had

had any idea of the other's whereabouts. As soon
as we reached the skerm, I took my two gun-carriers
and a couple more boys with axes, and went to chop
out a bees' nest I knew of close by. It proved to
be a well-stocked one, and we got from it, I
should think, from 15 to 20 lbs. of splendid
honey. Whilst we were engaged chopping, one of
my Kafirs who had wandered some distance away,
came running up, saying there was a white rhinoceros
lying asleep not a hundred yards off. Thinking the
noise must have already disturbed it, I did not
consider it worth while to go and see ; but, when
we had taken all the honey, I thought I would just
walk to where it had been, and was very much
surprised to find the confiding beast still lying fast
asleep. It must have been deaf, for we had been
making a tremendous noise and chatter for the last
half-hour, certainly not more than 150 yards away
from it. I walked close up to it and whistled, when
the sleepy animal stood up, and I shot it behind the
shoulder ; it ran about 100 yards and then stopped,
and a second bullet in the shoulder killed it. It was
a cow, and very fat ; so, leaving some Kafirs to cut
her up, I returned straight to the skerm with the
honey, and sent more boys to help carry the meat.

By this time it was quite dark, and W. was
waiting for me to begin supper. Whilst chopping
out the honey I had heard two shots, and found on
inquiry that they had been fired by my comrade,
who had killed a black rhinoceros down near the
elephants' drinking-place. That night, two lions
drank at the small hole of water close to our skerm,
and then walked up a path just behind us, roaring
terrifically the while. They were so near, that some
of the Kafirs got uneasy, and threw stumps of fire-

wood and shouted at them.   On going down to the
large pools of water the next morning, we found
that no elephants had drunk there during the night ;
but, in order to give them another chance, instead
of pushing on at once with the ivory to the waggons,
we made a round amongst the hills to the north-west,
returning to our skerm again at nightfall.   As soon
as the day dawned, we sent a couple of Kafirs down
to the water to see if any elephants had been there,
and on their return in a quarter of an hour with the
joyful tidings that a fine troop of bulls had drunk
during the night, we at once started in pursuit.   We
found they had come down from the right-hand side,
and returned on their own spoor, feeding along nicely
as they went, so that we were in great hopes of overtaking them without much difficulty.   Our confidence,
however, we soon found was misplaced, for after a
time they had ceased to feed, and, turning back
towards the N.E., had taken to a path, along which
they had walked in single file and at a quick pace,
as if making for some stronghold in the hills.   Hour
after hour we trudged on, over rugged stony hills,
and across open grassy valleys, scattered over which
grew clumps of the soft-leaved machabel trees, or
rather bushes ; but, though the leaves and bark of
this tree form a favourite food of elephants, those
we were pursuing had turned neither to the right
nor the left to pluck a single frond.

After mid-day, the aspect of the country changed,
and we entered upon a series of ravines covered with
dense, scrubby bush.   Unfortunately the grass had
here been burnt off, but for which circumstance the
elephants, I feel sure, would have halted for their
mid-day sleep.   In one of these thickets we ran on
to three black rhinoceroses (*R. bicornis*) lying asleep

When we were abreast of them they got our wind, and, jumping up, rushed close past the head of our line, snorting vigorously. It was a family party, consisting of a bull, a cow, and a full-grown calf; they passed so near us that I threw at them the thick stick which I used for a ramrod, and overshot the mark, it falling beyond them.

Shortly after this incident, we lost the spoor in some very hard, stony ground, and had some trouble in recovering it, as the Kafirs, being exhausted with the intense heat, and thinking we should not catch the elephants, had lost heart and would not exert themselves, hoping that we would give up the pursuit. By dint of a little care and perseverance, however, we succeeded, and after a time again entered upon a more open country. To cut a long story short, I suppose it must have been about two hours before sundown when we came to a large tree, from which the elephants had only just moved on. At first we thought they must have got our wind and run, but on examination we found they had only walked quietly on. We put down the water calabashes and axes, and the Kafirs took off their raw-hide sandals, and then we again, quickly but cautiously, followed on the spoor. It was perhaps five minutes later when we at last sighted them, seven in number, and all large, full-grown bulls. W. and I walked up to within thirty yards or so, and fired almost simultaneously; he at one standing broadside, and I at another facing me. Our Hottentot boy also fired, and, as the animals turned, a volley was given them by our Kafirs, about ten of whom carried guns. Not an elephant, however, seemed any the worse, and they went away at a great pace. Judging from the lie of the land ahead that they would turn to the

right, I made a cut with my two gun-bearers, whilst
W. kept in their wake.   Fortune favoured me, for
they turned just as I had expected, and I got a
splendid broadside shot as they passed along the
farther side of a little gully not forty yards off.
The Kafir having, as he ran, reloaded the gun which
I had already discharged and on which I placed most
dependence, I fired with it at the foremost elephant,
an enormous animal with long white tusks, when he
was exactly opposite to me.   My boy had put in
the powder with his hand, and must have overloaded
it, for the recoil knocked me down, and the gun
itself flew out of my hands.   Owing to this, I lost
a little time ; for when I got hold of my second gun
the elephants had turned back again (excepting the
one just hit) towards W. and the Kafirs.   However,
I gave another a bullet behind the big ribs as he was
running obliquely away from me.   The first, which
I had hit right in the middle of the shoulder, was
now walking very slowly up a steep hill, looking as
though he were going to fall every instant ; but,
nevertheless (as until an elephant is actually dead,
there is no knowing how far he may go), I determined
to finish him before returning to the others.   On
reaching the top of the hill, and hearing me coming
on not a dozen yards behind him, the huge beast
wheeled round, and, raising his gigantic ears, looked
ruefully towards me.   Poor beast, he was doubtless too
far gone to charge, and, on receiving another ball in
the chest, he stepped slowly backwards, and then
sinking on to his haunches, threw his trunk high
into the air and rolled over on his side, dead.

During this time, the remainder of the elephants,
harried and bewildered by the continuous firing of
W. and our little army of native hunters, had come

round in a circle, and I saw the four that still
remained (for, besides the one I had killed, two more
were down) coming along in single file, at the long,
quick half run, half walk, into which these animals
settle after their first rush.   I at once ran obliquely
towards them ; but, before I could get near, one
more first lagged behind, and then fell heavily to the
ground, so that there were but three remaining.
W., being blown, had been left behind ; but most
of the Kafirs were still to the fore, firing away as
fast as they could load, from both sides.   It was
astonishing what bad shooting they made ; their
bullets kept continually striking up the ground all
round the elephants, sometimes in front of their
trunks, sometimes behind them, and ever and anon
one would come whistling high overhead.   It was
in vain that I shouted to them to leave off firing and
let me shoot ; their blood was up, and blaze away
they would.

Just as I was getting well up alongside, the
elephants crossed a little gully, and entered a small
patch of scrubby bush, on the slope of the hill beyond,
in the shelter of which they at once stopped and faced
about, giving me a splendid chance.   I had just
emptied both my guns, hitting one animal full in
the chest, and another, that was standing broadside
to me, in the shoulder, when loud lamentations and
cries of " Mai-ai ! " " Mai mamo ! " burst from my
Kafir followers close behind.   At the same time my
two gun-carriers, throwing down their guns, ran
backwards, clapping their hands, and shouting like
the rest.   Turning hastily round, I saw a Kafir
stretched upon the earth, his companions sitting round
him, wailing and clapping their hands, and at once
comprehended what had occurred.   The poor fellow

who lay upon the ground had fired at the elephants,
from about thirty yards behind myself, and then run
up an ant-hill, just as another Kafir, who preferred to
keep at a safer distance, discharged a random shot,
which struck poor Mendose just between the
shoulder-blades, the bullet coming out on the right
breast. I ran up at once to see what could be done,
but all human aid was vain—the poor fellow was
dead. At this moment two more shots fell close
behind, and a minute or two afterwards W. and our
Hottentot boy John came up. One of the three
elephants had fallen after my last shot, close at hand,
and a second, sorely wounded, had walked back right
on to W. and John, who were following on the
spoor ; and the two shots I had just heard had sealed
his fate. The third, however, and only surviving
one out of the original seven, had made good his
escape during the confusion, which he never would
have done had it not been for the untimely death of
Mendose.

The sun was now close down upon the western
sky-line, and little time was to be lost. The Kafirs
still continued to shout and cry, seeming utterly
paralysed, and I began to think that they were
possessed of more sympathetic feelings than I had
ever given them credit for. However, on being
asked whether they wished to leave the body for the
hyænas, they roused themselves. As luck would
have it, on the side of the very ant-hill on which the
poor fellow had met his death was a large deep hole,
excavated probably by an ant-eater, but now un-
tenanted. Into this rude grave, with a Kafir needle
to pick the thorns out of his feet, and his assegais
with which to defend himself on his journey to the
next world, we put the body, and then firmly blocked

up the entrance with large stones, to keep the prowling hyænas from exhuming it.   Poor Mendose! he
was an obedient, willing servant, and by far the best
shot of all our native hunters.

The first thing to be done now was to cut some
meat from one of the elephants, and then get down
to a pool of water which we had passed during the
hunt, and make a "skerm" for the night.   On
reaching the nearest carcase, which proved to be in
fair condition, I was much surprised to see my Kafirs
throw aside every semblance of grief, and fight and
quarrel over pieces of fat and other tit-bits in their
usual manner.   Even the fellow who had had the
misfortune to shoot his comrade, though he kept
asserting that "his heart was dead," was quite as eager
as the rest.   In the evening they laughed and chatted
and sang as usual, ate most hearty suppers, and
indeed seemed as if all memory of the tragedy which
had occurred but a few hours before, and which at the
time had seemed to affect them so deeply, had passed
from their minds.

Thus ended the best day's hunting, as regards
weight of ivory, at which I had ever assisted.   The
next day we set the Kafirs to work with three
American axes, and before nightfall the twelve tusks
(not one of which was broken) were lying side by
side, forming one of the finest trophies a sportsman's
heart could desire to look upon.   The largest pair
of tusks weighed 57 lbs. apiece, and the smallest 29
lbs. and 31 lbs. respectively—a very fair lot of bull
ivory.

A few days later, at the valley of Dett, we had a
day's elephant-shooting of a very different character.
We had arrived there the evening before, and had
found the ivory I had left there untouched by human

hands, though the hyænas, guided by the scent, and despite the depth at which it was buried, had scratched away the sand, and exposed the uppermost tusks to view.

Dett, as I have said before, is a long valley, running into one of the tributaries of the river Gwai, with a swampy bottom and large beds of reeds, amongst which appear here and there a few open water holes. Near its upper end, and two or three miles above the first of these pools, it is bounded on one side by dense jungles of wait-a-bit thorn, which extend for many miles in a westerly direction. These great thorn jungles are called " sinangas " by the Kafirs, and it is deemed dangerous work following elephants into their dark recesses, as the beasts seem to consider them their own particular domain, and look upon any intrusion as a personal insult. What constitutes the danger is this : the bush is so dense and thorny that, except where elephants, buffaloes, or rhinoceroses have opened up paths, through which they crash without difficulty, it is in many parts quite impenetrable, and thus one is liable, when charged, to get stuck fast, and caught like a fly in a spider's web. The uniform sombre grey of these leafless thorn jungles (for not until the rains fall do the leaves sprout) assimilates, too, so well with the dull leaden colour of an elephant's skin, that, though such a large beast, he is invisible except at very close quarters; and often, when following on spoor in such a locality, the first warning I have received of the proximity of a herd of these animals standing asleep has been the rumbling of their intestines, they themselves being completely invisible within a few yards. Elephants, as a rule, are more vicious in these sinangas than elsewhere, and there are very few native hunters who will follow spoor far within them.

Our camp—where I had buried the ivory—was situated at some considerable distance down the valley, and about eight or ten miles from the sinangas I have just mentioned. On the night we reached Dett, whilst sleeping there, we heard elephants drinking at a water hole not far up the valley, and at the first dawn of day, after having a cup of hot coffee, we went and took up the spoor. The elephants, a fine troop of eight or ten bulls, had been feeding quietly along all night, through the large open grassy forests which border Dett, always heading, however, towards the sinangas, where we guessed they were bent upon standing during the heat of the day. It was, however, not until an hour or so past mid-day (as they had pursued a circuitous course backwards and forwards) that our conjectures were confirmed, and we entered the thick bush. About an hour later, we came up with them, standing some fifty yards away, on our right, under a clump of camel-thorn trees, and in a rather open place compared with the general density of the surrounding jungle. Besides the small troop of bulls we had followed, and which were nearest to us, there was a very large herd of cows standing just beyond, which, as we had not crossed their spoor, had probably drunk at Sikumi—a water hole not many miles distant—and come to this rendezvous from the other side.

Taking a hasty gulp of water, we at once walked towards them. As we advanced, the slight rustling of the bushes must have attracted the attention of one of the bulls, for he raised his trunk high in the air, and made a few steps forward. " I'll take him,

and do you fire at the one with the long white tusks
on the left," whispered W.   " Right you are ! "
was the reply, and the next moment we fired.   I
just had time to see my elephant fall on his knees,
when he was hidden by the troop of cows that,
awakened from their sleep by the shots, and not
knowing exactly where the danger lay, came rushing
towards us in a mass, one or two of them trumpeting,
and others making a sort of rumbling noise.
Seizing our second guns and shouting lustily, we
again pulled trigger.   Our Hottentot boy John,
and five of our Kafirs, who still carried guns, also
fired ; on which the herd turned and went off at
right angles, enveloped in a cloud of dust.   My
gun had only snapped the cap, but my Kafir, to
whom I threw it back, thinking in the noise and
hurry that it was discharged, reloaded it on the top
of the old charge—a fact which I only found out, to
my sorrow, later on.   The cloud of sand and dust
raised by the panic-stricken elephants was at first
so thick that we could distinguish nothing ; but,
running behind them, I soon made out the bull I
had wounded, which I recognised by the length and
shape of his tusks.   He was evidently hard hit, and,
being unable to keep up with the herd, he turned
out, and went off alone ; but he was joined almost
immediately by four old cows, all with small, insignificant tusks, and, instead of running away, they
walked along quite slowly, first in front of and then
behind him, as if to encourage him.   Seeing how
severely he was wounded, I at once went after him,
accompanied only by my two gun-carriers, Nuta and
Balamoya, W. and the rest of the Kafirs going on
after the troop.   My bull was going so slowly that
I had no difficulty in threading my way through the

bushes and getting in front of him, which I did in order to get a broadside shot as he passed me. One of the four cows that still accompanied him walked along, carrying her head high and her tail straight in the air, and kept constantly turning from side to side. "That cow will bother us; shoot her," said Nuta, and I wish I had taken his advice; but her tusks were so small, and the bull seemed so very far gone, that I thought it would be a waste of ammunition. I therefore waited till he was a little in front of where I stood, and then gave him a bullet at very close quarters, just behind the shoulder, and, as I thought, exactly in the right place; but he nevertheless continued his walk as if he had not felt it. Reloading the same gun, I ran behind him, holding it before me in both hands, ready to raise at a moment's notice, and, the four cows being some twenty yards in advance, I shouted, hoping he would turn. The sound of my voice had the desired effect; for he at once raised his ears and swung himself round, or rather was in the act of doing so, for immediately his ears went up my gun was at my shoulder, and as soon as he presented his broadside I fired, on which he turned again, and went crashing through the bushes at a trot. I thought that it was a last spasmodic rush, and that he would fall before going very far; so, giving the gun back to Nuta to reload, I was running after him, with my eyes fixed on the quivering bushes as they closed behind him, when suddenly the trunk of another elephant was whirled round, almost literally above my head, and a short, sharp scream of rage thrilled through me, making the blood tingle down to the very tips of my fingers. It was one of the wretched old cows, that had thus lain in wait for me behind a dense patch of bush.

Even had my gun been in my hands, I should scarcely have had time to fire, so close was she upon me ; but, as it was, both my Kafirs were some fifteen yards behind, and the only thing I could do was to run. How I got away I scarcely know. I bounded over and through thorn bushes which, in cold blood, I should have judged impenetrable ; but I was urged on by the short piercing screams which, repeated in quick succession, seemed to make the whole air vibrate, and by the fear of finding myself encircled by the trunk or transfixed by the tusk of the enraged animal. After a few seconds (for I don't think she pursued me a hundred yards, though it seemed an age), the screaming ceased. During the chase, the elephant was so close behind me, that looking over my shoulder was impossible, and all that I did was to dash forward, springing from side to side so as to hinder her from getting hold of me, and it was only when the trumpeting suddenly stopped that I knew I was out of her reach. I was barelegged—as I always am when hunting on foot—and my only garment before the beast charged was a flannel shirt ; but I now stood almost *in puris naturalibus*, for my hat, the leather belt that I wore round my waist, and about three parts of my shirt, had been torn off by the bushes, and I doubt if there was a square inch of skin left uninjured anywhere on the front of my body !

After the cow left me I ran on about fifty yards (for I thought that if she heard my voice close at hand she might come on again), and then shouted out the names of my two gun-carriers, who at once answered and soon came running up, both with their guns, which I was afraid they had thrown away. "Amehlo 'mahlope, soree!" said they—literally,

I

" White eyes, sir ! "—a Kafir idiom for " What a
narrow escape ! " I told them to take up my spoor,
so that I might get my hat and then follow up the bull,
from which I had been driven away, as I felt sure he
had not gone very far after receiving the last shot.
Just as we were starting Nuta called out, " Look at
the dust ; there they go ! " and on doing so, I saw
a cloud of dust rising above the bush some two
hundred yards away to our right, towards which,
thinking it was raised by the four cows, and that the
bull might still be with them, we at once ran. On
cutting the spoor, however, a glance showed us that
the cows were alone—the bull, I now felt sure, having
remained behind, too badly wounded to keep up
with them any longer. The cows were going at a
run, and, being probably satisfied with driving me
away, had left their wounded lord to his fate.

Being pretty well fagged with the exertion to which
the old cow had put me, and feeling confident that the
wounded bull was not very far from where I had last
seen him, I sat down at the foot of a camel-thorn
tree, whilst one of my boys climbed up to see if he
could see him standing anywhere in the surrounding
bush. In about ten minutes he came down, not
having been able to make out anything, and we
started back, intending first of all to recover my
hat—of which I already felt the need, the sun
being intensely powerful—and then to take up the
spoor of the wounded elephant. We had gone
perhaps a hundred yards, when our attention was
arrested by some one shouting a short distance ahead.
We stopped to listen. Shortly after the shouts were
repeated, this time quite close. At the same moment
I saw the tops of some bushes in front shaking
violently, and then made out the outline of an

elephant's back and head coming towards us. I at once understood that the shouting came from one of our Kafirs, who was trying to turn the elephant and drive him back towards W. or one of our hunters who carried a gun. Catching up a handful of sand, and throwing it into the air, to see how the wind was, I placed myself in such a position that the elephant, if he held the same course, would have to pass close by me above the wind, thereby offering me a splendid broadside shot. But *l'homme propose, et Dieu dispose* ; for when he was only about thirty yards off, coming steadily along at a quick walk, and just as I saw that he was followed by four quite small calves, the Kafir who was running him about, and who knew nothing of my position, again shouted a little to my right, on which he turned from his course and came straight down towards where we stood. Seeing this, I shouted as loud as I could, hoping he would turn again and still offer me a broadside shot ; but I suppose he was tired of being trotted about in the hot sun, and thought it time to expostulate ; for, instead of swerving, he raised his head, spread his huge ears, and came on straight towards us. Feeling sure that he would charge directly he made us out, I just waited till his head came through a bush close in front, and then fired into his chest, bringing him to his knees. He was up again in an instant, and crashed away through the bushes to my left, whilst the four calves came straight on, and ran close past us on my right. Seizing my second gun from the hands of Balamoya— for the first time since it had snapped the cap at the commencement of the hunt—I threaded my way through the jungle so as to intercept him ; and as he was badly wounded and had settled into a slow walk, I easily succeeded, and running a little ahead,

let him pass me broadside on within thirty yards.
Taking a good sight for the middle of his shoulder,
I pulled the trigger. This time the gun went off—
it was a four-bore elephant gun, loaded twice over,
and the powder thrown in each time by a Kafir with
his hands—and I went off too! I was lifted clean
from the ground, and turning round in the air, fell
with my face in the sand, whilst the gun was carried
yards away over my shoulder. At first I was almost
stunned with the shock, and I soon found that I could
not lift my right arm. Besides this, I was covered
with blood, which spurted from a deep wound under
the right cheek-bone, caused by the stock of the gun
as it flew upwards from the violence of the recoil.
The stock itself—though it had been bound round,
as are all elephant guns, with the inside skin of an
elephant's ear put on green, which when dry holds it
as firmly as iron—was shattered to pieces, and the
only wonder was that the barrel did not burst.
Whether the two bullets hit the elephant or not I
cannot say ; but I think they must have done so,
for he only went a few yards after I fired, and then
stood still, raising his trunk every now and then,
and dashing water tinged with blood over his
chest. I went cautiously up to within forty yards or
so of him, and sat down. Though I could not hold
my arm out, I could raise my forearm so as to
get hold of the trigger ; but the shock had so told
on me, that I found I could not keep the sight within
a yard of the right place. The elephant remained
perfectly still ; so I got Nuta to work my arm about
gently, in order to restore its power, and hoped that
in the meantime the Kafir, whose shouting had
originally brought the elephant to me, would come
up and be able to go and fetch W. No doubt, if I

had shouted he would have come at once, for he could not have been very far off ; but had I done so, the elephant might either have charged or else continued his flight, neither of which alternatives did I desire. After a short time, seeing no chance of aid arriving, and my nerves having got a little steadier, I took my favourite gun from Nuta, and, resting my elbow on my knee, took a quiet pot shot. I was, however, still very unsteady even in this position, but I do not think the bullet could have struck very far from the right place. The elephant on receiving the shot made a rush forwards, crashing through the bushes at a quick walk, so that we had to run at a hard trot to keep him in sight. He now seemed very vicious, for, hearing a dry branch snap, he turned and ran towards us, and then stood with his ears up, feeling about in all directions with his trunk to try and get our wind.

Nuta, who up to this day had always been a most staunch and plucky gun-bearer, now seemed seized with a panic, and refused to bring me the gun any more, calling out, "Leave the elephant, sir ; this day you're bewitched, and will surely be killed." However, as the elephant was evidently very severely wounded, I had no idea of giving over the chase as long as I could keep up, and, after bestowing a few Anglo-Saxon idioms upon Nuta, I again ran on. The bush now became very thick, and, as the elephant was going straight away, I could not get a chance of a shot. About a mile farther on, however, we came to one of those large open turf flats which occur here and there in the midst of the sinangas. It was quite a mile square, and perfectly bare, with the exception of a few large camel-thorn trees, which were scattered about in clumps. On reaching this opening, the elephant, instead of turning back into the bush, as I should have expected, kept his course, making straight for the farther side, and going at that long, swinging walk, to keep up with which a man on foot must run at a fair pace. I had now been a long time bare-headed, exposed to the heat of the fierce tropical sun, and the kick I had received from the gun had so much shaken me, that I felt dead beat, and could scarcely drag one leg after the other. I saw that I should never be able to run up to within shot of the elephant, which was now about 150 yards ahead; so, taking the gun from Nuta, I told him to try and run right round him, and by shouting turn him back towards me. Relieved of the weight of the gun, and being a splendid runner, he soon accomplished this, and standing behind the stem of a camel-thorn tree a long way in advance, halloed loudly. Accordingly, I had the satisfaction of seeing the elephant stop, raise his ears, look steadily in the direction of the noise, and then wheel round, and come walking straight back towards the jungle he had just left, taking a line which would bring him past me, at a distance of about fifty or sixty yards. I stood perfectly still, with Balamoya kneeling close behind me; for, though elephants can see very well in the open, I have always found that if they do not get your wind, and you remain motionless, they seem to take you for a tree or a stump. To this I now trusted, and as the elephant came on I had full leisure to examine him. The ground between us was as bare as a board, except that it was covered with coarse grass about a foot high, and he looked truly a gigantic and formidable beast; his tusks were small for his size, one of them being broken at the point, and I do not think they could have weighed much over 30 lbs. apiece. He came steadily on, swinging his trunk backwards and forwards, until he was about seventy yards from where I stood, when suddenly I was dismayed to see his trunk sharply raised, as if to catch a stray whiff of wind, and the next instant he stopped and faced full towards us, with his head raised, and his enormous ears spread like two sails. He took a few steps towards us, raising his feet very slowly, and bringing them down as if afraid of treading on a thorn. It was an anxious moment; he was evidently very suspicious, but did not know what to make of us, and had we remained motionless I believe he would still have turned and walked on again. " Stand still!" I whispered between my teeth to Balamoya; but the sight of the advancing monster was too much for him—he jumped up and bolted. The instant he moved, on came the elephant, without trumpeting, and with his trunk straight down. Though very shaky just before, the imminence of the danger braced up my nerves, and I think I never held a gun steadier than upon this occasion. As he was coming direct at me, and as he did not raise his trunk, his chest was quite covered; there was therefore nothing left but to fire at his head. He came on at an astonishing pace, and I heard only the " whish, whish" of the grass as his great feet swept through it. He was perhaps twenty yards off when I pulled the trigger. I aimed a little above the root of the trunk and just between the eyes, and directly I had fired I ran out sideways as fast as I could, though I had not much running left in me. Looking over my shoulder, I saw him standing with his ears still up and his head slightly turned, looking towards me; the blood was pouring down his trunk from a wound exactly where I had aimed, and, as it was inflicted by a four-ounce ball, backed by a heavy charge of powder, I cannot understand why it did not penetrate to his brain ; it had half-stunned him, however, and saved my life, for, had he come on again, it would have been utterly impossible for me, fatigued as I was, to have avoided him. After standing still for a short time, swaying himself gently from side to side, he again turned and took across the flat. Nuta, seeing what had happened, instead of trying to turn him again, cleared out of his road, and, making a large circle, came back to me. Perhaps it was as well he did so.

I now gave up the pursuit, for I was completely fagged out, and laid myself down in the shade of the nearest camel-thorn tree, and after an hour's rest, as the sun was getting low, I started back. At length I rejoined W. and all the Kafirs, at the spot where we had put down the calabashes and axes on first sighting the elephants. Every one looked very glum, and I soon found that W. had been equally unfortunate with myself, so that between the lot of us we had not bagged one single elephant.

I felt sure, however, that the bull I had first wounded was not very far from where I had last seen him, and so, after drinking a little water, of which I was much in need, we all went to try and ferret him out. After a good deal of trouble we hit off my spoor, and at last found my hat stuck in a thick thorn bush, which was further decked with my leather belt and the greater portion of my shirt. We found from the spoor, that the cow had pursued me right up to this bush, and then turned back, and I cannot help thinking that it was to her having smelt the hat that I owed my escape. We now looked for the bull's spoor, and soon found it besprinkled with

blood ; but after following it for a very short distance,
it became obliterated by the tracks of a large part of
the herd, which had turned back and crossed over it
during the hunt.   All our efforts to get it away
were fruitless, and at last, when the sun went down,
we were obliged to give it up and make for the
nearest water hole, which we reached after about an
hour and a half's walk in the dark.   A herd of
buffaloes had been there just before us, and trampled
and wallowed in the shallow pool, till they had
rendered the water quite undrinkable to any one but
a thirsty hunter.   Here we slept.   We were without food or blankets, though for my part I did not
think this much of a hardship, as I was too fatigued
to feel hungry, and the nights were getting warm.
The cut on my cheek was about two inches long,
and deep, extending up under the cheek bone.
Having neither needles nor thread to sew it up, and
it being in an impossible place to bandage, there was
nothing for it but to leave it to nature.   Luckily,
being in perfect health, it healed up straight away
by first intention, in spite of being left exposed to
the sun ; and though I still bear a scar, which serves
as a souvenir of the most unfortunate and eventful
day's elephant-shooting in which I ever took part, I
was able to shoot again in about ten days' time.   My
shoulder was much bruised, and I must have ruptured
some of the fibres of the muscles, for it was more
than three months before I could hold my arm
straight out at right angles to my body, though I
could shoot with it perfectly well all the time.

Want of food forced us to abandon the search for
the wounded elephant—which in such bush, and
without spoor, would have been rather like looking
for a needle in a bundle of hay—so we made our

way next day down the valley to our camp. In the afternoon, W. went out and shot a black rhinoceros, whilst I occupied myself in picking out the little black ends of the wait-a-bit thorns which were pretty evenly distributed over my person. The next day, we again made a start for Linquāsi, and, whilst crossing a large open glade, came across a herd of buffaloes, two of which W. shot. One of these was a very fat cow, and the meat delicious, being tender and juicy, and fully equal to the best beef. That evening we slept at Chuma-Malisse.

On the following morning, about two hours after leaving camp, and whilst passing through a belt of young forest, we had the luck to run right into a herd of elephant cows. It was a strong temptation to shoot, but I judged it better not to reopen the wound on my cheek, and so only ran with W., and helped to load and hand him the guns. He killed three, and our Hottentot boy also bagged one, besides a small thing that one of the Kafirs knocked over, which ought never to have been shot, and which I do not count. On sighting these elephants, we had put down the water calabashes, and laid a large thin sheet of meat, about a yard square, cut from the ribs of one of the buffaloes, on a patch of grass, and in their flight they ran right over these things, breaking two calabashes, whilst one of them trod fair in the centre of the piece of buffalo meat, which was only about half an inch thick, and stamped a hole through it just the size of her foot. That same day we chopped out all the tusks, and the next evening reached Linquāsi, where we found our bullocks, horses, dogs, and indeed everything else at the waggons, safe and in good order.

PLATE V

1. WATERBUCK ♂ (Cobus Ellipsiprymnus).

   Shot in the Mashuna country, Sept. 17, 1880.
   Length of horns, 2 feet 7 inches.

2. POOKOO ANTELOPE ♂ (Cobus Vardoni).

   Shot on the Chobe river, July 7, 1874.
   Length of horns, 1 foot 4 inches.

3. POOKOO ANTELOPE ♂ (Cobus Vardoni).

   Shot on the Chobe river, Aug. 12, 1874.
   Length of horns, 1 foot 4 inches.

4. REEDBUCK ♂ (Cervicapra Arundinacea).

   Shot on the river Tati, Dec. 2, 1880.
   Length of horns, 1 foot 2 inches.

5. REEDBUCK ♂ (Cervicapra Arundinacea).

   Shot on the river Chobe, Nov. 1, 1879.
   Length of horns, 1 foot 1½ inch.

6. LECHWE ANTELOPE ♂ (Cobus Leche).

   Shot in the swamps of the Lukanga river, about 14° south
      latitude. Jan. 7, 1878.
   Length of horns, 2 feet 1 inch.

7. LECHWE ANTELOPE ♂ (Cobus Leche).

   Shot on the river Chobe, July 12, 1879.
   Length of horns, 2 feet 3 inches.

PLATE V

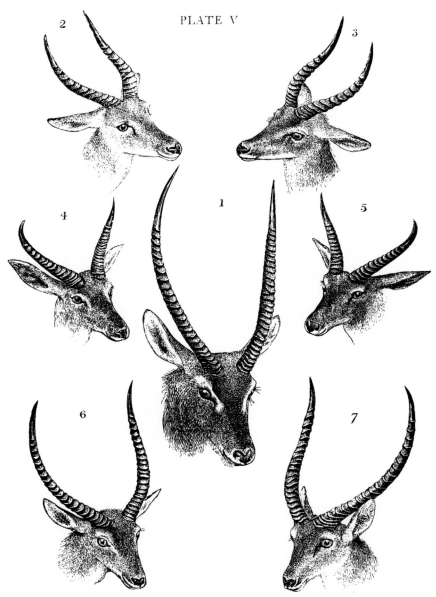

CHAPTER VII

UNTIL the latter end of November we continued
hunting with varying success, sometimes in the
neighbourhood of the Gwai river, at others in the
dense wait-a-bit thorn jungles to the north and west
of Linquāsi, and by that time the rainy season having
fairly set in, we trekked back again to Gubulawayo,
carrying with us nearly 5000 lbs. weight of very
fine ivory. During the summer months we spent
the greater part of the time trekking about the country
trading, and made an excursion across the high and
open downs lying to the south-east of the Matabele
country, to the junction of the Ingesi and Lunti rivers,
where we found some hippopotami, but did not shoot
any, though we had very good sport amongst the
herds of blue wildebeests, zebras, and roan antelopes,
which frequented the flats. In March 1874 we
trekked down to Tati in company with Messrs.
Fairbairn and Dawson, two young Scotsmen, who
had been trading with Lobengula, and were now on
their way to Bamangwato with two fine loads of ivory.

Our intention was to hunt during the coming winter in the country bordering on the Chobe and Zambesi rivers, making a point of visiting the Victoria Falls during the season.   As, during the months of January and February, torrents of rain had constantly been falling, the whole country between Gubulawayo and Tati had been converted into a marsh.   Travelling by African bullock waggons is slow work at the best of times, but in order to give an idea of how slow it may become in the interior at the end of a very wet season, I will here chronicle the fact that on this journey it took us twenty-three days to reach Mengwe, which is only fifty-nine miles by road from Gubulawayo, although we worked on an average seven or eight hours every day.   The waggons were continually sinking right up to the bed plank in the boggy ground, and over and over again the bullocks sank one and all up to their bellies in the mire. Whenever this happened we had to off-load the waggons, dig out the wheels, and place logs of wood and chopped brushwood in front of them to prevent them again sinking.   At the end of a hard day's work we often found ourselves only a few hundred yards from where we had started in the morning.   We broke, too, thirteen disselbooms,[1] all of which had to be replaced at a considerable expense of time and labour. Still we always went forwards, and at length reached Tati.   Here we met Mr. J. L. Garden and his brother Lieut. Garden, and as the objects they had in view were very much the same as our own, except that they were doing for their pleasure what George Wood and I were making a business of, we soon arranged to travel together as far as the Zambesi.

[1] Disselboom is the pole of the waggon to which the two hind bullocks are yoked

Thus on a clear, bright African winter's morning, May 6, 1874, we trekked away from the Tati *en route* for the still distant hunting-grounds of the Zambesi. Altogether we formed quite a caravan, as our party consisted of Mr. and Lieut. Garden, and their English servant Tofts, with three waggons, and Wood and myself with two.

As the road from Tati to the Zambesi is so well known to English traders and hunters, and has been so lately described by Dr. Holub, and by many other travellers before him, I will not trouble my reader with any description of it, but will conduct him at once to our camp on the head waters of the river Daka (pronounced Deykah) situated about sixty miles due south of the Victoria Falls, which we eventually reached on June 10. At Daka we were occupied for some days in constructing strong enclosures for our cattle and in laying in a supply of game meat for the use of our people and dogs, who were to remain at the waggons whilst we were away hunting. At last, on June 22, we made a start for the falls, the route to which from Daka lies through a hilly country for the first thirty miles or so, intersected by several small streams all flowing eastwards. Then come a succession of broad sand-belts thickly timbered with fine goussy trees, between which again and the river is a tract of about the roughest country in the world, cut up, as it is, into innumerable steep sides, precipitous ravines and gullies, which find their way down to the deep narrow chasm at the bottom of which the Zambesi runs, in a boiling, seething torrent, for many miles below the great falls.

Early on the morning of the third day after leaving the waggons, and whilst skirting the edge of a sandbelt covered with rather thick bush, we heard an

elephant call close to us,—not the loud scream which
these animals give when angry, but something very
much resembling the cry of a baboon ; so like, indeed,
that many of our Kafirs, who had not much experience
of these animals, said it was one.   All our Bushmen,
however, declared it at once to have been an elephant,
so we immediately called a halt, and, putting down all
our traps, entered the bush to look for spoor.   At a
short distance from the edge, the jungle became exceedingly dense, though not thorny, and about twenty
feet high.   We now advanced slowly and cautiously,
and had not proceeded a hundred yards when we came
upon elephant spoor.   The soil was soft sand, and the
footmarks had the appearance of being but that instant
imprinted, and were certainly not five minutes old.
We now spread out in a line, of which I was the left-
hand man, and with the exception of my own especial
Kafirs I was soon out of sight of the rest of the party.
The wind was in our favour, so we only had to
advance cautiously till we sighted the elephants, having
agreed before separating that whoever saw them first
should not fire, but send Kafirs to call the rest, that
we might all get a chance.   In this manner I was creeping forward, step by step, when suddenly one of my
Bushmen touched me gently on the arm, with a whispered " —s—s," and upon turning and following the
direction of his hand and eyes, I beheld the dim outline of an elephant looming through the dense, sombre-
coloured, leafless bush.   He was standing broadside
on, a little to my left, and after I had once seen him it
was easy enough to make him out, for he was not
over fifteen yards from us.   I could see that he was
a bull, nearly full grown in point of size, though the
smallness of his tusks showed that he was still
young.   When I first saw him he was standing per-

fectly still, but as I looked he stretched out his trunk,
and breaking off the end of some small branches con-
veyed them to his mouth, and commenced quietly
chewing them.   After peering carefully round without seeing any more elephants, I sent a Kafir to let
my friends know.   He had scarcely left me when
three shots fell to my right, and before I could raise
the gun to my shoulder, the huge beast before me
wheeled round and was off.   A hare could not have
turned and got under way more expeditiously, or
more silently.   But though his quickness saved him
from a broadside shot, I was in time to give him a
four-ounce ball in the hip, and calling on my favourite
Bushman, "Hartebeest," to run on the spoor, we
were soon hard on his tracks.   He did not run
straight, but doubled about in the bush, and the soil
being soft and sandy the Bushman was enabled to run
at full speed, I myself, being in excellent condition,
keeping close to his heels.   We had run for perhaps
a mile or so, when a perfect fusillade opened not far
to our right, and I was thinking of leaving the spoor
and cutting across in the direction of the shots,
making sure my companions were engaged with the
troop, when the Bushman suddenly exclaimed,
"Nansia! Nansia!" (There he is) and I just caught
a glimpse of my own elephant standing with his ears
raised, listening intently.   He must have been
bothered by the shots that had just been fired, and
perhaps had got somebody's wind, for at this moment
he turned and came crashing down in my direction.
Seizing my gun, I gave him a good shot right in the
shoulder as he passed, within ten yards I verily believe
of where I stood ; upon which he pulled up immediately, and facing round in our direction, raised his
trunk and ears, and gave vent to two or three short

sharp screams of rage.   His shoulder being broken, however, he was unable to charge, and upon receiving three more bullets fell to the earth dead.   This was my first elephant this year.   When at length we all met again, I found that my companions had killed two more, both young bulls about the same size as mine, and the six tusks averaged about 20 lbs. apiece.   Besides those killed, Wood had wounded a full-grown bull with fine tusks, but eventually lost him owing to the thickness of the bush.

As soon as our Kafirs had once more all assembled at the spot where the blankets and other baggage had been left, we despatched them in three parties to chop out the tusks, whilst we ourselves set to work to prepare a breakfast, for which the cool morning air and the excitement of the hunt had given us a keen appetite, and after having very leisurely discussed an ample and substantial meal, of which some slices of fried heart, fresh from one of the newly-slain elephants, formed a not unimportant feature, we proceeded (guided by the loud cries and diabolical singing of the Kafirs) to inspect the nearest of our three prizes, which was not more than 300 yards distant.

The huge carcase, or rather what remained of it, lay on one side, as it had fallen, with the legs extended. Behind the ribs and just over the belly the Kafirs had peeled off a large slab of skin, about three feet square, and through the trap-door thus formed dragged out the stomach and intestines ; they had also cut out the heart, liver, and lungs, so that what was left was merely a hollow shell, in the lower half of which the blood had formed a pool a foot deep.   Into this cavity they and the Bushmen now kept entering by twos, disappearing entirely from sight, searching eagerly for small pieces of fat along the backbone and about the kidneys, and bathing in and smearing themselves all over with the blood. This is a common practice amongst all the natives in the interior of Africa whenever large game, such as elephants or rhinoceroses, are killed, particularly if they happen to be the first of the season. Whether they imagine that this bath of blood gives them courage or not, I cannot say. They do not wash it off again, but let it dry on them and remain there till it gradually wears or gets rubbed off. Up to the time of our arrival on the scene there had been very little progress made at chopping out the tusks, each one having left this part of the business to his companions, and devoted all his own time and attention to securing tit-bits of fat juicy meat and roasting the same over the fire that had been kindled near at hand. Our presence, however, soon changed the aspect of affairs, and, at last, by an hour after mid-day, the six tusks were laid side by side, each native had his bundle of meat and fat tied up with strings of bark, and we were once more ready to resume our journey. Had there been water in our immediate vicinity we should have remained and passed the night here, but, the nearest stream being at a considerable distance, we deemed it best to push on.

A walk of some eight or ten miles through low, sparsely-wooded hills brought us to a small river, and, it being then pretty late, we forthwith made our camp near the summit of a piece of rising ground on its farther side. Of course we had an extra yarn that evening, and, seated round the cheery blaze of the log fire, fought the battle o'er again and killed our game once more. Our native followers, too,

K

revelling in an abundance of the fattest and most esteemed portions of the three elephants, danced and sang *à qui le mieux* ; and, lastly, a few prowling hyænas, having smelt out the meat that hung in festoons on all the trees around our camp, commenced to serenade us with their dismal, melancholy howls. But at length sleep, " tired nature's sweet restorer," began to steal over us, so, calling to the Kafirs to cease their wild and noisy performances and make up the fires, especially that which, with an eye to the morrow's breakfast, we had lighted over a hole in the ground containing a huge junk of elephant trunk, we wrapped ourselves in our blankets and were soon oblivious of all the cares and troubles of this world.

At last, on Saturday, June 27, from the top of a high sand-belt, we caught the first distant view of the far-famed Victoria Falls of the Zambesi. Our guide had evidently taken us very much out of our direct course, for, instead of hitting off the river exactly at the falls as we ought to have done, we were now far to the eastward ; but we all felt grateful to him for the mistake, for otherwise not only should we have missed the glorious bird's-eye view of the whole valley of the Zambesi, which we were now enjoying, but also should probably not have examined, as we did on the following day, the remarkable chasm through which the river runs below the falls.   From where we stood the *coup-d'œil* was truly magnificent ; we must have been fully twenty miles distant, but the immense volumes of spray which, like white feathery clouds, rose high into the air from the long, narrow chasm into which the river (more than a mile broad) madly plunged, seemed scarcely a couple of miles off.

With Mr. Garden's glass we could see, through

the less dense portions of the spray, the broad blue river, studded with thickly-wooded islands, and even distinguish here and there the tall thin stems and graceful feathery crowns of several lofty palm-trees. Between our station and the river lay spread out beneath us the rough, rugged country of which I have before made mention, cut up in all directions by innumerable fissures and ravines, whose very inequalities, aided by the enchantment distance invariably lends, rendered it pleasant to the eye, though to walk across, it is one of the most awkward bits of country I know of.   On the other side of the river rose, one behind the other, range beyond range of low, well-wooded hills, the farthest of which, blending with the distant horizon, bounded one of the most beautiful panoramas that it has yet been my fate to look upon.

Our Bushmen and Kafirs from the Matabele country could not understand the cloud of spray at all, and made the most naïve remarks concerning it, asserting it to be steam rising from boiling water, and then asking our guide how their people had managed to make so large a pot !   As it was still early when we first sighted the falls we hoped to be able to reach them or their immediate vicinity before nightfall ;   but never were erring mortals more deceived, for, owing to the numberless ravines, each one deeper and more precipitous than the last, we were still when the sun went down at least eight or ten miles from the wished-for goal, though not more than one from the deep chasm at the bottom of which the river runs below the falls.   That night we camped on the summit of a small round hill, and were lulled to sleep by the deep continuous roar of the most glorious waterfall in the world.

Although the Victoria Falls are only 18 degrees south of the equator, still the nights at this season of the year are very cold. In the day-time the temperature is about the same as on a summer's day in England, but the atmosphere, being much drier, not so oppressive. This is, of course, the cold season of the year, and even by the end of August there will be a change indeed.

On the morning of the 28th we started to see the falls at close quarters, resolving to cut straight down to the river, and then skirt along the edge of the chasm through which it here flows. This chasm is in itself a most wonderful sight, and in many respects, I think, must resemble the deep canyons in North-Western America. The sides of this curious cleft in the earth's surface are more than precipitous, they are overhanging, and at its bottom, at a depth of many hundred feet, the river runs in a boiling, seething torrent.

We now followed the course of the river, often making long detours to avoid the many precipitous gullies. On the way Mr. Garden shot a water-buck cow, bringing it down on the spot with a ball through the neck, and, as we had not yet breakfasted, we forthwith cut out the liver, and, kindling a fire, soon made short work of it.

As we neared the falls we found that the river ran in sharp zigzags, doubling backwards and forwards across its general course, so that by cutting from point to point we did not go over one-fourth of the ground we must have done had we followed the edge of the chasm. At last, about mid-day, we stood on the brink of the falls themselves. How I wish I could give you some idea of their wonderful grandeur and beauty! But the task is far beyond me. Imagine a river more than a mile broad, suddenly tumbling over a precipice 400 feet in depth, which runs in a perfectly straight line across its entire breadth ; and perhaps from these naked facts, imagination may picture in some degree how grand a sight must be that of the Victoria Falls of the Zambesi. The river tumbles into a narrow rent in the earth which runs right across its course. This rent, due to some convulsion of Nature, is only about 100 yards in breadth, and the outlet from it, which is near the northern bank, is still narrower. Both sides of this fissure, a mile in breadth, into which the river plunges, are perfectly precipitous, so that one can walk along the edge as far as the outlet, right opposite the falls, and on the same level as the river above them. The even face of the falls is marred by two islands, both near the southern bank, one of which was named Garden Island by Dr. Livingstone ; this, however, does not much matter, as, owing to the dense spray which ascends from the chasm high into the air, more than 200 or 300 yards can never be seen at once. As we stood facing the falls the roar was deafening, and so dense was the spray that, except when a puff of wind blew it momentarily aside, we could see absolutely nothing. But these glimpses were magnificent. One stands, it must be understood, on the very edge of the chasm, on a level with the river above, and only separated from the cataract by the breadth of the opening (about 100 yards), into which it dashes, so that when a sudden puff of wind blows away the spray immediately in front one sees the beautiful blue river, studded with thickly-wooded, palm-bearing islands, seemingly as still and quiet as a lake, flowing tranquilly on heedless of its coming danger, till with a crash it leaps in one splendid mass of fleecy, snow-white foam into an abyss 400 feet in depth.   At whatever part one looks, the rays of the sun shining on the descending masses of foam form a double zone of prismatic colours, of whose depth and brilliancy no one who has only seen the comparatively faint tints of an ordinary rainbow can form any conception.   Such are the Victoria Falls—one of, if not *the*, most transcendently beautiful natural phenomena on this side of Paradise.

Mr. Garden, who has also seen the Falls of Niagara, considers that, taken all round, the Victoria Falls are superior in grandeur and magnificence, though in the former the volume of water is greater than in any part of the latter ; but comparisons are odious, and, no doubt, each excels in different ways. Anywhere within a hundred yards of the cataract the spray, of course, wets one through in no time, and near the edge it is like standing in a pond.   The narrow rent which serves as the river's outlet doubles round and runs for 500 or 600 yards parallel with the chasm, and then again doubles backwards and forwards several times in a zigzag course, as before described.   On the point of land thus formed, the ground, from the continuous drenching of the spray, is always damp and boggy, and on it is a thick grove of large trees of a species unknown to me, and, in some parts, of dense underwood composed of clumps of palm-bushes and other shrubs.   This damp and shady retreat forms (especially during the hot weather) a favourite resort of elephant and buffalo, besides water-buck, koodoo, impala, etc.   The fresh spoor showed us that a herd of buffaloes had not long left before our arrival, and the huge footprints of elephants and hippopotami bore evidence that some of these animals had also been here very recently. Before leaving this glorious scene, we went up to look at the entrance to the gorge into which the river rushes as it emerges from the chasm of the falls, when, as we approached the edge, I, being first, perceived, not twenty yards in front of me, through the dense misty spray, a small antelope, which I took for a reed-buck. It was standing browsing literally on the very brink of the awful abyss, utterly regardless of the roar of the falling masses of water, the drenching, penetrating spray (which by this time had chilled us to the very bone), and, worse than all, of the ruthless intruders upon its moist domain. A bullet from Mr. Garden's rifle, which broke its foreleg, was the first intimation it received of our whereabouts, and another through the shoulder settled it. After the Kafirs had carried it beyond the reach of the spray, to skin and cut up the meat, my attention was called to it by one of my Matabele Kafirs crying out : " What sort of a buck is this ? It isn't a reed-buck—look at its tail ! " And on doing so I at once saw that it was a species with which I was quite unacquainted. It was a female, about the size of a reed-buck, but rather heavier in the body, and in colour a sort of foxy red, with long curly hair on the back and haunches. We at first imagined it to be a lechwe ewe, but on asking our Zambesi natives, they pronounced it to be a pookoo, an antelope discovered by Dr. Livingstone, and named by him after Major Vardon—(*Cobus Vardoni*). They said there were very few about here, but that higher up the Zambesi, on the northern bank, and on the southern bank of the Chobe, they were common ; and this we afterwards found to be the case.

Above the falls, from the point some sixty miles

distant where it is joined by the Chobe, the Zambesi
flows through low, undulating forest-clad sand ridges,
which culminate here and there in abrupt rocky cliffs
or stony hills.   Its banks, and the islands with which
its broad blue bosom is studded, are decorated with
graceful, feathery palm-trees of two varieties, under
which, on the northern shore, many a small cluster
of neat-looking native huts may be seen.   Everything in the vicinity of this glorious river looks
green and smiling.   Its waters are of a deep blue,
pure and clear as one could wish.   In the still, deep
reaches at the tail of the islands, or the quiet shady
coves formed by some point of land, herds of hippopotami disport themselves in almost complete security;
whilst from the trees and bushes which line its banks
strange birds, scared by the approach of the intruder,
wing their way to more secure retreats ; and now
and again may be seen the handsome white-headed
fish-eagle, as he soars in graceful circles high overhead, or, seated on the topmost branch of some
withered tree, gives vent from time to time to the
loud shrieking cry peculiar to the eagle tribe.

Even in a fertile, well-watered land, the first sight
of a beautiful river is always pleasant ; but after our
long journey through the unspeakably dreary, sandy,
thirsty, silent, lifeless wastes, that stretch in unbroken
monotony from the very banks of the Zambesi to
the far-off Limpopo, the sight of the glorious sheet
of running water, and the semi-tropical luxuriance
and verdure of the surrounding scenery, burst like
a vision of Paradise upon our thirsty gaze.   I may
as well here say that we saw the river Zambesi and
the Victoria Falls under the most favourable circumstances, for during the past season the rains having
been unprecedentedly heavy, and not being long

over, the river was still, on our arrival, excessively
high, and the volume of water at the falls much
greater than is usually the case, for, with the
exception of where it was broken by the two islands
I have before mentioned, the face of the falls presented one even, uninterrupted sheet of foam, and
nowhere were the rocks to be seen that marred its
regularity when Mr. Baines made his excellent and
very precise drawings of it in 1862. I myself
subsequently paid a second visit to the falls in the
following October, at the very end of the dry season,
when the river was at its lowest ; and although they
were still a grand sight, and at the same time the
spray being very much less, a far more extended
view was obtainable than on my first visit, yet to
my mind the effect was not to be compared with
that produced by the fall of the far greater volume
of water which I then saw.

During the two following days, Monday and
Tuesday, we remained at our camp near the falls,
making short excursions up and down the river, and
ever and again returning to feast our eyes once more
on the mighty cataract ; and on Monday night, the
moon being at its full, we went to view the falls by its
light. Its pale, soft beams were, however, unequal
to the task of piercing the dense volumes of silvery
spray, on which they nevertheless imprinted a most
perfect double lunar rainbow, whose soft tints rivalled
in beauty the more gaudy colours of its diurnal
relative.

During these two days very many natives came
across in canoes from their villages on the northern
bank (the southern side is here uninhabited, owing
to fear of invasion by the Matabele), bringing baskets
of corn, maize, beans, and ground-nuts for sale.

Their canoes are simply logs roughly hollowed out and rounded off at the ends, and are very crank-looking craft ; they are usually paddled by two natives, one in the bow and the other in the stern, and will not carry more than one passenger, who sits in the middle.

Along the banks of the river about here we found that the natives had dug a great number of pitfalls, about ten feet in depth, to entrap hippopotami, elephants, or buffaloes, which, being always placed in the pathways made by these animals, and neatly covered over with dry grass, are most difficult to detect, even when one knows there are such things about ; but the unconscious traveller, ignorant of anything of the sort, is almost sure to be engulfed in one of them sooner or later. This happened to two of our party, neither of whom, luckily, was in any way hurt, after which we adopted the plan of letting one of the Kafirs walk in front, who gave us due notice of their whereabouts, by either uncovering them with an assegai or falling into them, an example which we were, of course, careful not to follow.

But all this time the season was fast advancing, and it behoved us to push on in search of elephants ; so on Tuesday evening we held a council of war, in order to decide to what part of the country we should next direct our steps. Like the celebrated house mentioned in the Bible, we were divided amongst ourselves, Wood wishing to turn back and strike through the hills eastward to the country near the river Gwai, where he and I had made so successful a hunt the preceding year, whilst I myself was bent upon following the Zambesi to the westwards, hoping to meet with a hunter's paradise in the unknown country in that direction, and Mr. Garden and his

brother inclined to my opinion ; so it was finally
settled that Wood should take fourteen of our Kafirs
and Bushmen, and make tracks eastwards, taking
with him the tusks of the three elephants already
shot, which he would forward at the earliest opportunity to the waggons at Daka ; whilst I, with ten
Kafirs and two Bushmen, together with the Gardens
and their whole retinue, should proceed up the river.

CHAPTER VIII

Koodoo—Impala—Tenacity of Life—Water-buck—A New Servant—
The " Chobe " River—Pookoo Antelopes—Buffaloes—A Wounded
Cow—Elephant-shooting—Lions at Night—Abundance of Buffalo
—The " Pookoo Flats "—Mosquitoes and Tsetse-Flies.

It was on the 1st of July 1874 that we broke up
our camp at the Victoria Falls, where we had passed
a pleasant week, viewing and reviewing from every
point of vantage this grandly beautiful work of
Nature.

Following the course of the river, and keeping
close along the bank, we found the walking in most
parts very tolerable, though in places the sand-belts,
thickly timbered and covered with dense underwood,
came right down to the water's edge. Just before
sundown, as we were making a cut across a neck of
land to avoid a large bend of the river, I descried the
head and ears of a koodoo cow, gazing intently at
us from the edge of a patch of bush, and calling
Captain G.'s attention to it, he immediately fired,
but the range was rather far, and whether the shot
took effect or not, I cannot say ; at any rate the
animal bounded away through the bushes, followed
by several more, including two bulls. One of these
latter carried a very fine pair of horns, so I seized my
ten-bore rifle from the hands of the Kafir who was
carrying it, and ran at my utmost speed, skirting

along the bush, in the hope of cutting them off as
they emerged on the farther side. I was just in
time, for the koodoos having, as I had anticipated,
turned up wind, passed me in single file at not more
than 120 yards' distance. The largest bull — a
magnificent specimen of perhaps the handsomest
antelope in the world—came last, and as he cantered
easily by, I took him just in front of the shoulder to
allow for the rate at which he was going, and fired.
The shot, which told loudly as it struck, brought him
to his knees, but springing up again, he turned at
right angles to his former course and came bounding
along straight in my direction. Any one unacquainted
with the habits of the animal would have sworn that
he was charging ; but I knew well that it was but the
spasmodic rush which all animals make, after receiving
a ball through the heart. When within a few yards
of where I stood, he fell headlong to the earth, but
regaining his legs made another short rush, and then
falling forwards once more—with such force as to
break the bone of the lower jaw against a large piece
of stone—lay still for ever. This was the finest
koodoo I had yet shot, and indeed one of the finest
I had ever seen, and with admiration I gazed on its
graceful proportions, and small game-looking head,
surmounted by the long spiral horns. The rest of
our party now coming up, we resolved, as we were
only a few hundred yards from the river, to camp on
the spot, so, kindly assisted by Mr. Garden, I set to
work to carefully remove the skin from the head and
neck of my prize, which I was determined to preserve
in toto, with the long beard under the throat, and the
mane on the back of the neck. I may here say that
the horns of this koodoo measured 43 inches in
perpendicular height, that is, in a straight line from

point to base.   On examination, we found that my
bullet had struck it in the centre of the shoulder, and
going right through the heart, lodged under the skin
on the other side.   Early the next morning we came
across an immense herd of impalas, one of which I
shot.   My bullet—a ten to the pound—struck it as
it was running straight away, and entering by the
left thigh, tore a passage through the entire length of
its body, passing out on the breast, and yet this
animal—not much larger than a springbuck—ran at
least 400 yards after receiving such a wound, and
had it not been for the excellent spooring of one of
my Masaras, would have eluded us after all, in the
jungle, and become a prey to the vultures and
hyænas.   The tenacity of life exhibited by wild
animals in South Africa, and I suppose all over the
world, is really extraordinary, and many instances of
it have come under my own personal notice so
wonderful, that I hardly like to recount them.   In
the afternoon, as we were skirting along the river, a
small herd of water-buck rushed out from a patch
of reeds, crossing about 100 yards in front of us as
they made for the jungle.   As they passed we fired,
wounding two, but though there was a good deal of
blood on the spoor, and we followed them a considerable distance, they made good their escape.   Later
on we met a small party of natives, who had come
across from their village on the other side, to hunt.
They were all armed with huge spears, but their
hunting seemed to be confined to visiting and keeping
in order a lot of pitfalls—of all of which we had
fortunately managed to steer clear—and despatching
with the aforesaid spears any animals that were
unlucky enough to tumble into them.   In the
evening one of these men came to our camp, saying

he wanted to work for one of us, and after a good
deal of interpreting, engaged to follow my fortunes
for three months, for the consideration of a cotton
blanket, to be paid at the end of that time.   He was
a fine, broad-shouldered fellow, as black as ebony,
always good-tempered and willing, and proved a most
excellent servant.   Like most of the natives who
inhabit the fertile banks of the Zambesi, he was fat
and sleek, and presented a strong contrast to my
spare-made, sinewy Makalakas and Masaras.   At the
spot where we camped that night, the river was more
than a mile broad, running over a shallow rocky bed,
and presenting the appearance of a rapid, though no
rocks were apparent above its surface.   As I looked
across this vast expanse of rippling broken water, the
crest of every tiny wave gilded by the rays of the
setting sun, I thought it one of the most perfect of
the many beautiful views I had yet seen along the
banks of the Zambesi.

Early on the morning of the following day, as we
were passing through a patch of terribly dense jungle
that came down to the water, we cut the fresh spoor
of three elephant bulls, and following it, all but got
up to them (in fact, I had just caught a glimpse of
the hind-quarters of one), when the wind suddenly
veering, they smelt us, and were off in the twinkling
of an eye; of course we ran on the spoor, but in
such jungle it was hopeless, for whereas they crashed
down all before them, we had our work cut out to
force a passage at all, and so had to give it up as a
bad job, cursing the adverse fate that had, as it were,
dashed the cup from our very lips, for had the wind
remained favourable but a few moments longer, we
might have crept close up to them, and obtained a
splendid standing shot.   In the afternoon Mr. G.

shot a water-buck bull, about three parts grown, and although the meat of this species of antelope is very coarse and ill-flavoured, we found its marrow bones exceedingly good, and they proved a welcome addition to our supper.   The next day was Saturday (July 4), our fourth day since leaving the falls, and shortly after noon we reached "Umparira," the town I have before mentioned as situated just at the junction of the Chobe and Zambesi rivers.   We here found two Griqua hunters in the service of Mr. Westbeech, and as they were thinking of returning in a few days to his waggons, at Pandamatenka, I persuaded them to take the head and horns of the koodoo I had shot a few days before with them, giving them at the same time a letter to their "Baas," begging him to be kind enough to forward them to my own waggons at Daka at the first opportunity.   These Griquas told us they had killed an elephant bull close at hand that very morning, and had only just returned from it.   This elephant was one of four that had come down in the night and drunk only a few hundred yards from their camp; being apprised of which fact by some natives, who had found the fresh spoor, they followed them into the dense bush close to the river, and coming up with them, broke the shoulder of one at the first discharge, and finally killed him.   This, they said, was the first elephant they had killed this season, as having suffered severely from fever they were still very weak, and consequently unable to do much hunting.   One of them, Jacob Ourson by name, told us he had been some distance up the Chobe the preceding year, and gave us some information about the country.   He said the sand-ridges along the river were covered with dense jungle, in which, last year, he had found elephants plentiful, and buffaloes innumerable. Umparira is a horrid-looking place, situated in a marsh between the two rivers, suggestive of nothing but fever, ague, and mosquitoes. It is a most unhealthy spot, and the graves of three English traders, who died there of the deadly malarial fever, attest the fact. It is just my idea of Eden in *Martin Chuzzlewit*, and the very look of the place is almost enough to give one ague. Having delayed a considerable time talking to Jacob Ourson, it was late before we again made a start, and that night we camped at only a few miles' distance from Umparira. The Chobe, near its junction with the Zambesi, is a fine deep river, several hundred yards in breadth. The word " Chobe " (which, according to Dr. Livingstone, is the name by which this river was known to the Makololo in the time of Sebituane) we found to convey no meaning to the natives now living along its banks, who have no particular name for it, but call it differently opposite each town, and " Chobe " is very likely only the name of some particular part, or of the headman of some town on its banks whom the great explorer visited.

The next day (Sunday), we continued our journey westwards along the southern bank of the Chobe, which here runs nearly due east. As we had been informed, we found that a dense continuous jungle, interspersed with large forest trees, came down in most parts almost to the water. This jungle-covered land rises in some places abruptly, in others in a gentle slope, leaving along the shore a margin of open ground (from 10 to 100 yards broad), covered with short grass, and formed, no doubt, of alluvial deposit. On the other side of the river, as far as the eye can reach, stretches a wide expanse of flat, marshy country, intersected by numerous deep, well-defined

streams, that here form a sort of network between
the Chobe and the Zambesi. As we proceeded,
traces of the presence of elephants and buffaloes
became more and more frequent, and we kept a sharp
look-out for fresh spoor ; from time to time herds of
pookoo antelopes (a rare species of water-buck only
found along the banks of the Chobe and Zambesi
rivers), disturbed by our approach whilst feeding
close along the water, eyed us curiously, and then
bounded up into the jungle. Three of them,
however, fell to our rifles in the course of the forenoon, one of which—a young ram—was the first of
these animals I ever shot. As it was Sunday, and we
wished to cut up the meat of the three pookoos, we
came to a halt soon after mid-day, and finding a
convenient place, cleared a spot just within the edge
of the bush, where we might arrange our camp for
the night.

About a couple of hours before sundown, being
tired of sitting still, and wishing to see if there were
any elephant spoor about in the neighbourhood, I
called up my Kafirs, and started on a tour of
inspection. As we advanced into the bush, we found
the tracks of elephants and buffaloes crossing and
recrossing it in all directions, so much so indeed
that I almost expected to run across a herd of the
former that very evening, and felt sure I should see
some of the latter coming down to drink before long.
About an hour's walk from our camp I crossed an
open valley, running down at right angles to the
river, between two sand-ridges covered with dense
jungle, down which ran several large game paths,
leading to the water, and well trampled by buffaloes
and elephants. From the great quantity of spoor—
of all dates up to the preceding night—I had no

doubt that this valley formed a favourite route to and from the river, and made a mental note of it, as a good place to watch for them on moonlight nights. As it was already late when I started, I had not gone very far beyond this point, when, warned by the disappearance of the sun behind the tree-tops that not much more than half an hour's daylight remained, I turned to retrace my steps, in order to reach camp before dark.   On again arriving at the open valley mentioned above, I found it occupied by a large herd of two or three hundred buffaloes, that had emerged from the surrounding jungle during my absence, and were now feeding quietly down towards the river for their evening drink.   Though I hardly liked to fire, for fear of disturbing elephants, some of which might, for all I knew, be within hearing, yet, on the other hand, I had a strong desire to secure a nice fat buffalo steak for supper, and at last forgetting all more prudent resolves, and sympathising with the feelings of my Kafirs, who kept entreating me to shoot them a fat cow, I took my four-bore elephant gun and advanced towards the still un-conscious herd, resolved to kill one if possible. Those that were nearest were about 120 yards from the edge of the bush, beyond which there was no shelter, save that afforded by a few large scattered goussy trees.   However, by creeping cautiously forward on my hands and knees, I managed to get within 80 yards or so, when an old cow observing me, raised her head and gazed steadily towards where I crouched.   There was no time to be lost, as I saw she was thoroughly alarmed, so, singling out a fine fat cow, that stood broadside on close beside her, I raised my heavy gun, and taking a quick aim behind her shoulder, fired.   The

loud bellow that followed the shot told me she was
hard hit, but I could see nothing, for the whole herd,
startled by the report of the gun, rushed together in
wild affright, and now stood in a dense mass, facing
towards their hidden foe, effectually screening the
wounded cow from my view. In another instant,
seemingly satisfied that something dangerous was
near, they turned about and galloped away across the
valley, making for the bush on the opposite side,
and on the dust raised by their many feet subsiding,
I beheld the one I had wounded still standing where
she had been shot, and thought she was about done
for ; but on seeing me step from behind a tree, she
immediately wheeled round and made for the jungle.

When the herd ran together, after I had fired,
with several nasty-looking old bulls in their front,
my native attendants had all retreated precipitately
to the edge of the bush (with the exception of one
of the Masaras, who was carrying a small gourd of
water slung on an assegai over his shoulder), or I
might have given the cow another shot with my
second gun before she turned to run. Although
evidently severely wounded, she still managed to get
over the ground at a great rate, and entered the
bush at least 100 yards in advance of myself and the
Bushman, who were following at our best pace, the
Kafirs carrying my guns being a considerable distance
behind. Just within the edge of the jungle was one
very thick patch, unlike the greater part, covered
with foliage, and behind this the wounded buffalo
turned and stood at bay waiting for her pursuers.
Not thinking of this stratagem (a very common one
with both buffaloes and elephants), and imagining
her to be a considerable distance ahead, I ran into
her very horns before I saw her, and she at the same

time seeing me at once charged, with eyes on fire, and her nose stretched straight out, grunting furiously. Luckily she was not standing head on, but broadside to me, and so could not come straight at me, but had first to turn round the bush. This gave me time to spring through the bushes to one side, as she rushed past, when she immediately made at the Bushman, who, springing into a small sapling, just swung his body up out of reach as she passed beneath. So close was she, that, as the calabash full of water, which he had been carrying slung on an assegai, fell to the ground behind him, she smashed it to atoms, either with her feet or horns, just as, if not before, it touched the ground. After this she turned and stood under the very slender tree on which the Bushman hung, looking up at him, and grunting furiously, but not attempting to butt the tree down, which I think she could have accomplished had she but tried. At this instant the Kafir who carried my ten-bore rifle, reaching the scene of action unperceived by the buffalo, fired at and missed her, on which she again retreated behind the bush from whence she had first charged. By this time, however, I had my second elephant gun in my hands, and creeping up gave her another bullet on the point of the shoulder, just as she caught sight of me and was again turning to charge. On receiving this second ball, she fell to the ground, and, snatching up an assegai and followed by several of the Kafirs, we ran in and despatched her before she could rise. She proved to be a dry cow in splendid condition. The sun was now down, so we lost no time in cutting up the meat and starting for camp, which, after an awkward walk in the dark through the thick thorny bush, we at last reached. On my arrival, I found that Mr. Garden, who, like

myself, had gone out for a stroll in the afternoon,
had not yet returned. Captain Garden during my
absence had shot another " pookoo " antelope, which
made our fourth that day. As the night was very
dark, and the bush unpleasantly thick to get through
even in the daytime, we began to think Mr. Garden
must have missed his way, and were just about to fire
a couple of shots to guide him, when we heard voices
in the distance, and a few minutes later he stepped
into camp, and we were all of us soon deeply interested in the contents of a pot of " pookoo " stew.
Mr. G. had shot an old buffalo bull with his 500-
bore Express rifle, and brought the grim-looking
head back to camp with him. It must have been a
very old animal, for the face was almost devoid of
hair, and the horns very close set, but like those of
most of the buffaloes in this part of the country, not
at all wide spread, though very deep and rugged, and
gnarled as the trunk of an old tree. Mr. Garden
had also noticed a good deal of elephant spoor, and
as in this dense jungle we were unanimous that it
would be useless to hunt in company (as in all probability more than one elephant would seldom be seen
at once), I resolved to separate from my kind friends
on the following day, and henceforth hunt alone.
Accordingly, early the next morning, when crossing
the valley where the preceding evening I had shot
the buffalo, we cut the fresh spoor of elephants that
had passed to and from the river during the night, I
proposed to my friends that they should follow them,
and leave me to proceed farther up the river. To
this they would not agree, but insisted that I should
take the spoor and let them push on, as they said
they would be sure to find other spoor before long ;
and we thus finally settled it, and with hearty wishes

for mutual success, and the hope that before long we should meet again, we parted. I lost no time in making arrangements to follow the elephants, and after putting down my blankets and other baggage with all the buffalo and pookoo meat, and leaving two Kafirs in charge, at once started in pursuit, taking care to have all the calabashes filled with water, and not forgetting the large American axe to chop out the tusks in case of success. On carefully examining the spoor, my Bushmen reported that there were four elephants, one large full-grown bull and three younger ones. For about half a mile they had followed one of the paths leading up the valley, and then leaving it turned into the neighbouring jungle, heading down the river in the direction from whence we had come that morning. They had been feeding quietly along, and I felt sure that we should come up with them before long if they did not get our wind. But that this contingency would happen I was very much afraid, for the wind kept veering and chopping about in a most distressing manner, and as the elephants too held no particular course, but kept doubling about in all directions, I began to fear they would surely scent us before I could get up to them. Besides this, the jungle was fearfully thick, and in many places we found it difficult to creep through it at all. After proceeding in this manner for about three hours, following slowly and carefully on the spoor, several unmistakable signs showed us that we were not far behind our game, and might expect to come up with them at any moment, and very shortly afterwards, the Masara who was carrying my gun, and taking the spoor, suddenly stopped and pointing forwards, ejaculated the one word "Nansia" (There they are), immediately followed by "Ee-ya-balecka"

(They're running away).   At the same instant
I caught a glimpse of the outline of a huge grey
mass that was passing at a half walk, half run,
not more than thirty yards from us.   The sharp-
scented brute was not in full flight, and had
probably only got the merest whiff of tainted
wind, but there was not an instant to lose, so, seizing
my gun and holding it in both hands, the muzzle
pointed forwards, ready to be raised to my shoulder
at a moment's notice, I dashed through the jungle as
fast as possible in order to intercept the elephant I
had seen and give him a shot in the shoulder at close
quarters.   In this way, only thinking of the one I
had already seen, I ran almost under the tusks of
another huge old bull that, still unconscious of any
danger, was standing, head on to me, behind a dense
bush.   On hearing the rustling I made, he raised
his head and trunk, showing a fine thick pair of tusks,
and at the same time spreading his enormous ears
stared hard with his vicious-looking eyes towards
where I stood.   Now was my chance : scarcely half
a dozen yards separated us, and as his head was raised,
and he held his trunk high in the air, moving it
quietly backwards and forwards to try and get my
wind, his whole chest was exposed ; so quickly bringing my gun to my shoulder, and aiming for the heart,
I fired.   The heavy recoil turned me right round,
and when I again faced about, the elephant had
vanished in the dense bush.   However, I felt sure he
would not go very far with such a wound, so bidding
the Bushman, who was now beside me, to run on the
spoor, I lost no time in following him, and after
threading our way for a couple of hundred yards or
so through the jungle, running as fast as circumstances
would allow, we once more came up with him.   He

was evidently done for, and only walking slowly along, swinging his trunk from side to side. Some of my Kafirs having run round in front of him, now commenced to shout, on which he turned and came walking slowly back again towards me. As he passed at not more than twenty yards from me, I gave him another four-ounce ball in the centre of the shoulder, which brought him to a stand, and after receiving another immediately afterwards from my second gun, he fell flat on his side stone dead. On examination, we found him to be a fine old bull, with a perfect pair of tusks, weighing nearly 60 lbs. apiece, and I felt very well pleased at having secured him with so little trouble. The work of chopping out the tusks, and cutting out the fat and the best portions of the meat, occupied the greater part of the afternoon, so that when we reached the river at the drinking-place from whence I had taken the spoor in the morning, and where the two Kafirs had been left in charge of the baggage, it was already late, therefore I at once set to work to clear a piece of ground just within the bush and close to the water's edge, for as this was evidently a favourite drinking-place for elephants, I determined to remain in the same camp and hunt the surrounding jungle during the following week or so.

Scarcely had we got everything ship-shape, when, just as, seated on my bed of dry grass, I was about to commence a supper of fried elephant's heart, washed down with a cup of bitter tea, one of the Kafirs reported that a large herd of buffaloes were coming down the valley to the drinking-place, on which I got up, and went to the edge of the bush to have a look at them. The whole of the open ground was literally covered with their massive dusky forms, which in the dim twilight appeared twice their natural size. Though it is difficult to speak with any degree of accuracy as to numbers, I think there could not have been less than from two to three hundred, the greatest part of them being cows, and young animals not yet full grown, though here and there I distinguished an old bull, one of the patriarchs of the herd. They were advancing rapidly towards the river, and soon, preceded by an old cow, which from time to time stopped and sniffed the air suspiciously, their foremost ranks stepped knee-deep into the water, and after drinking their fill, gradually gave place to those in the rear, and again commenced feeding quietly up the valley. Until twilight had given place to a clear starlight night, I watched this interesting scene, standing just on the edge of the jungle, and not twenty yards from the nearest of them. Being well supplied with meat, I did not attempt to molest them, and soon the last of the herd, having satisfied his thirst, disappeared in the darkness of the night, and I once more returned with renewed energy to my interrupted supper. About an hour later, just as, wrapped in my kaross, I was falling asleep, a troop of lions commenced to roar not far down the river, and I roused myself to listen to their deep-toned muttering voices. They seemed to be advancing steadily along the river towards our camp, roaring grandly at intervals, and at length reached the place, not thirty yards away, where the buffaloes had drunk. Here they gave tongue in splendid style, making the whole forest resound again, and causing me to sit up and clutch my rifle involuntarily. Several times during my three years' wanderings in the far interior of Southern Africa, have I, when camped in a patch of bush, or lying at a shooting-hole on the edge of some lonely pool or river, thus heard a troop of lions roar in my immediate vicinity, so close indeed, sometimes, that I could hear the hiss of their breath after each purr ; and though it is now the fashion to depreciate the courage of the lion, the power of his voice, and everything else concerning him, yet it is a fact that, under such circumstances, several of them roaring in unison will make the whole air in their immediate vicinity vibrate and tremble, and I know of nothing in nature more awe-inspiring, or on a dark night more calculated to make a man feel nervous.   As a matter of fact, however, according to my experience, there is very little to fear from lions when they roar freely, as they only do so after they have satisfied their hunger, whereas, when on the look-out for a meal, they are as still as the grave, or only give vent to a low purring growl, which, though uttered close at hand, seems to come from a long way off.   Such at least has been the case on the occasions when they have attacked my oxen at nights, or whilst prowling about trying to do so, but kept off by the dogs.   On the present occasion these lions soon passed our camp and continued up the river, their voices growing fainter and fainter, till at length they died away in the distance, and I fell asleep.

Before sunrise the next morning, leaving the camp in charge of my two youngest Kafir boys, I started into the jungle with the rest in search of elephants, and had not proceeded 300 yards before crossing the fresh spoor of two bulls that had drunk during the night close to our camp, but so noiselessly as not to have awakened either myself or any of my Kafirs.   We at once followed them, and they led us for two or three hours through the thick jungle, going westwards, almost parallel with the course of the river ; but as is so often the case when elephant-hunting on foot, just as we were close up to, and expecting to sight them at every instant, they got our wind and decamped. Thinking that as they had not been much disturbed in this part of the country, they perhaps would not run far in such thick bush, I directed my two Masaras to take the spoor at their best pace, but though we stuck to it for good three hours, running and walking alternately, it was useless, and I finally gave it up. All the time we were thus following them, the elephants had been doubling about in every direction in the bush, constantly manœuvring so as to get our wind, by which means they kept themselves informed of our whereabouts, and avoided a closer acquaintance. Several times the spoor showed us where they had been standing, no doubt listening intently, and sniffing the air for some sign of our approach.

I may here say that whilst following these elephants early in the morning from the river, and before they got our wind, we came across two large herds of buffaloes, and on again returning to camp, after having been fairly outwitted by our would-be victims, we passed close to another large troop, that, having lain asleep in the deepest recesses of the jungle, during the heat of the day, were just commencing to feed down towards the river for their evening drink.

The number of buffaloes about this part of the Chobe is really astonishing,[1] and in no other part of the country that I am acquainted with, have I found them so numerous. They are quite a nuisance to the elephant-hunter, for not only do they continually

---

[1] This was written in 1874. The buffaloes have now been driven farther westwards, but beyond the Sunta outlet they are still to be met with in great numbers.

trample out the fresh spoor, and make it most difficult to follow, but often by lying quite close to where elephants are standing, and then running towards them on the hunter's approach, give notice that danger is at hand.

At the point where we struck the river on our way back—some three or four miles to the westward of our camp—stretched a large flat piece of ground, in some parts over half a mile broad, lying between the steep forest-covered, jungly sand-belt and the bank of the river. This flat might be from six to eight miles long, and lay in the form of a semicircle, in a bend of the sand-belt, that rose abruptly behind it, and ran down to the water at each extremity. The greater part of this extensive tract—once no doubt the ancient bed of the river—was open, though here and there patches of bush were scattered over its surface, and near the river grew many very fine wide-branching camel-thorn trees (*Acacia giraffæ*). On coming down from the jungle, about an hour before sundown, and looking across the open ground towards the river, I beheld several herds of " pookoo " antelopes, some impalas, and a small family of graceful striped koodoos—amongst them a grand-looking old bull—whilst far to my left the foremost ranks of a herd of buffaloes were just emerging from the bush, the fourth troop I had seen that day. Thoroughly disgusted with the result of my day's work in pursuit of the elephants, and in order to take the edge off my disappointment, I resolved to lay aside my rule never to shoot game (so long as I had any meat left in camp), and secure, if possible, a good specimen of the head of a male " pookoo," and accordingly on the way home killed two fine rams. The horns of one of these, which I now have in my possession, measured 16 inches, which is about the extreme length they ever attain.

The number of pookoo on these flats quite surprised me. Sometimes troops of more than fifty of them were to be seen together, males and females mixed, or again small herds of ten or fifteen old rams, forming, I suppose, a sort of bachelors' club. On my first arrival I found them very tame, and up to the time of my visit they had evidently had but very little experience of firearms. Owing to the great numbers of these antelopes, I christened this place the "Pookoo Flats," by which name I shall henceforth refer to it.

Although the nights were still very cold, yet in the early part of the evenings, huge black mosquitoes, as vicious as bull-dogs, already commenced to make their presence disagreeably felt : little did I dream what was in store for me during the hot weather later in the season ! In the daytime, too, "tsetse" flies, whose numbers increased daily as the season advanced, were very troublesome. Nowhere does this virulent insect exist in such numbers as to the westward of the Victoria Falls, along the southern bank of the Zambesi and Chobe. It is usually found in great numbers near the river, becoming scarcer and scarcer as one advances inland, till at a distance of a few miles it disappears, except in some particular patches of forest. Along the water's edge they are an incredible pest, attacking one in a perfect swarm, from daylight till sunset, and without a buffalo or giraffe tail to swish them off, life would be unendurable. The well-known African traveller, Andersson, says their bite has not been inaptly likened to that of a flea. My experience is that it is far more severe, and that about one in every ten bites (that perhaps

touches a nerve) closely resembles the sting of a wasp
or bee, as it will cause one when seated to spring up
as if pricked with a needle.   As they are possessed
of a long probe, a thick flannel shirt offers no
protection against these most abominable of all
created insects—direct descendants, no doubt, of the
flies that plagued Egypt.   Though, during 1872-73,
I had hunted elephants on foot in fly-infested
countries, yet never had I met with them in sufficient
numbers to cause much annoyance ; but along the
Chobe river, during the months of September and
October, hunger, thirst, fatigue, and all the other
hardships that must of necessity be endured by the
elephant-hunter, sank into insignificance as compared
with the continuous unceasing irritation caused by the
bites of the " tsetse " flies by day, and three or four
varieties of mosquitoes by night.   What a glorious
field lies open there for an enthusiastic entomologist !
I think that this plague of " tsetse " flies, along the
Chobe and Zambesi, is due to the enormous numbers
of buffaloes that frequent their banks, as they always
seem very partial to those animals.   The bite of
this remarkable insect, as is well known, though
fatal to all kinds of domestic animals, is innocuous
to every species of game, and to man.   A general
belief exists, that amongst domestic animals, the
donkey, dog, and goat are exceptions to this rule,
but this is a mistake, for I have seen all three die
from the effect of its bites.   That all the natives
living in the " fly " country possess both dogs and
goats, I admit, but these have been bred there from
generation to generation, and have become acclimatised, whereas, if you take either a goat or a dog
that has been bred outside the " fly " country, into
a district where the " tsetse " is found, it will die in

nine cases out of ten, and the original progenitors of
the animals the natives now possess were no doubt
such exceptions to the general rule. Even now, the
natives told me, out of a litter of pups, born in the
country and of acclimatised parents, some always die
of " fly " symptoms. The " tsetse " fly is about the
same size as a common horse fly, of a dull greyish
colour, with bars of a pinky tinge across the body ;
its wings, however, do not lie in the form of a
penthouse, but are like those of an English house
fly, only longer. Animals, such as horses and oxen,
that have been bitten by the " fly " during the dry
season, usually live on until the commencement of
the rains, but seldom survive long after the first
shower has fallen. It often happens that when
hunting with horses, outside, but close to, the " fly "
country, one is led in the ardour of the chase into an
infested district ; if such is the case, and it is uncertain
whether the horse has been bitten or not, the truth
can be ascertained by pouring a few buckets of water
over him, when, if he has been " stuck " (as hunters
call it), his coat will all stand on end, like that of a
lung-sick ox. On several occasions, horses have been
purposely taken into parts of the " fly " country, where
elephants were known to be plentiful, in the hope that
by their aid their owners would be able to shoot
enough ivory to compensate for the loss entailed by
their inevitable death, for, of course, in tolerably open
country a man ought to be able to kill very many more
elephants on horseback than on foot. My comrade
W. once made an experiment of this sort, and he
informed me that at the end of two weeks his horse
grew too weak to hunt with, and at the end of three
could not carry him at all, though it did not die for
some time afterwards. But to return to my journal.

The three following days I remained in the same camp, hunting in the neighbouring bush with the very worst of luck, for though each day I got the fresh spoor of elephants, on all three occasions they winded me and decamped before I caught sight of them. I never saw such a place as this bush for the wind, which never seemed to blow for two minutes together from the same quarter. This I attributed to the different currents of air that were continually blowing over the open marshes on the other side of the river, and seemed to form eddies in the jungle. It was most disheartening, as in elephant-hunting on foot everything depends upon keeping below the wind of these keen-scented brutes, and here this was almost impossible. My only consolation lay in the hope that as the season advanced, and the weather became hotter, the winds would drop and the air become stiller. On each of these three days we encountered more than one large herd of buffaloes, but having meat I never fired a shot at them for fear of disturbing more valuable game. On the Thursday night a troop of elephant cows came down to drink close to our camp, trumpeting and splashing about in the water for a long time. The spoor of this troop I followed the next day, though unsuccessfully, as I have before said.

On Saturday morning (July 11), after burying the tusks of the bull I had shot the preceding Monday, being tired of my camp and the bad luck I had met with there, I packed up all my traps and made another start up the river. Whilst crossing Pookoo Flats early in the morning, I saw a black rhinoceros cow with a small calf not much larger than a pig, that, on getting our wind, at once made for the jungle at a quick trot, besides some koodoos,

M

zebras, and as usual any amount of impalas, pookoos, and baboons, which latter quaint-looking beasts swarm along the Zambesi and Chobe. When near the upper extremity of the flats we cut the fresh spoor of a troop of elephant cows, so, after putting down all the baggage and leaving two of the Kafirs in charge till our return, I at once set the Bushmen to follow them. The spoor took us right through the belt of jungle which lines the river, and out into a forest of goussy trees with very little underwood on the other side. Here it became involved in a labyrinth of other spoor of elephants that had only passed a short time before, and all the science of my two Bushmen (and better or more experienced hands on a game trail I never saw) did not suffice to unravel it, so at length I was forced to give it up. On the way back to the river we again crossed the spoor of two elephant cows, accompanied by several young animals of various sizes, so, thinking they would probably not be very far off in the bush, I followed them, and about an hour later the Bushman who was in front suddenly crouched down, and after peering eagerly through the jungle in front of him for a few moments, turned and whispered the well-known "Nansia" (There they are). The wind was perfectly fair, blowing strongly from the elephants towards where we stood, so taking my gun I walked quietly forwards to reconnoitre. As we had divined from the spoor, there were only two cows worth shooting, the largest of which was standing broadside to me, so, creeping noiselessly to within twenty yards, I gave her a ball in the very centre of the shoulder. The shot was followed by a rush, as the affrighted herd crashed through the bush, breaking everything before them, and not giving me a chance at the other cow

with my second gun.   The one I had fired at I
saw from the first was mortally wounded, and after
running 150 yards or so she fell dead, shot right
through the heart.   On cutting her up she proved
to be excessively fat ; but though an old cow
her tusks were not very large, only weighing 9 lbs.
apiece.

I set the Kafirs to work to chop out the ivory
and cut out the heart and inside fat at once, and
as, of course, very much less time and labour have
to be expended on a cow than on a bull elephant
(the bones in the head of the latter being not only
much larger, but in addition very much harder than
in the former), we managed to reach the place
where the traps had been left before sundown, and
at once made for the bank of the river some few
hundred yards distant, in order to camp near the
water.

As we were nearing the river I observed the
figure of a man dressed in European clothes creeping
forwards step by step, closely following a Kafir boy
who kept pointing forwards, evidently to some sort
of game that they were stalking.   This I soon made
out to be Tofts, Mr. G.'s servant, intent upon stalking a pookoo.   So intent was he upon his object that
I managed to approach from behind and touch him
on the shoulder before he observed me.   Our greet-
ing frightened away the antelope, which, as I had
plenty of good fat elephant meat, did not much
matter.

Tofts told me that Mr. Garden was at his camp
about a mile away, but that Captain Garden had
gone farther up the river in company with Henry
Wall (a Bastard man from Graham's Town, who had
entered Mr. Garden's service at Tati, as interpreter

and overseer over all the waggon-drivers and Kafirs).
Of course, on hearing that Mr. Garden was so near,
I relinquished the idea of camping where I was, and
under Tofts' guidance started forthwith for his
bivouac, which we reached shortly after dusk.

OLD 4-BORE DUTCH ELEPHANT GUN.
Used by the Author in 1873-74.

PLATE VI

1. IMPALA ANTELOPE ♂ (Æpyceros Melampus).

    Shot on the Chobe river, July 29, 1877.
    Length of horns, in straight line from point to base, 1 foot
    7 inches.

2. IMPALA ANTELOPE ♂ (Æpyceros Melampus).

    Shot on the Chobe river, Aug. 14, 1879.
    Length of horns, in straight line from point to base, 1 foot
    8 inches.

3. SPRINGBUCK ♂ (Gazella Euchore).

    Shot near the Molapo river, June 28, 1876.

4. SPRINGBUCK ♂ (Gazella Euchore).

    Shot at great Chwai salt-pan, Jan. 10, 1881.

5. BLESBUCK ♀.

    Shot on the Transvaal flats, Feb. 28, 1879.

6. HORNS OF GREY RHEBUCK.

    From near Grahamstown, Cape Colony.

7. HORNS OF RED RHEBUCK.

    From near Grahamstown, Cape Colony.

8. BUSHBUCK ♂ (Tragelaphus Sylvaticus).

    Shot near Port Elizabeth, Cape Colony, March 1876.

9. SPOTTED BUSHBUCK ♂ (Tragelaphus Scriptus).

    Shot on the Chobe river, near Linyanti, July 27, 1879.

10. BLUE WILDEBEEST ♂ (Catoblepas Gorgon).

    Shot on the Mababe plain, Oct. 26, 1879.
    Spread of horns, 2 feet 2 inches.

PLATE VI

1

2

3

5

4

6

7

8

To face page 164.

10

9

CHAPTER IX

Hippopotami—Lechwe Antelopes—Difficult Shooting—Elephants on the "Chobe"—A Plucky little Calf—A Canoe Ride—Makubas and their Island—Return to "Pookoo Flats"—400 lbs. of Ivory.

On our arrival we found that Mr. Garden was still down at the river, but in a few minutes he returned, with two guinea-fowls that he had just shot. These birds abound all along the river, roosting at nights in large flocks in the trees close to the water's edge, and are, in my opinion, when young, the best eating of all the game birds found in the interior of South Africa. Over a savoury stew of elephant's heart, we recounted to one another our several experiences during the past week. Mr. Garden had had no luck with the elephants ; for, though there were lots of them about, he had been, like myself, much bothered by the currents of wind in the thick bush. Just opposite this camp, on the other side of the river, or rather on an island in the marsh on the other side, for the country seemed flooded in every direction, was a small native town of some six or eight huts. These natives had paid several visits to my friend's camp, and he had been with them in their canoes to shoot hippopotami—which are plentiful in the Chobe—but without success, as they were afraid to paddle near enough to these much-dreaded monsters to allow him to shoot with any certainty, for the head of the hippopotamus, which is only kept above the surface for a few seconds at a time, offers a very small mark. As I have said, these animals are abundant in the Chobe, as also in the Zambesi, and usually congregate together in herds of from three or four to twenty members, though the old bulls are often seen alone. They remain in the river all day, but at night come out and feed along the banks, sometimes wandering to a considerable distance from the water. According to the natives—and they ought to know—they are very vicious, and it is dangerous to approach them in canoes, as they have a nasty trick of diving down and seizing these flimsy craft from beneath in their huge jaws, crushing them of course like nutshells. When shot they immediately sink to the bottom, and, if lean, and the weather be cold, will not rise to the surface for many hours, but in warm weather, and when fat, they come to the top in a much shorter time.

The next day being Sunday, and as I had been working hard all the week, I did not go out hunting, but remained in the camp with Mr. Garden. About mid-day some natives came across from the little village opposite, bringing a few sweet potatoes and ground-nuts for sale, which I purchased for elephants' fat. On making inquiries about the different sorts of game to be found in this part of the country, they told me there were lots of " lechwe " in the marsh on the other side of the river, and as this was a species of antelope quite new to me, a specimen of which I longed to obtain, I persuaded them to take me across at once, to try and get a shot at one, as on the following day I wished to continue my journey up the river. We soon crossed the main stream, which seemed to be very deep, when, laying down their paddles, my boatmen took to long poles with a fork at the end,

and punted for about a mile and a half across some
flooded grassy land, where in parts there was barely
sufficient water to float the canoe, and we were just
approaching some low swampy ground that appeared
above the water level, when far to our right one of
the natives descried some lechwes, on which the head
of the canoe was turned in their direction, and
cautiously propelled through the reeds and grass
towards them.   When near enough to make them out
I could see that there were about twenty, all rams,
as their long lyre-shaped horns proved (for the ewes
of this species are hornless).   They were standing
up to their bellies in water, but after watching
us for a short time, and when we were still 300
yards distant, they made for the drier ground, headed
by a splendid old ram with a remarkably wide-set
pair of horns, of which I ardently longed to become
the possessor.   Taking off my veltschoons, I jumped
out of the canoe, and tried to cut them off, by
running obliquely towards the same point for which
they were heading, and partially succeeded, for as
they came bounding along in single file, I managed
to get within 200 yards or so of the hindmost, but
on firing had the mortification of seeing the mud
fly up, short of, and slightly behind him.   I, however,
loaded and followed them up again, and soon
saw other herds dotted about the marsh, like springbucks on the open plains of the Transvaal Republic.
Yet, despite my utmost efforts to stalk or cut them
off, often wading waist-deep in water, I found it
impossible to get anywhere near them on the bare
open marsh, and at last, having fired away the last of
the ten bullets I had brought with me to no purpose,
returned about sundown to the canoes, very tired, and
with my naked feet very sore and much cut about by

the grass, reeds, and worst of all, the sharp edges of the shells of a sort of fresh-water mussel. Had I had a small accurately-sighted Express rifle the result would no doubt have been very different; but it must be remembered that my whole armoury consisted of only two four-bore elephant guns, and a ten-bore rifle, with scarcely any grooving, and for which I had only spherical balls, which latter was the one I used on this occasion. However, though unsuccessful so far, I resolved that I would not quit the Chobe without obtaining a good specimen of the head of one of these rare and beautiful antelopes. When first they make up their minds to run, these lechwe buck stretch out their noses, laying their horns flat along their backs, and trot like an eland, but on being pressed break into a springing gallop, now and then bounding high into the air like impalas. Even when in water up to their necks they do not swim, but get along by a succession of bounds with great rapidity, making a tremendous splashing and general commotion. Of course when the water becomes too deep for them to bottom they are forced to swim, which they do well and strongly, though not as fast as the natives can paddle, and in the rainy season when the country is flooded great numbers are driven into deep water and speared before they can again reach the shallows where they can touch ground. It is owing to their being thus driven about and harried by the natives in canoes, I suspect, that they are so wild, as I don't think they can often have heard the sound of a gun before.

On the following day, Monday, July 12, I again parted from Mr. Garden, and started away westwards, along the southern bank of the river, and soon finding traces of elephants, turned off to make a reconnaissance in the neighbouring jungles, but, though rousing two herds of buffaloes, and a black rhinoceros with a small calf, I did not chance across any fresh spoor of the animals of which I was in search, so, returning to the water in the evening, I slept at a distance of only three or four miles from where I had camped the preceding night. The next day I made a new start, determined to keep straight on till sundown, unless I crossed the spoor of elephants that had drunk during the night, but the sun was scarcely an hour high, when, as I walked in front, my eyes were gladdened by the sight of the fresh footprints of a fine bull, and another half-grown ; on walking a little way into the jungle on their track, so as to examine the spoor minutely, and settle about how long ago they had passed, we soon found, from the freshness of the leaves, broken twigs, and other indications, that they must have drunk just about daybreak, and as they were feeding along in fancied security, I felt sure they were still not far distant. The bull, we found by the spoor, had something the matter (probably an old bullet) with his right fore-leg, which he brought round at each step with a sweep, making a semicircular furrow in the sand. It seemed as though we might be led to a consider-able distance from the river, so I told all my Kafirs except my two gun-carriers to run back and fill the calabashes with water as quickly as possible, and then with my two attendants commenced strolling quietly along the spoor, which was thickly strewn with leaves and chewed bark, expecting the boys to catch us up in a few minutes ; suddenly, as I was thus sauntering along with my eyes bent on the ground, never dreaming of anything of the sort, a slight rustling in front of me caused me to look up, and there, not twenty yards off, stood a fine bull elephant quietly feeding on the dark green leaves of a shrub, with the name of which I am unacquainted ; he was standing with his wounded foot doubled backwards, and just resting with the point of the toe on the ground, leaning all his weight on the other foot. The second elephant, whose spoor we had seen, I then made out standing about twenty yards to the left. It appeared to be a half-grown beast, with tusks of about 6 or 7 lbs. weight—not worth shooting—who knows ? perhaps it was a young sweetheart who had voluntarily left the herd to tend her injured lord, whose game leg, no doubt, had caused him to separate from his comrades. As I looked, she raised some sand with her trunk, and poured it on to the back of her head, just between the ears. Why she did this I leave to some wiser man than myself to determine, but do it she did. Fearing a sudden eddy of wind, which was now favourable, I at once, without waiting for the Kafirs, took my gun, and crept cautiously forwards on my hands and knees, determined to get as near as possible, and make sure of him with a bullet in the chest. I will here say that I consider there is no danger in creeping right up to a single elephant, though I do not think it advisable to approach within thirty yards or so of a large herd, as it often happens that in their first panic, they do not know exactly where the shot was fired, and come rushing down in a mass right on to the spot where the hunter stands, making it difficult for him to get out of the way. On this occasion, keeping the thickly-foliaged bush on which he was feeding between me and him, I crept round the side of it, and was then so near to him that he could almost have touched me had he stretched out his trunk, when I saw, that, whereas one of his tusks was curved right up in a semicircle, the other, which was shorter, stood straight out. It seemed strange as I watched him blinking his sharp twinkling eyes, and quietly munching the bundles of leaves that he kept conveying to his mouth with his trunk, that he should be so utterly unconscious of my presence. However, it was now time to act, so waiting till he again raised his trunk, I aimed so that the bullet should pass through the top of his heart and up into the lungs, and fired. On receiving the shot he recoiled on to his haunches, but recovering, spun round and went off at a great pace, using his game leg as though there were nothing the matter with it, and followed his young companion, a glimpse of whose hind-quarters I just caught disappearing through the bush. With such a wound I knew he would not go far, and he soon settled down into a walk, so running in front of him, I gave him a second ball in the shoulder as he passed, when he stopped, and after swaying backwards and forwards, and breaking all the bushes within reach, he sank slowly down, leaning against a small tree, which his weight, though bending it double, was not sufficient to break, so that he died thus, half propped up, with his head quite loose, and neither of his tusks resting on the ground. The Kafirs, now coming up in hot haste, were much surprised to find the elephant already dead, and I set them to work at once to chop out the tusks. One of these, as I have said, was curved to a remarkable degree, and when extracted from the skull, described considerably more than a half-circle, the other being absolutely straight. They were both within a pound of the same weight, scaling nearly 40 lbs. apiece. As the sun was not yet two hours high, I chopped out the tusks at once, and after burying them at the

foot of a large baobab tree, to be picked up on my
return, continued my journey westwards along the
river. About mid-day I met some of Captain Garden's
boys carrying four bull tusks ; Captain G. himself I
did not see, as he had taken a round in the sand-belt
in the hope of cutting fresh elephant spoor.   His boys
informed me that there was no bush along the river's
edge farther on, and no elephant spoor, and that their
master had only met with one troop of bulls since
parting from his brother, when he with Henry
Wall had shot two of them. They were now on
their return down the river to Mr. G.'s camp at
Pookoo Flats.   In spite of this discouraging news, I
determined to follow the course of the river for another
day or two at least, and so continued my journey.
All that day (Tuesday) and the following I trudged
along, but saw not a sign of elephants ; but about
10 A.M. on Thursday morning, I cut the fresh spoor
of a troop of cows that seemed to have drunk late in
the night.   Filling the calabashes with water, I at once
started on their spoor. They had been feeding
about nicely, and digging up roots in all directions,
and at mid-day it became evident that I was not far
behind them. Just then a black rhinoceros, that
was sleeping a little to one side of the elephant spoor,
got our wind, and jumping up came tearing close
past in front of us, snorting like a steam engine.
A little farther on, and when we must have been
within a few hundred yards of them, the elephants
also winded us and ran. We at once commenced to
run on the spoor, at a steady jog-trot, and in a
quarter of an hour or so had the satisfaction of
seeing a small calf pegging along in front of us.
On approaching the little beast, it put on a spurt
and began screaming lustily. This, I think, must

have brought the elephants to, as only a few hundred yards farther on we came up to them all standing. One of them, a splendid cow, brought her trunk round with a sweep, and trumpeted, probably to call the little calf, which was now behind us. As she did this, she offered me a splendid shot, for I was now within eighty yards, so I gave her a four-ounce bullet, which catching her just behind the shoulder, must, I think, have passed through her heart, and smashed her off-leg, as she came to the ground with a crash, and never rose again. At the shot the rest of the herd rushed away at a tremendous pace; I had already had a good run on the spoor, and running in this heavy sand, and under a tropical sun, is no joke; however, I managed to get pretty well up to them again, and gave the best cow I could see a ball on the hip. She at once left the herd, and followed by a good-sized calf, started off at a long swinging walk, that gave me all my work to keep up with. Another shot from behind, how-ever, slackened her pace considerably, and enabled me to pass her and give her a third shot in the shoulder. This I at once saw was a mortal wound, for the poor beast commenced to throw large quantities of blood from her trunk; after standing under a tree for a short time, her limbs began to tremble, then she made a few steps backwards, and sinking on to her haunches, threw her trunk high in air, and rolled over on her side stone dead. The calf, which was quite large enough to pound one to a jelly, and had teeth protruding six inches beyond the lip, was now beside himself with rage, and with ears ex-tended, and trumpeting loudly, charged viciously at any one who approached within fifty yards of his dead mother. Once I let him come on to close quarters,

and then dashing a heavy assegai into his face, sprang
past him at the same time.   This feat, which after all
required nothing but a little presence of mind and
judgment, seemed greatly to astonish the Kafirs,
who declared that "to-day have we seen that the
white man's heart is hard."   The assegai stuck fast
in the thick part of his trunk ; however, he managed
to twist the end of his trunk round the shaft, which
he broke, though he first succeeded in extracting the
blade.   I then threw another assegai through his ear ;
this he could not get rid of, and at last rushed away
with it still dangling.   I was very glad he had at last
made up his mind to decamp, as it would have been
a thousand pities to shoot such a plucky little beast,
and I had really begun to think that I should be
obliged to do so before I could take possession of
his mother's carcase.   Both these elephants were
excessively fat, and the first I had shot had a beautiful
pair of tusks, long, white, and without a crack, and
weighing 17 lbs. apiece.   Whilst we were engaged
in chopping out the tusks, some Makuba Kafirs came
up.   They told me that whilst going down the river
in their canoes, they had seen the two boys whom I
had left in charge of my things sitting on the bank,
who informed them that their master, a white man,
was on elephant spoor.   Soon afterwards they heard
my shots, and in the hope of getting a little meat, at
once started for the scene of action.   When I told
them that after my boys had cut off what they
wanted, they might take the two elephants *in toto*, their
delight was unbounded.   Long had it been, and long
would it be again, I expect, before they would get
such a gorge of fat meat.   Two of them were instantly despatched to call the entire population of the
village from which they hailed to help to cut up and

carry the meat, and I feel sure that not one scrap of meat or bone of those two elephants was left to fatten the vultures or hyænas.

Upon questioning the men as to whether there were any elephants farther up the river, they informed me that about two days' journey to the westward, and not far from one of their towns, a large troop had been drinking for some time past, and offered to take me, my Kafirs, and all my belongings in their canoes to the town in question, in order that I might shoot them some more meat. Of course I was delighted at the idea, and on the following morning, five canoes having been told off for the accommodation of myself and party, I once more made a start up river. My two Bushmen, Hartebeest and Arotsy, walked along the bank, so as not to miss the spoor of any elephants that might have drunk during the night, but I went by canoe and enjoyed a delicious rest. I really did enjoy this canoe trip most thoroughly, and as we glided over the clear and rippling water, fanned by a cooling breeze and free from the persecution of the detestable "tsetse" flies, my mind recalled many a pleasant day spent in times gone by upon the quiet reaches of my dear old native Thames. Every now and then, however, a herd of graceful lechwe antelope, plunging through the shallow water, the blowing and bellowing of hippopotami, and now and then a hideous crocodile, lying like a log upon the sand, broke the association of ideas, and recalled the fact that many a mile of land and water lay between me and the old country.

Late on Saturday afternoon we reached the Makuba village, for which we had been making. It was situated upon an island at a spot where the river opens out into a sort of marshy lake, and about 400

yards from the mainland. In the evening I shot a
lechwe antelope, a young ram, and the first of this
species I had yet bagged. This I gave to the
villagers, who in return gave me some splendid fish,
a sort of perch, just caught or speared. These fried
in elephant's fat were delicious and a real treat.

Shortly after dark we heard a black rhinoceros
drinking on the mainland, and snorting violently
every now and then. After a bit he retired and all
was once more still ; not for long, however, for it
was soon evident, from the splashing and occasional
trumpeting, that a large herd of elephants were
drinking and bathing themselves just opposite our
island, and not 500 yards from us.

The next day was Sunday, but believing that " the
better the day, the better the deed," I followed the
elephants, and came up to them about mid-day.
There were no bulls amongst them, but some of the
cows had fine long white tusks. Suffice it to say that
I killed four of them, every scrap of meat and all the
bones of which were carried by the Makubas to their
island during the three following days. This meat
was a godsend to these poor people, who, being
refugees from the Barotse valley, had no corn, and
were only eking out a precarious subsistence on fish,
palm nuts, and some aquatic plants. The feasting
and dancing that were carried on night after night
as long as I remained here, vouched for the capacity
of their stomachs, the lightness of their hearts, and
the untiring vigour of their limbs—both legs and
arms ; and I think that the advent of the fair-skinned
stranger, who supplied them with such an abundance
of meat, and what they prize above all earthly bless-
ings, fat, will ever be remembered by them with
feelings of unmitigated pleasure.

On this island I remained for eight days, or rather
I slept there, for every day I went either up or down
the river to look for elephant spoor. However, I
saw none. The troop out of which I had shot the
four had made tracks for more secure retreats. In
addition to the want of sport, too, the stench upon
the little island was becoming unbearable, so on a
Monday morning I once more packed up my traps,
and made a start down the river, as I thought I
should be more likely to find elephants, and bulls
too, in the thick jungles near the mouth of the Chobe,
than in the more open country farther west.

On the fourth day I again reached the " Pookoo
Flats " without having met with any elephant spoor
whatever. Here I fell in with Henry Wall and
Tofts, who told me that they had been to the
waggons at Daka, and returned to this part of the
country with my comrade Wood, who having found
no elephants in the hills to the eastward of Daka,
towards the river Gwai, where we had shot a great
many the preceding year, had brought one of our
waggons and the horses to a pan, situated about
twenty miles to the south of the Chobe, and just
beyond the range of the tsetse fly. As the waggon
was so near, and I now had over 400 lbs. of ivory,
which was just as much as my boys could carry, I
resolved to proceed to the waggon, and getting a
Bushman from Henry Wall to show me the way, I
started on the following day, and reached Wood's
camp late in the afternoon. The next day we were
joined by Mr. and Captain Garden. They had shot
two bulls since I last saw them, one a very fine one,
whose tusks weighed nearly 70 lbs. apiece. Wood
had also shot a splendid bull close to the waggon,
only three days before my arrival. Here we remamed

N

for some time searching unsuccessfully for elephants, both on foot and horseback, so I made up my mind to return to the " Chobe," and if I found no elephants in the thick bush, to follow the course of the river very much farther westwards than I had done on my first trip.

SINGLE 10-BORE RIFLE.
Used by the Author from 1876 to 1880.

CHAPTER X

Pookoo Antelope—Shooting Lechwe—Up the Chobe—Strange Experience with Elephant—Canoe Trip through Marsh Lands of Chobe —Buffalo—Island Inhabitants—Palm Wine—Situtunga Antelopes —"Umbaracarungwe" Island—Dense Thorn-bush.

THUS, towards the end of August, I once more found myself on the southern bank of the Chobe, about twenty miles to the west of its junction with the Zambesi. It was dusk when we reached the river, and too dark to shoot anything that evening, although I wanted meat. Early the next morning, however, I knocked over a solitary old pookoo ram ; whereupon I called a halt, and my hungry Kafirs, lighting a fire, roasted and ate the greater portion of it on the spot. As the name of pookoo probably conveys but a very slight idea to the majority of my readers, I will here say a few words about this, one of the least-known of all South African antelopes.

The only place where I ever met with this species was in a small tract of country extending along the southern bank of the Chobe for about seventy miles westward from its junction with the Zambesi. They are never found at more than 200 or 300 yards from the river, and are usually to be seen cropping the short grass along the water's edge, or lying in the shade of the trees and bushes scattered over the alluvial flats which have been formed here and there by the

shifting of the river's bed.   That they exist, however,
eastwards along the southern bank of the Zambesi as
far as the Victoria Falls (about sixty miles from the
mouth of the Chobe) I think probable, as I saw one
shot on the very brink ; but, though I followed the
river's bank all the way, I never met with another
till I reached the Chobe.   The natives report them
common on the eastern bank of the Zambesi, north
of Sesheke.   From a plate in Dr. Livingstone's
first book, I always imagined that the pookoo was
found at the Lake Ngami ; but, as he makes no
mention of it in the letterpress before reaching the
Zambesi, and as neither Andersson nor Baldwin, who
both visited the lake, seems to have known of its
existence at all, this is perhaps erroneous.   In size
they stand about the same height at the shoulder as
the impala, but, being much thicker-set and stouter-
built, must weigh considerably more.   The colour is
a uniform foxy red, the hair along the back about the
loins being often long and curly ; the tips of the ears
are black.   The males alone bear horns, which are
ringed to within three inches of the point, and curve
forwards like those of the lechwe, to which animal
they are very closely allied.   The longest pair I have in
my possession measure sixteen inches, which is about
the extreme length they ever attain.   These antelopes
are usually met with in herds of from three or four
to a dozen in number ; but on one of the alluvial
flats to which I have before referred I have seen as
many as fifty in one herd.   Sometimes ten or a dozen
rams may be seen together, or a solitary old fellow
quite alone.   I have often seen these antelopes feeding
in company with a herd of impalas, and then their
heavy thick-set forms contrasted strongly with the
slim and graceful proportions of the latter animals.

The meat of the water-buck is usually considered to be more unpalatable than that of any other South African antelope ; but, if it will give any one satisfaction to know it, I can conscientiously say that that of the pookoo is several shades worse.   In conclusion, I have found that they and their congener the lechwe are wonderfully tenacious of life, and will run long distances after receiving wounds that one would think ought to be immediately fatal.   But to resume.

Breakfast over, we continued our journey westwards, following the course of the river ; and about mid-day fell in with some natives, who had come across from the island on which their little village was situated to collect firewood.   Two of these men I at once recognised as individuals who had taken me in their canoe to shoot lechwe buck during the preceding month, and on their asking me if I would not try my luck again (for on the former occasion I had been unsuccessful), I promptly accepted the invitation.   After giving my own Kafirs directions to prepare a camp on a point of land a little farther on, I stepped into the canoe, and started for the flooded land on the other side of the river.   On passing the little village, and our object being made known to the inhabitants, several men and boys jumped into their canoes and followed us, hoping to come in for a share of the meat, should I be successful in killing anything.   The paddles were then laid aside, and the canoes propelled by means of long poles with a fork at the end, towards a bit of land about a mile distant, that rose slightly above the water's level.   The average depth was about two feet, but in places it was so shallow that, there not being sufficient water to float the canoes, the natives had to get out and drag them along until it became deep enough to punt. In most parts of this marsh the tops of the grass growing on the bottom rise above the surface of the water, so that it often presents the appearance of a huge grass-field, through which it is difficult to believe it possible to paddle a canoe, for miles and miles in every direction. Scattered all about are clumps of palm bushes, growing on what must once have been ant-heaps.

We soon caught sight of several herds of lechwe bucks feeding out in the open marsh, and standing as they usually do, up to their bellies in water ; but they were excessively wild, and would not let us approach within 300 or 400 yards.

At last we sighted a large herd feeding close to the edge of a long strip of dry land that rose slightly above the level of the water, and, by keeping the canoes in a line behind a large clump of palm bushes, managed to approach unperceived to within about 200 yards of it. Telling the natives to remain perfectly still, I pulled off my veltschoons and took my gun, and by the aid of the long grass managed to reach the edge of the dry ground, without exciting any suspicion amongst the lechwe. The grass being here very scanty, I had to lie quite flat, and crawl along like a snake, pushing my rifle in front of me. In this way I had advanced about fifty yards, when, on slightly raising my head to reconnoitre, I saw a fine old buck, with a beautiful pair of horns, staring steadily in my direction, and, as the wind was all right, I knew that he had made me out. I was within 150 yards of him ; so, rising quickly to a kneeling position, I took rather a full sight on his chest as he stood facing me with his head up, and fired. The bullet told loudly on him, and, as the rest of the herd bounded away, the stricken animal remained standing, with his head down and mouth open, and his tail held straight out. The herd, after running about 100 yards, turned and stood looking towards the wounded one, as if waiting for him ; so, hastily reloading, I ran towards them, hoping to secure another buck, for I felt sure the first I had fired at was done for. They allowed me to get within 150 yards, when some ewes began trotting away, followed by the rest in single file. Two splendid old rams stood nearest me, and, taking one of them just behind the shoulder as he turned to run, I fired, and heard the bullet strike distinctly ; but, in spite of it, he went off after the rest. The sound of the shot seemed to act as a tonic on the one first wounded, who at once started off at a great pace, skirting along the water ; so, telling the Kafirs to follow the other, I took a man and a boy with me and went after him. He soon took to the water, and made across a broad flooded valley towards a large extent of dry ground on the farther side.

It was easy to follow him, even when not in sight, as, besides the bloody traces he left on the dry ground, the blades of grass that grew above the water were besprinkled with blood from his mouth and nostrils, so that I felt sure the bullet had passed through one of his lungs. Thinking the best plan would be to leave him to himself for a bit, I turned back, and made all haste in the direction of the one I had wounded at the second shot, as I did not know exactly where I had hit him, and thought he might require another bullet. We soon found the spoor of the Kafirs following on the bloody tracks of the buck, and shortly afterwards perceived them wading towards us across a broad expanse of shallow water,

On coming up they reported that the wounded lechwe had left the herd and made for a branch of the river where the water was deep, across which he had swum, when they were forced to abandon the pursuit. As it would have taken a considerable time to get the canoes round to the spot where he had crossed this branch of the Chobe, and it being late, I reluctantly gave him up, and started back for the place where I had left the one first wounded.

As I had anticipated, the loss of blood had soon told upon him, and we found him lying in a patch of grass, not far beyond where I had last seen him. When we were about thirty yards off, he sprang up and again made off, but had not gone many yards when I knocked him over with a bullet behind the shoulder. He was a beautiful animal, very thick-set and heavy, of a bright bay colour, with white belly and black points on the legs, and carried a lovely pair of horns, beautifully ringed, and curving well forward at the points. This being the first lechwe ram that ever fell to my rifle, I was much pleased at my success, and removed the skin of the head with the greatest care ; and then, it being too late to think of going after the other, I returned to camp for the night.

The next morning I again went across to the marsh after the lechwe, and had the good fortune to shoot a magnificent specimen, the finest ram out of a very large herd.

In the evening, after returning to camp, I shot two buffaloes out of a large herd that came down to drink a few hundred yards farther up the river.

After consigning the heads and skins of the lechwe antelopes to the care of the natives, by the aid of whose canoes I had shot them, and dividing the greater part of the meat of the two buffaloes amongst them, I again made a start up the river in search of elephants.

I will here make an extract verbatim from my diary, written on the spot, and then give an account (explain it I cannot) of a very curious experience that happened to me :—

"*Monday, August* 24.—Shot two elephant cows.

"*Tuesday.*—Went to chop out the tusks of the two elephants, but found that one had got up in the night and gone off. As I gave her two four-ounce bullets behind the head as she lay on the ground, I cannot understand it at all. I followed on the spoor till sundown to no purpose, and did not get back to the river till midnight, half dead from thirst."

I will now give a fuller account of this incident.

A little after mid-day we crossed the spoor of a large herd of elephant cows that had come down to the river to drink during the preceding night. As I knew, from former experience, that the elephants about here seldom stood except at long distances from the river, I did not for a moment imagine, it being already so late, that it would be worth while following them; but, wishing to reconnoitre the neighbouring jungle, to see if there were much spoor about, I told my Kafirs to make a camp and dry the meat they were carrying, and then struck off into the forest, accompanied only by my two gun-carriers, Hellhound and Arotsy. Just along the river's bank ran a strip of very dense jungle, perhaps half a mile broad, beyond which was open grassy forest, interspersed with patches of thick bush.

Shortly after emerging from this belt we again crossed the spoor (which I had not been following), and walked along it for a few hundred yards, when we came to a spot where the elephants had evidently tarried a long time, as the soft sandy soil was dug into holes and ploughed up in all directions, no doubt in search of roots. I began to get interested, and regretted having left my best running Bushman behind. After following the spoor for half a mile or so farther, we again came to a place where they had routed up some hundred yards of ground, and from whence it seemed they had not long moved on. I now felt sure of coming up with them, and, in point of fact, after tracking them for another hour in a semicircular course, I sighted, standing under some large trees, a small troop that had lagged behind the main body. Amongst these there were four good cows, and a lot of young things, ranging from the size of a pig upwards. As I looked at them, trying to pick out the best, a little calf kept endeavouring to insert its head between its mother's fore-legs and get at her breasts : she, however, pertinaciously warded off her thirsty offspring, and at last, losing all patience, gave the little animal a butt with her fore-head that sent it flying several yards. The finest elephant, carrying a pair of long white tusks, stood nearly facing me ; so, advancing cautiously to a tree about thirty yards from her, I took a sight on her chest, and aiming on one side of her trunk, fired. With a roar she turned, and crashed away with the rest at a tremendous pace ; seizing my second gun from the hands of Hellhound, who stood beside me, I gave another a good shot in the ribs, and followed on at my best speed. After going a hundred yards the cow first shot fell dead, the bullet having passed through her heart.

My guns were by this time both reloaded ; so, calling on my attendants to keep close, I made a spurt and got up to within fifty yards behind the elephants. The one I had wounded with the second shot showed no signs of flagging, nor, indeed, could I distinguish her amongst the others : so, pulling up, I gave the biggest cow a shot straight from behind, about the hip, and a foot above the root of the tail, which brought her to the ground instantly, with all four legs sprawled out like a spread eagle. However, she very soon picked herself up, and walked slowly forward, with her head raised and tail carried straight in the air. Thinking from her bearing she wanted to charge, I took the second gun, and running up noiselessly in the soft sand to within thirty yards of her, shouted, expecting her to turn and take a look at me preparatory to making a rush, which would have given me time to nip any such intention in the bud with a four-ounce bullet ; but on my shouting, to my very great astonishment, instead of turning she lowered her head and tail and went off at a great rate.

Running out sideways, I gave her another bullet just behind the ribs, which only seemed to accelerate her pace. After this we had a long chase, very tiring in the hot sun and deep sand ; but not until I had given her two more bullets obliquely from behind did she show any signs of giving in. At last, however, she swerved from her course, enabling me to make a considerable cut, when I got a broadside shot at her which brought her down with a crash, leading me to think I had broken her shoulder.

On going up to her, she commenced making the most violent struggles to rise, jerking up her head and swinging herself almost into a sitting position ; so, running round behind, and waiting till she fell back again flat on her side, I placed the muzzle of the gun between her ears, within six inches of the back of her head, and fired, on which she lay perfectly still. Arotsy, one of my gun-carriers, now went behind her to cut off her tail, but on lifting it, finding it devoid of hairs (for the animal was old), he did not think it worth taking. My other gun-carrier remarking that she still kept opening her mouth, I took the gun from him and again fired another bullet into the back of her skull, close to its junction with the vertebræ. This time I placed the muzzle within an inch of the skin, and the smoke from the powder came curling out of the hole in a thin blue wreath.

I then sat down behind the dead animal's head (for dead I thought she surely must have been) for about a quarter of an hour, during which time she lay as still as the grave. So I left her, and went to the elephant first killed, and, as soon as my attendant had cut out the heart and inside fat, started for the river, reaching the camp, which was not more than two miles distant, about sundown.

At first dawn next day we set off to chop out the two pairs of tusks, as I wished to push farther on up the river. We soon reached the first elephant, and, leaving three Kafirs with it, I went with the rest to the other one, and before long came to the place where I had left it the preceding evening; but, to my surprise and horror, instead of the bulky carcase and long white tusks, I saw only its impress in the sand and a large pool of blood, which it had thrown out with its trunk as it lay on the ground. Though I could scarcely believe my eyes, the fact remained. The elephant, after having received five four-ounce bullets in the body and two in the back of the head, had got up in the night and gone off! Truth is

stranger than fiction, it is said, and certainly this
anecdote of mine is very strange, and yet absolutely
true in every detail.

Little more remains to be said. I at once took
the spoor, and followed it till the sun went down,
and, could I but have got water, would have followed
it for ten days more.   When I relinquished the
pursuit, we were many miles from the river, and
(not having carried water) suffering from a thirst
such as those only can appreciate who have walked
during a long day in deep sand, under a blazing
tropical sun.

The forest being pretty open, and the moon
about full, we got along well enough, and at last,
about midnight, we struck the river at a point at
least twelve miles from our camp, which we did not
reach much before daylight. I think it is usually
believed tsetse fly will not bite at night ; but along
the Chobe river (where they swarm), and by moonlight, I can feelingly say that this is a mistake.
They kept flying up from the ground on to my
naked legs, and bit as furiously as in the daytime ;
and, judging from the deep curses and loud slaps
behind me, I had no doubt they were paying similar
attentions to my Kafirs.

My first care on reaching camp was to boil a pot
of tea and roast a few slices of elephant's heart, after
discussing which I wrapped myself in my kaross and
slept till late the next day.   In the afternoon,
getting tired of sitting still, I again packed up my
traps, and at sundown camped some ten or twelve
miles farther up the river.

On Thursday morning I had just shot a fine
impala ram, which my Kafirs were in the act of
skinning, when two canoes hove in sight, paddling

rapidly in our direction, and a few minutes later their occupants were standing beside us. All four of these men I at once recognised, as they had followed me for meat during my preceding trip up the river in July. One of them had only one eye, the other, with the greater part of the flesh from that side of his face, having, according to him, been torn out, when a boy, by a hyæna. I should say he had not been a beauty to begin with, and his misfortune had certainly not added to his attractions. These men expressed themselves as very pleased to see me again, saying that all the people in the marsh were on the look-out for me, as they had finished the meat of the seven elephants I had shot them last month, and hoped I had now returned to again make them happy with a fresh abundance of fat flesh.

After a few inquiries as to the whereabouts of the elephants, they informed me that there were some on an island far out in the marsh, to which they wished to take me ; and as nothing pleased me better than the prospect of penetrating into this interesting and unknown country, I at once acceded to their proposal, and agreed to wait where I was till the following day, when they promised to return with a sufficient number of canoes and men to carry my whole party and traps across the marsh. That night I retired to rest with a light heart, building all sorts of castles in the air. A troop of lions passed up the river soon after the moon rose, roaring magnificently, at one time being not a hundred yards from our camp.

A little before noon the following day my one-eyed friend and his comrades arrived, bringing with them thirteen canoes, each manned by two natives. They said that to get to the island where the elephants were we should have to coast along the bank to a place they named (near which I had shot the four cows in the preceding month) before striking out into the marsh ; so, distributing my Kafirs and baggage amongst them, we started.   The canoe prepared for me was the largest of all, and in the centre of it were a mat and small wooden stool for me to sit on.   After punting along for an hour or so, one of the Kafirs espied a black rhinoceros standing amongst some bushes close to the water's edge ; so, having as yet no meat for my large party, I at once landed with my elephant gun and walked up to him.   When within about twenty yards the animal either saw or heard something, for, wheeling round with a snort, he faced us, holding his head high in the air ; the next instant a four-ounce ball, catching him in the throat and probably injuring his vertebræ, knocked him down, and he lay sprawling about, raising his head continually and beating it violently against the ground, whilst snorting loudly.   Taking my small ten-bore rifle, I ran up, and watching my opportunity, put a ball just behind his ear, which, penetrating to his narrow brain, at once put a stop to his struggles.   On examination, he proved to be a black rhinoceros bull, that is, one with the long prehensile lip, of the so-called variety *R. keitloa.*   The horns, which I still have in my possession, measured 2 ft. 1 in. the anterior one, and 1 ft. 4 in. the posterior.   He proved to be as lean as a crow, yet my hungry followers cut up and stowed away in their canoes every fraction of the meat in a marvellously short space of time.

In the afternoon my boatmen paddled me cleverly behind a patch of reeds close up to a herd of hippopotami, and, on one of them showing his head close to me, I fired, the bullet cracking loudly on his skull. On being struck he made a mad plunge forwards, bringing his fore-feet clean out of water, and then disappeared. Some of the natives said he was killed, and would come to the surface if I would only wait a little ; but I myself did not think so, for, if shot in the brain, they usually sink like a stone without any commotion. Yielding, however, to their entreaties, I waited an hour or so, and then, nothing having appeared, we continued our journey. In the evening I shot a fine old wart hog, with large tusks.

At daybreak we again embarked in our little fleet, still skirting along the shore of the marsh in a south-westerly direction. Where the main channel of the Chobe was, I did not know ; as far as we could see to the north and west, the whole country was a sheet of water, interspersed with islands, and intersected here and there by deep streams. There is always a cool breeze blowing across these watery wastes, even during the heat of the day ; and then, again, one there escapes tsetse flies, which make life unendurable on the mainland—so that altogether I never enjoyed any part of my wanderings so much as this canoe trip. In every direction, herds of the graceful lechwe, one of the handsomest of South African antelopes, were to be seen standing about in the shallow water ; but they were very shy, and would not allow the canoes to approach within shot. Wild-fowl, geese, duck, and teal, of many kinds abounded, and I noticed also several species of bitterns, egrets, ibises, and other water-loving birds that I had never seen before ; whilst my attention was constantly attracted by the shrill, plaintive cries of large white-headed ospreys, as they sailed in graceful circles overhead.

We had scarcely left our camp half an hour, when, on rounding a point of land, I perceived, far ahead, a long, black line creeping slowly from the water's edge towards the jungle, which we soon made out to be a herd of buffaloes. The natives of course begged me to shoot a fat cow, and, as I wanted a good piece of meat for myself, I resolved to make the attempt. Before we had got anywhere near them, they had disappeared in the bush; so, disembarking, I took the spoor and followed, when, just as I sighted them, they got my wind and made off. The bush, however, being thick, they did not go very fast, and kept continually stopping to look round, and after a short run I managed to kill a young bull and a nice fat cow, besides wounding an old fellow who seemed inclined to make himself disagreeable.

On returning to the river with the meat, I found my fleet augmented by the arrival of three more canoes, whose owners said their town was on an island not far off, from whence, hearing my shots, they had at once come across, in the hope of finding that something had been killed, for a share of which they might come in. These men told me that in some thick beds of reeds near their town were some situtunga antelopes. This antelope, of which I shall have more to say later on, is the *Tragelaphus Spekii* of naturalists, and, like every other animal, is known by different names in different parts of the country. At Lake Ngami, for instance, it is called " nakong," on the lower Chobe situtunga and puvula, whilst on the upper Kafukwe river it is known by the name of " n'zoe," and at Lake Bengweolo, according to Dr. Livingstone, " n'zobe." As I longed to obtain a specimen of this rare and beautiful antelope, and as besides it was necessary the Kafirs should partially

o

dry the buffalo meat before proceeding farther, I resolved to devote the rest of the day to their pursuit. Promising my informants fat and meat in case of success, I started, telling my two gun-carriers to follow meanwhile the spoor of the buffalo I had wounded, and despatch him, as I felt sure he could not have gone very far.

A paddle of some two miles brought us to a small island, the residence of my guides. On this little patch of dry ground, not more than thirty yards square, and nowhere rising more than three feet above the level of the water, some seven or eight families of natives had made a temporary home. In the centre and highest part of the island they had cleared away the underwood, and erected a few flimsy sort of huts, made either of reeds or by stretching grass mats on poles. On my walking amongst them, clad solely in a coloured cotton shirt and an old felt hat, there was a wild stampede amongst the women, who, catching up their dusky offspring, rushed away, shrieking with fear, from the fair-skinned, bearded apparition. One of my guides, after shouting to them that I was harmless, brought me a small stool, neatly cut out of a solid block of wood, on which I sat down at the foot of a small palm tree, and looked about me. Curiosity before long conquered all other feelings in the minds of the fair sex, and I was soon surrounded by the entire female and juvenile population of the encampment, who kept staring at me in the most embarrassing manner, laughing and pointing at me all the time, and making remarks, none of which, perhaps luckily for my feelings, I was able to understand. I was the first white man any of these women and children had ever seen, though some of the men said they had seen Livingstone—whom they

called " Ra-Monare " (Sir), when he passed through
the Barotse valley some twenty years ago. Several
of the women held out their babies to have a look at
me ; but they must have previously told them that
the devil was white, as the little imps, one and all,
screamed in a most appalling manner and struggled to
get away. After a while, one of my guides brought
me a calabash of palm wine, the first I had ever seen,
and a wooden bowl of palm nuts (very nasty).

This wine is of a clear bluish colour, and tastes at
the same time both sweet and acid : it is never drunk
cold, but always first warmed over the fire, which
removes a tendency it would otherwise have to make
one sick. It is said to be very intoxicating, but,
though I drank a great deal, I never found it so.
To collect the juice from which palm wine is made,
little earthenware vessels are tied on to the stems of
the trees, just below wounds purposely made in the
bark, from which the sap trickles. As I looked
round me I saw some of these ingenious contrivances
attached to all the palm-trees on the island. The
only food these people had, besides fish, was some
very uninviting-looking stuff closely resembling saw-
dust in appearance. This I found was made from
the roots of the palm-tree, which are first roasted
under the ashes, and then hammered, when this
substance falls out from between the fibres. The
description I have given applies to all the people I
found living in the marsh of the Chobe during my
visit in 1874.

Through my interpreter I gathered that, being
dissatisfied with the government of Sipopo, the
paramount chief of the Barotse, they had fled from
the Zambesi a few months previously, and, being
without corn or any other sort of food, had lived

ever since on nothing but fish and palm roots, which
accounted for the pains they took to show me
elephants, the death of one of which bulky animals
they knew would secure them an abundance of fat
and meat, the favourite diet of an African at any
time.   All these natives possessed little prick-eared,
jackal-looking dogs, which must have accommodated
themselves to the fish diet of their masters.

After spending an hour in examining the various
contrivances of these people, I again embarked and
paddled off in quest of situtunga antelopes.   Much
to my regret, however, both on this and subsequent
occasions, my endeavours to obtain a specimen of
this rare and beautiful water antelope were vain.
They are only to be found in dense beds of reeds
through which it is difficult to propel a canoe ; and
even in districts where they are plentiful, one seldom
meets with them.   When approached (I speak from
native report) they do not attempt to run away, but
immersing their whole bodies—leaving only their
noses and the tips of their horns above water—trust
that they will be unobserved.   In this way the
natives paddle quite close, and spear them as they
stand.   The skins of these antelopes, many of which
I saw, are of a uniform light greyish-brown colour,
with very long fine hair, the horns of the males being
about two feet in length, and of a spiral form, like
those of the koodoo, or, better still, the inyala of the
south-east coast.   The feet of this species are of an
enormous length, which no doubt is a provision of
nature to enable them to walk across the soft, boggy
marsh land in which they live, in which an animal
with a short hoof would assuredly sink.

On my way back I shot a lechwe ewe, which I
gave to my guides, and which they handed over to

their womenfolk, amidst much clapping of hands and
other manifestations of joy, and I have no doubt it
proved the best meal the poor creatures had had for
many a long day.

Whilst returning to camp, my conductors speared
two fine fish (a species of perch), which, fried in
elephant's fat, formed a welcome addition to my
supper.   They throw these spears with considerable
accuracy into the midst of a shoal—whose course is
marked by the ripples on the surface—trusting to
chance to impale something, and for every fish they
bring to bag make, on an average, about a hundred
casts.   These spears are very ingeniously made, and
are barbed in a fearful manner ; the small end of the
shaft, which is long and tapering, is usually inserted
into a hollow reed, which counterbalances the weight
of the iron head, and floats to the top.   My gun-
carriers had, during my absence, followed and killed
the buffalo bull I had wounded in the morning,
so that there was an abundance of meat for all my
numerous followers.

Before daylight the next morning I stirred up the
Kafirs, and set them to work to tie up the meat and
get the canoes packed, and just as the sun was rising
we were again under way.   After skirting along the
shore for some two hours, we reached the point where
it was necessary to quit the mainland and strike across
the marsh to the islands where I hoped to find
elephants.   As we advanced into the verdure-studded
swamp, the long line of forest-covered sand-ridges that
bounded it to the south grew gradually blue in the
distance, and finally disappeared altogether.   About
two hours before sundown we reached a large island,
where my guides wished me to pass the night ; so,
concluding that they knew best, we at once went

ashore, and set to work to form a camp under some
fine forest trees, about twenty yards from the water's
edge. Towards evening I took my ten-bore rifle, and,
accompanied by some natives, went for a stroll, hoping
to fall in with a pig, or perhaps get a shot at a lechwe
near the water.

The soil of this island, which must have been
several miles in circumference, consisted of fine white
sand, into which one sank ankle-deep at every step.
It was for the most part quite open, with patches
of palm (growing principally round ant-heaps) and
clumps of large forest trees scattered here and there.
We had gone about a mile from camp without seeing
anything, when we suddenly came upon a small troop
of tsessebe antelopes, accompanied by one old blue
wildebeest bull, feeding out in the middle of a large
opening. Wishing to secure the tail of the wildebeest
with which to keep off the tsetse flies, etc., I fired, but
missed him. After reloading, I was again running on
to try for another shot, when, looking to my right, I
saw a black rhinoceros cow with a half-grown calf
coming towards me. On this I relinquished the
pursuit of the wildebeest, and resolved to try and bag
the larger animal, regretting that I had not brought my
big-bore elephant gun with me. The rhinoceros had
evidently been disturbed by the shot, but did not
know quite what to make of it. She was about
200 yards off, and coming straight on towards me
at a quick walk, and turning uneasily from side to side
at every few steps ; so I stood behind a little cluster of
palm bushes and waited for her. She came steadily on,
followed by her calf, until within about fifty yards,
when she must have got a whiff of my wind ; for,
wheeling suddenly, she started off at right angles at a
quick trot. Taking her just behind the shoulder, I

fired, on which she broke into a gallop, snorting
loudly ; but, after running for a couple of hundred
yards, she pulled up and sank down on to her knees
stone dead, and I despatched the calf with another
bullet.   One of the Kafirs now instantly started at full
speed for the camp, to call all the people to come and
carry the meat.   On examination this proved to be
the common black rhinoceros of the interior (*R.
bicornis*).   Her anterior horn measured 21 in. in
length, and the posterior 5 in.

Before the sun was well down the air was filled
with huge long-legged black mosquitoes, which
attacked my legs and arms with a ferocity and
perseverance worthy of a better cause, and forced me
to beat a hasty retreat to camp, where I was able to
escape from their attentions by sitting in the smoke of
the wood fires (a very unpleasant alternative).   These
atrocious insects, and the risk of fever in its most
malignant form, are the two drawbacks to a sojourn
in these otherwise interesting swamps.   The short
winter was now over, and the nights were so hot that
I could not bear a kaross over me, except towards
morning ; yet, to protect myself from the mosquitoes,
I was obliged to pile green wood on the fire, and
arrange it so that the smoke blew over me in a thick
cloud, which kept them off pretty effectually.

During my absence quite a small army of fresh
arrivals had joined my camp, all of whom had come
across in canoes from the various little islands where
they were living, in the hope of getting meat, so that I
now had at least one hundred hungry mouths to feed.

About an hour before noon the following day,
after a pleasant voyage amongst some little gems of
islands—several of them inhabited, and on many of
which grew clusters of the tall, graceful palms—and

passing numberless herds of lechwe, that added life
and beauty to the scene, we reached our goal, viz.
two densely wooded islands, separated from one
another by a narrow channel not more than 10c
yards wide. The larger of these islands, called by
the natives "Umbaracarungwe," is of considerable
extent, and as far as my eye could reach I could
trace the blue outline of the forest with which it was
covered. The other, though considerably smaller
than its neighbour, must yet have been fifteen miles
or so in circumference, and as I still had at least
seven hours of daylight, I determined to commence
its exploration without delay. Stranding the entire
fleet of canoes, and leaving some of the natives
to form a camp (amongst them two of my own
Makalakas, who had come with me from the Matabele country, and both of whom had got a touch of
fever), I at once started, striking into the jungle so
as to cut through to the farther side of the island,
from whence I intended to skirt round its edge, outside the bush, until I again reached the canoes. In
this way I judged that I should cross the spoor of
any elephants that might be there at the point where
they had come down to the water to drink on the
preceding night.

On entering the jungle my heart sank. During
my experience of elephant-hunting I had seen some
nasty bits of bush, but never anything to be compared
to this island fastness. The underwood, thick and
thorny in itself, was interspersed with bushes covered
with dense foliage—though at this season of the year
everything on the mainland was leafless—and the
whole was matted and woven together by the long
branches of a low tree that I had never seen before,
with smooth, soft, green bark and enormous thorns

about two inches in length, straight and sharp as a
needle.   Altogether, it was the most disagreeable
place one could well imagine in which to fight a
wounded elephant, and I had small hopes of meeting
with much success.   Before proceeding many yards
we found traces of the handiwork of elephants,
which had been here two days ago, and were
perhaps still on the island.   All round the jungle and
between it and the water ran a margin of open
ground varying from 10 to 100 yards in breadth,
making the walking very easy.   As we advanced
we came across great quantities of buffalo spoor
and the huge footprints of elephants, none of which
latter were fresher than those we had noticed on
the point of the island.   Looking now to the north
and west there were no more islands to be seen,
but extending to the distant horizon stretched one
unbroken bed of reeds, through which, say the natives,
the main branch of the Chobe runs.   We had made
the circuit of perhaps two-thirds of the island, when
one of my men caught sight of a large python lying
under a bush, which, in company with some of his
friends, he proceeded to attack.   Before the huge
reptile seemed to think of bestirring itself, a barbed
spear was driven through its body just behind the
head, pinning it to the ground, and almost at the
same instant two or three more through different
parts of its back.   Another man then sawed its head
off with a large broad-bladed assegai, and the other
spears were withdrawn ; but the body still continued
to writhe in a wonderful manner.   This python was a
female, measuring fifteen feet in length, and the natives,
after removing the skin, which I bought, carried it
entire to camp, as the meat and fat of these reptiles
are considered by them to form a very choice dish.

We had just turned the corner of the last bay, at the farther extremity of which lay the canoes, when we sighted a large herd of buffaloes feeding knee deep in the marsh about 100 yards from the shore; so, it being necessary that I should keep my large party in good humour with an abundance of meat, I resolved if possible to shoot a fat cow. The animals were coming back towards the jungle, so I took up a position behind a bush and waited for them, and, as they advanced, fired at a cow, bringing her to the ground, bellowing. On this the herd turned and took to the water again; but as they ran I fired with my second gun and made a lucky shot, breaking the spine of a young bull, and of course completely disabling him. I then ran up to the cow, which was struggling to rise, and finished her with another ball behind the ear, whilst the natives went in and despatched the wounded bull with their assegais. The herd not seeming to like the open turned after going a short distance, and came back again at a gallop towards the jungle, seeing which I threaded my way along just within the edge of the bush and cut them off. When they were about fifty yards from me I shouted, on which they pulled up, and stood one and all with their noses raised, sniffing the air and gazing towards where I was hidden. Profiting by this pause, I took a quick aim at a fat cow and fired, tumbling her on to her head. At the shot the whole herd came on with a rush, not thinking of me, probably, but wishing to gain the shelter of the bush, and to avoid being run over I had to throw down my gun and hastily ascend a small tree. After finishing the third buffalo, and cutting out its tongue, I walked on to the canoes, as I felt ready for supper.

On my arrival my two Makalakas told me that

PLATE VII

1. TSESSEBE ANTELOPE ♂ (Alcelaphus Lunatus).
   Shot near the river Daka, Oct. 13, 1877.

2. TSESSEBE ANTELOPE ♀ (Alcelaphus Lunatus).
   Shot in the Mashuna country, Sept. 22, 1880.

3. LICHTENSTEIN'S HARTEBEEST ♂ (Alcelaphus Lichtensteinii).
   Shot on the Manica plateau, Dec. 22, 1877.

4. LICHTENSTEIN'S HARTEBEEST ♂ (Alcelaphus Lichtensteinii).
   Shot on the Manica plateau, Dec. 28, 1877.

5. HARTEBEEST ♀ (Alcelaphus Caama).
   Shot at Boatlanarma valley, Feb. 13, 1879.

6. HARTEBEEST ♂ (Alcelaphus Caama).
   Shot near Selinya, Dec. 28, 1880.

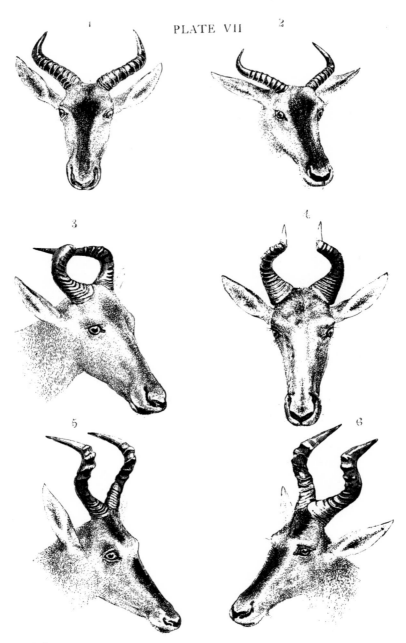

PLATE VII

To face page 202.

during the afternoon a troop of ten bull elephants had come out of the jungle on the other island at a point about 200 yards off, and after drinking and walking along the shore for a short distance again entered the bush. Fancy elephants in this age so little disturbed as to drink in the daytime, and what a glorious sight it must have been to see these gigantic animals walking in the open with their slow majestic step. But now I feared they must have heard the shots I had just fired, yet as the natives assured me that a gun had never before been fired on these islands, I still had hopes that, not knowing what it was, they might not have taken alarm, and in effect hearing one trumpet at no great distance soon after dark I felt sure that such was really the case, and had it not been for the mosquitoes, should have felt perfectly happy and contented.

CHAPTER XI

Adventure with Elephants—Return to Mainland—Two Elephant-
hunts—Ten killed—Schinderhutte ; Tragic End—Two Buffalo
Bulls—Encounter with a Lioness—Return to Tati, and England.

THE next day was the 1st of September, and as the
sun, which in far-off England heralded the death of
many a plump partridge, raised his fiery face above
the eastern horizon I stepped into my crank Makalolo
canoe and was soon paddling over to Umbaracarungwe, the larger of the two islands, with great
hopes of soon making the acquaintance of the
elephants. Instead of skirting the bush, I struck
straight into the centre of the dense jungle, and had
not advanced a mile when my Bushman Arotsy, who
was in front looking for spoor, stopped and pointed
silently to the ground, where, deeply impressed in
the soft yielding sand, I saw the giant footprint of
the mightiest beast that walks the earth—an African
bull elephant. We soon found that although they
must have plainly heard the shots I had fired at the
buffaloes the preceding evening they had utterly dis-
regarded them, and had been feeding about in all
directions ever since. This made their spoor very
difficult to follow, and great caution was necessary to
prevent their getting our wind and decamping quietly
before we sighted them ; for although they had paid
no attention to the report of a gun, all animals have

an instinctive aversion to the smell of man, and I felt that the merest whiff would make them run like the most experienced of their kind. The bush was frightfully thick, just as bad as that on the smaller island, with, however, here and there open places in which grew only a few camel-thorn trees (*Acacia giraffæ*); but I thought that if I could only get well up to them I should be able to make sure of one, which was as much as I hoped for. After following several blind leads, taking the spoor of single elephants that had gone away feeding a short distance and then rejoined the herd, my Bushman suddenly gave a start and became rigid, with one arm pointing forwards, and there was little need to ask him what he saw. The elephants were about 100 yards to our right, on the edge of a good-sized opening, across which they had just walked. They were then standing still, four of them being quite outside the bush under a tree, off which one of them had just broken a large branch, so as the more easily to get at the tender shoots, from which the leaves were sprouting. One of these was a fine full-grown bull, with perfect tusks, which, though short, were very thick. They were standing most unfortunately as regarded the wind, and I feared they would scent us every instant. I would have retired and gone round them, but momentarily expected a puff of air, and so thought it better to try and get up to them without delay. Therefore, taking my gun, I at once advanced towards them across the open, trusting that they were too pre-occupied to notice me. But an unkind fate was against me ; even as I started I felt a puff of wind from behind, and simultaneously saw the trunks of the elephants slightly raised to catch the taint. It

was enough ; they did not stop to ask questions, but
wheeled round towards the bush with marvellous
despatch. Though I stood fast, and raised my gun
the instant I saw the trunk of the big bull turned up,
he was round before I could fire. I managed to put
a bullet in just behind his ribs, which made him roar
and sit back on his haunches ; before he could recover
I seized my second gun from Hellhound, and gave
him another bullet in the hip, on which he jerked
himself up, and rushed into the bush after the rest.

Calling to my two gun-carriers to load and follow,
I ran on with Hartebeest (the best runner among
my Bushmen) after them. They had cleared a broad
path before them, and raised such a dust in the loose
sand that it was impossible to see anything. However, I trusted to the sagacity of my Bushman (a
better servant in the hunting veldt I never saw),
and, keeping his dusky form in view, dived through
the thorny jungle close behind him. Suddenly he
halted, and, looking forwards, I caught sight of the
tops of the elephants' ears above the bush. They
had come to the water's edge, and stood turning and
looking about in all directions. My gun-carriers
were nowhere in sight, and I did not dare call out,
as the elephants would then have run on again, so I
waited ; they, however, did not stand many seconds,
but stepped out in single file across the open place
to their right, swinging their trunks backwards and
forwards. It was a bitter moment ; eight of them
had passed broadside to me at not more than thirty
yards' distance, and I was without a gun and dared not
call. There were four old bulls, the rest being not
quite full-grown. The tusks of all the old ones were
rather short, but looked thick and heavy. The one I
had first wounded was not amongst them, and had

probably turned out in the jungle behind.   Thinking
they had all passed, I now ran out into the opening,
shouting with concentrated intensity, in company
with my Bushman, "Leta imbopo!" (Bring the gun),
when another young bull, with long thin white tusks,
emerged from the bush behind, and, catching sight
of us, at once charged, trumpeting shrilly.   "Balecka,
soree!" (Run away, sir), shouted the Bushman,
and we made a dive back into the bush, each
successive scream making me, at any rate, spring
forward with wonderful energy.   Our pursuer did
not come far beyond the edge of the bush, but
turned and went after his companions.

My two gun-carriers now came up, and, running
on the spoor, we presently sighted the elephants again,
going at a quick walk through the jungle.   I told
Hartebeest to try and run round and head them
towards me, hoping to get a good broadside shot as
they passed ; but before he managed to do so, I myself
got pretty well up on the near side, and gave two bulls
each a good shot behind the shoulder.   Had the
country been tolerably open, I should probably have
bagged them both, as, being close, I felt sure the bullets
went somewhere near the right place ; but in such
dense bush as was this, it was impossible to do much,
for an elephant bull, even when shot clean through the
heart, does not fall at once, but will often run several
hundred yards first.   And neither do they always bleed
externally, so that there is no guide as to which spoor
one ought to take.

At the shots there was a roar and a rushing and a
crashing, a cloud of dust was raised, and everything
had disappeared.   I was just preparing to try and take
up the spoor of the wounded animals, when loud shouts
ahead announced to me that the herd had run on to

Hartebeest. Directly afterwards I saw three, a little to my right, coming back towards me, and stood fast, hoping to get a good chance as they passed. There were two young bulls in front, followed by an old one. The first two went by; but the old fellow, either catching a glimpse of me, or more probably getting a whiff of my wind, spun round, raised his huge ears, and at once charged, but without screaming. I was ready, and put a ball into his chest below his raised trunk, which brought him to his knees; he was up again in no time, and, turning, broke back into a terribly thick piece of jungle. However, I stuck close to him, and after a quarter of an hour's dodging, during which time I gave him two more bullets, he at last lurched forwards on to his head, and then rolled over sideways, stone dead. On cutting him up afterwards, we found that two out of the three bullets fired at him had passed through the top of his heart!

I now plunged into the bush again, to look for the blood spoor of the others I had wounded, but had not gone far when I perceived a young bull with nice white tusks coming along with his ears raised, and turning his head from side to side. Taking up a handful of sand to see which way the wind was, I placed myself so that he would pass close by without scenting me. As he walked past he offered a splendid shot, and, taking him just behind the shoulder, I pulled the trigger; but the report was merely the puff of the powder alone, my gun-carrier in the hurry having put in no bullet. Imagine my disgust! The elephant hearing the cap snap, at once rushed forwards, and we followed at our best pace on the spoor. When within ten yards of a patch of high, dense jungle, Hellhound turned with horror-struck look, saying, " Ee-aisa, soree ! " (He's coming this way,

sir). Seizing the gun, I let him get past me, and
stood ready. I could hear the bushes rustling, and
soon saw the tops switching, but nothing more. The
next instant, however, the head of an elephant, with
the immense ears outspread, and the little eyes
twinkling wickedly, burst into sight ! He, too, saw
me at the same moment, and, thinking no doubt that
he had me, at once commenced to trumpet, having
remained quiet until then—a sign he meant mischief.
He held his trunk down, so that I could not get a shot
at his chest, and cannot say that I took much of an
aim at all, for there was no time ; but, getting the
sight somewhere on his head, I fired, and then threw
myself out sideways under the bushes. Looking
round, I saw my antagonist retreating backwards with
his trunk raised perpendicularly in the air, evidently
stunned and dazed, but otherwise none the worse.
He now walked to about fifteen yards from where I
lay, and again stood, densely thick jungle intervening
between us. I took my second gun (after noiselessly
loading the one I had just fired) from Arotsy, who
had stood fast behind me, and gave him a bullet
through the bush. On receiving this attention he
walked on, and after going a short distance, again
stood, feeling about for the wind with his raised trunk.
He now offered a splendid shot, as the bush between
us, though thick, was low, and his whole shoulder was
exposed. Covering him carefully, I pulled the trigger,
but the only sound was the snapping of the cap, on
which I bobbed down instantaneously. The elephant,
hearing the click, spun round and stood with ears
raised, looking towards whence the sound had
proceeded ; but we all lay like hares, and, seeing
nothing, he again walked on. Hastily putting on
another cap, I then stood up, and, getting another

P

beautiful broadside shot, I pulled the trigger, but again only the cap snapped.[1] But this time the elephant spun round, and charged at once in the direction of the noise, trumpeting fearfully. I made a dive sideways, not daring to run, as he would certainly have seen me. The huge beast luckily did not hit us off quite correctly, but came to a halt not ten yards away, turning from side to side, and testing the wind with the upturned end of his trunk.

At last, to my intense relief, in which no doubt my two companions shared, he went off at a run. I now thought of giving him up, which I would not have done had not my gun played me false ; but at the instant hearing voices to my right, which I recognised as those of my own Makalakas, of whom I had seen and heard nothing during the hunt, shouting " Nansi, soree ! " (There he is, sir), I took my other gun and again went forwards. On crossing an opening I caught sight of my irascible friend going along just within the edge of the bush on the farther side. My Kafirs were shouting like fiends beyond him ; so, imagining the row would turn him, I skirted along the edge of the bush in the hope of cutting him off, but I never saw him again. He broke right through my line of beaters, and going to the water's edge, crossed over to the other island, and the canoes not being handy, I had to stop.

I now fell in with the main body of my followers, who had carefully kept out of sight during the hunt. I told them I had killed one elephant, at which they seemed greatly delighted, and we at once set off

---

[1] These missfires were probably owing to some minute piece of leaf or bark, or other foreign body, which, as I passed through the jungle, had fallen into the leathern powder sack slung at my side, and choked up the bottom of the nipple, as, on pouring a few grains of powder into it from the outside, it at once ignited.

together for the carcase. I then took my own Makalakas and Bushmen, and again struck into the jungle, hoping to come across one or other of the elephants I had wounded. But, though I spent several hours at it, it was in vain, for the whole jungle was trampled in all directions with spoor in such a way that my Bushmen could make nothing of it, and I finally gave it up and returned to the dead elephant. My naked legs and arms had suffered considerably from the thorns, one of which, that had been driven about an inch deep into the calf of my leg, I only extracted with the greatest difficulty. The major part of my shirt, too, had remained behind me on different bushes, and altogether I no doubt presented a very forlorn appearance. The marsh natives, having heard the elephant screaming, imagined that I had been actually caught and had only escaped by dodging his feet and creeping away between his hind legs. This story was handed from mouth to mouth until it reached some of the traders with Sipopo, who, going out of the country before they saw me, carried the report south with them ; so that when I again reached the Matabele country in the following December, all my friends congratulated me on my miraculous escape !

My first care was to go down to the canoes, which had all been brought round as close to the dead elephant as possible. Then I had a good bathe and wash, and after putting on a clean shirt and extracting most of the thorns from my legs, I felt myself again. By this time every fraction of the elephant, except the skull, skin, and vertebræ, had been brought down to the water-side. The huge bones, after being chopped into small pieces, were boiled in large pots, on which all the fat which is contained in their cellular structure was melted out and floated to the top of the water. The trees around the camp were red with festoons of meat, and as the elephant was excessively fat (and a Kafir would sell his soul for that delicacy), there was great rejoicing and feasting that night throughout my bivouac. The tusks, I forgot to say, though short, were thick and heavy, weighing 52 lbs. each.

Before dawn next morning I was aroused by a great commotion and chattering, and on inquiring what the matter was, I learned through my interpreter that a messenger had arrived, bringing a report that an expedition sent out by Sipopo was approaching, to clear these marshes of inhabitants. I pooh-poohed the idea, and still believe the intelligence was false, for what booty could Sipopo expect to obtain from these wretched people ? But a panic had seized them, and all argument was useless, and as I did not quite fancy being left without canoes on this island, there was no alternative but to pack up my traps and sub-mit to being again paddled back to the mainland. This was a great disappointment, as I had hoped to spend at least another week pottering about in the marsh. I have omitted to say that on this large island, and also on the one where I shot the buffaloes, I found great numbers of tsetse flies, though I saw none of these insects on any of the smaller islands I visited. Eleven canoes were told off to carry me, together with my servants and baggage, and all the rest went off to see after the women and children. Nothing of any consequence occurred on the return journey, and late in the afternoon we again reached the mainland, after an absence of four days. That evening I camped at several hundred yards' distance from the river, in order to escape from the mosquitoes, which were now as numerous and troublesome along the water's edge as on any of the islands out in the marsh.

On Thursday, September 3—the day after my return to the mainland—my star was in the ascendant, as on it I shot five elephants out of one herd, besides a fine eland cow. The latter was one of a large herd that I came upon standing just by the water's edge on leaving my camp at first dawn of day. There was not a single bull amongst the lot, so, picking out a cow with nice long horns, I fired with my elephant gun, and breaking her neck, she fell on the spot in about a foot of water, so that we had to drag her several yards to dry land before we could cut her up. She proved to be a fine young cow in good condition, of the grey desert species, without a vestige of a stripe on her. Her horns, which were very fine, measured 33 inches in length, curving slightly outwards at the points. After cutting out her tongue, breast, and heart, and putting the horns in a tree, I gave the rest of the meat to my canoe-men, who here left me.

I then again followed the edge of the marsh— which trended nearly due south—accompanied only by my own Kafirs. About a mile farther on was a large shallow lagoon, separated from the marsh by a narrow strip of land, and there we found the spoor of a very large herd of elephants that had drunk during the night. The sun was scarcely an hour high, so putting down my baggage, and leaving two of my Makalakas, who were still suffering slightly from fever, to look after everything, I at once started in pursuit. Just within the goussy forest, which here extends almost to the water, the elephants had dug up at least an acre of ground in search of roots, and I had good hopes of soon overtaking them ; but

as after this they had not again loitered, it was already
late in the afternoon when we at last caught sight of
them, and we had trudged over many a weary mile
of deep sand since leaving the river.   Though the
sun was still intensely hot, I came up with them in
an immense opening in the forest, devoid of any
covert whatever, except that afforded by a few leafless
mopani trees, scattered here and there, and some
wretched little thorn bushes of the wait-a-bit variety,
only three or four feet high.

When I caught sight of the herd they were at
least a mile off, and advancing slowly in dense black
masses, and after accurately ascertaining how the
wind was by letting fall a handful of fine sand, I
deemed it advisable to attack them from the other
side.   This was one of the largest herds of elephants
I had ever seen ; I am afraid to say how many of
them there were, but I think there must have been
from 100 to 200 at least.   Excepting a few young
bulls, easily distinguishable from their superior size,
they were all cows and young animals.   To my left
I could see one fine young bull, with long white
tusks, standing with some others round the stem of
a solitary mopani tree, but to get at him I must
have passed close to a lot of cows, across ground as
bare as a board ; so, resolving to keep an eye on him,
I turned my attention to a cow with long perfect
ivory, that was directly facing me.

About fifty yards from her were two or three
slender mopani bushes, not sufficient to cover a rat,
but it was all there was ; so, holding my gun before
me with both hands, ready to be raised at a moment's
notice, and crouching forwards, I advanced quickly.
I was still some ten yards from the bush, when she
saw me through it, and at once raised her head,

spread her ears and looked, and the next moment, seeming to make me out, was just swinging round, when I gave her a bullet between the neck and the shoulder, bringing her to her knees.

At the shot there was a tremendous commotion ; but the behaviour of this large body of elephants was very different from that of a small herd, which would instantly have rushed away in a wild panic. Those farthest off did not seem to know where the danger lay, and came running up towards me at a shambling sort of trot, many of the cows with their trunks high in the air, trumpeting shrilly and making a curious rumbling noise. Taking advantage of the confusion, I gave another young bull a shot behind the shoulder, and then hastily got the guns reloaded. By this time the elephants had organised themselves into bands, and were moving off in different directions in large troops, but not going very fast. The cow I had first shot now fell, and the young bull I saw was also done for. At this juncture Hartebeest outflanked the herd in which was the young bull I had seen standing under the mopani tree, and they all now came back right for me in a long line ; so much for me, indeed, that I had to make tracks hastily to get out of the way, as in this open country I did not dare approach within a hundred yards or so after the first shots. As the young bull passed me I aimed well forwards, and saw the dust fly from him just in the right place behind the shoulder. At the shot a cow came rushing down towards us, trumpeting loudly, with her trunk in the air ; but, not seeming to make us out, was just turning, when I gave her a ball with the second gun. After this I killed another cow with a single bullet, which went clean through her heart, and must have broken her

shoulder on the other side, for she fell as if struck
by lightning, and never rose again.

There were now two down and three wounded.
The young bull I had just shot was standing not far
off, and even as I turned to look at him he lurched
backwards, throwing his trunk high in the air, and
then fell on his side, and I knew his race was run.
The larger bull and the wounded cow had both
separated from the herd, but whereas the latter was
following on the tracks of her companions, the
former was walking slowly off by himself at right
angles.   On my getting up near him he turned, and
raising his ears, stared at me, and I thought he meant
to charge, but he was probably too far gone, poor
brute.   As he again turned I got a splendid chance
at his shoulder, and gave him a fatal shot through
the top of the heart, on receiving which he walked
steadily forwards, and then fell with a crash on his
broadside, his legs seeming to be swept from under
him.   The other elephants were by this time all out
of sight, except the wounded cow, who was going
off at a good pace in the distance.   When I had got
within a couple of hundred yards of her she was
headed by some of my Kafirs, and, on their shouting,
turned, and came walking back towards me.   I stood
where I was, just by an apology for a bush, thinking
she would pass on one side or the other and give
me a broadside shot, but on she came, nearer and
nearer, till it was evident that she was heading
exactly for where I was standing.   When she was
within forty yards Hellhound lost heart, and either
ran or moved off backwards, and, on seeing him stir,
the elephant, who, so long as we remained still, had
not observed us, immediately raised her ears, and
came on with uplifted trunk, screaming loudly.

However, I was ready, and planted a ball fair in her chest, when she stopped, and, turning, went off at right angles, holding her head high, but, before having gone a hundred yards, she suddenly fell dead, the last shot having pierced her heart.

Thus ended one of the best days I ever had with elephants ; and, as regards numbers, quite the best up to that time, for never before had I shot more than four to my own gun out of one herd. The tusks of the two young bulls weighed 25 lbs. and 14 lbs. respectively, and the cow I first shot was particularly fine, her tusks weighing over 17 lbs. apiece.

It was now much too late in the afternoon to think of chopping out the tusks, so having cut out the heart of one of the cows for myself, and the inside fat of all the five (this was soon done by sending two Kafirs to each elephant), we started for the river, and reached our camp near the lagoon about two hours after dark.

Soon after leaving the dead elephants we sighted a fine troop of giraffes—one of the most beautiful ornaments of South African forests—and not long afterwards a large herd of elands (all cows) ; both these animals abound in this dry and sandy, yet thickly wooded country.

On reaching camp I was surprised to see a dozen fires, and on coming up found about twenty of my canoe friends, who, either not believing in the reported raid of Sipopo or having trusted their goods and chattels to the care of friends, had again followed me for meat. Of this I was very glad, for I knew that now not a particle of the five elephants would be wasted, for these men would establish two camps, and carry meat and water backwards and forwards until they had dried and brought every fraction, even to the bones, down to the river.

After burying the tusks of the elephants under a large tree near the water's edge, which we could not fail to recognise on our return, I again pushed forwards, skirting along the marsh in a southerly direction. Singular to say, the pookoo antelopes, which were so abundant some thirty miles farther back, had now entirely disappeared, though the character of the country and the vegetation remained precisely the same in every particular. I cannot think of any reason to account for the curious localisation of this species.

Next day (September 6) we again kept on along the edge of the marsh, and saw much game—giraffe, elands, koodoos, impalas, blue wildebeests, tsessebes, wild pigs, and out in the marsh numberless lechwes. We also crossed some elephant and a few rhinoceros spoors, not very old, though these latter animals are rather scarce all along the Chobe. About two hours past mid-day, coming to some well-worn elephant paths with recent tracks upon them, leading to and from the water, I resolved to pass the night in their vicinity ; so, putting down the baggage, I left most of my Kafirs to form a camp, and then with the rest took a stroll forwards, to reconnoitre the land and pass away the time until sundown. We had not left the camp a mile behind when we espied the black massive forms of a herd of buffaloes lying asleep in the shade of some large goussy trees, just on the edge of the sand-belt, and not 100 yards from the water. As we passed they got our wind, and the whole herd, after running together and eyeing us for a few moments, turned and took themselves slowly off, enveloped in a cloud of dust. A short

distance farther on, we came upon five old bulls
feeding on the short young grass, beneath some tall
acacia trees.   So intent were they upon their occupa-
tion that, although they were heading towards us,
they seemed utterly unconscious of our presence.

Motioning to my Kafirs to remain behind, I
advanced noiselessly to a tree, certainly within twenty
yards of the foremost, and then, standing clear of the
trunk, I shouted out, "Halloa there!"   Instantly
the five ponderous heads were raised, and five sets
of eyes stared with a wondering, inquisitive sort of
gaze at the unwonted intruder.   Only for a few
moments, though ; then, headed by a grey, almost
hairless old fellow, they turned and went off at a
lumbering gallop into the adjacent bush.   A mile or
two farther on, we passed another enormous herd of
these animals, lying, like the first we had seen, just
on the slope of the sand-belt, where they had no
doubt been sleeping during the intense heat of the
day.   This part of the country must have been
utterly undisturbed by human beings for some time
past, or buffaloes would never lie like this all day
long, and in full view, so close to the water.   As I
had meat, and, moreover, feared lest a shot might
disturb more valuable game, I did not think of
molesting them, and reached camp again a little
before sundown, just in time to see three tall, graceful
giraffes issue from the forest a little distance beyond,
and stalk across the intervening flat, swishing their
long tails to and fro, on their way down to the water.
It is a curious sight to watch these long-legged
animals drinking, and one that I have had several
opportunities of enjoying.   Though their necks are
long, they are not sufficiently so to enable them to
reach the water without straddling their legs wide

apart. In doing this, they sometimes place one foot in front, and the other as far back as possible, and then by a series of little jerks widen the distance between the two, until they succeed in getting their mouths down to the water ; sometimes they sprawl their legs out sideways in a similar manner.

During the night no elephants came down to drink, as I had hoped they might do, by the paths near which we had camped ; so next morning I again pushed on, and made a good day's march. In the evening, being rather short of meat, I shot a tsessebe antelope, in very fine condition. Though the meat of these antelopes is tolerably good, the fat, like that of the wildebeest, turns hard, unless very hot, and sticks to the palate in a most disagreeable manner.

The following day (September 8) was another red-letter day in my hunting annals, as on it I again shot five elephants out of one troop, all cows. I came up with them late in the afternoon, having followed the spoor since sunrise, in deep sand, and under a sweltering sun. We got them at last standing in a small patch of bush, though the surrounding forest was pretty open. On my firing at a fine cow, a number that I had not seen, and that, having been roused suddenly from a sound sleep, did not know exactly where the danger lay, came running down towards us from both sides. Our position at one moment seemed critical, and had any vicious old cow got our wind, she might have made it warm for us. As it was, our shouts at length turned them, and, my guns being reloaded, I broke the shoulder of one of them just as she was swinging round, and, on despatching her with a second bullet, saw, for the first time, that she had but a single tusk, which was, however, remarkably long and white. I then made all haste after the retreating herd, which, being large, did not go very fast, and after a severe run managed to kill three more, all full-grown animals, with fair tusks. My Bushman Hartebeest ran splendidly, and succeeded in heading a small herd away from the main body, and in turning them back towards me. Of these I killed two, and, had I not exhausted my stock of bullets—of which I only had seventeen to start with—I could without doubt have killed more, as we ran them regularly to a standstill.

During the intensely hot weather in September and October, just before the rains fall, elephants soon become fatigued if driven about and exposed to the fierce sun. When they get hot and tired they insert their trunks into their mouths and draw out water from their stomachs, which they dash over their breasts and shoulders to cool themselves ; and when the supply of water is exhausted they will sometimes throw sand over their bodies, which one would suppose would only make them hotter than they were before. Though, as I have said, elephants get knocked up comparatively soon when hunted during the hot weather, yet, as may be imagined, it is killing work following them on foot at that season, in deep sandy ground and under a tropical sun, and with nothing to drink but a very limited allowance of water carried in a gourd, which soon gets lukewarm from the intensity of the heat.

Two of the cows just shot carried very fine ivory, and the single tusk of the second killed, which was almost straight, was exceptionally long, protruding nearly three feet beyond the lip ; it, had, however, a bad crack in it. I will take this opportunity of saying that when an elephant has only one tusk the bone on the other side is quite solid, and shows no sign of a hollow where the fellow ought to be. It is far from uncommon to meet with one-tusked animals amongst elephant cows in South Africa, though rarer amongst the bulls.

It seems dreadful to slaughter so many of these huge creatures merely for their tusks ; for, if there are no Bushmen or other natives about, the carcases are abandoned to the hyænas and vultures. But *il faut vivre.* Ivory is the only thing obtainable in this country with which to defray the heavy expenses of hunting ; and if you depend on your gun for a living, as was my case, it behoves you to do your best when you get a chance. It is true that within a week I had killed ten elephants ; but from this date (the 8th of September) until the 20th of November, though I was hunting continually the entire time, and tramped over an enormous extent of wild and utterly uninhabited country, I only saw one more of these animals (a young bull) in all that time. I mention these facts to show how much work an elephant-hunter has often to go through, taking it all in all, for each animal killed.

Whilst following on the spoor of the elephants, I was surprised, upon issuing from a thick goussy forest, to find myself suddenly in face of a hill of considerable height. As this was the first hill of any sort or kind I had seen since leaving the Victoria Falls, and as it is certainly the only eminence within a radius of very many miles, I viewed it with great curiosity, and could I have afforded the time would certainly have ascended it. As it was, however, the spoor, after approaching pretty close to its foot, again led us away in a contrary direction. I afterwards heard from the marsh natives that their name for this hill is " Umgooloo." This is the same hill

KNOCKED UP. WAITING FOR THE COOL OF NIGHT TO GET BACK TO THE WATER.

which Livingstone mentions by the name " Ngwa,"
and which is known to Khama's people at the present
day as " Goh-ha."

By the time that the last elephant was disposed of,
and my scattered followers had reassembled, it was
late in the afternoon, and we were all of us terribly
distressed for want of water ; so, as there was a
moon, I resolved to wait for the cool of night to get
back to the river.

Although we had followed upon the spoor of our
victims for a great distance, they had pursued a zigzag course, so that we were not so far away from the
marsh as I had imagined. Still, it was not much before
midnight that our ears were at length greeted by the
distant croaking of many thousands of frogs, and a
few minutes later I was having calabashes of water
poured over my head, and washing some of the dirt
from my grimy person. By good luck we had hit off
the marsh pretty close to our encampment, which we
at length reached about half an hour afterwards.

During the next two days, whilst most of my
Kafirs were away chopping out the tusks of the five
elephants, I took my two gun-carriers with me and
examined the country farther on ahead. I found that
just beyond my encampment the country between
the marsh and the forest-clad sand-belt opened out
into an enormous alluvial flat, scattered over which
were here and there patches of bush and clumps of
tall acacia trees. After leaving the sand-belt and
getting a good distance out into this flat in the
direction of the marsh, the top of Mount Umgooloo
at length appeared in the distance, rising higher
and higher above the tree-tops as I proceeded. On
this flat I saw several ostriches, and great numbers of
zebras and tsessebe antelopes.

As with the ivory that I had previously buried I
now had as much as my Kafirs could possibly carry,
and as I was many days' journey distant from my
waggons, I resolved to return thither at once with
what I had, and then try my luck again amongst
the mountains to the eastward of the Victoria Falls.
So, on Friday, September 11, I made a start, and
ultimately reached Daka (where my waggons were
standing) on Saturday evening the 26th, after an
absence of three months.   On the last day, starting
from Gazuma just at sunrise, I walked on ahead of
my Kafirs, and, passing Pandamatenka about mid-day,
at last reached the waggons a little before sundown,
which, though I do not know the exact distance, I
look upon as a very good day's work, as I carried my
heavy elephant gun and the sun was intensely hot.
My Kafirs, who were carrying heavy loads, did not
arrive till late the following day.   During my return
journey I shot one more elephant (to which I have
before referred), and several buffaloes and antelopes
for food.   The death of two of these buffaloes is
perhaps worthy of notice.

Early one morning, as I was walking in front of
my Kafirs, I espied two old bulls just ahead—the
one lying down, and the other standing.   As I
wanted meat I at once made preparations to circumvent them, so, taking my favourite elephant gun, and
closely attended by Hellhound, who carried its fellow,
I crept up to a bush within fifteen yards of the
nearest, which was lying fast asleep, and at once
rudely disturbed its slumbers with a four-ounce ball
behind the shoulder.   On receiving this mortal
wound, the stricken animal rolled on to its back with
all four legs high in the air, whilst its comrade, a
hairless old brute, with horns worn down to mere

stumps, instead of running off, only wheeled round and looked at me in a way very suggestive of charging. But, if such were its intention, it was never acted upon, for with a bullet from my second gun I brought it bellowing to its knees. At the shot the one first wounded got on its legs again, and they then both ran together, and, after swaying backwards and forwards, fell alongside one another, so close indeed that in its death struggles the one kept kicking its dead comrade on the nose. One of these buffaloes had been fearfully lacerated and bitten about the neck and the tops of the shoulder-blades, only a short time previously, by a lion, which, however, it had evidently at last succeeded in beating off. The wounds smelt most offensively, and the meat of the shoulder-blades was quite green, and utterly uneatable. This old fellow would, no doubt, have been extremely vicious, and it was lucky that I made short work of him. Before proceeding on our way, my Kafirs dragged the carcases round, and left them with the noses touching, looking into one another's eyes, in which position the skulls and horns no doubt remain to this day.

On my return to the waggons I found that the Gardens had already trekked out, and that George Wood was away hunting to the eastward. On Monday morning, after a full day's rest, the first I had had for several months, I again left the waggons, striking into the hills to the north-east of our camp, and then working my way down to the Victoria Falls. From the falls I walked back to Daka in two days, shooting and cutting up two zebras on the road. On this trip I saw no signs of elephants, nor was I more successful during the latter half of October. On the 2nd of November a large herd of

buffaloes came up the Daka river to within a few
miles of our camp, thirteen of which we shot, Wood,
whom I had met, killing seven, and I myself six.   It
must not be thought that these buffaloes were shot
for sport, as we killed so many in order to dry a
supply of meat for use along the road to Tati for
ourselves, Kafirs, and dogs.   Setting two Kafirs to
each buffalo, we had all of them skinned and cut up,
and although a good deal of the meat was rather
high when we got it to the waggons, it was none the
less palatable to the dogs and Kafirs on that account.

At length, on the 8th of November, George
Wood trekked out with the waggons along the
regular caravan road, whilst I, taking my own Kafirs
and Bushmen with me, and a few trading goods,
started for Wankie's Town, which is situated about
eighty miles to the east of the Victoria Falls, from
which place I intended to cut right across country
to Thamma-setsi, where I had arranged with my
companion that he should wait for me with the
waggons.   This plan was carried out without
any mishap, and I again reached the waggons
on November 20, bringing with me over 300 lbs.
of fine ivory that I had bought from Wankie.
On my return journey I saw several enormous herds
of buffaloes, and a good many rhinoceroses of both
the black and white species, but not a single fresh
elephant spoor.   The following day we shot a black
rhinoceros bull close to the waggons.   Some days
later, on reaching the Mitengue river, we met Mr.
Schinderhutte, a man who had been many years
trading and hunting in the interior, and was then
on his way with a load of goods to Westbeech, at
Pandamatenka.   This was the third occasion upon
which I had met Schinderhutte ; he was a fine,

handsome man, and I have been told, a very agreeable and well-informed one when he was sober. Some months later this man came to a dreadful end. He was again on his way to the Zambesi with two waggon-loads of goods, amongst which was a hogshead of Cape brandy, to which he paid the most marked and unremitting attention, till at last he went half mad, and in a fit of delirium-tremens commenced shooting his oxen as they were trekking along. One day one of his Kafir servants demanded his payment, and on being told that his time was not up, became insolent, on which Schinderhutte, taking a loaded rifle from the side of the waggon, blew his brains out, the ill-fated Kafir falling dead alongside the fore-wheel. According to the account given by one of his drivers, this act seemed to sober him a little, and he never afterwards left the waggon without taking a loaded rifle with him. One day, however, he disappeared. Search was made for him the following morning, and some portion of his remains found, the rest having been eaten by the hyænas. There is no doubt that he was killed by Makalakas and Bushmen in revenge for what was nothing more or less than the cold-blooded murder of their comrade, but the exact circumstances of the tragedy are not, and probably never will be, accurately known. The day after they had killed him, the natives looted the waggons, stealing all the guns, powder, sugar, etc.

With Schinderhutte were my old friend Dorehill and Mr. Frank Oates, a most kind-hearted and amiable gentleman, and a great ornithologist, whom I had had the pleasure of meeting the preceding year in the Matabele country. They were on their way to the Zambesi, to see the falls and get a little big game shooting. As the unhealthy season was just commencing, I strongly urged them to put off their projected trip until the following winter. Dorehill yielded to my arguments, and returned with Wood and myself to Tati. Mr. Oates, however, decided to go on and risk it. He reached the falls safely, but soon afterwards was stricken down by the deadly fever, of which he ultimately died in the following February, close to the sources of the Tati river.

On December 3, whilst trekking along the bank of the Tati river, and when about forty miles distant from the gold-mine, I at last shot my first lion. Many people may think it strange that I should have been so long—nearly three years—living almost entirely in the wilderness, in countries where lions were plentiful, and where I was continually hearing them at nights, and yet never have seen one; but such is the case, and never since the three lions at Goqui in July 1872, until that day, had I seen another of these animals. Being nocturnal animals, and accustomed to lie asleep in beds of reeds and thick patches of bush during the daytime, it is mere chance work ever coming across them, especially in the "fly"-infested districts, where dogs cannot be used. On this occasion, as Dorehill and myself were riding along through a patch of bush, our ears were suddenly saluted with a muffled growling that we did not immediately interpret. The next instant, however, Hartebeest rushed forwards, pointing with his assegai, and shouting, "Isilouan! isilouan!" (Lions! lions!) I saw nothing, but galloped through the bush in the direction he pointed Dorehill heading a little to the right. A few moments later, coming to a more open part, I saw two large lionesses trotting

along in front of me. Upon hearing me behind
them, they both stopped, and standing broadside to
me, turned their heads and looked towards me.
Pulling in my horse, I jumped to the ground, upon
which they started off again at a gallop. I fired at
the hindermost one as she ran, and evidently struck
her, for she threw up her tail and gave a loud growl.
They now went into a patch of short mopani bush,
beyond which the country was open forest, with no
underwood. At first they trotted out into this open
forest, but the wounded one not seeming to like it,
turned, and squatting on the ground, crept back like
a cat, with her shoulders above her back, and her
eyes all the time fixed upon me, until she reached a
little thorn bush, under which she stretched herself
at full length, and lay watching me with her head
couched on her outstretched paws. All this time
the other lioness was standing in the open, and I was
just going to dismount and fire at her, when, turning
towards me, she trotted a few steps forwards, and
then, throwing her tail two or three times straight
into the air, came galloping forwards, growling
savagely. Turning my horse's head I pressed him
to his utmost speed, closely pursued by the lioness.
I do not know how near she got, but her loud purring
growls sounded unpleasantly close. As soon as the
growling stopped, I knew she had given up the
chase, and so rode round in a half-circle to get a view
of her. She then trotted to a large mopani tree, in
the shade of which she stood. When I rode to
another tree about sixty yards off, she lowered her
head and stood looking at me, snarling savagely,
with her tail held straight in the air. I think that
she had done her best to catch me, as her flanks were
heaving like those of a tired dog, with the exertion

of her run. Feeling sure that she would charge again as soon as she recovered her breath, I steadied myself and fired from the saddle, but missed her. She never took the slightest notice of the shot, but continued snarling and growling. Resting the butt of my rifle (a single ten-bore muzzle-loader) on my foot, I now reloaded with all expedition, and fired again, the lioness all this time having preserved the same position, standing exactly facing me. This time I struck her right in the mouth, knocking out one of the lower canine teeth, breaking the lower jaw-bone, and injuring her neck. She fell to the shot instantly, and lay quite still. I thought she was dead, but took the precaution to reload before riding up to her. On dismounting and walking towards her, she raised herself on her fore-quarters, when I gave her a ball in the shoulder which effectually settled her. Dorehill now came up with the Kafirs. He had seen the other lions, a male and two females, for there were five altogether, but they had given him the slip in a patch of thick bush. We now went to look for the one I had first wounded, but though there was a little blood under the bush where she had been lying, we could discover no further trace of her, and the ground being very hard no sign of her spoor was visible, even to the keen eyes of the Bushmen. So, after skinning the one I had killed, which was in beautiful condition, we returned to the waggons. A few days later, on December 11th, we reached the Tati, where we met with a warm welcome from Mr. Brown, the hospitable trader, so well known for his kindness and courtesy to all who have travelled in the interior of South Africa. Here I found a bundle of letters from home—the first I had received since leaving the Diamond Fields, nearly three years previously. Owing to news contained in these letters, I now determined to take a run home to England, and thus, on February 1, 1875, turned my face southwards, and travelling through the Transvaal and Natal territories, reached Durban in April, where I embarked for the old country.

List of Game shot from 5th June to 5th December 1874

Elephant .	.	.	. 24
Rhinoceros (black)	.	.	5
,, (white)	.	.	4
Hippopotamus .	.	.	1
Buffalo .	.	.	. 19
Giraffe .	.	.	2
Zebra (Burchell's)	.	.	7
Wart Hog	.	.	. 4
Lion	.	.	. 1
Eland	.	.	. 1
	Carry forward	.	68

	Brought forward	.	68
Koodoo .	.	•	. 3
Sable Antelope.		.	. 1
Roan Antelope.		.	. 1
Tsessebe .	.	•	. 3
Water-buck	.	.	. 1
Lechwe .	.	•	. 3
Pookoo .	.	•	. 7
Impala .	.	•	. 5
Steinbuck	.	•	. 1
	Total .		. 93

PART II

CHAPTER XII

Land at Algoa Bay, 1876—The Giraffe and its Habits—Giraffe-hunts
—Amandebele Marauders—Adventure with Lion—Narrow Escape
—Westbeech the Trader—Chase after Gemsbuck—Horse killed
by Lions ; wound the Male ; found dead by Bushmen soon after.

On the 15th of March 1876 I once more landed at
Algoa Bay and immediately set about organising
another expedition to the interior. With the
details of my journey from the coast I will not
weary my readers. Suffice it to say that after four
months' continuous travelling by bullock waggon
I at length reached the Matabele country. At
Kanye, near Secheli's, I met my old friend, Mr.
Dorehill, who then joined company with me ; and,
on arriving at Tati, we fell in with two English
gentlemen, Lieutenant Grandy, R.N., and Mr. Horner,
who had come up country on a hunting trip, and
had only arrived a few days before ourselves. As
it was now too late in the season to think of visiting
any of the more distant hunting-grounds in search
of elephants, either in the neighbourhood of the
Zambesi, or in the Mashuna country, the four of us
chummed together, and passed the remainder of the
year in short hunting excursions up and down the
Tati, Shashi, and Ramokwebani rivers. During the
month of October Lieutenant Grandy and myself
made an excursion to Gubulawayo, the capital of

Lobengula's country, leaving our friends still hunting in the Tati district, where we rejoined them again in the beginning of November. During this period the chief object of our pursuit was the giraffe, about which I will here take the opportunity of saying a few words.

This animal, though its range has been sadly reduced since the days of Gordon Cumming, is nevertheless still to be found in considerable numbers over a vast extent of country to the south of the Zambesi river. In parts of the Kalahari desert it is said to abound, and in all the dry sandy district between Bamangwato and Lake Ngami, and thence to the Mābābe, Chobe, and Zambesi rivers, it is also very numerous. Along portions of the Botletlie river, and in the waterless but forest-clad sand-belts on the southern bank of the Chobe, it is particularly plentiful. In the country between the Chobe and the Zambesi the giraffe is also found, in the neighbourhood of Linyanti ; but is not nearly so numerous there as on the other side of the former river. Immediately north of the Zambesi it is unknown, though it appears to be plentiful in parts of Central and Eastern Africa. In some parts of the Matabele country it is also common, but until within the last few years was never found eastwards of the river Gwelo, though it was always very plentiful in the sand-belts to the westward of that river. This fact is the more curious since the soil, vegetation, and general appearance of the country are precisely similar on both sides of the river, which during a great portion of the year is only a succession of pools, and therefore does not offer the slightest obstacle to any animal desirous of crossing it. During the last three or four years a few giraffe have extended their range farther eastwards, and in 1880 there were a few on the upper Gwenia, and in the vicinity of Jomani. Up till then, however, none appeared to have crossed the Se-whoi-whoi river. The fact that the giraffe, like the gemsbuck and eland, is most common in portions of the country where water is usually very scarce, and sometimes altogether wanting, would seem to show that, like those animals, it can subsist for a considerable period without drink, and many people declare, indeed, that it never does drink. This, however, is erroneous, as upon many occasions I have myself seen it in the very act ; and a curious sight it is to watch these long-limbed brutes straddling out their fore-legs gradually, until their mouths reach the water.

The giraffe is both fleet and enduring, and it is only a fairly good horse that can gallop clean past one. As, however, they seldom put out their full pace until hard pressed, they can be shot without much difficulty, even with a bad horse, by making him spurt up to within 100 yards or so of their sterns, and then dismounting quickly, giving them a bullet from behind just above the root of the tail. Owing to the shortness of their bodies any ordinary rifle will drive a bullet so placed right into the heart or lungs, and I have seen several giraffes killed in this manner by a single ball from a Martini-Henry carbine. As the chase of the giraffe is considered by many Englishmen who have distinguished themselves in the hunting-grounds of Southern Africa to be the sport *par excellence* of the country, I will reproduce some notes from my diary about this period, bearing upon the subject.

On the 2nd of November, the day after the return of Captain Grandy and myself to Tati we sent over a waggon to Ramokwebani drift, nineteen miles distant, following on horseback the next day. Our intention was to trek up and down the Ramokwebani river for a month or so, halting for a few days wherever we found good grass for our oxen, and game in sufficient quantities to keep our numerous retinue of native servants in meat. On the evening of our arrival Dorehill and I rode down the river to look for a head of game, and whilst pursuing two koodoo cows, suddenly saw a herd of seven giraffe in full flight about a quarter of a mile to our right. We at once left the animals we were pursuing to turn our attention to the nobler quarry, and galloping obliquely towards them, soon began to lessen the distance between us. I was badly mounted, my horse being not only slow, but excessively lazy, requiring a constant application of spur and sjambok to keep him going. However, as I have said before, giraffes, if not hard pressed, do not go at a very great pace, so that before long we were within 100 yards of them. Even in the ardour of the chase, it struck me as a glorious sight to see these huge beasts dashing along in front, clattering over the stones, or bursting a passage through opposing bushes, their long, graceful necks stretched forwards, sometimes bent almost to the earth to avoid horizontal branches, and their bushy black tails twisted up over their backs. And how easily and with what little exertion they seemed to get over the ground with that long, sweeping stride of theirs! Yet they were going at a great rate, for I felt that my old nag was doing his best, and I could not lessen the distance between us by an inch. I now saw that Dorehill was about to make a push, and as the horse he was riding was pretty fast, I knew that he would press them into a

much quicker pace, and leave me behind altogether :
so reining in I jumped off, and taking as steady an
aim as my arm, tired with flogging, would allow,
fired at a large dark-coloured cow, that looked to
me in good condition.   The bullet clapped loudly,
and I saw her stagger, but recovering immediately,
she went on, though slightly in the rear of the
others.   At this moment my friend jumped off
close behind them, and gave another cow a shot.
I was now a long way behind, but my horse, though
slow, possessed good staying powers, so that by dint
of keeping on at a hard gallop, and cutting angles
when I could, I again crept up, and gave my cow
another shot, quickly followed by a third, which
brought her to the ground with a crash.   She was
not yet dead, however, for as I approached she reared
her lofty head once more, and gazed reproachfully at
me with her large soft dark eyes.   For the instant,
I wished the shots unfired that had laid low this
beautiful and inoffensive creature.   But now the
cries of my Kafirs and Masaras, following like
famished wolves on the blood spoor, broke upon
my ear ; so, stifling all remorseful feelings, I again
raised my rifle and put an end to the miseries of my
victim, whose head, pierced with a heavy bullet, fell
with a thud upon the ground, never to be raised
again.   Leaving some of the boys to cut up the
meat, I rode on with the rest to look for my friend,
whom I found beside another prostrate giraffe which
he had killed a little farther on.   As the one I had
shot was the fatter of the two, we left the Kafirs here
and went back to mine.   It was now late ; so hastily
dividing the boys into two parties, and bidding them
sleep by the two giraffes respectively, and cut them
up and bring in the meat on the following day, we

ourselves started for the waggons with our gun-carriers, who also carried a few of the choicest portions of the meat. I may here remark that it is difficult to imagine anything more tasty and succulent than a steak off a young giraffe cow, when in good condition, though it may be that hunger, the sauce with which I have always eaten it, has something to do with this opinion. Whilst riding back to the waggons along the river bank, I shot a fine koodoo bull.

On the afternoon of the following day, we inspanned the waggon, and trekked down the Ramokwebani. Dorehill rode on in front, and coming across two giraffes on a large flat near the river, had a glorious run after them across the open, and galloping right past the one, killed the other, a young bull, on the edge of a little gully, close to which, and within twenty yards of the carcase, we outspanned for the night.

Being now well supplied with meat, we resolved to shoot no more giraffe until it was all finished ; but on the following day, some Masaras coming to the waggons and begging us to kill some game for them, as they were hungry, we thought that we might again take the field with good consciences ; so, telling them they must try and show us some big game, either eland, buffalo, or giraffe, we saddled up and followed them forthwith.

Crossing the river, they made straight for a range of hills running parallel with it ; and before we had proceeded very far, their sharp eyes detected in some hard ground the spoor of a herd of giraffe, which, on further inspection, turned out to be quite fresh. Whilst following it we put up a large snake, which we promptly despatched with sticks. It proved to be a mamba, a poisonous species, and measured over ten feet in length.   The giraffes had been feeding about in all directions, crossing and recrossing their own spoor continually, and it required all the skill of our crafty guides to get it away; but they were hungry, and lightly indeed must the animal tread that a half-famished Masara will not track to its hiding-place.   All at once they stopped short, and, pointing to the ground, pronounced the well-known word "Balegeelee!" (They've run), and, glancing downwards, we saw, from the now deeply-cut hoof-marks, and the displaced sand, that such was indeed the case.   The keen-scented animals had probably got wind of us, and of course made off.   No time was to be lost; so, taking our guns, we bade the Bushmen and our own boys run on the spoor.   They at once went off at a good sharp pace, the two Masaras leading, and, after running for about a mile and a half, brought us down to the river again, which the giraffes had crossed.   After toiling across the broad expanse of soft white sand, for there was not a drop of water within six feet of the surface, the Bushmen again took up the running, but had not proceeded far when they stopped short, at the same time crouching down and pointing eagerly forwards with their assegais.   They had sighted the giraffes, as we ourselves did almost immediately afterwards. They were standing about 300 yards off, looking back towards us, seven in all,—four cows, two half-grown calves, and a huge patriarchal old bull, whose lofty head towered high over those of his comrades.   Beyond them the veldt was pretty open for about 1000 yards up to the edge of a mopani forest.

"Now for a run!" said Dorehill, and off we

R

went. For an instant the giraffes stared wonderingly towards us, and then, twisting up their long black tails, galloped away at a swinging pace. My friend, being mounted on a very fine horse, distanced me considerably, though I was able to keep close enough to enjoy a very fine view of the chase. The horse and his rider seemed to be straining every nerve, whilst the long sweeping stride of the giraffes gave one the idea that they were not exerting themselves to any great extent. Nevertheless they were doing their best, for, before they reached the bush, the gallant chestnut had borne his rider first level with and then clean past the old bull, who at once, swerving to one side, went off at right angles ; and, just as the cows were gaining the shelter of the forest, Dorehill jumped off close behind them, and as the report of his rifle rang out, I heard the bullet clap loudly, and at the same time saw a dark-coloured cow throw out her legs spasmodically, evidently hard hit. Before my friend was in the saddle again I passed him, and my old horse, responding to my call and spurting gamely, soon brought me close up behind the giraffes. Hastily glancing through them, I noted the one just wounded by my companion, and then, picking out a light-coloured cow that I thought looked the fattest of the remaining five, I pushed close up alongside of her, and turned her away from the others ; but the bush being rather thick, it was some time before I could get a chance of a shot, though I stuck close to her. The bush through which the chase led consisted principally of large mopani trees growing pretty close together, and the judgment with which the giraffe, though going at a great pace, steered her course through them, breaking the smaller opposing branches, or gracefully bending

forward her long neck so as to pass beneath stouter
ones that sometimes almost grazed her shoulder, was
a most curious sight, though one to which I had
little time to attend, as I had all my work cut out
to find a path for myself.   At last we reached an
opening in the forest, which gave me a chance of
which I was not slow to take advantage.   Springing
off about fifty yards behind her, and just as she was
gaining the bush on the farther side of the opening,
I gave her a shot high up in the hip, which, entering
obliquely, must have penetrated to her heart, for
after receiving the wound she ran barely 100 yards,
and then, standing still for a few moments, fell down
backwards, stone dead.

As soon as some of the Kafirs came up, I left
them with the carcase and hastened to rejoin my
friends, whom I found with the rest of the boys
cutting up a very fat cow.   After taking all the inside
fat and the best parts of the meat for ourselves, we
rode home to the waggons, leaving the remainder for
the Bushmen, one of whom at once started off to
fetch all his people.   Early the following morning,
whilst sitting at the waggons, we were surprised to
see a long line of Kafirs approaching from the other
side of the river.   Their large ox-hide shields and
short stabbing assegais at once announced them to be
Amandebele on some marauding expedition.   When
within 100 yards of our camp, they halted, and a
few of the headmen came up to the waggons, and,
after first telling us a lot of ridiculous lies, at length
admitted that they had been sent out by their chief,
Lobengula, to murder any strange Bushmen or Kafirs
whom they might find hunting in his veldt.   Of
course we said nothing about our friends the Masaras,
for whom we had killed the giraffes, and who, I

fear, would have had but a sorry time of it had they chanced to fall into the hands of these ruthless murdering scoundrels, whose greatest happiness is to stab to death defenceless and unresisting women and children, and in whose vocabulary such words as pity or mercy find no place.

After a prolonged parley, and when all the usual questions had been asked and answered—during which time our interlocutors had been eyeing with greedy looks the giraffe meat which was hanging in festoons from the neighbouring trees—they asked us to saddle up our horses and try to shoot something for their hungry followers, who, they averred, had been without food for two days. Glad to get quit of them so easily, we willingly agreed to do our best, and had the horses brought up forthwith. Suffice it to say that we shot that afternoon a solitary old giraffe bull, and on the following day three cows, all of which we gave to the Amandebele ; and then, breaking up our camp, trekked higher up the river.

During the following fortnight we continued hunting on the upper course of the Ramokwebani, shooting several handsome specimens of the larger antelopes, and four buffaloes, which are about the last that have been shot in that part of the country. Towards the end of the month we crossed over to the river Tati, striking it about forty miles above the settlement. It was whilst we were here that I met with an afternoon's sport, of which I will now give an account. The two or three preceding days having been so rainy that we had been unable to do any hunting, we were out of meat, and our gang of about a dozen Kafirs and Bushmen consequently were making sad inroads into our stock of corn

—a state of things to be remedied as soon as possible.

The morning of the day of which I am speaking broke dull and rainy, and during the forenoon heavy showers kept continually falling. About two o'clock, however, the rain cleared off, and, although the sky still remained cloudy and overcast, I thought that I might venture out for an hour or two's ride without fear of a wetting ; so, calling for my horse—poor Bottle, whose untimely fate I will recount later on —I at once saddled up, and, taking a few boys with me, rode along the waggon-road which here follows the course of the river. We had not proceeded more than a mile before cutting the spoor of some five or six koodoo cows that seemed to have only just passed. The spoor being so fresh and, as the ground was soft and wet with the recent rain, very easy to follow, I took it, and in a short time sighted the koodoos, of which, after a short chase, I shot one, and, leaving the Kafirs to cut up the meat and carry it to the waggons, rode on by myself, not caring to turn back after having been out so short a time. I had ridden at a walk through the bush for about an hour, when I sighted a small herd of tsessebe antelope feeding quietly down an opening in the forest. With them were two young fawns, which, from their diminutive size, I judged to be but a few days old. Being anxious to catch a few young antelopes, and having several cows in milk at the waggons, I thought that this would be a good oppor-tunity, and anticipating but little difficulty in running down such tender-looking creatures, at once rode out into the open and gave chase. Never was erring mortal more deceived. The two little tsessebes, young though they were, ran every bit as fast as

the old ones ; indeed, sometimes when I made a spurt
in the hope of cutting them off, they passed their
dam at greyhound speed, and appeared in the van
of the herd.   At last, disgusted and disappointed, I
pulled up in mercy to my horse, which I felt had
had enough of it.   After off-saddling for a short
time, I then rode in the direction of the waggon-road,
and had just emerged from the bush upon a large
opening, from whence I could see the line of dark
thorn trees that marked the course of the river
Tati, when my attention was attracted by something
behind a bush about 300 yards distant, which
looked very like the ears and horns of some animal
gazing in my direction.   Riding slowly forwards, my
suspicions were soon confirmed, for a noble old roan
antelope bull trotted out a few yards from the shelter
of the bush, turned and stared at me for an instant,
and then with a whisk of his tail cantered away,
followed by about ten others that had been lying
down behind the bushes, whilst the bull apparently
kept on the look-out for danger.   For an instant,
thinking of the hard run my horse had just had, I
hesitated whether or no to pursue ; but as Bottle on
sighting the game cocked his ears, raised his head,
and altogether seemed anxious for the sport, I determined to have a short run and endeavour to secure
a good head.   Riding at a hand gallop, I was soon
close behind them ; and as the bull that brought up
the rear of the herd turned to see what was behind
him, I jumped off, and gave him a shot just as he
was galloping away.   Before I could again get within
shot they entered a patch of thick bush.   Through
this they went but slowly, and in an open glade just
beyond the whole herd came to a halt and faced
about, so that as I burst suddenly from the thick

foliage in their rear I was close upon them. My sudden apparition of course caused a panic, and away they went again at top speed. I saw at a glance that the bull was not there, and thinking that he must have turned out or fallen dead in the thick bush behind, gave a cow a shot as she galloped straight away, which, striking her just at the root of the tail, brought her to the ground at once, powerless in the hind-quarters. On riding up and dismounting to give her the *coup de grâce*, she tried to drag herself towards me on her fore-legs, her eyes glaring like those of a wounded buffalo. She then made a loud squealing noise, when I put a term to her suffering with a bullet through the shoulders. As she had a very fair pair of horns, I cut off her head and hid it in a thick bushy tree, trusting that no harm would befall it before the Kafirs could fetch it when I sent for the meat next morning. Then breaking off a dry stake, and tying a large bunch of dry grass on the end of it, I stuck it into the ground alongside the carcase to keep off the vultures (this plan answers sometimes, though not always, but I know of no other that ever does, though I have heard of and tried many). Trusting to Providence on the score of lions and hyænas, I now took the spoor backwards into the bush to look for the wounded bull, and see if there was any blood. I soon hit it off, and, finding a great deal of blood, followed it, not expecting that the wounded beast would go very far. After spooring for about a mile the traces of blood became less and less frequent, and at length only a few drops appeared at long intervals. Still, as the ground was soft and damp the spoor was easy enough to follow, until after another mile or so I found myself among the tracks of the whole herd, that must have run

round in a half-circle in order to rejoin their wounded
comrade. I now gave it up, the more especially as
it was getting very late ; and although I knew I was
close to the waggon-road, I did not know exactly
how far I was from the waggons ; so, turning my
horse's head, I rode straight for the river, about two
miles distant. When within a few hundred yards of
the bank the remains of an old cattle kraal, huts, etc.,
attracted my attention, as, from the position of several
large thorn trees in the vicinity, I thought I recognised it as the spot where, two years before, I had
passed two or three rainy days. With my thoughts
thus engaged, I rode forwards at a slow walk, my eyes
always fixed on the remains of the old huts, and was
within about seventy yards of the kraal fence, when,
glancing to the front, I saw, lying straight in my path,
a small yellow thing, and as instantly as my eye fell
upon it I knew that it was a lion, for I could see
the yellowish eyes, and the lines from the corners
of them, quite plainly. He was lying exactly facing
me, with his head couched on his outstretched paws,
on a piece of bare, sandy ground, and just between
two little stunted wait-a-bit thorn bushes. So close,
however, did he manage to squeeze his body against
the ground, that I think, if it had not been for his
eyes, I should have taken his head, pressed close
down between his paws, for one of the little ant-
heaps that one sees all over the country. Whether
the dampness of the grass and bushes, which no
doubt formed his usual lair along the river's edge,
had caused him to come up to this dry patch of
ground, or whether he had seen the horse approaching from afar, and was lying in wait for us with any
dire intent, I cannot take upon myself to say. At
any rate, there he was, not fifty yards off, straight

in my path, with his eyes intently fixed upon the advancing horse, and I did not stop to ascertain his intentions, but the instant I saw him pulled in and dismounted. As I lifted my rifle he just raised his head about six inches. Fear that he would bound away made me fire rather hurriedly; but the roar that instantly followed the shot let me know that he had got the bullet somewhere. Owing to the dampness of the air, the smoke hung in such a manner that for several seconds I could see nothing of the lion, which kept up a loud and continuous roaring. But as it cleared off I saw him tumbling about on his head, with his right fore-leg swinging in the air. Before I could get another cartridge in my rifle, however, he recovered from the shock he had received, and shambled off into the thick wait-a-bit thorn bushes that skirted a deep gully just behind the old kraal. I must confess that I did not like exactly following him into this low thorny scrub, where one could not see ten yards ahead, alone and without dogs; but, at the same time, I longed to possess his hide, and, moreover, thought I had given him a deadly wound, for as his fore-arm swung loose from the shoulder, I knew, from the position in which he was lying when I fired, that my bullet must just have grazed past his cheek, struck him on the point of the shoulder, and then, as I imagined, raked him, passing in all probability through one of his lungs. Leading my horse by the bridle, I now took the blood spoor, which followed the waggon-road into the gully, down whose bed it then turned towards the river, which was less than one hundred yards distant. The opposite bank of this gully being steep and high, I thought I should stand a better chance of seeing

the lion by going along the top of it—at the same
time taking him at an advantage—than by following
the bed.   So leading Bottle to the top, I there left
him, and walked along the edge of the steep bank,
holding my rifle in readiness, and keeping a sharp
look-out on all sides.   All at once, about thirty
yards in front, I saw, just appearing above the edge
of the bank, something that looked like the top of
a lion's mane as it waved slightly in the wind.   I
was not left long in doubt, for suddenly a shaggy
head was popped up just for a second of time, and
then both head and mane disappeared.   Thinking
he was still there, I got to a place from whence I
could command a view of where I had just seen him,
but on attaining it had the mortification to find that
he had made off.   The sight of me, instead of
rousing him to resent the injury he had already
received, had only decided him to decamp afresh.
I now went down into the bed of the gully and
again took up his spoor, which, after reaching the
river's edge, turned into a patch of fearfully thick
and thorny bush.   I was peering through this and
thinking it would be madness to crawl into it after
a wounded lion, when with a hoarse growl the brute
raised himself up not fifteen yards off, looked
towards me, showed his teeth, and then, his heart
again failing him, crept away with as much speed
as his wounded state would allow.   Although so
near me, the thickness of the scrub rendered the
chance of a successful shot so uncertain that I did
not think it advisable to fire.   Just then a heavy
shower of rain commenced to fall, the sun, too, was
all but down, so I thought it the wisest plan to ride
back to the waggons and return on the following
day with the dogs, feeling sure that the lion was so

badly wounded that he would not be very far from
where I had left him ; indeed, my chief fear was
that he would die before morning and the hyænas
destroy the skin.   Going back to my horse, that
was still standing where I had left him, I at once
mounted and rode along the track at a brisk canter
towards the waggons.   I was riding along thus,
the rain coming down pretty sharply, when I saw,
standing looking at me, not 100 yards from the
road, a fine old roan antelope bull.   Pulling in, I
at once jumped to the ground, which decided him
to decamp.   Just as he turned, however, I fired,
and saw by the rush he instantly made that he was
hard hit.   Jumping on my horse, I was soon hard
upon his heels ; but he did not lead me far, falling
dead before he had run 150 yards.   He carried a
fine head, which I instantly set to work to cut off.
Then, once more remounting, and carrying the
head before me across the saddle, I rode as fast
as I could to the waggons, which I reached about
half an hour after dark, in time to recount to
my friends, over a rough but substantial dinner,
the excellent afternoon's sport that I had met with,
and my sanguine hopes of bagging the wounded
lion on the following day.

   At dawn next morning we were stirring, and by
sunrise were half-way to the spruit where I had
last seen the lion, having left orders for the waggons
to inspan and follow us at once.   On reaching the
spruit we off-saddled the horses, and, leaving a Kafir
in charge of them, proceeded with the dogs and the
rest of the Kafirs and Bushmen to look up the lion
on foot.   Though some heavy showers had fallen
during the night, we were still able to get the spoor
away through the patch of bush in which I had last

seen him ; and not fifty yards farther on the behaviour of the dogs showed unmistakably that he
was still close at hand. A regard for truth forbids
me to pronounce a very glowing eulogium upon the
courage displayed on this occasion by our mongrel
pack. At the mere scent of the lion all but two
rushed precipitately past us, not forwards, but backwards, with their tails between their legs, some of
them yelping with fright ; nor did they put in an
appearance again until the hunt was over. Two
veterans, however, an old dog half paralysed in the
hind-quarters, and a one-eyed bitch, stood their
ground, and, with the hair on end all along their
backs, growled savagely. Even these two would not
go far in front of us. Whilst poking about looking
for the spoor we came to the place where the
wounded beast had lain all night, and from which he
must just have crawled away as we came up. He
seemed to have lost a good deal of blood, and had
champed and chewed every bit of stick within his reach.

There was now no more difficulty about taking
the spoor, as the footprint showed very plainly in
the soft ground, wet and muddy with the night's
rain ; but the bush being pretty thick and in leaf,
we only advanced very cautiously, step by step,
expecting every instant to see the lion. After proceeding for some distance in this manner, it became
evident to me that as we advanced so he constantly
receded, creeping from bush to bush, so that we
never could get a view of him, and I began to fear
that this sort of thing might go on for an indefinite
period. I therefore proposed to Horner that he and
I should take up a position on some higher ground
along the river, a little on ahead of where I judged
the lion to be, leaving our friends and the Kafirs to

To face page 253.

CLOSE QUARTERS; TATI RIVER, NOVEMBER 22, 1876.

keep the spoor and drive him past us. We had not quite reached our post, however, when of a sudden he commenced to roar. At the same instant Grandy called out, " There he is—I see him," and fired, and then said, " That's hit him ; that's knocked him over." I at once ran down to him, and saw the lion lying crouched down, with his head under a horizontal willow branch. All this time he had kept up, without cessation, one continuous roaring. I had just raised my rifle to fire, when Horner, who was a little to my left, anticipated me. The lion at once ceased roaring, and disappeared over the bank amongst the overhanging willows. As the river was full, and running strong at the time, I did not think he would like to take the water, and ran along the bank to intercept him as he came up again. He soon did so, and, seeing me, I suppose, commenced to roar again. He was now, however, invisible in a patch of bush, but, as he never stopped roaring, I could tell his whereabouts pretty well. As he had shown himself so pusillanimous both on the previous evening and during the whole morning, knowing, too, that I had hurt him severely, and believing that Grandy had hit him too, I hardly expected he would charge, or I might have been more careful. As it was, however, I was peering about into the bush to try and catch sight of him, holding my rifle advanced in front of me, and on full cock, when I became aware that he was coming at me through the bush. The next instant out he burst. I was so close that I had not even time to take a sight, but, stepping a pace backwards, got the rifle to my shoulder, and, when his head was close upon the muzzle, pulled the trigger, and jumped to one side. The lion fell almost at my very feet, certainly not six

feet from the muzzle of the rifle. Grandy and
Horner, who had a good view of the charge, say
that he just dropped in his tracks when I fired,
which I could not see for the smoke. One thing,
however, I had time to notice, and that was that he
did not come at me in bounds, but with a rush along
the ground. Perhaps it was his broken shoulder
that hindered him from springing, but for all that
he came at a very great rate, and with his mouth
open. Seeing him on the ground I thought that I
must have shattered his skull and killed him, when,
as we were advancing towards him, he stood up
again. Dorehill at once fired with a Martini-
Henry rifle, and shot him through the thigh. On
this he fell down again, and, rolling over on to his side,
lay gasping. We now went up to him, but, as he
still continued to open his mouth, Horner gave him
a shot in the head. I now examined my prize with
great satisfaction. He was an average-sized lion,
his pegged-out skin measuring 10 ft. 3 in. from nose
to tip of tail, sleek, and in fine condition, and his
teeth long and perfect. Grandy and Horner must
both have missed him when they first fired, as we
could find no mark of their bullets on the skin ; so
that when he charged, the only wound he had was
the one I had given him on the previous evening.
This bullet had merely smashed his shoulder-blade
and lodged under the skin just behind it. The
bullet with which I so luckily stopped him when
charging, had struck him fair on the head, about
half an inch above the right eye ; here it had cracked
the skull, but, without penetrating, had glanced
along the bone and come out behind the right ear.
I believe that this shot must have given him con-
cussion of the brain, and caused his death, and that

when he stood up after, it was merely a spasmodic action, for the shot that Dorehill gave him was only a flesh wound through the thighs, and the last shot that Horner gave him in the head as he lay on the ground had passed beneath the brain pan. By the time that I had skinned the lion, the waggons came up, and I then sent all the spare Kafirs to fetch the meat and head of the roan antelope cow that I had shot the preceding evening, telling them to take my horse's spoor backwards until they came to the dead animal. A little after mid-day they returned, telling us that they had found three lions at the carcase, or, to speak more correctly, at what had once been the carcase, for they had left but little of it, except bones. Thinking that the lions might still be there, Grandy, Horner, and myself at once saddled up and went to see ; but we had our ride for nothing, as the brutes had prudently retired, and we found nothing but vultures picking the bones they had left. They had also pulled the head out of the thick bushy tree in which I had hidden it, and quite spoiled it.

During the two following days, Dorehill and I shot three roan antelopes and four giraffes, two of the latter very fat. We then stood over two days, drying the meat and rendering down the fat ; and on the following day inspanned and started for the settlement, which we reached on November 28, after an absence of just four weeks.

Here for the first time I met Mr. George Westbeech, the well-known Zambesi trader, whom, curiously enough, I had never before seen, although upon several occasions during the last four years I had often been in his immediate neighbourhood. Mr. Westbeech is one of those many English and

Scotch men whose innate love of enterprise, combined with indomitable perseverance, has led them to try their fortune in every unexplored corner of the globe, and it is the individual efforts of a host of such men in different parts of the world that have won for Great Britain the goodly share of the earth's surface which she at present possesses. This energetic Englishman first opened a trade with Sipopo, king of the Barotse, in 1871, and until the assassination of that potentate in 1876 yearly brought out from the Zambesi country from 20,000 to 30,000 lbs. of ivory. Since that time, the country having been in a state of anarchy, the trade has, of course, very much fallen off. In 1873 Mr. Westbeech visited the Barotse valley, where he remained as the guest of Sipopo until June 1874. He there met a Portuguese trader, Joao Ferreira, spoken of by Cameron, and is himself the Englishman "Georgo" referred to by him.

On the 1st of December, as it was necessary for me to fetch some property belonging to me that was lying on the Diamond Fields and get back again to the interior by the end of the rainy season, I bade adieu to my friends at Tati and trekked away to the south, following the main waggon-road leading to Bamangwato. I took both my waggons with me and three horses, and was accompanied by two Europeans — Mr. Edwin Miller, a young colonist and a first-rate game shot, who was in my service, and a Mr. Bell, who had made an unsuccessful trading trip to the Zambesi, and to whom I was now giving a passage to the Diamond Fields. On my journey down country and back again, which occupied the best part of five months, only one incident happened worth relating, and as the full account of

this adventure, written upon the spot to my friend
Mr. Alexander Brown, now lies before me, having
been sent by him to help me to compile these journals,
I think my best plan is to reproduce it just as I then
worded it.

MY DEAR ALICK—To ease my distracted mind,
I will now give you a full and particular account of
what has befallen me during the last two days. At
Goqui (let me not omit the one sweet drop in my
cup of bitterness) I shot a fine old red hartebeest
bull, a solitary old fellow. On Sunday night I slept
about six miles on the Tati side of Serule, and
finding a pan of water near at hand, remained there
all Monday, trekking on again in the evening to
Serule. Having ridden out on horseback as the
waggons were travelling, I came across a family of
Bushmen, one of whom, upon my questioning him,
said he could surely show me gemsbuck on the
following day, if I would remain at Serule and be
guided by him. Of course I was only too glad to
spend a day in such a pursuit, and so remained at
Serule that night, the Bushman sleeping at the
waggons. Next morning we made an early start,
Miller riding the yellow nag, whilst I rode Bottle.
I suppose we had ridden about six miles when we
cut the fresh spoor of a herd of gemsbuck. The
veldt was here very open, but the tracks led us into
a sand-belt, which gradually grew thicker and thicker,
till at last it became difficult to ride through, even
at a walk. From where the bush was densest, however, they fed back again towards the open country,
and at last, when about 300 yards from the
edge of the bush, I saw a large animal that I
knew was one of the gemsbuck make a dash past.

Seizing my rifle, I rode after him, and saw another following the first. As I knew they were making for the open country, I just let them go at their own pace, and did not attempt to fire, thinking to make surer of my shot when we were out of the bush. They were two bulls, I think, with splendid tails and large black patches on the hind-quarters, and long shining black horns of at least the average length. They ran very nicely and smoothly, neither swerving to the right nor to the left, but holding a straight line, though going at a great pace. On reaching the open ground at the foot of the sand-belt, one of them turned short off, and went away like the wind, making back for the bush again, so I held on after the other. I now pressed up to within about fifty yards, and springing off, believe I should in all human probability have given the gemsbuck a good shot, as he was running straight from me, well within range, and there was not a bush between us; but just as I was going to fire, Bottle ran right in front of the muzzle of my rifle. I raised it at once, and was intending to put it back to half-cock, when he gave me a pull, and my finger being on the hair trigger, the gun went off in the air. I did not think this would matter much, as there being more than a mile of flat before us, I imagined I could gallop up again in no time. However, I was mistaken, for after going a couple of hundred yards at a gallop, Bottle suddenly stopped dead in spite of all my spurring; in fact, after never having once played me false during the last two months, he most un-expectedly, and just when I particularly wanted him to be on his best behaviour, resumed the tricks which he often used to play me when I first bought him, and of which I thought I had entirely broken him.   The gemsbuck, having all this time been going at a hard gallop, was 500 yards ahead, when, by dint of spurring, I got my horse started again.   Little by little I crept up to within 300 yards of the chase, when I felt that Bottle was again going to pull up.   Wild with rage and mortification, I dropped the reins, and raising my heavy rifle above my head, and holding it just in front of the hammer, struck the poor beast with all my force between the ears.   He fell in his tracks like an ox that is poleaxed, shooting me over his head—for he was still going pretty fast.   After I had disengaged myself from him, he soon stood up, and I then, to my astonishment, saw that he had not turned a hair, there not being a drop of sweat upon him, except under the saddle, neither was he panting in the least.   In fact, he had simply refused to run out of " pure cussedness," and lost me this, my first chance of killing a gemsbuck, and now heaven knows when I may get another.   But now for the pith of my story.   Riding back to Serule, I at once inspanned, and at ten o'clock P.M. outspanned a few miles short of Pelatsi.   As the Bushman told me there were also gemsbuck about Pelatsi, and I wished to ride out to look for some on the following day, I did not tie Bottle up, but left him loose to feed round the waggons all night, as I had no corn to give him, and the Bushman declared there had been no lions about here for years.

About 2.30 A.M. I was awakened by my boy January, who, in a stage whisper, announced to me : "Sir, daar's en ding op de paard" (Sir, there's a thing on the horse).   Scarcely thinking it possible that it could be a lion, but yet not knowing what other thing could be "op de paard," I took my rifle and followed the boy along the oxen, which were tied up in the yoke. Miller went with me too, and advancing cautiously to the fore yoke, I could see the indistinct dark form of the horse lying stretched upon the ground about five-and-twenty yards off; at the same instant, too, I heard a low grating growl, which let me know at once what the thing was that was on the horse. It was a cloudy, misty sort of night, but yet the light of the moon above seemed to pierce, and partially illumine, what would otherwise have been a pitchy darkness. As we advanced towards the horse, I saw two lions rise from behind it and make off, muttering curses upon our importunity as they went. Miller wanted to fire, but as their distinct forms were almost instantly lost in the gloom, I restrained him, as I thought a shot might frighten them away altogether, whereas if they were undisturbed they might return and remain by the carcase until daylight, when we might come to conclusions with them. Acting upon this, I returned to the waggon, and had not been there five minutes when I heard the lions at the carcase again. Taking our karosses, Miller and I now crept along the line of oxen, and lay flat on our bellies by the fore yoke, watching for about an hour. All this time the lions kept scrunching up the bones and tearing at the flesh of my dead horse without intermission, now and again grunting and growling, seemingly over disputed pieces of meat, and all this time the oxen, the nearest of which was only twenty-three measured paces from the horse's fore-foot, kept quietly standing up and lying down, poking one another with their horns, or catching their legs in the "reims,"[1] and the fore oxen kept ringing the

---

"Reim" is the soft though raw-hide thong used universally in South Africa for tying up bullocks or horses.

bells which were tied round their necks. Like Daniel, they didn't care a bit for the lions, and the lions didn't care a bit for them. Now and again I could see one of the lions rise from behind the horse, and placing its fore-paws on the carcase, raise its head and look towards us, its cocked ears being plainly visible against the sky-line ; then in a noiseless, ghostly manner it would seem to sink into the ground again. About ten yards to my right hand there was a little bush, a bit nearer to the lions, so I crept up to it without appearing to attract their attention. As I sat here I began to fear that, as day broke, and before it got light enough to see to shoot, they would decamp, and the idea struck me that it would be as well to creep up to a little bush that was about eight yards from the carcase—the wind being favourable—as I should then be so near that, even if I could not see the sight of my rifle, I should have been almost certain to hit one, had they showed any signs of decamping. Lying flat on my belly and pushing my rifle cautiously in front of me, I had advanced about six yards, and thought I had the little bush well between me and the lions, when suddenly the form of one seemed to rise from the earth, and with its fore-paws on the body of the dead horse, commenced looking intently towards me. I could now see the outline of the beast's shoulders, with the head surmounted by the rounded ears, quite distinctly, and levelling my rifle, was debating whether or not to fire, when with a loud growl she—for it was the lioness—sprang away, and at the same moment I saw the indistinct outline of another rise from the carcase and follow her. Thinking that there were only two of them, and that I had made a mess of the whole business, I stood up, and was on the point of advancing towards the horse, when a very nasty gurgling sort of growl arrested my footsteps. I could see nothing, but knew that a third lion was in my close vicinity, so, cocking my rifle, I held it with the muzzle advanced, and my finger on the trigger, ready for accidents. After standing thus for a few seconds, straining every sense to try and discover the whereabouts of the lion, I sat down, and then edged gradually away to a little leafless bush a few yards to my right. There was now a sort of greyish light which rendered objects much more distinguishable than they had been an hour previously, yet though I commanded a clear and unobstructed view of the dead horse, the outline of which was becoming plainer every instant, I could see no sign of the lion, though I knew he was not twenty yards away. It was now getting so light that I raised my rifle, and looking along the sights found that I could see pretty well, though the ivory foresight glimmered rather large in the nick. Another five minutes passed, and to me who had been watching since it was quite dark it seemed nearly light. I looked towards Miller and Bell, and saw them quite distinctly lying flat on their faces between the two spans of oxen, and then glancing again towards the dead horse, my eyes suddenly became fixed upon the greenish-yellow eyes of the lion, which was lying between me and the horse, its tawny body pressed flat upon the yellow sand, and its great head couched upon its outstretched paws. For the last hour I must have been constantly overlooking it, for, as we afterwards found by actual measurement, there was only a space of twelve paces between us. The beast's eyes were concentrated upon me with a most unpleasant intensity, and I saw that his tail, with a fine black bunch at the end of it, was twitching from side to side with little nervous jerks. Well, I thought he meditated an attack. Very likely he didn't, but he really looked uncommonly disagreeable, and I was sitting in a cramped and awkward position to receive a charge, so, taking as good an aim as I could for the centre of his head, I fired. With a loud grunt he stood up on his hind legs and rolled over backwards, and for some seconds lay still. Before I could get another cartridge in, however, he regained his feet and made off after the other two (a lioness and a nearly full-grown cub), that we now saw rise from under a bush some 200 yards off. Miller did not fire until the lion had regained his legs, letting slip the golden opportunity when his ideas were deranged by my shot, and missing him, unfortunately, when he did fire. We now took up his spoor on foot. At first there was only a little blood, but after a bit the blotches became larger and more frequent, and seemed to be thrown from his mouth. I feel sure that I hit him right in the face, and fancy the bullet must have glanced from his lower jaw-bone, which in a lion is very solid. To make a long story short, we followed the spoor for several miles, and at last, as it appeared evident that the lion had not received a mortal wound, gave it up. I would have held on longer, but my bad leg became very painful,[1] and the bush was in most parts too thick to follow a wounded lion on horseback ; so I at length returned to the waggon even more mortified at the loss of this lion than I was at that of the gemsbuck on the previous day. I have now made a skerm round the dead horse, and this evening shall set a gun, and then trek on about a mile and await the result ; but, successful

---

[1] I had hurt my leg badly about a fortnight previously in a fall from my horse whilst chasing a giraffe, cracking the tibia so that some of the serum ran out, and formed a lump on the bone.

or unsuccessful, I shall resume my journey to-morrow. His wound, I am afraid, will prevent the lion from returning, but I confidently expect the lioness to put in an appearance.   I made this morning two fatal errors.   The first was endeavouring to get too close, for had I waited at the bush within twenty yards of the lions, I believe I could have had a quiet pot shot at them by daylight.   The other was not to have saddled up the yellow horse.   This I thought of, and was actually on the point of creeping back from the bush to give the order, when I thought that the possible benefit was not worth the risk of disturbing the lions.   Here you have the whole story, and will I am sure be able to understand and appreciate my feeling of bitter disappointment.

December 7th.—The lions did not return last night.   Had I not wounded the male they no doubt would have done so.   They may come to-night, but I cannot afford to wait any longer on the chance, for time is now precious.   Thus, most disgracefully to me, has ended this little episode in my hunting career. I could bite my tongue and tear my hair with vexation.   However, the whole affair is past and done with now, so I must try and gradually recover my equanimity, which has not been so much disturbed by the loss of my horse—though that is no trifle—as by my failing to kill the lion. . . .

Three months later, I learned from my friend Mr. Matthew Clarkson that the Bushmen had found my lion lying dead, a few days after I wounded it.   They brought him the skin to buy, and told him that my bullet had broken the beast's lower jaw, and lodged in his neck.   As lions are so few and far between about that part of the country, I think there can be no doubt as to its identity.

CHAPTER XIII

ALL over the interior of South Africa, wherever game
still exists in sufficient quantities to furnish them
with food, lions are to be met with, and are equally
plentiful on the high, open downs of the Mashuna
country, amongst the rough, broken hills, through
which run many of the tributaries of the Zambesi, in
the dense thorn-thickets to the west of the Gwai river,
or in the marshy country in the neighbourhood of
Linyanti. As, however, they are nocturnal in their
habits, and usually lie asleep during the daytime, in
beds of reeds, or in the midst of dense thickets, it is
only by chance that one comes across them, even in
parts of the country where, from hearing their voices
at nights, and constantly seeing their spoor, there can
be no doubt that they are plentiful. All the Dutch
hunters in the interior, as well as many Europeans,
who pretend to higher scientific attainments, say that
there are at least three distinct species of lions in
South Africa ; while some assert that there are four
or even five. Their distinctions are all based upon
the length and colour of the mane, the general colour

of the coat, the spots on the feet, and the comparative
size of the animals.   For my part, and judging from
my own very limited experience of lions, I cannot see
that there is any reason for supposing that more than
one species exists, and as out of fifty male lion skins
scarcely two will be found exactly alike in the colour
and length of the mane, I think it would be as reasonable to suppose that there are twenty species as three.
The fact is, that between the animal with hardly a
vestige of a mane, and the far handsomer but much
less common beast with a long flowing black mane,
every possible intermediate variety may be found.
This I say emphatically, after having seen a great
many skins, and I entirely deny that three well-
marked and constant varieties exist.   On June 6,
1879, I came across two fine old male lions on the
Mababe flat, lying together under the same bush,
and shot them both.   One was a full-maned lion with
a very dark-coloured skin, the other a very light-
coloured animal with scarcely any mane at all.   In
size they were as nearly as possible equal, the skins,
when pegged out, measuring 10 feet 10 inches and 10
feet 9 inches respectively.   A few months afterwards
Mr. H. C. Collison and myself again came across
two lions, the one dark-coloured, with a full, blackish
mane, the other a yellow-looking animal with but
little mane.   A day or two later we shot two lionesses.   The one killed by my friend carried in her
womb three cubs (two males and a female) that
would probably have seen the light a few hours later.
Of the two male cubs the one, owing to the dark
colour of the tips of the hairs, was almost black,
whilst the other was reddish yellow.   The skin of
the female cub was also of a light colour.   Now, I
firmly believe that the two male cubs would have

grown up, the one into a dark-skinned, black-maned lion, the other into a yellow lion with but little mane ; and further than this, I believe that the two pairs of males I have mentioned above were cubs of the same litters, and had been hunting in company since their cubhood. This is only surmise, but the Bushmen bore me out in my opinion, saying, when I told them what I thought, " Yes, that is true ; we knew them well ; they are children of one mother." How to account for the variation in the length and colour of the mane in different individual lions I do not know. The theory, that it depends upon the density and thorniness of the jungles they inhabit, which pulls out and destroys their manes to a greater or lesser extent, I do not consider tenable, as on the high open plateaus of the Matabele and Mashuna countries, where scarcely a thorn-bush is to be seen, lions of every variety as regards length and colour of mane are to be found, and the same variations also occur amongst those found in the neighbourhood of the Tati, where the country is for the most part covered with thick thorny jungles. I have never seen the skin of a wild lion with a mane equal in length to that attained by the greater part of the lions one sees in menageries. All wild lions with a full mane have two small tufts of hair, one on the elbow, and the other in the armpit ; but I never yet saw one with any long hair along the belly, between the forearm and the flank, as may be seen in almost all menagerie lions in this country. I do not say that cases do not occur of wild lions becoming equally hairy, but they must be very rare, otherwise I should have met with some amongst the large number of skins I have seen. The coat of the wild lion is very short and close, whilst that of lions kept in this country becomes very much

longer, and usually of a redder colour than the pale
yellow or silvery-grey hue of the wild animal.   I
could pick out the skin of a menagerie lion from
amongst a hundred wild ones.   Climate and regular
feeding must, I think, have a good deal to do with
the luxuriant growth of mane almost invariably to be
observed in lions in confinement.   If these causes are
not sufficient to account for the great difference which
undoubtedly exists between the ordinary wild lion of
Africa and his caged relative, I do not know what
other suggestion to offer.   Nothing can be more
disappointing to the youthful sportsman, fresh from
England, and accustomed to the full flowing manes of
the lions in the gardens of the Zoological Society, or
the representations of the wild animal to be seen in
works on natural history or picture books, than to
shoot him in his native haunts, and find him almost
destitute of mane, for, after all, what is a lion without
a mane but the shadow of the noble beast one has
mentally pictured to oneself?   As regards the size of
the South African lion, the following are the lengths
of the pegged-out skins of six full-grown males shot
by myself, and carefully measured with a tape-line :—
viz. 10 feet 3 inches, 10 feet 6 inches, 10 feet 9 inches,
10 feet 10 inches, 9 feet 7 inches, and 11 feet 1 inch.
These are the lengths of the skins after having been
pegged out and stretched to a certain extent.   However, after having flayed it, I carefully measured the
naked carcase of the largest lion.   From the top
of the front teeth to the end of the tail it measured
9 feet 7 inches, laying the tape along the curves of the
body, and as all the gristle and meat of the nose had
been cut away with the skin, and at least an inch
must have been lost with the tuft at the end of the
tail, I think it would have measured all but 10 feet

before it was skinned, even without making any allowance for the mane. A lion shot one night in the cattle-kraal at Tati by Messrs. Brown and Doby in 1877, by the light of a lantern, weighed 376 lbs. My friend Brown told me that although it was a large lion it was in very low condition. The pegged-out skins of nine lionesses shot by myself measured from 8 feet 10 inches to 9 feet 7 inches.

It has always appeared to me that the word "majestic" is singularly inapplicable to the lion in its wild state, as when seen by daylight he always has a stealthy, furtive look that entirely does away with the idea of majesty. To look majestic a lion should hold his head high. This he seldom does. When walking he holds it low, lower than the line of his back, and it is only when he first becomes aware of the presence of man that he sometimes raises his head and takes a look at the intruder, usually lowering it immediately, and trotting away with a growl. When at bay, standing with open mouth and glaring eyes, holding his head low between his shoulders, and keeping up a continuous low growling, twitching his tail the while from side to side, no animal can look more unpleasant than a lion ; but there is even then nothing majestic or noble in his appearance. When a lion jerks his tail two or three times in quick succession straight into the air, look out, for such a demonstration is almost always followed by a charge, though this preliminary is not always gone through before charging. From my own observation, I should say that lionesses usually give birth to three cubs ; but, from some cause or other, many appear to die when very young. In the interior of South Africa one more commonly meets with four or five lions consorting together than with single animals, parties of ten or twelve being not uncommon.

A party of twelve lions would probably consist of say two males, three or four full-grown females, and half a dozen large cubs, which, except that they are slighter built, would appear, if not very closely looked at, to be almost as large as full-grown lionesses. In July 1880 I came one day upon a lion, three full-grown lionesses, and three small cubs. Now, if each of these lionesses had had a couple of large cubs, the whole party would have formed what one would be justified in talking of as a troop of ten lions. As to the character of the lion, I myself consider him to be a far more dangerous animal to meddle with than any other in South Africa. However, I write this under correction, as I have only killed sixteen lions to my own rifle, which is not a sufficient number upon which to base one's verdict as to the general disposition of an animal. That more accidents have happened in encounters with buffaloes than with lions is not that the former is a more dangerous animal than the latter, but because, for every lion that has been killed in the interior (within my own experience at any rate), at least fifty buffaloes have been brought to bag. Hunting lions with dogs usually reduces the danger to a minimum, as the beast's attention is, as a general rule, so occupied with the yelping pack that surrounds him, that he pays no attention to his more formidable enemies ; it sometimes happens, however, that he dashes straight through the dogs at his human adversary. If mounted, too, the hunter's skin is often saved by the fleetness of his horse ; for, except in forest which is too thick to allow one to gallop at full speed, or where the soil is deep, soft sand, I do not think an average lion can overtake an average horse. If on foot, however, and without dogs, though there is little danger in attacking lions, in the first instance, yet to follow up a wounded one is very ticklish work, especially in long grass or thick cover, for there is probably no animal of its size in the world that can conceal itself behind so slight a screen, or rush upon its pursuer with such lightning-like rapidity. I have never seen a lion bound ; they always appeared to me to come along like a dog at a clumsy-looking gallop, though they get over the ground at a great pace. From what I have seen, I do not think that lions have any fixed way of killing game, but believe they employ different tactics against different animals. I have seen a horse, a young elephant, a sable and a roan antelope, killed by a bite in the throat, which must have caused death either by dividing the jugular vein or by strangulation. I have seen, too, a horse and several zebras killed by bites on the back of the neck behind the head. Buffaloes are, I fancy, sometimes killed by dislocation of the neck, which is done by the lion springing on to their shoulders and then seizing their noses with one paw, giving the neck a sudden wrench. I have seen and shot numbers of buffaloes that, after having been terribly bitten and scratched by lions about the neck and on the tops of the shoulder-blades, have finally made their escape. I have never met with an instance of a lion carrying an animal that it has killed ; and, as far as I know, their invariable practice is to drag the carcase along the ground, holding it the while by the back of the neck. This they do with even the smallest antelopes, such as the impala, and I do not think that a South African lion would be capable of lifting such a heavy beast as a bullock from the ground, as the North African species is said to do, much less of springing over a high fence with one. The fact that one does not hear of regular man-eating lions, that for a long period have been constantly in the habit of preying upon human beings, as is the case with tigers in India, is due, I fancy, not to the difference in the nature of the animals, but to the superior boldness of the African natives over those of India, for even amongst the least martial tribes of South Africa, if two or three people are killed by a lion, the population of the surrounding country is roused, and a party being formed, the lion is usually surrounded and stabbed to death with assegais ; whilst, amongst such warlike tribes as the Matabele, if a lion only kills an ox, or even a goat, its fate is usually sealed, or even if not killed, it gets such a scare that it is glad to quit the district. Such a thing as a man-eater, or even an habitual cattle-slayer, would never be tolerated for an instant. Nevertheless, many natives are killed every year in those parts of the country where lions are plentiful. In 1875, five lions came up the Inquisi river, and killed four Matabele women working in their maize-fields not far from the town. The next day the whole male population turned out, and following up the lions killed four of them, one making good its escape. In 1876, a Kafir boy who was herding my friend Mr. Brown's goats at Tati was seized, killed, and eaten by a lioness, as he was returning home with his charge one afternoon, and when only a few hundred yards from and within sight of the houses. The next day my friend and all the whites who were then at Tati turned out and hunted up the lioness. She was found close to where she had killed the boy, and shot by Hendrick Viljoen (a son of old Jan Viljoen). The teeth of this lioness were worn down to mere stumps, and there is no doubt that the infirmities of old age, and the lack of strength requisite to catch and kill wild animals, had driven her to attack a human being.

In 1879, another case occurred at Tati of a man being killed by a lion, which I will here relate as I heard it from my friends Messrs. Brown and Phillips. A young Matabele warrior belonging to the Imbezo regiment having fled from the harsh rule of Lobengula, was on his way to join Kuruman, a chief living in the Rustenburg district of the Transvaal, and claiming to be the eldest son of Umziligazi, and the true heir to the Matabele throne. He was accompanied in his flight by the girl of his choice, who was, like himself, a true Matabele of pure Zulu blood. Upon reaching Tati, he did not go to the houses, as he feared to meet other Matabele, who might recognise him as a fugitive, but crossed the river which runs below them at a distance of about 200 yards. In the evening, leaving the girl concealed amongst the bushes on the farther bank of the river, he went and explained his circumstances to Mr. Brown, who gave him some food. It happened that my friend was upon the point of making a journey to the Transvaal, and had his waggon ready loaded up for an early start the following morning. Seeing this, the fugitive begged to be allowed to accompany him as far as Bamangwato, and his request being granted, he tied his shield on to the waggon, and saying he would join my friend the following morning along the road, recrossed the river. About midnight the half-dozen white men who were then at Tati were awakened by loud shrieks and wails of "Mai-māmo! mai-māmo!" (The lion has taken my man! the lion has killed my man!) Rushing out to see what was the matter,

T

they found the poor girl, minus all the small amount of clothing which usually formed her full dress, sobbing and wailing pitifully. Her story was this—" When my man returned with the food and pot which the white men gave him, we made a small fire and cooked and ate it, and then lay down to sleep in the shelter of a bush. We had only a very small fire, as we were afraid to make a larger one for fear of attracting attention. I was cold and did not sleep, but my man slept. When the night was very black I saw an animal prowling round us. Starting up, I shook my man, crying out, 'Awake! awake! here is a hyæna.' At the same instant the beast rushed upon us, and seizing my man by the head, dragged him away. I still thought it was a hyæna, and seizing my man's knobkerry, rushed after him into the darkness. My man never cried out nor spoke. When I was close upon the beast that I still thought was a hyæna, I saw by its size and the long hair on its head and shoulders that it was a lion. Then my heart died, and I did not strike it, but, dropping the knobkerry, ran through the river and up to the white men's houses ; and it was only when I got close to them that I was able to cry out." The next morning Messrs. Brown, Phillips, Walsh, Dr. Bradshaw, and a few Boers that were there, followed up the lion, and shot it close to the remains of the unfortunate man. The bereaved girl returned to her friends in the Matabele country, and last year I heard that one of the king's brothers had taken her to wife. A popular error concerning the lion is that it is a very clean feeder, and never eats the flesh of any animal that it has not killed itself. The South African lion is often a very foul feeder, and according to my experience, prefers eating game that has been killed by

man, to taking the trouble of catching an animal for
itself.   Often when elephants have been shot, lions
will prey upon the stinking carcases as they lie festering in the rays of a tropical sun and at last become
a seething mass of maggots, returning night after
night to the feast, until no more meat is left.   This
occurs in parts of the country abounding in game,
where it would give a party of lions but little trouble
or exertion to catch a zebra, buffalo, or antelope, and
procure themselves a meal of fresh meat.   In the
same way, no matter how plentiful game may be,
lions will almost invariably feast upon any dead animal
left by the hunter, from a buffalo to a steinbuck, that
they happen to come across.   In eating the carcase
of a large animal, lions always either tear open the
belly near the navel and first eat the entrails, liver,
etc., or else commence near the anus and eat the
meat of the hind-quarters.   They often pull out the
entrails, and rolling them into a heap near the carcase,
cover them over with earth and sand, no doubt for
the purpose of preserving them from the vultures,
which they know will visit the carcase during the daytime.   At night they return and unearth and eat the
dinner they have taken such pains to preserve.   I
suspect that this is only done in places where lions
are liable to be interfered with by man, and do not
dare to lie during the day close to their kill, as is
their usual custom ; but I have met with instances of
it on three different occasions.   When lions are met
with in the daytime they almost invariably retreat
before the presence of man, even when disturbed at
the carcase of an animal which they have just killed,
and when they are presumably hungry.   If pursued
or wounded, however, they may be expected to
charge, and, *ceteris paribus*, I have found in my small

experience that a far larger proportion of them do charge than of any other animal in Southern Africa with which I am acquainted ; and as their powers of concealing themselves, and their quickness and agility in attack, are far greater than in the elephant, buffalo, or rhinoceros, I pronounce them to be more dangerous animals to meddle with than any of these. As with men and all other animals, individual lions differ so much in disposition one from another that it is impossible to tell from one's experience of one what the next is likely to do, and I do not consider that any man has a right to say that lions are cowardly beasts, because the two or three that he has shot have not happened to show fight, but have perhaps exhibited great pusillanimity. At night, and when urged on by hunger, lions are sometimes incredibly daring ; in fact, as old Jan Viljoen once said to me, " A hungry lion is a true devil, and fears nothing in this world." In illustration of the audacity and perseverance sometimes displayed by lions when desperate from hunger, I will give a short account of some incidents that occurred at our camp near the Umfule river on the nights of June 30 and July 1, 1880.

Having formed a camp on the banks of a small stream, a tributary of the Umfule river, Messrs. Jameson, Collison, and myself went away on the 30th of June to the north-east in search of elephants, leaving Dr. Crook, a gentleman who had accompanied Mr. Jameson from the Diamond Fields, and who was not a very ardent sportsman, in charge of the encampment. Besides Dr. Crook, there remained at the waggons a young colonist, Ruthven by name, in Mr. Jameson's employ, a lot of colonial coloured drivers who were going away hunting in the " fly " country on the following day, and at least twenty

Matabele Kafirs. The camp was arranged thus :—
In the centre stood our four waggons, parallel with
one another, enough space being allowed to admit of
the horses being tied between them. In front of the
waggons was our cattle-kraal, containing nearly sixty
oxen, made very high and strong ; whilst surrounding both the kraal and the waggons, and leaving the
latter standing in an open space about sixty yards in
diameter, was a second strong, high fence. At intervals round the inside of this fence, and of course
within the space, the different parties of Kafirs had
made their sleeping-places, each party keeping up one
or two fires, so that the whole camp must have presented a very animated appearance.

On the evening of the 8th of July we returned
home, and were surprised to find our camp deserted.
Riding into the enclosure we found a cross, and the
letters R. R. deeply cut on the stem of a tree that
grew on one side of the kraal, and at its foot a
newly-made grave. Full of conjecture as to what
these evidences of disaster might signify, we at once
galloped along the broad track left by our four
waggons, and half an hour later found them standing
on the bank of the Umfule itself, where Dr. Crook
had made a new encampment. In answer to our
inquiries we learned the following story. In the
dead of night of the very day on which we left the
waggons, every one was awakened by the shrieking
of Mr. Jameson's pet baboon, " Susan," that was
fastened just in front of one of the waggons, and at
the same time a horse was heard struggling between
the waggons. Ruthven and a Bamangwato boy
named Buckram rushed forwards to see what was the
matter, and found old " Jordan," one of Mr.
Jameson's horses, struggling in the clutches of a lion.

Upon their shouting and waving their blankets, the beast left the horse and made good its retreat in the darkness. Jordan, though badly bitten on the back of the neck just behind the head, and scratched about the throat, had not sustained any very material injury, but the wounds would not heal up, and eight months afterwards, when I last saw him, they were still sloughing. After this the fires were kept up, and nothing further occurred to disturb the peace. The following morning Dr. Crook found the hole in the fence through which the lioness had crept. Here he set two guns with strings tied on their triggers and brought across the gap in the fence in such a way that if the lioness were to return by the same path during the coming night she would in all probability shoot herself. When evening came, Ruthven and two colonial boys (waggon drivers) did not turn in, but sat up round a fire, hoping to get a shot at the lioness should she return and make an attack from another quarter. It was ten o'clock by the doctor's watch when old Umzobo, a Matabele man, who was in charge of my property whilst I was away hunting, and who was at that moment sitting by a fire along-side of my waggon, said to a young Kafir near him, "Blow up the fire, I hear something moving outside the fence." The boy was in the act of doing as he had been told, and the fire was just blazing up, when the lioness suddenly appeared in their midst and seized old Umzobo from in front by the leg, making her teeth meet behind the shin-bones. With great presence of mind, the old fellow forced his hands into her mouth one on each side, when she let go and seized Impewān, another Kafir of mine, by the fleshy part of the buttock, just as he was preparing to make tracks. Feeling an unpleasant sensation behind, he instinctively put his hand there, when the lioness, quitting her first hold, instantly seized it, and was dragging him away into the darkness, the poor fellow all the while shrieking with terror and agony, when Ruthven fired.   The shot frightened the lioness, and she released Impewān and disappeared in the darkness.   Immediately after Ruthven fired, two other shots fell in quick succession.   Dr. Crook, awakened by the growling of the lioness, the shrieking of the Kafirs, and the reports of the rifles, jumped out of the waggon and ran to see what had happened. At the fire where Ruthven had been sitting he found Norris, one of the coloured drivers, crying over a prostrate figure, which upon turning over he found to be poor young Ruthven with half his head blown off.   How this untoward accident happened will never be exactly known, but there is no doubt that it was owing to one or other of the drivers losing their wits at the sudden and alarming nature of the disturbance, and pulling off their guns at random. I think myself, that Ruthven must have been sitting down when he fired, and that he then stood up suddenly, bringing his head close to the muzzle of one of their guns.   He fell dead, poor fellow, with his head in the fire.   Having restored some sort of order amongst the panic-stricken Kafirs, dressed the wounds of those that had been bitten, and covered poor Ruthven's body with a blanket, Dr. Crook again turned in.   At twelve o'clock one of the set guns went off, but no other sound broke the stillness of the night.   At 2 A.M. the other gun went off, and the Kafirs all said they heard a low groan at the same time.   As may be imagined, no one slept during the remainder of this eventful night.   At daylight the doctor, hearing cries of " Gwasa ! Gwasa ! " (" Stab her! Stab her!"), went out and found that the lioness, that had thrice returned to the attack, had met her fate at last, and lay dead before the muzzle of the second gun, and just at the gap in the fence through which she had entered the encampment on the first night. The bullet had passed right through her heart. The first gun had not injured her, and could not have been properly set. This lioness was apparently in the prime of life, with a good coat and fine long teeth; she was, however, very thin, and had nothing in her stomach, and no doubt was desperate from hunger. The following day Dr. Crook buried poor Ruthven, and then moved the camp to the Umfule, where, as I have related, we found him. About a fortnight after these events had occurred, I myself had a very lucky encounter with a family of lions, which I do not think it will be out of place to relate here. Mr. Collison and myself were riding along one evening accompanied by a lot of Mashunas, a few miles to the eastward of the Hanyane river, when I espied an ostrich running parallel to our line of march at a distance of several hundred yards to our right. Thinking I might get a shot by cutting across the bird's course, I at once galloped in pursuit, leaving my friend with the Kafirs. After riding about a mile and a half at a stiff gallop, I eventually did get a long shot, but missed. Shortly after firing I heard another shot, which I subsequently found had been fired by my friend at an eland. I now rode slowly back towards where I had left the Kafirs, and just as I sighted them also came in sight of a small herd of tsessebe antelopes that were feeding down an open valley. As it was now very late in the afternoon, and time to think about making a camp, I thought I had better shoot one of these

animals for dinner, as there were both wood and
water near at hand. Riding up towards them, I
proceeded to carry out my designs. With my first
shot I struck one too far back, and thinking to lose
him, I fired at another that was standing broadside on about 250 yards off. This one I hit fair in
the shoulder, and he fell dead after running but a
short distance. The one I had first wounded was now
standing with its head down and mouth open looking
very sick, so I rode towards it, thinking I should be
able to secure it as well. When I had approached
to within 150 yards of it, however, it looked up, and
then galloped away as if there was nothing the
matter with it. Piqued at such conduct in a beast
that I had thought completely in my power, I at
once gave chase, but the harder I galloped the faster
the wounded tsessebe ran, till at last, in mercy to my
horse, that I felt was getting very tired, I pulled in,
fairly beaten, and rode slowly back towards where I
had left the Kafirs at least three miles away. As I
was thus riding listlessly along through rather an
open country, dotted all over with patches of forest
and bush of a few acres in extent, I saw a lion
suddenly emerge from a thicket to my left and
canter across the open, about 150 yards in front
of me, towards another patch of bush. One glance
at his heavy form showed me that he was a very
large animal, with a fine flowing black mane. To
gather up the reins and, putting spurs to my tired
nag, gallop as hard as I could to cut him off from
the bush, was the work of a second. However, he
reached the bush, which was not far distant, about
sixty yards in front of me, but instead of entering it,
faced round and stood looking at me. As I had
undone the rimpy that I always have, running from

a ring on the bridle, to my belt, to check a horse in case he wishes to bolt when I dismount, I did not like to get off, not feeling sure that the horse would stand, but pulling him broadside, fired from the saddle. As the horse was still panting from the effect of the gallop after the tsessebe antelope, I could not get a steady aim, and missed. The lion did not budge, but still stood in the same place, eyeing me attentively. Hastily pushing in another cartridge, I then sprang to the ground, resolving to take my chance as to whether the horse would stand, and make as sure as possible of my shot at the lion ; just as I raised my little rifle the grim-looking beast turned his head and glanced over his shoulder, an action which is said by old Dutch hunters to be a certain preliminary to a charge. However, a second later I fired, bringing him on to his head with his tail in the air, roaring tremendously. I then reloaded and mounted my good horse, that had stood motionless beside me all this time, unmoved either by the report of the rifle or the hoarse growling of the lion. His race was, however, run, for, after pushing himself along the ground for about twenty yards by a series of kicks from his hind legs, he rolled over on his side, a sure sign with a lion that he is dead or dying. Riding alongside of him, I dismounted and admired at my leisure one of the noblest prizes that have as yet fallen to my rifle. In dying this lion made a most terrific noise. He kept filling his lungs with air, and then emitting roars which might have been heard (and which the Kafirs did hear) miles away. He was an enormous brute—the largest I have yet killed, and had a beautiful sleek coat and a lovely mane, long and flowing, black on the shoulders, and bright yellow on the cheeks. The measurements

To face page 283.

ENCOUNTER WITH LIONS; MASHUNA LAND, JULY 16, 1880.

of his skin and carcase I have given in another place. I now halloed for the Kafirs, and at last saw two running towards me. Great was their surprise upon finding me standing over the body of a magnificent lion, instead of, as they had expected, a wretched tsessebe antelope. I was stooping over my prize, toying with the mane, when one of the boys, seizing me by the shoulder, cried excitedly, "Look, look, sir! look at the lions!" Hastily raising my eyes, and following the direction of his outstretched hand, a sight met my eyes that made my heart jump. At a distance of not more than 250 yards from where we stood, three great lionesses were stalking slowly across a little open glade, walking in single file, one behind another. At the heels of the hindmost ran three little cubs, not much bigger than cats. As the grass had been burnt off just here, I had a splendid view of their massive thick-set forms, but wasted no time in looking at them. Hastily mounting my horse, I cantered past behind them just as they entered a patch of bush. The sun was now down, so there was no time to lose, there being but a short allowance of twilight in these latitudes. I now walked my horse along within the bush parallel to the lions, which, although they were not sixty yards off, did not appear to notice me. The grass, however, not having been burnt off within the bush, was so long that I could only just see the outline of their backs. Soon the foremost lioness walked slowly over the sloping side of an enormous grass-covered ant-heap, exposing her massive shape well to my view. As I hastily dismounted she observed me, and turning her head stood looking at me, but without moving her body. The next moment I fired, and rolled her down the sloping ant-heap with her

legs and tail in the air. The other two now turned
their villainous greeny-yellow eyes upon me, and I
was afraid the one with the cubs was coming at me,
which would have been awkward, as my rifle was
only a single-barrelled one, and I should scarcely
have had time to reload. For a few seconds they
gazed towards me with lowered heads, then with a
loud purr and a sweep of their tails sprang away and
trotted off through the grass. By this time I was
again in the saddle with my rifle reloaded. I could
see the lioness I had just wounded still struggling in
the grass, and so rode towards her with every sense
on the alert. When I was about twenty yards from
her she righted herself, and, lying on her outstretched
paws, raised her head and looked fixedly at me, on
which I put a bullet into the centre of the white
patch in her throat, firing from the saddle. Her
head dropped at the shot, and I knew she was done
for. All this, which has taken some time to relate,
did not occupy many seconds. I now galloped
through the open bush in the direction taken by the
two remaining lionesses, and almost instantly saw one
close in front of me. At the same moment she saw
me, and facing round stepped a few paces towards
me, holding her head low, and twitching her tail
savagely from side to side. I felt positive she was
on the very point of charging, and so fired at her
from the saddle without losing an instant. I this
time made a very pretty shot—more by good luck,
doubtless, than anything else—striking her in the
very centre of the nose, half-way between the eyes
and the muzzle. From the position in which she
was holding her head, this shot smashed right into
the brain, and she fell all of a heap in her tracks.
Had I struck her between the eyes, the bullet would

in all probability have glanced from her skull. There now only remained the lioness with the three cubs, and her I could see nowhere, though I felt certain she was not far off. The light was getting so bad in the shade of the trees that I could scarcely see the sights of my rifle. I was standing at the foot of a large ant-heap, on the top of which grew a bush and a tree, so dismounting, I led the horse a little way up it (the ant-heap was at least thirty feet in diameter at the base), and looked all about me through the bush and long grass. I was beginning to feel rather lonely, for the gloom of the evening was fast deepening, and though I knew that two lions lay dead, I did not know exactly how near me the mother of the cubs might be. Suddenly I heard " yap, yap, yap," behind me, and looking round saw one of the little creatures emerge from the long grass and come trotting towards me. It came to within a yard of my horse's hind-legs and then trotted back again towards the grass, being met half-way by the other two, when all three of the little beasts stood together about ten yards from me.

From the moment I saw the first cub I had not moved, but stood straining my eyes in the direction from which it had come, to try and get a view of the lioness. My horse too had been standing like a statue. I now thought it time to move, for I reflected that as the cubs were so near, their mother was in all probability not far off. I was in the act of mounting, and just swinging my legs over the saddle, when with open, snarling mouth, and giving vent to a succession of grunts, out she came straight at me. She had, of course, been watching me, and interpreted my moving as a demonstration against the cubs. To whisk the horse round the

side of the ant-heap, and gallop off at right angles
to the direction from which the lioness had charged,
was a manœuvre which I executed with great despatch.
I think she only came as far as the ant-heap, and
then retreated into the grass again with her cubs, for
though I galloped but a very short distance, and
came round to the other side immediately, I did not
catch sight of her. Just at this moment Collison
came up with a lot of the Kafirs.

It was now, however, so dusk that it was useless
looking further for the lioness in the long yellow
grass, and so she escaped. Had there been another
hour of daylight, the chances would have been very
greatly in favour of my killing her. As it was,
however, I was well pleased, for I had bagged three
full-grown lions with four shots. The rifle I used
was a single 450 Express by George Gibbs of
Bristol. The cartridges were loaded with $3\frac{1}{2}$ drams
of powder, and hollow bullets. As it was too late
to skin all the lions, I left the two females where
they were, and then went and camped alongside of
the big male. Just before daylight a hyæna came
and ate the meat off the ribs and hind-quarters of
one of the lionesses, quite destroying the skin. The
other was untouched. They were both very fine and
large, and in splendid condition.

The meat of the lion is very palatable, being white
like veal, and quite free from any smell or taste.
In fact, when cooked, no one who did not know
could possibly guess from anything in its appearance
or flavour that it was the flesh of a very indiscriminate-
feeding carnivorous animal. Jameson, Collison, and
myself, having one day shot two lions, and having
no other meat, cooked a large pot of it, and ate it
with great relish.

In concluding my remarks upon South African lions, I will only say that I have found them to be far less tenacious of life than any of the antelope tribe in the same country, and more easily disabled. When shot through the heart or lungs they die far more quickly than even a small antelope would do with a similar wound.

No weapon, in my opinion, can be more suitable for lion-shooting than a good 450 Express (made by such makers as Gibbs or Rigby, for example), with the ordinary hollow bullet ; and those writers who class such a soft-skinned easily-killed beast in the same category as the elephant, and advocate large rifles for both, and those, again, who contend that because a lion can be killed without difficulty with an Express, it is therefore unsportsmanlike to use a heavier weapon for an elephant, appear to me to reason from false premisses. There is relatively as much difference between the tenacity of life in the lion and the elephant as there is between a snipe and a wild goose, and it would be just as expedient to use the same-sized bullet for the two former animals as the same-sized shot for the two birds.

CHAPTER XIV

EARLY in April 1877 I again reached Tati, and after riding to Gubulawayo, to pay a visit to Lobengula, at once started for the Zambesi.

On this trip I was accompanied by two white men, Mr. Kingsley, an Englishman, and Mr. Miller, a young colonist and a first-rate shot. They were shooting on halves for me, *i.e.* I paid all expenses and found them in everything, on the condition that half the ivory of the elephants they shot belonged to me. I had, besides, several native hunters in my service. As, however, during the whole season the only elephants killed were a very small cow and two calves shot by Miller—the ivory valuing less than £2—this trip was a dreadful failure, pecuniarily speaking, and very nearly ruined me, as, expecting to find plenty of elephants up the Chobe, I had arranged the hunt on a large scale. We all hunted separately, so as to cover more country, but, with the exception of the three shot by Miller, and a small herd encountered by Mr. Kingsley, when he failed to score, none of us had the luck to come across any elephants at all.

It may be remembered that when I started down country, my friends Messrs. Dorehill, Grandy, and Horner had accompanied Mr. Westbeech to the Zambesi, having resolved to take the risk of being knocked over by fever, which is very deadly in that country during the rainy season. Lieutenant Grandy, who had come out to get some provisions, etc., at Tati, intending to return immediately, I met just before leaving.

He looked but the shadow of his former stout jovial self, but seemed to have shaken off the fever from which he had been suffering, and be on a fair way to recovery; I was thus much surprised and shocked when, some two months later, I heard of his death, which occurred at the Makalaka kraals on his return to the Zambesi, very shortly after I last saw him.

Poor fellow! he was one of the kindest-hearted and most jovial souls I have ever met; his untimely death added one more to the long list of old friends whose bones lie beneath the inhospitable soil of the interior of South Africa.

At Gerua I met my old friend Dorehill, who then travelled in with me to the Chobe; and at Pandamatenka we met Mr. Horner. Both these gentlemen had suffered much from fever; in fact, Mr. Horner had only clung to life by the skin of his teeth, and when I saw him it was still a question whether he would be able to retain his hold. Eventually, however, I am happy to say, he did recover.

As the country in which I hunted from May till November was for the most part the same through which I had travelled in 1874, and was, moreover, very barren in interesting experiences, I will not weary my readers with any detailed account of it.

U

I never saw an elephant the whole time, and my principal victims were buffaloes, of which animals I shot, I think, forty-five during the four months I was on the Chobe. I experienced a few charges from these animals, and had one rather narrow escape, which, however, I will not inflict upon my readers.

Though the buffalo of Central South Africa when wounded will usually charge its pursuer if it sees him close at hand, yet, if he is at a distance of over fifty yards, it will only do so in exceptional cases. Although many accidents happen in the pursuit of these animals, yet, in my opinion, the danger incurred in hunting them is marvellously exaggerated. Having shot altogether nearly 200 buffaloes to my own rifle, and followed very many of them when wounded into very thick bush, I think I have had sufficient experience to express an opinion on the subject. I know of several instances where buffaloes have charged suddenly, and apparently in unprovoked ferocity, upon people who never even saw them until they were dashed, in many cases mortally wounded, to the ground; but I believe that, in at any rate the majority of cases, if the whole truth could be made known, these buffaloes would be found to have been previously wounded by some other hunter, and finding themselves suddenly confronted by another sportsman in the thicket or patch of long grass to which they had retired to brood over their injuries, at once rushed upon the intruder, perhaps more from the instinct of self-defence than anything else.

Mr. Henry Barber, a great friend of mine, was very nearly killed in 1877 in this way, by a buffalo he never saw until it rushed upon him, and threw him into the air, inflicting a fearful wound, from which it is a marvel that he ever recovered.

FOLLOWING A WOUNDED BUFFALO IN THICK BUSH.

Now, Mr. Drake, another English hunter, had been shooting buffaloes there the day before, and I think it more than probable that the animal which so nearly killed my friend was one that had been wounded on that occasion.

Another very similar case occurred to a young Boer, Petrus Potgieter, several years ago on the river Impaqui.   One morning old Petrus Jacobs, the well-known old elephant-hunter, had been shooting buffaloes along the river, and besides killing some had wounded others.   In the afternoon young Potgieter was pursuing a herd of giraffes over the same ground, when one of the wounded buffaloes, which was standing in a patch of bush near to which he passed, rushed out and dashed both him and his horse to the ground.   The infuriated animal then made a charge at him, and, catching its horn in his coat, tore one side of it off.   Before receiving any further hurts Potgieter made his escape into a mopani tree, and the buffalo retired.   The horse died of its injuries.

I myself once had a horse killed under me by a buffalo.   This occurred in May 1874, when for the first time journeying from Tati to the Zambesi. The following account of this misadventure I have transcribed from the diary which I wrote at the time.

On the 20th of May 1874, after crossing the dry sandy bed of the river Nata, I rode out in search of game, and when the sun was about an hour high struck the spoor of two old buffalo bulls, and after a severe chase at last sighted them, looking, with their short legs and huge round sterns almost devoid of hair, very like rhinoceroses.   I waited till we reached a tolerably open piece of ground, and then, reining up short, jumped off about thirty yards behind the nearest, and taking steady aim, pulled the trigger, but, instead of hearing the anticipated report and answering bellow of the buffalo, my ears were greeted with a sharp metallic click that at once told me there was no cap on the nipple. Thinking it had been brushed off by one of the bushes whilst galloping in pursuit, and not imagining that such a thing was likely to occur again, I hastily put another on, and, jumping on to my horse, soon made up the lost ground and once more neared the old bulls, one of which being considerably in the rear of the other, I determined to confine myself to him. Just then he crossed a little dry gully, and, on reaching the opposite side, turned for the first time and eyed me savagely from beneath his close-set, rugged-looking horns.

I had now pursued the old brute for a considerable time, and this, of course, had not much improved his temper (which in an old buffalo bull is not at the best of times of the sweetest), so, expecting a charge, did not dismount, but, reining in my horse, took a quick aim and pulled the trigger with just the same result as before. The buffalo, probably not liking the idea of charging through the gully, turned, and again resumed his flight. Putting on a third cap, I now kept it down with my thumb, and was soon once more close behind him, and had galloped for perhaps a couple of minutes more, when, entering a patch of short thick mopani bush, he stopped suddenly, wheeled round, and came on at once, as soon as he caught sight of the horse, with his nose stretched straight out and horns laid back, uttering the short grunts with which these animals invariably accompany a charge.

There was no time to be lost, as I was not more
than forty yards from him ; so, reining in with a
jerk and turning the horse at the same instant broadside on, I raised my gun, intending to put a ball, if
possible, just between his neck and shoulder, which,
could I have done so, would either have knocked him
down, or at any rate made him swerve, but my horse,
instead of standing steady as he had always done
before, now commenced walking forward, though he
did not appear to take any notice of the buffalo.
There was no time to put my hand down and give
another wrench on the bridle (which I had let fall on
the horse's neck), and for the life of me I could not
get a sight with the horse in motion.   A charging
buffalo does not take many seconds to cover forty
yards, and in another instant his outstretched nose was
within six feet of me, so, lowering the gun from my
shoulder, I pulled it off right in his face, at the same
time digging the spurs deep into my horse's sides.
But it was too late, for even as he sprang forward
the old bull caught him full in the flank, pitching
him, with me on his back, into the air like a dog.
The recoil of the heavily-charged elephant gun with
which I was unluckily shooting, twisted it clean out
of my hands, so that we all, horse, gun, and man, fell
in different directions.   My horse regained its feet
and galloped away immediately, but even with a
momentary glance, I saw that the poor brute's entrails
were protruding in a dreadful manner.   The buffalo,
on tossing the horse, had stopped dead, and now
stood with his head lowered within a few feet of me.
I had fallen in a sitting position, and facing my
unpleasant-looking adversary.   I could see no wound
on him, so must have missed, though I can scarcely
understand how, as he was so very close when I fired.

However, I had not much time for speculation, for
the old brute, after glaring at me a few seconds with
his sinister-looking, bloodshot eyes, finally made up
his mind, and, with a grunt, rushed at me.   I threw
my body out flat along the ground to one side, and
just avoided the upward thrust of his horn, receiving,
however, a severe blow on the left shoulder with the
round part of it ; nearly dislocating my right arm
with the force with which my elbow was driven
against the ground ; and receiving also a kick on the
instep from one of his feet.   Luckily for me, he did
not turn again, as he most certainly would have done
had he been wounded, but galloped clean away.

The first thing to be done was to look after my
horse, and at about 150 yards from where he had
been tossed, I found him.   The buffalo had struck
him full in the left thigh ; it was an awful wound,
and as the poor beast was evidently in the last
extremity, I hastily loaded my gun and put him out
of his misery.   My Kafirs coming up just then, I
started with them, eager for vengeance, in pursuit of
the buffalo, but was compelled finally to abandon the
chase, leaving my poor horse unavenged.

When buffaloes have not been thinned out, they
are usually found in herds of from 50 to 200 or 300
animals.   Old bulls are often found alone, but more
generally speaking in twos, threes, or fours.   Along
the Chobe I have seen as many as fifteen old buffalo
bulls consorting together, and upon several occasions
small herds of eight, nine, and ten old patriarchs.
These little herds of bulls are much more easy to
approach than a large herd of cows, amongst which
there are always a few wary animals on the look-
out for danger.   I have not found old buffalo bulls
more dangerous than herd animals.   Unless they are

To face page 294.

ADVENTURE WITH A BUFFALO; RIVER NATA, MAY 20, 1874.

wounded, they retreat, at any rate in the great majority of cases, before the presence of man ; and when wounded they are not more dangerous than herd animals under similar circumstances.

To my mind there is no more exciting sport than following into thick covert the blood spoor of a wounded buffalo. Step by step, with rifle advanced and on full cock, the hunter creeps forward with every sense on the alert, expecting at every instant to see the creature's dark, massive form. It is perfectly wonderful how difficult it is to distinguish the dusky black shape of a large animal when standing motionless in the gloom of dense bush. If, however, your eyes are trained to such work, so that you are pretty sure of spotting the buffalo, if not before, at any rate at the same moment that he sees you, the danger of the proceeding is much diminished, as these animals almost invariably stand at right angles to their spoor, and upon sighting their pursuer, first look at him and then swing themselves head on, before charging. This gives one just time, if cool and ready, to put a bullet into them between the neck and shoulder, which usually, if it does not floor them, makes them give up the idea of charging. When once started, however, a buffalo is a very difficult animal to stop.

Once, in 1874, when hunting with George Wood near the Chobe, we came upon an old buffalo bull lying down in some long grass. My friend gave him a bullet as he lay, upon which he jumped up and stood behind some mopani trees, only exposing his head and hind-quarters on either side their stems. After eyeing us for a few seconds, he turned and went off at a gallop, but before he had gone many yards Wood fired at him with his second gun and

knocked him over ; he was on his legs again in a
moment, and wheeling round came straight towards
me at a heavy gallop, his nose stretched straight out
and grunting furiously. When he was about twenty
yards from me, I fired with my large four-bore
elephant gun, and struck him fair in the chest.
This staggered but did not stop him, for, swerving
slightly, he made straight for the Kafir carrying my
second gun ; this the man at once threw down, and
commenced climbing a tree. The buffalo just brought
his right horn past the tree, and scraping it up the
trunk so as to send all the loose pieces of bark flying,
caught the Kafir a severe blow on the inside of the
knee, nearly knocking him out of the tree.   The
sturdy beast then ran about twenty yards farther,
knelt gently down, and stretching forth its nose
commenced to bellow, as these animals almost always
do when dying ; in a few minutes it was lying dead.

Buffaloes that have been wounded by lions are
usually, and not unnaturally, ill-tempered.   One
cold winter morning in 1873, I left my camp before
sunrise, and had not walked a quarter of a mile
skirting round the base of a low hill, when, close to
the same path I was following, and not twenty yards
off, I saw an old buffalo bull lying under a bush.
He was lying head on towards us, but did not appear
to notice us.   My gun-carriers were behind, having
lingered, Kafir-like, over the camp-fire, but had they
been nearer me I should not have fired for fear of
disturbing elephants, of which animals I was in
search.

As I stood looking at the buffalo, Minyama, one
of my Kafirs, threw an assegai at it from behind me,
which, grazing its side, just stuck in the skin on the
inside of its thigh.   Without more ado, the ugly-

looking old beast jumped up and came trotting out, with head up and nose extended, evidently looking for the disturbers of its peace, and as Minyama was hiding behind the trunk of a large tree, and the rest of the Kafirs had made themselves scarce, it at once came straight at me, grunting furiously. I was standing close to a very small tree, not more than six inches in diameter, but as I was unarmed, and to run would have been useless, I swarmed up it with marvellous celerity. The buffalo just came up and looked at me, holding his nose close to my feet, and grunting all the time. He then turned and went off at a lumbering canter, and I then, for the first time, saw that he had been terribly torn and scratched on the hind-quarters and shoulders by lions. Had he tried to knock my little sapling down, he might, I think, easily have accomplished it ; as it was, my legs being bare, and the bark of the tree very rough, I had rubbed a lot of skin off the insides of my knees and the calves of my legs.

All representations of South African buffaloes charging with their heads lowered are purely imaginary, as they never do so ; but on the contrary invariably hold their noses straight out, and lay their horns back over their shoulders. They lower their heads just as they strike.

As with all dangerous animals, it is impossible to judge by the speed with which buffaloes run away from you, of that which they are capable of exerting when the positions are reversed. Considering their heavy build they are marvellously swift, and even in the open, a fairly good horse will have to do all he knows to keep in front of one, while in bush, anything but a very quick animal stands a good chance of being overtaken. In 1873, a buffalo cow, although

very severely wounded, ran down in the open a horse
Lobengula had lent me, and on which my Hottentot
driver was mounted ; she struck the horse as it was
going at full speed between the thighs with her nose,
and, luckily, striking short, knocked it over on one
side, and sent its rider flying, but before she could
do further damage a bullet through her shoulders
from George Wood incapacitated her for further
mischief.

Buffalo calves are born in January, February, and
March, several months later than the calves of the
various species of antelopes living in the same country,
which are born from September to Christmas-time.

The largest buffalo horns I have myself brought
home, and which I think are about as large as one
is likely to get in the interior (though they are said
to attain to a greater size along the coast), measure
as follows :—Greatest spread measured in a straight
line from bend to bend, 3 feet 8 inches ; depth over
forehead, 1 foot 3 inches ; length of each horn along
the curve, 3 feet.   This buffalo was shot near
Linyanti on the Chobe.

2. Horns of buffalo bull shot near the river
Ramokwebani.   Greatest spread measured in a
straight line from bend to bend, 3 feet 6 inches ;
depth over forehead, 1 foot 5 inches ; length of each
horn along curve, 2 feet 11 inches.

3. Horns of buffalo cow shot near Linyanti, river
Chobe.   Greatest spread measured in a straight line
from outside bend, 3 feet 4 inches ; depth over
forehead, 7 inches ; length of each horn along curve,
2 feet 4 inches.

During the year 1877 I shot near Linyanti some
lovely specimens of that most exquisitely beautiful
little antelope, the Chobe bushbuck (*Tragelaphus*

To face page 299.

BUSHBUCKS FROM THE RIVER CHOBE.

An intermediate form between the Bushbuck of South Africa (*Tragelaphus sylvaticus*) and the Harnessed Antelope of North-Western Africa (*Tragelaphus scriptus*).

sylvaticus or *scriptus*).   Two of these specimens are now in the collection of the British Museum, in a very good state of preservation.

This lovely little creature is not only in itself one of the most beautiful of South African antelopes, but is of considerable interest from a scientific point of view, as it forms a connecting link between the dark-coloured bushbuck of the Cape Colony (*Tragelaphus sylvaticus*) and the smaller but more beautifully-marked harnessed antelope (*Tragelaphus scriptus*) of North-Western Africa.   As, between the Chobe bushbuck and the Cape bushbuck, many intermediate forms occur in different localities, more or less striped and spotted, some specimens of which I laid before the Zoological Society on June 21, 1881, I think it only reasonable to suppose that intermediate stages might also be found between the bushbuck found on the Chobe and the harnessed antelope, and have little doubt that further investigation will show that the Cape bushbuck and the harnessed antelope are specifically identical, and merely local varieties of the same animal.   In October I returned to my waggons at Daka, very much disgusted at my want of luck with the elephants.   However, I determined not to give up the game yet, but, instead of going out, as usual, to spend the unhealthy season in the uplands of the Matabele country, to cross the Zambesi and seek fresh hunting-grounds in the unknown countries to the north of that river.

With this intention I sent my waggons out to Tati in charge of Miller, and keeping four donkeys to carry my baggage, and my Basuto servant Franz to look after them, was ready to start on my journey of discovery towards the end of the month, just as the rainy season was commencing.

On this expedition I was accompanied by Mr. L. M. Owen, a gentleman well known in the colonies as a splendid rider and a very daring leader of volunteers in many of the Kafir wars.

He had come in on a shooting excursion to the Zambesi, and I had met him for the first time some two months previously on the banks of the Chobe. Unfortunately we did not hit it off very well together, as much through my fault, no doubt, as his, owing to what I may call incompatibility of temper.

HORNS OF BUFFALO BULL.
Shot on the banks of the Ramokwebani river.
Scale 1 inch to the foot.

HORNS OF BUFFALO COW.
Shot near Linyanti, on the river Chobe.
Scale 1 inch to the foot.

CHAPTER XV

On October 30, eight days after leaving Pandama-tenka, we crossed the Zambesi at Wankie's Town, swimming the donkeys through the river at the tail of a canoe without much difficulty. At this time of year the heat in the Zambesi valley is intense, and very enervating and oppressive. On November 3 the thermometer marked 87° at day-dawn, the coolest time in the whole twenty-four hours. At mid-day, in the shade of very thick-foliaged trees, with a breeze blowing beneath, it ranged from 103° to 110° as long as we were on the river.

November 6th.—Reached Mwemba's kraal about 9 A.M. He is supposed to be the biggest man amongst the Batongas. He told us we were the first white men he had ever seen, and was also very much surprised and pleased at the sight of the donkeys. Many of the Batonga men in this part of the country go perfectly naked, without the slightest vestige of cloth or skin about them. Two days before reaching Mwemba's, Owen shot a lioness. I fired at her first but missed her most disgracefully, though I was very close to her. She was in the last stage of emaciation from old age and want of food, and would, I think, have died a natural death in the course of a few days. She was nothing but a bag of bones covered with a mangy old skin, and her teeth were worn down to the gums.

November 13*th.*—Reached the river Chaiza, near which there are several Batonga kraals. On an island near here, Lorenço Monteiro, a half-caste Portuguese trader, has established himself, with a large following of Shakundas. From him we got reliable information about the road, and he also got us two guides to Nhaucoé, the nearest Portuguese trading station. In the afternoon there was a row at the next kraal between the Batongas and some Shakundas, one of whom had ill-treated a Batonga woman. The Batongas demanded payment ; the Shakundas refused, and fired upon them, but without doing any damage. The Batongas then came on with their assegais, killing one Shakunda and wounding another.

November 14*th.*—A deputation of Batongas came up to demand the life of the Shakunda they had wounded yesterday ; they were only armed with assegais and shields of ox and buffalo hides. On their arrival they all squatted under a tree close to our encampment. The Shakundas must, however, have foreseen this, and collected all their men from the surrounding kraals during the night, as they came over in force, most of them armed with flint-lock muskets, and a few with bows and arrows, and after a good deal of talking, the Batongas resigned their claim and returned to their kraal.

November 15*th.*—Got rid of our Kafirs from Wankie's.

November 16*th.*—After a good deal of trouble, got five Shakundas to go with us to Nhaucoé, three on land, and the other two, with some of our traps, in the canoe. At last, about 2 P.M., we once more made a start, and, thinking that anxiety and trouble were over for a time at least, I stepped along with a lighter heart than I had had for many days. Fortune, however, seemed still unpropitious, for we had not proceeded far before meeting a large army of Batongas, fully three hundred strong. At this juncture, one of our Shakundas, and most of our own Kafirs, became invisible ; so we ourselves drove the donkeys along, and went up to where the foremost Batongas were commencing to assemble under a large tree, to have a parley with them. If they are to be believed, they have suffered grievous wrongs at the hands of the Shakundas, who, as they assert, have been in the habit of murdering them, ill-using and kidnapping their women and children, burning their corn, stealing their goats, etc. They further said that, hearing that two Englishmen were at Chaiza, they had come to ask our intervention and assistance to conclude a final peace with Monteiro and his people, and therefore begged us once more to go back with them. This wish, which under the circumstances was tantamount to a command, we very unwillingly complied with. On reaching our camp it was too late to enter into any negotiations with the Portuguese that day, though I sent my Basuto servant over to the island to apprise him of the expressed wishes and intentions of the Batongas. According to him, all the fault lies on their side, and he accuses them of having treacherously murdered several of his people, and otherwise interfered with Portuguese trade. The night was cloudy and overcast, and a little rain fell. Though the Batonga army was encamped all around us, they were very orderly, and gave us no trouble whatever. During the night the Shakundas on the island beat their war drum and bade defiance to their enemies, who only listened to them in sullen silence.

November 17*th.*—The Batongas now talked no more of peace, but declared they would drive Monteiro and his followers off the island. Small bands of ten or a dozen kept continually coming in from the surrounding kraals, all decked out in war costume. Some of them were, with their large feather-dresses, as ferocious-looking savages as I have seen, and, barring the head-dresses, about half of them were perfectly stark naked. There was only one gun, an old Portuguese flint-lock, in the entire Batonga army; but they were very rich in assegais, none carrying less than four, and many of them eight, of these weapons. About 10 A.M. the Shakundas were reinforced by about thirty of their people from up the river, who came down to the island in ten canoes. The big war drum was then beaten with more vigour than ever, and all sorts of warlike and defiant antics gone through in sight of the Batongas, who sat squatted in bands under different trees, listening to orations from their different leaders, which, to judge from the violence of the gesticulations, must have breathed nothing but blood, slaughter, and vengeance. For about four hours this sort of thing continued; but, as there were 500 yards of blue water between the contending parties, and both seemed afraid to act on the offensive, it looked as if the whole thing would end in smoke. At last, about 2 P.M., two Shakundas came across from the island in a

canoe, and, after about an hour's conference with
the Batongas, came up to our hut, and told us that
everything was settled. How, I do not know,
unless it was owing to the arrival of a Portuguese
trader from Nhaucoé with a strong detachment of
Shakundas, all armed with guns, which had taken
place during, or just prior to, the conference. In
the evening, the Batongas retired to their several
kraals, blowing what seemed to be shrill notes of
defiance upon their reed trumpets. Later on, I
went across to the island to see the newly-arrived
Portuguese. He was a small, sallow, dried-up-looking
specimen of humanity, Samoés by name. He had
with him several girls, whom he wanted to sell for
ivory.

November 18*th*.—Still detained here for want of
carriers. Bought a canoe for three and a half
fathoms of cloth ; sent messengers to the Chief of
the Batongas, asking for carriers and guides to
Nhaucoé. In the evening our messengers returned,
bringing seven Batonga carriers sent by the Enduna
to help us on. The entire clothing worn by four
of these men consisted of eight porcupine quills
stuck through holes in their ears. In the evening
bought a second canoe for two cotton sheets, a yard
of limbo, and half a pound of beads.

November 19*th*.—Packed up the donkeys, the
canoes, and the carriers, and once more made a start
for Nhaucoé. Saw some hippopotami in the river,
and several fine flights of Egyptian and spur-winged
geese in the course of the morning. About four
in the afternoon we reached some Batonga kraals,
from one of which a fellow emerged carrying a huge
musical (or, rather, unmusical) instrument. The
dreadful contrivance consisted of a few flat pieces

x

of hard wood laid across calabashes of different sizes. The whole affair was suspended in front of the musician by a strap which passed over his shoulders, and was fully as large as a street organ. The flat pieces of wood when struck emitted a hollow, deafening, and altogether most diabolical noise, which one could hardly believe that even a Zambesi Kafir could be brought to consider in any way musical. This musician was accompanied by two accomplices, one of whom beat upon a hollow buffalo horn with a stick, and the other merely rapped two pieces of wood one against the other, all three of them going through a sort of slow dancing step, and howling a dismal sort of chant (a few words reiterated over and over again) in time to the music. This band accompanied us to our sleeping-place, and serenaded us in the most persevering manner. About nine o'clock, however, a heavy rain came down, which rather damped their ardour.

November 20*th.*—Before daylight in the morning the Batonga band again struck up, and played without cessation until we struck our camp. Soon after starting I shot two waterbucks ; and Owen, who was in one of the canoes, shot a large crocodile, measuring thirteen feet long. In the evening I went after two hippopotami that were disporting themselves in the river just opposite to the spot which we had selected for our camp ; but the narrow, crank canoe was so unsteady that I could not shoot with any accuracy. One of them came up about 150 yards away, and then, opening its huge jaws to the fullest extent, sprang half out of the water, and threw itself over sideways.

November 21*st.*—Reached Sambwero's, where we breakfasted. We passed a great many Batonga

kraals, deserted by their owners, who had been
driven across the river during the late raid made
upon them under Portuguese authority.   Many of
the huts and corn-bins had been burnt.   At this
place there stands on the bank of the river a square
house, with two compartments, having a verandah
all round it, which we afterwards learned had been
built about two years previously by a Portuguese
trader.   In the afternoon we continued our journey,
and that evening slept near some Batonga kraals
that had been burnt by the Shakundas.   Just at
sundown about fifty Kafirs came down to our camp,
each of them carrying from four to eight assegais.
The Enduna told us that all their towns and corn-
bins had been burnt, they themselves shot down,
and their women and children killed or carried off
into slavery by the Shakundas in the service of
Portuguese during the late raid.   They now appeared
to be living in the bush, with the remnants of their
flocks and herds, the best way they could.   He gave
us two goats, saying he was very pleased to see
Englishmen again, as he knew them to be men who
did not trouble people like the Portuguese.   From
the description he gave us of the last three Englishmen he had seen, they must have been Dr. Livingstone,
Charles Livingstone, and Dr. Kirk.   When we asked
him if he had ever seen donkeys before, he said,
" Yes ; they had had one with them."

November 22*nd.*—Early in the morning a man
came down and presented us with another goat.   In
the course of the forenoon we passed through a
great many villages, all burned off during the raid ;
and at the little river Lufua we found a large party
of Kafirs, who seemed to have returned to the ruins
of their homes to brood over their misfortunes.

They repeated the same tale of women killed and carried off, corn burned, etc., which we had heard before, and, to illustrate the way in which they had been shot down, one of them laid a lot of twigs one across another in a heap, each twig representing a dead man. In the afternoon we passed through a lot more burnt villages and found the remains of two Batongas (a man and a woman) lying in the footpath. Many bodies had been dragged into the neighbouring bush by the hyænas, and the stench was often offensive as we walked along the bank. In the evening we reached some Banyai kraals that had also been burnt and plundered.

November 23*rd.*—Passed through a country that must have been thickly populàted by Banyai before the late raid. Now, however, most of the towns were deserted, and we saw nothing but old women, the young ones having all been carried off into slavery. As we passed along, the people turned out *en masse*, and accompanied us, clapping their hands, dancing, and the women making a peculiar shrill quavering cry, which was taken up from kraal to kraal, and from hill to hill, on both sides of the river. They evidently thought us representatives of a people who differed altogether in thought, sentiment, and action from the Portuguese, as they overloaded us with praises, calling us "children of the Almighty," and the "people who did not kill or plunder." In the evening we reached Mamba. A few miles below this, the river Sanyati empties itself into the Zambesi from the south, just at the western entrance to Kariba Gorge. Thanks to the rain, which had cooled the ground, the last four nights had been less oppressive than any we had had since leaving Wankie's. The women were here very demonstrative in welcoming us, though what they imagined two Englishmen were going to do for them I cannot conceive. Some of them prostrated themselves before us, and rolled about in the dust. In the course of the day we saw several herds of hippopotami.

November 24th.—In the morning I went down to look at the mouth of the Sanyati river, about six or eight miles off. The bed of the Sanyati is one mass of huge boulders of rock, and about 150 yards broad; but when I saw it, which was certainly at the end of a remarkably dry season, there was but a mere driblet of water running into the Zambesi; but I can easily understand that after heavy rains it may be transformed into a roaring, seething torrent. The breadth of the Zambesi, where it runs through the narrow gorge of Kariba, in many places cannot be more than sixty yards— narrower than at any other place I had yet seen. It seemed to have worn a deep channel through the hard rock, through which it rushed with a strong current, full of whirlpools and eddies. From the high-water marks, I should think that when in flood the Zambesi must here rise quite twenty feet above its lowest level, and its breadth would then be over 200 yards. To prove the narrowness of the river, I threw stones across it in many places, some of which fell a considerable distance on the farther side, though I had to throw without a run, and balancing myself on the tops of rocks.

November 25th.—To avoid the hills of Kariba, we left the river here, and took a path which passed at the back of them, through dry, desolate-looking mopani forests. About 11 A.M. we reached a pit dug by the natives, where we obtained enough water for ourselves and retinue. In the evening we went on to some Banyai kraals (headman Matua), having passed a great deal of eland spoor on the way. The only water here was in a deep pit dug by the Kafirs. About half an hour before sundown I went out with my rifle to look for koodoos, of which animals the Kafirs said there were some about. The sun was down, and twilight fast fading into dusk, when I came across a troop of eland cows. They saw me and ran ; but, following on, they turned to look at me, and one gave me a good chance. Though I could scarcely see the sight of my rifle, I gave her a good shot in the shoulder, on receiving which she only ran 100 yards or so, and fell dead. She was a perfect picture of an animal—a good deal smaller, I thought, than the elands I had shot to the south of the Zambesi, of a light red colour, fading into a creamy yellow shade, with nine very plainly marked white stripes on each side, and a very black line all down the centre of the back and tail. The black patches on the inside of the forelegs were also very large and black.

November 26*th.*—Reached the Zambesi again in the evening, just beyond Kariba Gorge. Saw several herds of game during the afternoon's march— koodoos, zebra, water–buck, and impala. The weather was still intensely hot, both day and night ; and, being damp and sultry, the heat was very oppressive. During the past week the thermometer had ranged from 103° to 110° in very dense shade, during the heat of the day, and never gone below 80° all night. Just before day-dawn the other morning it registered 87°.

November 27*th.*—Only made a very short day's journey, as the bush, being very thick, was difficult to travel through with the donkeys. Saw great numbers of hippopotami during the day, there being often two or three large herds of from fifteen to twenty in the course of a mile. Slept at the mouth of a small sand river, the Umtolanyange. A large troop of lions must have caught a head of game on the southern bank of the river, as they kept roaring in the same spot half the night.

November 28*th.*—Crossed the Losito river, and about 10 A.M. reached Nhaucoé at last.

November 29*th.*—In the afternoon, after a good deal of trouble with the Shakundas—who will do nothing for nothing, and uncommonly little for sixpence—we crossed the river, and a walk of seven or eight miles brought us opposite a little island (Cassoko), on which resides a Portuguese trader, Senhor Joaquim Mendonça. My boy Franz took the donkeys, and followed along the northern bank. We were now out of the Batongas, the aboriginal inhabitants of the country, and amongst the Shakundas, who are all freed slaves, or runaway slaves, of Portuguese from the countries near the mouth of the Zambesi. The most of them possess flint-lock muskets, and here they owed allegiance to Canyemba, a black man, who held some sort of official position under the Portuguese governor of Tete. Nearly all these fellows had been engaged in the late raid upon the Batongas. Whilst they were away from Nhaucoé, a party of Batongas came round in their rear and attacked the place, burning down almost all the houses ; the inhabitants left behind, however, all managed to escape in their canoes across the river. They were now living in little straw makeshifts for huts, on the white sand along the water's edge. There were the remains at Nhaucoé of about eight square houses with verandahs round them, the residences of Portuguese traders, living here two years ago. There were then, I afterwards learned, over twenty white men here; but they had all left, owing to the badness of trade. Senhor Mendonça alone remained. A half-caste Portuguese who was living here with the Shakundas came to see us, Gregorio by name. We heard afterwards that a few days before our arrival this gentleman had found out that one of his wives (one of very many) had mistaken another man for himself, and under that impression had committed herself considerably. Mr. Gregorio invited the pair of them to drink beer with him, and, whilst the lovers were enjoying the repast, shot them both dead. No questions were asked about the affair, though the other wives were probably more circumspect in the future. Upon our arrival opposite the island, Mendonça sent over a boat for us. On the highest portion of the island he had his dwelling-place, a square thatched house, with a wide verandah, in front of which, on a flagstaff, flaunted the Portuguese flag. Besides the large house, there were several store-rooms and outhouses, and below, occupying half the island, a village of Mendonça's slaves and dependants. Just at sundown two more Portuguese arrived here from Zumbo in a large flat-bottomed boat. One of them was going trading to the Manica country, in company with Canyemba, in a short time; and I afterwards met him there. This man, Mendonça told me later on, had left Portugal at his country's expense; the other, a little man with rather a pleasant face, had belonged to the Zambesi battalion which was sent from Portugal to take part in the Bonga war in 1867. Both of them seemed to be terribly knocked out of time by fever, from which the little man was still suffering. Mendonça

was a tall, spare man, well made, with regular
features, dark olive complexion, and fine black eyes.
Both now and upon my return from the Manica
country he treated me with the greatest kindness,
for which I shall ever feel grateful. He was, however, a slave-trader, and treated the natives with
great severity. As he expressed it, "Negro diablo ;
Africa inferno" (A black man is a devil ; Africa is
hell).

November 30*th*.—Brought all our goods across
from the northern bank of the river to Mendonça's
island, Cassoko, but left the donkeys in charge of
Franz and my Kafirs on the northern bank. The
first thing that jarred against my prejudices as an
Englishman the next morning was the sight of ten
Batonga women, just captured in the last raid, all
chained together. Each had an iron ring round her
neck, and there was about five feet of iron chain
between each ; some of them were women with little
babies on their backs, others young unmarried women.
Whilst I was here they were never loosened one from
another, but every morning they were sent over in a
large canoe to the southern shore, to hoe in a corn-field
all day in a row, all chained together ; at night they
were locked up, still all chained together, in a large,
square sort of barn. From the verandah depended
three raw hippopotamus-hide sjamboks, the lower part
of each dyed black with blood. During my stay
here, another little Portuguese, a fair-haired, light-
complexioned man, Manoel Diego by name, also an
old soldier from the Zambesi battalion, visited
Mendonça ; he had with him two very good-looking
young Batonga girls (victims of the last raid), one
about thirteen or fourteen years of age, the other
about ten, the best-looking specimens I had yet seen

of a very ugly race of people. He told me he had
just bought them from old Canyemba. The morning
after he came to Cassoko, he came up in a great rage
to Mendonça, telling him the two girls had escaped.
I was mightily glad to hear it. It appears that with
admirable pluck they had launched one of the large
canoes belonging to their master, and, in the absence
of the paddles, which were put away every night,
had paddled over to the northern bank, a distance
of many hundred yards, with their hands. Armed
Shakundas were at once sent out to try and recover
the fugitives; they were only too successful. On
the fourth day, having crossed over to look at my
donkeys, I met four Shakundas just embarking for
the island with the two poor young girls, who sat in
sullen silence, with bent-down heads, and "gyves
upon their wrists." My heart bled for them, and
had I had the money I would have bought them
from Diego. The one cost him a musket, for
which he told me he had given £2 : 10s., and the
younger one twenty rupees.

On my return to the island my boys informed me
that the two girls had been cruelly beaten, and one
of the sjamboks, dyed afresh with crimson stains, told
its own tale. It is horrible and unnatural to treat a
pretty young girl in this manner, and yet this same
Diego seemed a mild little man, with a very pleasant,
cheerful face. I have forgotten to mention how the
slaves are secured at night after being captured in
any considerable number. Large logs are cut by the
slaves, from nine inches to a foot in diameter, and
in these logs holes are chopped sufficiently large to
allow of a man's or woman's foot being put through;
other holes are then bored, and wooden pegs driven
in, which pass through the holes through which the

feet have been pushed, and only just leave room for
the ankle, rendering it impossible to withdraw the
foot.   In this manner five or six slaves are safely
fixed up in each log.   By day they march with the
forked stick round their necks, with which Dr.
Livingstone and other travellers have made the British
public familiar.   Here, perhaps, a few words concerning the "Basungo Canyemba," as he is termed
by the Shakundas, may not be out of place.   He is
a full-blooded black man, and came originally from
the Lower Zambesi, somewhere, I believe, in the
district of Tete.   He speaks Portuguese, and his sons,
who have been educated at Tete, both read and write
that language.   At present he lives on an island in
the Zambesi, just at the mouth of the river Kafukwe,
about twelve miles below Mendonça's island.   Upon
state occasions he comes out in a sort of Portuguese
uniform, with a sword.   He has a great deal of
power in these parts, having a very great number of
men all armed with flint-lock muskets, over whom
he seemed to exercise the most despotic power.
From what Mendonça told me, he seems to be constantly making raids upon any people in the neighbourhood of the Zambesi who have anything to be taken.
It was he who, with 600 guns, conducted the late
raid upon the Batongas, the effect of which I myself
had seen.   Mendonça also assisted with a body of his
dependants.   Sometimes he sends in large parties of
his men—two or three hundred—all armed with flint-
lock muskets, to hunt elephants.   When he makes
an attack upon a tribe, he goes, however, through
certain forms.   He sends a letter down to the
Governor of Tete, complaining of the injury done to
Portuguese trade and Portuguese subjects by a certain
tribe, and asking for a *permis de guerra*, or licence to

make war upon them, in order to chastise them for
their insolence.   As far as I could learn, I do not
think he finds much difficulty in getting these licences
granted.   But I am now commencing to relate not
what I have seen, but what I have heard, and reports
are not by any means to be relied on.   Still, he is a
man who possesses both the will and the power to
do immense harm—a slave-trader and a murderer.

I remained here on the island with Mendonça until
the 13th of December.   The smallpox was raging
among his people, two, three, and four of whom used
to die every day.   Owen, not considering it safe to
remain, went over and made himself a skerm on
the mainland, where Franz, my Basuto boy, was with
the donkeys.   During this time old Canyemba paid
us a visit in full dress, with a large cavalry sword.
Mendonça received him with several salutes of
musketry, and in an apparently very friendly manner,
though he afterwards informed me that he was an
awful scoundrel, and calmly added that he was not
the friend of Canyemba, but of Canyemba's ivory.
"That," said he, "is the friendship of a white man
for a black man."   I admired his candour and
marvelled at his hypocrisy.   A few days afterwards
Mendonça and I paid a visit to old Canyemba.   He
had a large barrack-looking house, and at the back,
and enclosed with a high palisade, were the residences
of the members of his harem, who, to judge from the
size of the enclosed space, must have been pretty
numerous.   His men had shot two hippopotami during
the night, and the heads had been cut off whole and
brought up to the house.   At dinner he gave us china
plates, knives and forks, and a better-prepared meal
than I had tasted for some time.   The following
morning we returned in canoes to Cassoko, which we

reached late in the afternoon after a pleasant voyage up the river, passing many herds of sea-cows *en route*. The mouth of the river Kafukwe is not very broad —about 150 yards, I think; but it looked very deep, and seemed to pour a very large body of water into the Zambesi. During my stay in Mendonça's island I shot five head of game, all on the southern side of the Zambesi. They were one zebra, one impala, one wild pig, one black rhinoceros, and one waterbuck. Owen shot on the north bank one zebra and two waterbucks.

On the night of December 9, my lazy boys allowed two of the donkeys to stay outside the kraal. The hyænas, which are very numerous and fierce about here, tackled them, and would have killed both had not Owen driven them off—it was a moonlight night—with repeated charges of buckshot. As it was, they killed the stallion, and mangled the other badly ; however, I sewed up his wounds on the following day, and he eventually recovered, only to die of something else. Two nights after this, the boys again left all the three donkeys out. I had been away hunting, and on my return, just at dusk, Franz shouted across the river that the donkeys were away. Mendonça at once called up a headman and a lot of slaves, and, giving them a lantern, told them to cross the river at once and take the donkeys' spoor, and not to leave it until they found them alive or dead. In a few minutes we were paddling across the river, but before reaching the shore we heard the hyænas making a tremendous noise, not very far away, and I knew that it was all up with my poor donkeys. We found the spoor, and, following it—guided, too, by the howling of the hyænas—at length came to the scene of the disaster. The hyænas made themselves scarce, and I had not even the satisfaction of getting a shot at one. We found little more than the skulls of the two sound donkeys; but, strange to say, the one that had been bitten before, and whose wounds I had sewed up, was standing under a bush not far off, and had never been interfered with at all. Slowly and sadly I led him back, cursing hyænas and Kafirs both loudly and deeply. The two Batonga boys, in whose charge the donkeys had been, had both bolted, nor did they return. I believe that I myself unwittingly contributed to the danger my donkeys ran from these ravenous beasts. When the first one was killed, I wished to poison all that remained of him. Now, I had with me two cartridge cases, one containing tartar emetic, and the other crystals of strychnine. When I opened the cartridges the crystals had turned to powder, and for the life of me I could not tell which was tartar emetic and which strychnine ; and, as both are disagreeable in their effects, I did not care about taking a dose to settle the question. So I tossed up which I should use—heads for the one, tails for the other. I set nine baits, and dosed them with the contents of the winning cartridge, which, I think, must have been tartar emetic. All the baits were taken ; the emetic no doubt having produced its natural effect, and the hyænas, by severe vomiting, having been rendered even more ravenous than they were before.

December 13*th*.—Started for the Manica country, under the guidance of four Shakundas that Mendonça gave me, though at considerable inconvenience to himself. Old Canyemba was going in himself in a few days on a hunting expedition, with a large body of men, and Mendonça thought it advisable for us

to get on in front of him. He gave me a letter to
a man trading for him, Da Costa by name, who left
the Zambesi about three weeks ago, and whom he
said we should find at Sitanda's Town. Sitanda is
the headman in the Manica country. Mendonça
told Da Costa in the letter that he must help us in
every way—give us men to show where the elephants
are, to carry the tusks, and to supply us with everything in the way of goods that we may want and
that he has with him.

December 14*th*.—Only got a very short distance,
owing to one of the Kafirs being ill.

December 15*th*.—Made a morning's journey to
Cambari's Town, an old Banyai, dependent for his
safety upon the caprice of Canyemba. He lived on
the banks of a little river called the Chongwe, which
runs out of the neighbouring range of hills into the
Kafukwe. From here our road lay through the
hills, which frowned above us, to the Manica country;
and, as rain threatened, we thought it best to stop over
for the day, and make a fair start on the morrow.

December 16*th*.—A heavy shower of rain commenced to fall before daybreak, and continued to do
so without cessation until late in the afternoon ; so
we had to lie up for the day, and amuse ourselves as
best we might in a Kafir hut, which old Cambari
kindly placed at our disposal.

December 17*th*.—Weather still looked very rainy,
and the high mountains in front of us, and through
or rather over which our road now lay, were shrouded
in thick mist. However, we made a start, and
before going far I shot an impala ram. Soon after
a heavy shower came on, during which we took
shelter in an old Kafir hut and made breakfast.
About 10 A.M. it again cleared up, and we got on

for a few miles, when a heavy rain came on once
more, which soon drenched us to the skin.   Soon
after we reached a small Banyai kraal, deserted by
its owners, but still in very good condition, and (the
weather still looking very unpropitious) did our best
to make ourselves comfortable for the night.   The
temperature seemed deliciously cool up here in the
hills, after the hot stifling atmosphere of the Zambesi
valley.

December 18*th*.—Day broke very wet and rainy,
so we remained where we were.   In the afternoon it
cleared up, so I went out and shot a wild pig.   A
Banyai here joined us from Cambari's kraal—a spare-
built, wiry little fellow, with his hair arranged in
long tassels or strings, which hung down on all sides,
over his eyes, and behind down to his shoulders.
He was about the wildest-looking individual I had
yet seen, wilder-looking than even the Bushmen of
the Mäbäbe—the *beau-ideal* of a savage, untamed
man.

December 19*th*.—Turned out a beautiful day, cool
and cloudy after the rain.   The path took us in
a north-westerly direction, continually ascending
towards the table-land of Manica.   Just at present
the country about here looked charming ; the young
grass—thanks to the heavy rains that had been falling
during the last fortnight—had shot up to a foot or
eighteen inches in height over hill and dale, every tree
and shrub was in full leaf, and everything looked green
and fresh and smiling.   A large proportion of the
trees and shrubs in these hills bear sweet-smelling
and handsome flowers, and I noticed more small wild-
flowers than I had seen in any other part of the
country that I had yet visited.   About two o'clock
we emerged from the hills, and stepped on to the

table-land beyond — great open plains, **or** rather rolling downs, intersected by ranges of low hills, for all the world like portions of the Mashuna country south of the Zambesi. I think we must have ascended quite 2500 feet above the valley of the Zambesi, and reckon we are now 3500 feet above sea-level. The temperature was delightfully pleasant, and quite fresh and cool after the stifling sultry heat of the Zambesi; the thermometer showed a difference of 20°. We stopped and made things square for the night at the first Manica kraal we reached, as rain threatened on every side. I went out to look for game, and, after a careful stalk in the open, got within 200 yards of a solitary old roan antelope bull, and killed him with my Martini-Henry rifle. His horns were small, though he was an adult animal.

December 20th.—Very misty morning, threatening rain; however, as the sun rose the mist dispersed, and we had a nice cool day. About mid-day we reached a small Manica kraal, where we remained for the rest of the day. In the afternoon I went out with my rifle, and shot a konze antelope, the first I had ever seen. He was a solitary old bull, and a fine specimen. I shot him just at the root of the tail, with a ten-to-the-pound bullet, but had a chase after him for at least four miles across the flats before I killed him. These antelopes very closely resemble the hartebeest of South Africa; the horns, however, are shorter, and flatter at the base, and the forehead is not nearly so elongated. The black mark down the front of the face of the hartebeest is also wanting in the konze, where the colour is of a uniform light red, with whitish markings on the tear bags under the eye; the general colour of the animal is a little lighter than that of the hartebeest, the tail, knees, and front of all

Y

four legs being black. On these flats there were great numbers of a small graceful antelope, much resembling, if not identical with, the oribi of the Cape Colony and Natal ; they were of a rich red colour, with conspicuous black tails. Like all other game about here, they were very wild and shy.

December 21*st.*—Went on to Chorumane's Town, situated on the little river Maiyune. On the road we passed a large herd of zebras, headed by two fine elands, standing in the open flat. About 2 P.M. a tremendous rain fell right over the town, inundating every hut, and before long the whole village seemed to be standing in a lake, and every hut was a foot deep in water. Towards evening the heavy rain stopped, but a drizzle continued to fall during the greater part of the night. By the help of some thickish lumps of wood, we managed to make our beds just above the water.

December 22*nd.*—Wounded an oribi very early in the morning, and followed it till nearly mid-day, as I was very anxious to obtain a specimen of this (to me) new antelope. However, at last it got into some long grass, and I had to give up the pursuit. In the afternoon I went out to look for game, and came across a troop of konze antelopes. After a good deal of trouble I at last got within 200 yards of one, and, firing with the Martini-Henry, knocked it down ; before I could get up to it, however, it recovered, and, regaining its feet, followed the herd. Thinking that it must soon give in, I followed it, running most of the way for more than an hour, but could never get nearer than 250 yards. The bullet had gone right through it, rather high up and a little behind the shoulders, and could only have just missed the lungs.

We could plainly see the blood running down on both sides, forming a dark streak on the light yellowish-red skin. At last I gave up all hope of running it down, and fired at the big bull of the herd at a distance of 250 yards. I made a lucky shot, as I was getting unsteady from hard running ; the ball caught him on the hip, and, as we afterwards found, travelled the whole length of his body and lodged in the neck. The animal, however, ran at least two miles before we finally brought him to a stand and assegaied him. This, I think, was a very old bull, as he was very much darker-coloured than the rest of the herd, and than the single bull I had shot two days before. All along his back the colour was a very rich dark red ; about a hand's-breadth behind each shoulder was a patch of dark grey about six inches in diameter ; the insides of the thighs and the belly were of a very pale yellow, almost white.

December 23rd.—Rained all day ; so we remained where we were, in a very leaky Kafir hut. I took advantage of the delay to skin and preserve the konze's head very carefully.

Christmas Eve.—Though it still looked very rainy, we packed up our things, and pushed on. About mid-day we reached an old deserted Kafir town. Here I shot a fine oribi ram, the first I had ever bagged. About 3 P.M. we came to a sort of shed. Here, a few heavy showers having fallen, and dense masses of rain-clouds closing in upon us from all sides, we resolved to sleep, and, by arranging two waterproof sheets over one end, we made ourselves pretty comfortable. About an hour before sundown the rain came down in torrents, and continued to fall without cessation during the entire night.

Christmas Day.—As day broke it was raining in

torrents, and we were enveloped on all sides in vast masses of dense mist. We managed to raise a breakfast of oribi and Kafir corn ; but for dinner (our Christmas dinner) we had absolutely nothing. I may say here that all the provisions we brought with us from Pandamatenka ran out before we left Mendonça's—coffee, sugar, tea, and everything else. Mendonça had nothing in the way of European provisions, having been absent for three years from Quillimane, so that since leaving the Zambesi we had lived entirely upon what I shot, and what we could buy from the Kafirs, and had had nothing to drink but water. In this dilemma, the weather showing no signs of improvement, we sent some of our boys on to the next town, which the Shakundas reported to be not far off, to buy some fowls and meal both for us and for themselves. About 2 P.M. the rain ceased, but it seemed probable that it would soon commence again. A herd of konze antelopes came down just opposite us, on the other side of the river, but, either seeing or hearing something suspicious, decamped. I went after them a long way, and eventually got a shot, but missed. The Kafirs we had sent on to buy provender for our Christmas dinner came back, reporting the town not far off, but the people refusing to sell except at most exorbitant prices. The clouds having now cleared a little, and being without food of any sort, we at once packed up and set off for the town, determined to buy something for dinner. When close to the kraal, a little before sundown, I espied a roan antelope a long way off ; however, by wading through a boggy marsh and a dense bed of reeds, where the water came up to my middle, I reached a mound with some bushes upon it, behind which I had last seen the roan antelope feeding.

Looking cautiously over the top, I saw the fine old bull lying down within eighty yards of me. At the same minute he got my wind, and sprang up, giving me a chance that I was not slow to take advantage of, and I planted a bullet right in the centre of his shoulder. He dashed away for about 150 yards at full speed, and then, pulling up, turned and presented his other shoulder to me, upon which I gave him a second bullet, which sealed his fate. The sun was now down, and torrents of rain, pouring from dense black clouds, drenched me through and through long before I could reach the Kafir town. Owen had managed to get a couple of leaky huts, one for our traps and the other for ourselves; but everything was dark and wet and dismal in the extreme, and the rain continued to fall in torrents. I at once sent all the boys to bring in the meat of the roan antelope, and when it came I managed to buy a little Kafir corn meal with some of it, off which we at last made our Christmas dinner at about ten o'clock at night, and by the fitful light of a lamp which we extemporised from a little marrow fat in a plate and a few shreds of blanket for a wick. Such is life! The only grain of comfort we had was the reflection that we were in a country never before trodden upon by even the wandering feet of a subject of Queen Victoria.

December 26th.—Raining hard as day broke, and no light to be seen in the sky at any point. As the next town was reported to be at a considerable distance, and the rain did not cease till late in the afternoon, we remained where we were. The Kafirs here were very difficult to deal with, and would sell us nothing except at the most exorbitant prices. Heavy rain came on again in the evening.

December 27th.—Rain again from early dawn till about ten A.M.   Being pretty well starved out, we were now obliged to push on to the next town, which we reached shortly before sundown, travelling all the day through fine forest country intersected by open glades, in most of which was a running stream of water.   Found tsetse fly abundant in these forests. In the afternoon Owen shot a konze cow.   On reaching the town (the largest we had yet seen), the Enduna shammed to be ill, and would not see us, nor would any of his people sell us anything or carry a message to him ; so at last I went to him myself, and managed to get a hut from him to put our traps in during the night.   I presented him with a fathom of calico, telling him at the same time we were hungry ; but all I got for it was about two pint beakers full of Kafir corn.   Neither he nor his people could be prevailed upon to sell us anything more.   These Kafirs evidently looked upon us with a jealous eye, and, not daring to resort to positive violence, put all negative obstacles in our way to prevent our farther progress into the country.   There is nothing about this people to admire.   They are not a fine-looking race, and very dirty and slovenly in their habits.   Their huts are a disgrace to even the lowest savages who have permanent dwelling-places.   Here there was any quantity of wood and grass, and yet their huts were one and all most wretchedly small, and, being only half-thatched, and seemingly never repaired, leaked like sieves.   They were also infested with rats, and a species of bug similar to the tampan of South Africa, but much larger and more venomous, its bite raising large lumps, which often turn to festering sores. Owen suffered very much from them, and nearly all my Kafirs swelled very much about the feet and

ankles.   Having nothing with which to keep off the
constant rain, and as we usually arrived too late at
the towns to make a shelter with boughs and grass,
we were forced to sleep in their filthy huts, and
suffered accordingly.   The headman of this town
was named Mashato.   There was a good deal of
tsetse fly, not only in the forest-clad sand-belts
through which we had just passed, but also in the
town itself.

December 28*th*.—Another rainy day, altogether too
wet to venture on with our things.   About mid-day,
however, it cleared up a bit, and by evening the sky
became pretty clear, and looked as if the rain, which
had now been continuous for three weeks, intended
to hold up for a bit.   About 3 P.M. I went out to
look for game, and, coming across a herd of zebras
and konze antelope, managed to kill two, one of each.
I also saw a single roan antelope and some reedbuck.

December 29*th*.—A fine bright day, though the
heavy dew made the walking through the long grass
unpleasant in the early morning.   Passed through a
beautiful-looking country for game, but only saw one
old konze bull, at which Owen had a shot.   After a
walk of about fifteen miles, we reached several small
kraals, where the people seemed much more friendly
than at the two towns we had last passed.   The old
Enduna did his best to make us comfortable, and
gave us the largest hut in the town to sleep in.

December 30*th*.—A fine day, and very hot.   Got
two fresh carriers to go with us as far as Sitanda's
kraal, which they say is three days' walk from here.
A two hours' walk brought us to Melimba's kraal,
who owns a few cattle.   The Enduna's son came
out to meet us, and sold us a little salt from the
Mashukulumbwe country, and a few ground-nuts.

He also brought a boy about ten years old for sale ;
he wanted three fathoms of white linen for him.
However, I had none to spare, as our stock was
getting very low.   A little farther on I shot a very
fine reedbuck ram ; its horns measured 15 inches along
the curve, and 12½ inches taking a straight line
from point to base.   After this, half an hour's walk
brought us to a little river, the Nwongwe, flowing to
the south-east ; and another mile, to a few small
wretched-looking kraals.   In the evening we found
that our two new carriers had run away, one of them
having met a creditor of his, who threatened him
with corporal chastisement if he did not stump up.
We at once sent his creditor after him.

December 31*st*.—My birthday. Detained here,
owing to our two carriers having decamped yesterday.
A hot sunny day.   It was now about the hottest time
of year, yet the thermometer only registered 84°
in the shade, which was from 20° to 25° less than the
heat we experienced daily during the six weeks we
were on the Zambesi in November and December.
Thus ended the year 1877.

CHAPTER XVI

January 1, 1878.—Went on westwards for about twenty miles, and slept on a little rivulet called Calolo, running towards the Kafukwe. Shot a reed-buck in the evening. There are several kraals about here, but we could not buy any corn, so that the people must be badly off for food this season. These Manica people are a miserable lot, unacquainted with several simple arts known to all other Kafirs and Bushmen that I have ever seen—such, for instance, as dressing skins. Either through laziness or stupidity, they are unable to make any use of a skin larger than that of an antelope of the smallest species, or a wild cat. The scanty clothing of both sexes consists of pieces of the inside bark of the machabel tree sewn together. They also make blankets of a considerable size of the same material. The Manica men all carry bows and arrows, the latter said to be poisoned.

January 2*nd.*—Walked on to the little river Kemba in the morning, a stretch of about fifteen miles. Although so much rain had fallen lately, there is no water between these two little rivers ; indeed, ever since leaving the Chongwe the country we have passed through seems badly watered. On the march I shot a zebra stallion close to the footpath. At this town we could get no corn, so had to send all the boys back to bring in the zebra meat, and, as they did not return till nightfall, we slept where we were.

January 3rd.—Went on to the next town, about eight miles distant in a northerly direction. Here we were again detained all day buying corn, as we heard that farther on there was a famine in the land, and we should not be able to get any. In the afternoon two or three thunderstorms broke around us, and we got two heavy showers of rain.

January 4th.—Went on in the morning to some more towns, where we breakfasted. In the afternoon made another move, and slept at a small pan of water. Went out in the evening with my rifle, and wounded a zebra, but lost it. I also saw a herd of konze antelopes and two eland bulls, but, being in the open, they saw me a long way off, and I could not get a shot, though I followed them till sundown.

January 5th.—Got on about twelve miles in a northerly direction. Saw a herd of zebras in the morning. Went out in the afternoon to look for game, but saw nothing. This is an infernal country to travel through ; there being a famine at the time of our visit, nothing was to be got from the Kafirs in the shape of provisions, except an occasional very small basket of corn, for which we had to pay a most exorbitant price. The farther, too, that we penetrated into the country, the scarcer the game became ; so that, if matters did not improve, we stood a very good chance of being starved. This night, as also yesterday and the night before, we were eaten up by mosquitoes.

January 6th.—Got on to a little town close to Sitanda's kraal, the chief of the country. Here we stopped, and breakfasted off a handful of ground-nuts, whilst messengers went on to announce our arrival About 2 P.M. they returned, saying that we were to come nearer to see the great man of the country, and at the same time bring a present for him. Half an hour's walk brought us within sight of a small collection of huts, where we were met by a young Kafir, who informed us that we rhust not approach nearer the chief that day, and at the same time pointed out to us the spot assigned for our encampment. That the chief of so small, poor, and miserable a nation should keep up so much state surprised us not a little. However, not wishing to be guilty of a breach of etiquette, and caring very little whether we saw him now or a month hence, or not at all, we complied with his wishes in everything, except that, instead of camping where he wished us, we moved down to the ready-made huts of the Portuguese trader, Joaquim da Costa, for whom we had a letter from Mendonça, and whom we had hoped and expected to find here. Unfortunately, however, having suffered much from fever, he had left for the Kafukwe five days before our arrival. At the same time we sent Sitanda a piece of coloured cloth and a cotton sheet, and an intimation that we were hungry. Presently a message came back thanking us for the present, and—curiosity having probably overcome dignity—requesting us to pay him a visit. So up we went. We found the old fellow a slight-built old Kafir, with an astute thin-featured face, sitting outside his hut with about a dozen cronies. When his people first come up to him to report any news, they roll on their backs in the dust before him, and subsequently, when talking to him, lie down on their sides and rub one shoulder in the dust at the conclusion of every sentence. He asked us what we had come to the country for, and when we told him we had come to hunt elephants and asked his permission to do so, he replied that we might hunt, but that one tusk of every elephant shot belonged to him as king of the country, and that we might keep the other; he then added that if we would give him a small present we could keep both tusks. This looked as if he either had a very poor idea of our hunting powers, or that there were very few elephants in the country; I think the latter was the true reason, and that it is all a myth about Manica being a good elephant country, as we had never seen so much as an old spoor, and we heard, too, that Da Costa did not buy a single tusk from Sitanda, who probably had not any for sale. However, we resolved that if there were no elephants here, we would cross the Kafukwe, and have a look for them in the Mashukulumbwe country. In the evening Owen complained of feeling ill.

January 7th.—Went down to Sitanda's cattle post, about four miles to the east. On the way I saw some konze antelopes and zebras, and wounded one of the latter, but, after following a long way on the blood spoor, I lost it. At the cattle post there were about fifty head of cows and oxen, and twenty small calves; these cattle were the smallest breed I had ever seen. I measured one of the largest cows (though they were all much of a size); she stood just 3 ft. 4 in. at the wither. Though so small, these little cows are capital milkers; they all had very small horns, and were really beautiful little animals. Went on from the cattle post to the

Lukanga river, where I shot a fine lechwe ram, an antelope that I did not expect to find in this part of Africa ; it was, however, identical in every respect with the lechwes I have shot on the river Chobe. The Situtunga antelope (*Tragelaphus Spekii*) is also found in the swamps of the Lukanga ; the natives here call it " n'zobe " ; at Lake Bengweolo, according to Dr. Livingstone, it is called " n'zoe." On returning, I found Owen much worse ; he had a bad attack of fever.

January 8th.—Owen very bad ; he had lost all power in his limbs. I did not know how it would end, but feared that it would put a stop to all our elephant-hunting and prospecting projects. This is a dreadful country to be sick in—nothing to eat, and hundreds of miles from the nearest white man. The mosquitoes were in incredible numbers ; luckily, Owen had his mosquito net with him. I, having left mine behind at the Zambesi, suffered horribly on the two previous nights, never having been able to close an eye ; to-day, however, I made myself a net of salampore, which I thought would answer.

January 9th. — My mosquito net answered capitally, and I arose next morning after a refreshing night's sleep, the first I had had for five nights. Went down to the Lukanga river again to look for lechwes, of which I at last spied a large herd, and by dint of a great deal of creeping and crawling through a boggy marsh, the water often up to my knees, I at last got pretty close to them. Whilst trying, however, to stalk a fine old ram feeding by himself, I disturbed some of the ewes, and they all ran. They soon stopped, however, to look round, and I got three shots into them, standing pretty thickly, killing two and wounding two more ; one of these had a hind leg broken, and after about an hour's chase through the swamp, we ran it in and despatched it with assegais. The other wounded one regained the herd ; so that I killed three, all ewes. Owen still very ill ; could not eat, and complained of great pain in the head.

January 10*th*.—As I feared, yesterday's work with the lechwes brought on an attack of fever; nor is it to be wondered at. I was at least six hours in the marsh, sometimes crawling on my hands and knees through black, stinking mud, festering beneath the rays of a tropical summer's sun, and the rest of the time wading up to my knees in mud and water ; but, as we had nothing to eat but Kafir corn, and there was very little game about here, I was obliged to go after these lechwes in the swamp. Owen very ill ; could neither sleep nor eat. I gave him a bottle of Warburg's fever tincture.

January 11*th*.—Down again with a very sharp attack of fever ; fearful pains in the head. Yesterday evening I bathed in cold water, which perhaps had something to do with it. My Basuto boy was also down. We were now in a pretty predicament—all down with fever of a very virulent form, and in the depths of a starving country. Eight wretched little Kafir fowls, about the size of a bantam, and just mere skin and bone, and a little Kafir corn and bad water, was absolutely all we had to eat and drink ; and if we had not got sufficiently well to have moved out of this accursed pestilential spot before our slender allowance was finished, it would have been a poor look-out indeed. Taking a straight line as the crow flies, we were more than four hundred miles from Inyati, the farthest trading outpost and missionary station in the Matabele country, which was the nearest point where we could hope to get anything like food for a sick man ; for Mendonça, though very hospitable, had nothing to eat himself but what he got from the Kafirs.   By the route we had to travel, we had to traverse at least seven hundred miles of wilderness before reaching this haven of refuge—a long and seemingly hopeless tramp for sick men.

January 13*th*. — Thanks to Warburg's fever tincture—which I believe to be the most powerful and effective medicine for this disease—the excessive and almost unbearable pains in my head had to a great extent ceased ; but I still felt very ill, and Owen and my Basuto boy were both very ill.

January 14*th*.—Dreadfully ill. Owen slightly better.

January 15*th*.—Better again.   Yesterday I went up to Sitanda's, at the same time giving a present, and asking for a man to show the way to where Da Costa was (only a day and a half distant), so that we might try and get some men from him to help us out of the country.   This he flatly refused to do.   The inhuman old barbarian, knowing the fatal virulence of this fever, evidently thought that if he could only prevent us from obtaining assistance, we must soon succumb to disease and hunger, and he would then be able to seize everything we had with us.   He also refused to sell us any sort of food, and must have sent word round to the adjoining kraals forbidding the people to sell us anything ; for at first they brought a few fowls and a little corn for sale, but now none came near us.

January 16*th*. — Can get no sleep at night. During the last three nights I have not slept a wink.

January 17*th*.—About midnight a steady rain

began to fall. It is now about 10 A.M., and the rain has not yet ceased. Everything looked unspeakably dismal and utterly miserable. If we only had something to eat, we might stand a chance of getting well ; but Kafir corn and water is all we have.

January 20*th.*—Owen a little better. Canyemba has arrived at last from the Zambesi, and we now confidently hope to get three or four boys from him to help us out of the country. A Portuguese trader, whom we saw at Mendonça's, had accompanied him ; but he had remained behind.

January 21*st.*—The Portuguese trader arrived about mid-day. He looked very ill, and was very much disgusted with the country. In the afternoon I went up to old Canyemba to try and get three boys from him to help us back to the Zambesi. However, though he had two hundred men with him, he would not give us one, nor help us in any way ; nor would he give us a man to carry the letter I had got from Mendonça to Da Costa, who was only a day and a half's walk from here, and who, on reading the letter from his master, would no doubt have afforded us every assistance in his power. I got a relapse of fever in the evening, and was very ill all night. It was evident that we must get away from here at all costs, as there was no doubt that it was a most particularly unhealthy spot ; and, besides that, there was no more food of any sort to be got. Tried to make an arrangement with the Portuguese to get a few pieces of calico from him and pay Mendonça, with whom I had left a few pounds, on my arrival at the Zambesi. However, he would not do it. Then asked if he would not let us have some, if we gave him Mendonça's letter to Da Costa, and signed a paper saying what we had received from him, and

asking him to return it to him. To this also he
would not agree. As a last resource, I asked him
if he would not buy a large-bore muzzle-loading
elephant gun. This he was willing to do, and drove
a hard bargain with me, only giving five pieces of
calico (24 yards) for a first-rate elephant gun, half a
bag of powder, and about fifty bullets.

January 22*nd.*—Still detained trying to get a
few carriers from some of the surrounding towns.
We found, however, that the heartless old brute
Sitanda had given orders that none of his people
were to carry for us, or to help us on in any way, no
matter what payment we might offer. There can
be no doubt of his motives ; he believed that if he
could only prevent us from effecting our escape we
should soon make our exit from this world, and he
would then be able to pounce down upon our things
like a vulture. I think he and his people were too
cowardly to resort to open violence.

January 23*rd.*—Sorted out our things, leaving
behind the greater part of our cartridges and many
other articles, so as to reduce what our scanty retinue
would have to carry as much as possible. In the
evening the Portuguese came down with a slave for
sale, a young Kafir, about eighteen or twenty years
of age. As it was of vital importance to us to get
carriers, I did not hesitate to buy him, and after a
good deal of haggling we managed to strike a bargain,
giving 320 loaded cartridges for this not very pre-
possessing-looking specimen of humanity. Like
many of the people about here, he had all his teeth
filed to sharp points. The Portuguese told me I
must watch him well in the daytime, and tie him up
at night ; however, I explained to him, through
one of my boys, that, although I had bought him, I

z

did not want to keep him for a slave, and that if he
would carry for me as far as the Zambesi, he might
go where he liked afterwards, or continue working
with me for wages.

January 24th.—At last, about 10 A.M., we managed
to make the first steps in our retreat from this
accursed spot, where we had spent eighteen miserable
days. Having had a relapse during the night, I felt
very ill and weak ; but necessity has no law, so we
crawled along as well as we could, and during the day
must have accomplished **several miles.**

January 25th.—Both of us very much knocked
up ; in the course of the day we managed to crawl
along about five miles. Nothing to eat but bare
Kafir corn and two small green pumpkins ; heavy
rain during the night. The whole country was now
covered with grass about six feet high, and the
vegetation was much ranker than I had seen it
anywhere south of the Zambesi ; the dew, too, fell
in wonderful quantities, and, added to the constant
heavy rain, made everything "demmed wet, moist,
and unpleasant," as Mr. Mantalini would say.

January 26th.—Staggered along a few miles
farther. Three very heavy thunderstorms, with
deluges of tropical rain, took place during the day.
With the weak and insipid food we had now to live
upon, we could gain no strength.

January 27th.—Forced to it by downright hunger,
we had to give the most exorbitant price of four
yards of calico for a little kid, which, when cleaned,
was no larger than an English hare.

January 28th.—During the night one of the
heaviest storms of rain burst upon us that it has ever
been my luck to have anything to do with. For
hours the rain poured down in torrents, and, as our

hastily constructed hut was by no means proof against its violence, we got a pretty good dousing. In the morning all our blankets and traps were so wet and uncomfortable that we thought it best to remain where we were, and dry our things.

January 29th.—The Kafir I bought from the Portuguese ran away, throwing down in the middle of the forest a very valuable breech-loading elephant gun. This, by following on his footsteps, we recovered. However, the villain had gone off with all our corn—a matter of the most vital importance in the present state of famine—and all my Martini-Henry cartridges.

January 30th.—Last night we had an awful night's rain, and got very wet. Coming in, we were much delayed and hindered by the constant rain, which fell night and day ; now it was just the same again. Everything seemed against us.

January 31st.—Cool, cloudy day ; looking very rainy. However, the rain held off, and we pushed on to the next town. I was now fast recovering from the fever, and, in spite of the wretched food we had to live upon, getting strong again ; Owen, however, was getting weaker.

February.—During the next ten days we made very small progress, as Owen was very ill and weak, and could not stand the walking. Comparatively speaking, I was myself now almost well again. The food, too, was now improving, as the mealies were getting ripe, and the pumpkins too. Owing to the slow rate at which we had been travelling, and the excessively high price of provisions, our calico was now reduced to two and a half pieces, and, at the same rate of expenditure, could not hold out until we reached Mendonça's ; and when our calico was gone, we should simply have starved to death. In this strait there was nothing to be done but to part company; so, leaving Owen with two whole pieces of calico and only two boys to feed, I took the remaining half-piece and all the rest of our boys, and pushed on, intending to send him back help on my arrival at Mendonça's. From where we parted there was a good footpath from town to town all the way back to the Zambesi; and, as Owen had only himself and two boys to feed, he had calico enough to buy all he wanted, travelling at his own pace as slowly as he liked, and thus not knocking himself up by over-exertion.

February 10*th.*—Parted with Owen, and walked hard all day, reaching just at sundown the little town where we had eaten our miserable Christmas dinner. In the afternoon, being hot, I imprudently bathed in a stream of cold running water. Whether it was owing to this or to over-exertion, I do not know, but that night I felt hot and feverish, and could not sleep, and knew I had another relapse of fever. For two days I pushed on, but then became so ill and weak that I had to lie still the following day. After crossing the Chongwe, I took a road to the right hand of that we came by, and passed two kraals with cattle; these cattle, however, were much larger than any at Sitanda's, being like those I had seen in the Mashuna country to the south of the Zambesi.

February 18*th.*—At last, thoroughly worn out with the fatigue of journeying through the high mountains which skirt the river, I once more reached the Zambesi, and, crossing over to Canyemba's island, slept there. During the whole of the return journey I never shot a head of game, being too ill and weak to go after those I saw.

February 19*th.* — Reached Mendonça's island, Cassoko, where I was very kindly received. On the following day I despatched two boys with a few provisions for Owen. These were all the people that Mendonça could spare; for, Da Costa having sent word to him that many of his men were ill with fever and unable to work, he had sent all his spare Kafirs to help him out with the ivory he had traded.

March 5*th.*—Owen reached here to-day in a very weak and dilapidated state.

March 21*st.*—Having bought seven pieces of calico (24 yards) and 5 lbs. of powder from Mendonça, we made a start for the Matabele country, intending to follow the northern bank of the Zambesi westwards, until we had passed the mouth of the Sanyati, and then to cross the river and strike straight across country to Inyati. Though I myself was now pretty strong again, Owen was so terribly weak and ill that we made but very slow progress, and did not reach Matua's kraal—where I had shot the eland cow coming in—until the 29th. Here I went out hunting, and shot a zebra mare. I only wounded her at the first shot, and had a very long chase before eventually killing her. I fancy I must have over-exerted myself, for that night I felt ill and feverish, and seemed to lose all my strength again.

April 1*st.*—Owen was now completely knocked up, and too weak to walk a step farther. In this state of things there was nothing for it but to make some sort of a portable bed and get Kafirs to carry him. This, after a considerable delay, I managed to do; and at last, on April 4th, we crossed to the southern side of the Zambesi. Here I hired eight strong men to carry Owen, each of whom brought a boy or servant to carry his blanket and cooking-pot,

so that my retinue numbered in all twenty men, for
whom I bought food enough to last eight days, as I
did not know whether there was any game or not
along the track.

April 6th.—Made a start soon after daylight.
The eight men who carried Owen worked by turns,
two at a time, and, going at a sort of half-trot, got
over the ground at a great pace where the walking
was good. In general, however, the walking was
very rough, up and down steep ravines, and through
long tangled grass. Our route led us in a line
parallel with the course of the Umay, a considerable-
sized river, running into the Zambesi from the south ;
and the frequent ravines we had to cross were formed
by the tributaries of this stream. Towards evening
we crossed fresh buffalo spoor, so I left the caravan
and followed it ; but, though I went a long way, I
could not come up with them, and only reached
camp a little before dark, quite tired, for I was still
very weak.

April 7th.—The Banyais (for to this tribe the
people belong who were working for me) refused to
carry Owen any farther unless I paid them the sum
that had been agreed upon beforehand. This of
course I could not do, knowing only too well that,
directly they had got their payment, they would run
away at night, and leave us to die in the wilderness.
However, after a great deal of talking and arguing,
and not before I had measured out the payment of
each individual separately and shown it to him, they
once more consented to go on ; and so, about mid-day,
we continued our journey. On the fourth day they
made another stand to get their payment, and once
more argued the point for several hours, but, finding
me firm, once more gave in. All this time we were

travelling through an uninhabited country, quite bare of game, though the pasture was good, and it being the rainy season, there was water in every pool. On the morning of the seventh day after leaving the Zambesi, we came upon a small herd of seven buffaloes, which unfortunately got our wind, and ran. I did my best to run up to them, but found myself terribly weak, and never managed to get within shot. In the evening, whilst the Banyais were making a camp, I went out again to look for game, and just at dusk saw a wild pig looking at me from the other side of a broad ravine. I fired at once, and knocked him over, but he recovered himself, and got into a patch of long grass. Following on the blood spoor for about fifty yards, we came upon him lying down. He at once jumped up, and made off again towards the dry rivulet at the bottom of the ravine. Before he reached it, however, my gun-carrier, "April," caught up to him, and stabbed him in the back with an assegai, when he turned round, grunting loudly. April got such a fright that he let go the assegai, and left it sticking in the pig's back, and before I reached the scene of action the brute had made good his escape into a large hole in the bank of the gully, assegai and all. Much disgusted, I went and in-spected the hole ; but, not liking to creep into it, and being unable to persuade any of the Kafirs to do so, returned to camp. During the night, lions roared loudly close to us. Early the following morning, April and some of the Banyais returned to see if they could not get the pig out of the hole, and soon appeared with the meat of the same. They told me they found it lying dead just outside the hole, April's assegai still sticking in its back.

April 15*th.*—Reached a Banyai town on the river

Gweo, a tributary of the Umay. It was only with the greatest trouble that I had persuaded the Banyai carriers to come thus far, and farther they would not go. We were now in a pretty mess. Owen could not walk a step ; we had only five boys, three of them mere striplings, and, worst of all, but two and a half pieces of calico left. I myself also was very weak and ill ; bad food, over-fatigue, and worry of mind that prevented my sleeping at night, had worn me to a shadow ; and I now got an attack of "shakes" (ague) every other day. However, there was but one thing for it, which was for me to push on to the Matabele country, and send help back to Owen as quickly as possible. In my weak state I almost despaired of being able to tramp so far ; but it was our only chance, for there was nothing left with which to pay men to carry Owen any farther, and we were still a long, long way from the Matabele country—ten days' hard walking for a healthy Kafir, across a very rough, broken country. Arrangements were soon made. I left Franz, my Basuto servant, to look after Owen, and a small boy whom Mendonça had given me to fetch wood and water, and took the other five Kafirs with me. I only took nine yards of calico with me, leaving the two whole pieces and all the beads with Owen ; which was a sufficient supply to enable him, with a little economy, to buy food enough to last at least six weeks, by which time, if I lived, help would have reached him from the Matabele.

April 17th.—Said good-bye to Owen, and started southwards. After a very tiring walk through a rough mountainous country, I reached a small town on the banks of the river Sengwe, where I slept. Near here there is a remarkable mountain standing by itself, and crowned with a mass of red-coloured rock, a landmark for miles round. This I called Mount Cromwell, in honour of him whom I consider the greatest of England's rulers. The following morning I shot an impala ram ; this meat was a godsend, and no doubt put a little strength into my wearied limbs.

April 22*nd.*—Reached Inyungo, Inyoga's town. This place was well known to me by name. It is from here that Lobengula, king of the Amandebele, receives an annual tribute of tobacco. Here I met a young fellow from the Matabele country. He told me that five days' hard walking would bring me to Inyati. Old Inyoga is a fine-looking old Banyai, but very poor, not having a single goat in his possession. He told me that the Matabele took everything from him. I wonder he does not retreat to the farther side of the Zambesi. I tried to get a guide to the Matabele from him, as the intervening country is uninhabited ; but, as I could not show them what I promised to pay, they would not trust me, so there was nothing for it but to strike straight through the country in a southerly direction. Gave away my last yard of calico, buying mealie meal for the road. Between the river Gweo, where I left Owen, and Inyoga's town, there were a great many buffaloes and black rhinoceroses. I never saw one actually ; but I came across any amount of fresh spoor. An elephant spoor I did not see, old or new, between Inyoga's and the Zambesi.

April 24*th.*—Left Inyoga's for the Matabele, the last stage in my journey. I soon got into a mass of rough, rugged, steep hills, dreadful walking for a man in my weak condition. Saw a black rhinoceros cow with a small calf ; but they got our wind, and I did not get a chance of a shot.

April 25*th.*—Shot a black rhinoceros bull early in the morning ; also saw some elephant spoor only a day old. Here I remained all day, and slept that night, drying meat on platforms of wood built over fires. From here until I reached the river Shangani, in the Matabele, I never saw a head of game, and only the spoor of one elephant bull.

May 3*rd.*—Reached a small Matabele outpost, about twenty miles distant from Inyati.

May 4*th.*—Reached Inyati, very exhausted in body, but joyful in mind, where I was heartily welcomed, and my wants attended to, by my kind friends and compatriots, the missionaries and traders of the Matabele country. The Rev. W. Sykes at once exerted himself to the utmost to get men to go to the relief of Owen, and two days after my arrival seven men started for the Gweo, carrying all the supplies and provisions that could be got together on the station. I am happy to say that they found Owen and my boy Franz both alive, and better in health than when I left them, and eventually brought them back to the Matabele country. After a three weeks' rest at Inyati, I went over to Gubulawayo, where I became the guest of the Rev. C. D. Helm and his wife, a German lady, and one of the kindest and most generous-hearted of women. Thanks to the wholesome food, and the unremitting kindness and attention which I received beneath their hospitable roof, I soon recovered my health, and in two months' time was strong and well enough to start upon another elephant-hunting expedition into the Mashuna country, having first had the satisfaction of seeing Owen safe in the care of the white men at Gubulawayo, and in a fair way to recovery.

CHAPTER XVII

HUNTING TRIP TO THE MASHUNA COUNTRY

Camp attacked by five Lions – Shoot variety of Game—Accident to Goulden—Griqua Hunters —Many Elephants killed—Shoot Sable Antelope Bull —" Situngweesa," Mashuna "god," and Lobengula —Enchanted Reed—Tragic Death of Quabeet : torn in pieces by Elephant—Elephant-hunt—Charged by Infuriated Cow and knocked down—Horse wounded—Twenty-two Elephants bagged.

EARLY in May 1878, as I have recounted in the last chapter, I again reached the Matabele country, but being in a very weak state of health, the result of long-continued semi-starvation, and the over-fatigue occasioned by having been obliged to walk day after day whilst suffering from repeated attacks of fever, it was not until August that I felt sufficiently strong to start upon another hunting trip ; but towards the end of that month, having obtained permission of Lobengula to hunt during the remainder of the season in the Mashuna country, I at once prepared myself for the journey, intending to join, and if possible hunt in company with, my friends Messrs. Clarkson, Cross, and Wood, who had left Gubulawayo in the preceding June.

On the 20th of August, in company with Mr. Goulden (Mr. Clarkson's partner), I made a start from the mission station of Inyati, taking the old hunting-road leading to the Northern gold-fields.

It was not until after crossing the Sangwe, Shan-

gani, and Vungo rivers—infested by lions—that we
found any game at all.   On the morning of the 30th,
however, shortly after crossing the last-named stream,
I shot a tsessebe antelope—one of three—and trekking
on again crossed the Gwelo, and reached the Gwenia
just before sundown.   Here we found the waggons of
the well-known old Dutch hunter, Jan Viljoen.   He,
together with all the males of his party, consisting of
one son and his two sons-in-law, was away hunting.
So far, Mrs. Viljoen informed us, they had met with
very few elephants.   Reports had come in, however,
she told us, that the Englishmen had been shooting
well on the other side of Umfule.   How I anathe-
matised the illness which alone had prevented my
being with them and sharing in their sport !   The
very day after old Viljoen and his party came here,
five lions attacked and killed two pack donkeys
belonging to him, which, through the carelessness of
the herd, had been left out at night.   The next morning the old man and his sons tackled the marauders,
and amongst them killed a lioness, the others making
good their escape into some reeds and long grass.

The following day we remained where we were
to give our oxen a rest, so I took a ride up the river
in the early morning, and shot two out of a small
herd of sable antelopes.

Two days later, on September 2nd, and shortly
before reaching the river Se-whoi-whoi, I came across
a solitary old sable antelope bull, with a fine pair of
horns, of which I wished to possess myself; but
fortune willed it otherwise, for after making two bad
shots, I eventually lost him amongst some stony hills
and thick underwood.   On my way back to the
waggons I gave chase to some zebras, and shot two
of them.   Just before sunset next evening we reached

the river Bembees, where we found a young Dutch
hunter encamped with his wife and family. As yet
he had shot nothing—I mean no elephants ; but his
Hottentot servant had bagged a fine cock ostrich, and
the day after our arrival he shot another, also in
good plumage. Between the Se-whoi-whoi and the
Bembees I saw a great deal of eland spoor, some only
a day old, but could not come across the animals
themselves nor any spoor fresh enough to follow.

Between Bembees and Sebakwe, Goulden and I
rode out to look for game, and meeting with a small
herd of koodoo cows, he shot one. On our way
back to the waggons we saw a fine cock ostrich, but
as my horse was slow, and I was armed with a ten-
bore rifle, I did not go after him. My friend,
however, being mounted on a very fast pony, gave
chase, and, in the ardour of pursuit, came foul of a
thick thorn bush, which dragged him from the saddle
and mauled him pretty generally, his face presenting
the appearance of a man's who has just had a domestic
squabble, or a severe encounter with a wild cat.

In the afternoon we trekked on to the Sebakwe
river, which is only about eight miles distant from
the Bembees, and into which it empties itself a few
miles below the drift. At daylight on September 5,
we crossed the Sebakwe, and after a four hours' trek
reached a gully with some water-holes in it. In the
evening, after inspanning, I rode on ahead of the
waggons, and shot a tsessebe antelope.

Early next morning we reached the river
" Umniati." The drift was very steep on both sides,
but we managed to get through without much
difficulty. Here I shot a waterbuck. I also saw a
herd of sable antelopes, and the fresh spoor of a
white rhinoceros, besides that of a single elephant

cow, not more than a day old. In the little rocky hills which here border the river, klipspringers are very plentiful.

The Umniati is one of the finest rivers that run northwards into the Zambesi from the watershed of the Mashuna country, and in many parts its large deep pools abound in hippopotami. In the hope of getting a shot at one, I walked several miles along the bank, crossing the river "Umgesi," which runs into it about two miles below the drift, but though I saw a great deal of spoor, some of it seemingly very fresh, I did not see any of the animals themselves. In the evening we trekked on again to the Umgesi, also a fine running stream of beautifully clear water. On the way Goulden shot a waterbuck cow.

September 7th.—Reached "Gwazān," a little river, with some fine pools of water, into one of which my waggon capsized. Luckily, it being lightly laden and the ground soft, no material damage was done, so that after off-loading, we soon righted and pulled it on to firm ground again. During the morning's trek we had crossed elephant cow spoor of yesterday and the day before, and in the evening I rode out and saw more, only a day or two old. They seemed to pass backwards and forwards about here, between the "fly"-infested country to the north-west, and the hills on the southern side of the road, and had I not been anxious to push on and join my friends, I would have remained for a week or so where I was, and hunted well through the hills in the direction of "Intaba Insimbi" (the mountain of iron).

The following day we remained at Gwazān to give the oxen a rest, so Goulden and I rode out to look for elephant spoor, but saw none. Whilst returning to the waggons we came across a small herd of roan antelopes, one of which I shot. In the evening, seeing a herd of sable antelopes feeding down a valley not more than a mile from the waggons, we again saddled up and rode after them   I soon shot the best cow amongst them—her horns measured 2 feet 8 inches along the curve — and then tried to bag the one bull that was with the herd — a fine old fellow, carrying a beautiful pair of horns. I gave him two good shots, and I could see the blood running from his nostrils ; but he nevertheless managed to climb a steep, rocky hill, covered with thick underwood, and disappeared on the farther side.   Up here I was obliged to lead my horse, and when I reached the top, of course the wounded antelope was out of sight.   As the sun was down it was too late to follow his spoor, so I was forced to leave him.   At dawn of day the next morning, I went back with my Kafirs to get the meat of the sable antelope cow, which we found untouched by either lions or hyænas.   On my way back to the waggons I came across another solitary bull, and shot him.   His horns, though very prettily curved, were small.

Just before sundown, as the waggons were trekking, a small herd of elands, whose spoor Goulden and I were following with the horses, winded us, and ran close past the waggons ; one of them, a young bull, my driver knocked over.

The following morning, September 10, we crossed the river Zweswe, and arrived after sundown at an encampment of Griqua hunters—the Neros—who have for many years earned a precarious subsistence in the interior by hunting elephants. That very day they had shot some close to their camp. It

appeared that two of their Kafirs having gone out
early to hunt, had come upon a large herd, which,
when fired upon, ran straight to the Griqua encampment—out of the frying-pan into the fire, in fact.
All hands then turned out, and between them—three
Griquas and several Kafirs—they killed eight, all
cows. This happened about mid-day, when we were
at Zweswe drift, only seven or eight miles away.
Had we only known what was going to take place,
we might with the greatest ease have inspanned that
morning, and come in for a share in the sport.

We heard from the Griquas that our friends had
their permanent encampment on the river Umfule,
only two waggon-treks from here. They said, too,
that they had already shot a lot of elephants, nearly
all fine bulls, and that on Sunday last, September 8,
Messrs. Clarkson and Wood rode right on to a large
herd, and shot eight of them, all good bulls. Also
that Mr. Wood's foreman—that is, the man given
him by the king as head man over his Kafirs—had
been killed by an elephant a few days before.

We were now certainly getting amongst the
elephants once more, and I hoped before long to
renew my acquaintance with them.

As it was a bright moonlight night, we inspanned
again about 10 P.M., and trekked on half-way to
Umfule, and a couple of hours' ride the next morning
brought us to our friends' encampment. They were
all away, however, having left the previous day for
the scene of the slaughter of the eight elephant bulls
shot on Sunday last, as they intended to form another
camp there and hunt from it, more to the north and
east, in the direction of the river Hanyane.

Upon receipt of this news I determined to follow
their waggon spoor, as I felt sure I should be able

to overtake them before sundown ; so, leaving directions with Goulden, who stayed behind, to send my waggon after me as soon as it arrived, I saddled up without delay. That morning, I forgot to mention, my dog caught a grys steinbuck, which, as far as I could judge, appeared to me to be identical with the grys steinbuck of the Cape Colony.

About mid-day, as I was riding quietly along the road, I espied a solitary old sable antelope bull, lying in the shade of a machabel tree, with a very fine pair of horns ; so, dismounting, I stalked up to and shot him, and then taking the skin of his head and neck to preserve at the waggons, placed the skull and horns in a tree on the roadside, where my waggon-driver, I thought, could not fail to see them. He was a very old bull, and when in his prime must have had a magnificent pair of horns, for even as it was, though very much worn down, they measured 3 feet 7 inches along the curve.

Late in the afternoon, while jogging quietly along, and just after crossing a little rivulet, I heard a shout, and saw three white men—at least three men wearing clothes and broad-brimmed felt hats—and several Kafirs, sitting on an ant-heap. Riding up to them, I found that, as I had already surmised, they were my old friends, Messrs. Clarkson, Cross, and Wood, and right glad was I to meet them once again. Our hearty greetings over, I learned that the eight elephant bulls they had shot four days previously lay just beyond the next rise, and that the waggon was outspanned a little farther on, on the banks of a small stream, a tributary of the Umfule. My friends had just returned from an unsuccessful chase after a lion, which the Kafirs had seen feeding on one of the dead elephants. They had sighted him—a fine male ;

2 A

but he was too wary, and managed to make his
escape in the long grass without offering a chance of
a shot. Early the same day, too, Cross had severely
wounded a fine leopard, which he first saw walking
over the prostrate carcase of one of the elephants ;
but it too crept away in the grass, and, as the dogs
would not take the spoor, he lost it.

We then walked back to the waggons, taking a
look at the huge, and now swollen and stinking
carcases of the elephants. They were all fine bulls,
and their sixteen tusks weighed from 30 to 55 lbs.
each.

That evening, over the camp fire, the forty odd
elephants shot by my friends, since I had last seen
them in the Matabele country, were killed over
again. They had had nearly all their sport to the
east of the river Umfule, near some Mashuna kraals,
called " Matja-ung-ombe " (the hill of cattle). The
chief of these kraals, Situngweesa, is considered a
very powerful " Umlimo," or god, by the Amandebele ; and, unlike most other Mashuna chiefs, who
are the victims of continual depredation, he is not
only left in the quiet enjoyment of his own, but often
receives presents of cattle, young girls, etc., from
Lobengula. It is very probable, however, that his
majesty—to use one of his own phrases—is only
fattening this false priest, and that one day he will
pounce down upon and massacre him and all his
people, and take his cattle and the ivory, of which,
it is said, he has a considerable store. This is only
surmise ; but even thus did Umziligazi, his father,
put to death, at one fell swoop, a whole bevy of
Makalaka gods, to whom, up till that day, he had
always shown great favour.

However, whatever may be the private thoughts

and intentions of their chief, the great mass of his people believe implicitly in the power of this Mashuna god, and my friends found it expedient to pay the old fellow a visit, to obtain his gracious permission to go and "kill the elephants nicely," for, until they did this, their boys would only hunt in a listless, half-hearted sort of way, constantly saying, "What is the use of your hunting elephants in Situngweesa's country without first getting his permission to do so?" But when, by the help of presents, the old fellow's good word was obtained, and Wood's head Kafir had been given a long reed, with which, when they were on the spoor, he was to bring the elephants back on their tracks, by first pointing the way they had gone with the enchanted reed, and then drawing it towards him, they at once seemed changed beings and hunted with the greatest alacrity ; and as, before my friends paid a visit to the seer, they had upon two or three occasions followed elephants without coming up with them, and were afterwards very successful, their belief in Situngweesa's power, and the efficacy of the enchanted reed, became more confirmed than ever.

It was whilst they were hunting at Matja-ung-ombe that Wood's head Kafir, a man named Quabeet, from the town of Inxoichin, was killed by an elephant. I give the story of this mishap as I heard it from Clarkson's own lips.

"Early in September, Messrs. Cross and Wood having taken the waggon to some neighbouring kraals to buy corn, I rode out by myself, and crossing fresh elephant spoor, followed it, and at length came up with the animals themselves—nine bulls, one of them an enormous beast without tusks. As soon as I fired upon them the tuskless bull turned out and went off alone, and I thought I had done with him. The elephant I had first fired at only ran a short distance, and fell dead. Quabeet and another Kafir of Wood's, who carried a gun, wounded and pursued another bull, which also turned from the rest as soon as he was shot. This I noticed as I galloped after the herd. I had just killed my second elephant, and had lost sight of the others, when my gun-carrier, Amehlo, came running up, pointing with his hand, and crying out, 'Sir, sir! there goes another elephant unwounded!' I did not see him at first, but after galloping through the forest for a short distance in the direction in which the boy pointed, I caught sight of him. As I did so, I heard an elephant trumpeting terrifically away to my left, and thought to myself that one of the Kafirs was being chased pretty smartly; however, I did not like to leave the elephant I was near, though had I known what was in reality taking place, I should most assuredly have done so. Well, I killed this third elephant, and then rode back to the one I had first shot, where I found all the Kafirs, with the exception of Quabeet. I then asked whom the elephant which had screamed so fearfully had been chasing, and the Kafir who had been with Quabeet said, 'Oh, he was chasing me!' and began to relate what an escape he had had. I then asked him where he had last seen Quabeet, and he said that when he left him he was still running after the elephant they had first wounded, and that he himself had given up the pursuit because he had trodden on a sharp stump of wood and hurt his foot. We then returned to camp, and Quabeet not making his appearance at dark, we thought he must have missed his way, and would turn up the following day. Early next morning we returned to the elephants, and after chopping out the tusks, retraced our steps to camp, which we reached late in the afternoon. Quabeet was not there; the sun set, and night again shrouded the surrounding forest in darkness, and he was still absent. I now felt sure that some accident had happened to him, and only guessed too truly that the awful and long-continued screaming I had heard whilst I was engaged with my third elephant had been his death-knell. The boys, too, cross-questioned the Kafir who had been with Quabeet, and convicted him of lying. I now determined that on the morrow I would take the spoor of the tuskless bull, for to him I could not help attributing the catastrophe which I felt sure had happened, and as he had turned out by himself when I fired the first shot, I knew I should have no difficulty in doing so.

" At break of day I left camp, and riding straight to where I had shot the first elephant, took up the spoor of the tuskless bull, and had followed it for maybe two miles when I came to a place where he had stood under a tree amongst some dense under-wood. From this place he had spun suddenly round, as the spoor showed, and made a rush through the bush, breaking and smashing everything before him. Fifty yards farther on we found Quabeet's gun, a little beyond this a few odds and ends of skin that he had worn round his waist, and then what remained of the poor fellow himself. He had been torn in three pieces; the chest, with head and arms attached, which had been wrenched from the trunk just below the breast-bone, lying in one place, one leg and thigh that had been torn off at the pelvis in another, and the remainder in a third. The right arm had been broken in two places and the hand crushed; one of the thighs was also broken, but otherwise the frag-

ments had not been trampled on." There is little
doubt that the infuriated elephant must have pressed
the unfortunate man down with his foot or knee, and
then twisting his trunk round his body wrenched him
asunder. This feat gives one an idea of the awful
strength of these huge beasts, and how powerless the
strongest of men—even one of " Ouida's " heroes—
would be, when once in their clutches.

By examining the spoor Clarkson found that when
this elephant charged, Quabeet was following another
—doubtless the one he had first wounded—and
thinks that in all probability the poor fellow never
saw the brute until it was close upon him ; and this,
I think, must have been the case, as it is astonishing
how difficult it is to see an elephant when he is
standing still amongst high and thick bush, especially
if one's attention is engaged with something else.

Poor Quabeet! I knew him well, and a real good
fellow he was. A Zulu by blood, he was born just
before Umziligazi left Natal on his flight northwards,
and was still quite a boy when he came to the
Matabele country. In the rebellion of 1870, when
the kraals of " Zwang Indaba " and " Induba "
fought for Kuruman against the present king Lobengula, he took part with the rebels, and received
several assegai wounds during the fierce hand-to-
hand combat that ended in the defeat of his party.
Requiescat in pace.

The day after I rejoined my friends we all rode
out to look for elephant spoor, directing our course
towards the " Hill of the Stump-tailed Bull," a large
round mount which stands by itself, close to the
junction of the Umbila and Umfule rivers, and
forms a conspicuous landmark. On the summit of
this hill, Wood told us, the veteran hunter Mr.

Hartley and his party shot, some years ago, an elephant bull with a stump tail, whence its rather curious name. At that time, he said, there was no tsetse fly on this side of the hill. We, however, caught some of these execrable insects upon our horses when still several miles distant from it, and had to make a hasty retreat in consequence. As we had been keeping a sharp look-out, we caught these flies—six altogether—as soon as ever they settled upon, and before they had time to "stick" our horses.

On our way back to the waggons we shot an eland bull and a wild pig, the latter in very good condition; and I may here say that in the opinion of most hunters there are few things more palatable than the flesh of a fat wild pig—his head baked to a turn forms a dish that an epicure would not despise. Upon reaching camp I found that my waggon had already arrived, having come on by moonlight.

My driver had, however, managed to miss the sable antelope's head that I had placed in a tree by the roadside, and it was owing to this circumstance that we killed a few elephants the following day, for, having sent two boys back at day-dawn to get the horns, they returned running, soon afterwards, shouting out something whilst still a good way off. At first we thought there were lions after the horses, and seizing our rifles ran down to meet them; but it turned out that as they were following the waggon spoor they had seen a small troop of elephants, and so had hastened back to tell us. Of course we at once saddled up, and riding to where the boys had seen them took their spoor, and before long came up with the animals themselves, a small worthless lot of cows. Of these we shot the six largest.

The next day Messrs. Wood and Cross rode back

to the camp at Umfule upon business, whilst Clarkson
and I took a ride to the eastward, but saw no fresh
elephant spoor.

September 16*th.*—Messrs. Wood and Cross having
returned the previous evening, we determined, since
we were getting no more fresh spoor, to inspan the
waggons and trek over to the river Umbila. This
we did, and reached the river by mid-day, where we
were occupied during the afternoon in making a fresh
camp. About here we saw a great deal of fresh
rhinoceros spoor, principally that of the white
species.

This evening we determined to leave the waggons
the next morning, and take a round on horseback
for ten days or so towards the north-east, as Wood,
who had hunted this country years before, thought
we should in all probability find elephants in the
thick groves of mahobo-hobo (a tree bearing a very
nice fruit, and only found, so far as I am aware, in
the Mashuna country) which lie between the Umsengaisi and Hanyane rivers. Our preparations were
soon made, and by an hour after daylight, on
September 17, we were on the march, taking with us
corn for the horses, and provisions for ourselves to
last a fortnight.

We had scarcely forded the Umbila river when
we crossed the fresh spoor of five or six elephant
bulls, which we at once followed. It was about
mid-day, and we were fast gaining upon them, when
they took a turn and made straight for the " fly."
As we had been all the morning upon the edge of
the infested district, we now kept a sharp look-out,
and it was not long before a " fly " was caught upon
Clarkson's horse, which we killed, and then again
took up the spoor, as Wood said the " fly " was not

very numerous about here ; and as we expected soon to come up with the elephants, we thought we might venture to follow them a little farther, keeping, of course, a sharp look-out all the time on our horses. It was shortly after this that the elephants we were following led us to the spoor of another large troop, also fresh. For some time the spoors were mixed, then that of the bulls turned to the left and again made for the " fly." Upon seeing this we resolved to leave the bulls—though we would far rather have shot them—and take the spoor of the troop, as it was leading us in a direction that would soon take us beyond the limit of the " fly." Shortly after making this turn we rode on to a black rhinoceros, the first animal we had seen that day. He honoured us with a hard stare, and then wheeling round trotted off, and disappeared in the bushes.

About 1 P.M. we off-saddled our horses for the first time that day, and had scarcely done so when three heavy shots, fired almost simultaneously, fell in the direction the spoor was taking, and at no great distance. Making sure it was some of Wood's Kafir hunters firing at the elephants we were following, we saddled up again, and cantered along the spoor, but, from the direction it took, soon found that the shots we had heard could not have been fired at the elephants. We now stuck to the spoor without a halt till about an hour and a half before sundown, when, fearing that it would get dark before we came up with them, we took our guns and galloped on, for the spoor was now becoming fresher every instant, and as the elephants were feeding nicely, easy to follow, by the machabel leaves alone, that lay scattered along the track.

I may here say that I was this day mounted on an

old horse in very poor condition, which I had bought
from Wood, my own having gone lame two days
before, and that all our horses had been the livelong
day under the saddle,. and like ourselves had had no
water.   Well, we had cantered along the spoor for
some distance, when we at last descried two elephants,
stragglers from the main body, and then the herd itself.   They were moving in a dense mass up a gentle
incline on the farther side of a dry watercourse, and
as the whole country about here is very sparsely
wooded, we had a magnificent view of them.   There
must have been at least sixty or seventy, great and
small, and a grand sight it was, and one not easily to
be forgotten, to see so many of these huge beasts
moving slowly and majestically onwards.   However,
as there was now but an hour of sunlight left, we
could spare but little time for admiration, and so
rode towards them, on murderous thoughts intent.
We crossed the dry gully, and passed within
150 yards of the two we had first seen, but they
never appeared to take any notice of us.   Just
as we neared the herd, one of the biggest bulls
turned broadside to us, and commenced plucking
some leaves from a bush, offering a splendid shot, of
which Clarkson was just going to take advantage,
when he saw us, and wheeling round, ran off.   As
he did so, I noticed that he had a stump tail. The
whole herd was now in motion.   At first they ran in
a compact body and at a surprising pace, raising a
dense cloud of dust, and in the confusion one of
them, half-grown, was knocked down, and must have
been trampled on and half-stunned, for he did not
get on his legs until the herd had passed, and then
at first ran back, away from his companions ; but
before long, finding out his mistake, wheeled about

and soon caught up to them again. We now galloped along, even with, and about 100 yards to the side of the foremost of them, shouting and hallooing, and thus drove them round in a large circle, our object being to tire them before we commenced firing. Though I had killed many elephants, yet having always before this season hunted on foot in regions infested by the tsetse fly, I had had no experience with them on horseback, so, having been told by my friends on no account to dismount, but to shoot from the horse's back, as, in case of a charge, I should have no time to remount, I endeavoured at first to comply with their instructions; however, my horse, worse luck to him, would not stand, but as soon as I dropped the reins, always walked or trotted forwards, thus making it impossible to get a shot. Seeing that if this continued, I should never shoot an elephant at all, I determined to dismount; so, cantering up alongside of the foremost, I jumped off, and gave a young bull a bullet behind the shoulder as he came broadside past me. He only ran about 100 yards, and then fell dead. After this I quickly killed two more with five shots—a fine cow and another young bull. The fourth I tackled, a bull with tusks scaling about 35 lbs., cost me six bullets, and gave me a smart chase, for my horse was now dead beat. I only got away at all by the skin of my teeth, as, although the infuriated animal whilst charging trumpeted all the time like a railway engine, I could not get my tired horse out of a canter until he was close upon me, and I firmly believe that had he not been so badly wounded he would have caught me. I know the shrill screaming sounded unpleasantly near.

Just as this bull fell, Wood and Cross came round

with what remained of the troop, and I met and turned them back again.   The poor animals were now completely knocked up, throwing water over their heated bodies as they walked slowly along, swerving first one way and then the other, as the cruel bullets struck them.   A good many had turned out, and made their escape in twos and threes, and as we had been picking out all the best, there were now not many left worth shooting.   My friends had fired away almost all their cartridges, but I had still thirteen left ; for, owing to my horse refusing to stand, I had not commenced firing as soon as they. As the elephants were now only walking, and sometimes stood all huddled up together in a mass, offering splendid standing shots, I felt sure of killing three or four more with my remaining cartridges, and should doubtless have done so had it not been for an accident that befell me, which happened in this wise. —Having picked out a good cow for my fifth victim, I gave her a shot behind the shoulder, on which she turned from the herd and walked slowly away by herself.   As I cantered up behind her, she wheeled round, and stood facing me, with her ears spread, and her head raised.   My horse was now so tired that he stood well, so, reining in, I gave her a shot from his back between the neck and the shoulder, which I believe just stopped her from charging.   On receiving this wound she backed a few paces, gave her ears a flap against her sides, and then stood facing me again.   I had just taken out the empty cartridge and was about to put a fresh one in, when, seeing that she looked very vicious, and as I was not thirty yards from her, I caught the bridle, and turned the horse's head away, so as to be ready for a fair start in case of a charge.   I was still holding my rifle with

the breech open, when I saw that she was coming.
Digging the spurs into my horse's ribs, I did my best
to get him away, but he was so thoroughly done that,
instead of springing forwards, which was what the
emergency required, he only started at a walk, and
was just breaking into a canter, when the elephant
was upon us.   I heard two short sharp screams above
my head, and had just time to think it was all
over with me, when, horse and all, I was dashed to
the ground.   For a few seconds I was half-stunned
by the violence of the shock, and the first thing I
became aware of, was a very strong smell of elephant.
At the same instant I felt that I was not much hurt, and
that, though in an unpleasant predicament, I had still
a chance for life.   I was, however, pressed down on
the ground in such a way that I could not extricate
my head.   At last with a violent effort I wrenched
myself loose, and threw my body over sideways, so
that I rested on my hands.   As I did so I saw the
hind-legs of the elephant standing like two pillars
before me, and at once grasped the situation.   She
was on her knees, with her head and tusks in the
ground, and I had been pressed down under her
chest, but luckily behind her fore-legs.   Dragging
myself from under her, I regained my feet and made
a hasty retreat, having had rather more than enough
of elephants for the time being.   I retained, however,
sufficient presence of mind to run slowly, watching
her movements over my shoulder, and directing mine
accordingly.   Almost immediately I had made my
escape, she got up, and stood looking for me with
her ears up and head raised, turning first to one side
and then to the other, but never wheeling quite
round.   As she made these turns, I ran obliquely
to the right or left, as the case might be, always

endeavouring to keep her stern towards me. At length I gained the shelter of a small bush, and breathed freely once more.

All this time I never saw my horse, which must have been lying amongst the grass where he had been thrown to the ground. I thought he was dead, or perhaps, to speak more truly, I was so much engrossed with my own affairs that I did not think about him at all. I stood now just on the highest ground of a gentle rise, which sloped gradually down to an open glade, in which, from where I was, I could see two dead elephants. Just then I saw a Kafir coming across the opening, and went down to meet him, leaving my elephant still standing on the spot where she had knocked me down. Being unarmed, for my gun had been dashed from my hand when I fell, I dared not go near her to look for it. Upon meeting the Kafir (Cross's gun-bearer) I hastily told him what had happened. The elephant was not now visible, being just beyond the crest of the rise, about 200 yards distant, but I only stopped to take some cartridges from my trousers pockets and put them in my belt, and then, accompanied by the boy, returned to the scene of the accident to look for my rifle and see what had become of my horse. On topping the rise, we saw him standing without the saddle, but the elephant had walked away, and was no longer visible. Going up to my horse, I found that he had received an ugly wound in the buttock from behind, from which the blood was streaming down his leg: otherwise, barring a few abrasions, he was unhurt. Whilst the boy was searching for my rifle, I looked round for the elephant, which I knew had only just moved away, and seeing a cow standing amongst some bushes not 200 yards from me, made sure it was the one that had so nearly made an example of me. The Kafir now came up with my rifle and saddle, the girth of which was broken. The rifle having been open at the breech when it fell to the ground was full of sand, so that it was not until I had taken the lever out, using the point of the Kafir's assegai for a screw-driver, that I managed to get it to work. I then approached the elephant, which all this time had been standing where I first saw her, and cautiously advancing to within fifty yards of her, took a careful aim, and gave her a shot behind the shoulder, which brought her to the ground with a crash. Pushing in another cartridge, I ran up and gave her a shot in the back of the head to make sure of her.

The sun had been down some time, indeed it was fast becoming dusk, so I shouted to attract the attention of my friends, whose shots I had not heard for some time past. I immediately heard an answering halloo, and soon met Clarkson, and walked back with him to a large ant-heap, where my comrades had off-saddled. I now found that my eye was bruised, and all the skin rubbed off my right breast, and I felt very stiff in the neck and down the back. I was smeared all over with blood, too, off the elephant's chest, on the back and on the left breast. This was all that was the matter with me, and a most wonderfully lucky escape I think it was. The elephant must have rushed against the horse from behind like a battering-ram, throwing me head-foremost to the ground, and the impetus of her rush must have carried her a little too far, for had I been in front of her knees, instead of behind them, nothing could have saved me. I think, too, that she was very severely wounded, and that this desperate charge must have so exhausted her that she let me escape more easily than she would otherwise have done : perhaps this, too, accounts for her not further molesting the horse.

It was now almost dark ; neither our horses nor ourselves had had a drink all day, and we did not know where we should find water, so we resolved to make for the Umsengaisi river, from which Wood did not think we were far distant ; it was not, however, until we had had a weary tramp of two hours or so in the dark that we at length reached it. Just where we struck it, the river was dry ; but after following down its course for about a mile, we found a rather muddy water-hole, which was nevertheless most acceptable under the circumstances. Having neither food nor blankets with us, we built a large fire, and proceeded to make ourselves as comfortable as we could.

Early the following morning we went to count and examine the dead elephants. I led my horse with me, after having washed his wounds well with cold water, intending to send him back to the waggons at the Umbila river as soon as my boys came up, for of all our Kafirs that had started with us the preceding morning, my friends' three gun-carriers were the only ones that had kept up with us, which was nothing to their discredit, as they were all carrying loads. The elephant's tusk had entered my horse's buttock near the anus, running obliquely into the rectum ; I had it syringed out morning and evening with strong carbolic lotion, and although for some time the poor beast seemed in a very precarious condition, in two months from then the wound had quite healed up, and he had entirely recovered from its effects. When we reached the dead elephants we found our Kafirs already there, and so made breakfast on the spot, and then proceeded to count the slain. We found altogether twenty-one dead elephants, two of them having but one tusk each. We afterwards picked up another which had gone away and died near the Umsengaisi, so that twenty-two in all had fallen to our rifles. I then sent two Kafirs to the waggons with my wounded horse, telling them to bring the one I had left there lame, back with them as quickly as possible. The Mashunas now commenced to arrive in large parties, eager for the meat, which we gave them on condition that they should chop out all the tusks, and carry them to the waggons at the Umbila river. The following day by noon all the tusks were out, and every elephant cut up. There had been no big bulls amongst this herd, but there were three whose tusks weighed from 35 lbs. to 45 lbs. each, and the forty teeth together must have scaled about 700 lbs. The last elephant which I had shot under the impression that it was the one which had caught me and struck my horse, turned out to be a cow that Cross had wounded just above the eye ; seeing her so near the horse, and so near to where I had left my elephant only a minute or so before, I naturally made the mistake.

Thus the elephant that had so signally discomfited me had gone off, though only to die, I am afraid, at no great distance, for the two shots I gave her were both good ones, which she could not long survive. I would have followed her spoor, as I should much have liked to possess myself of her tusks as a memento of the day's hunt ; but as we had driven the elephants all round about in every direction, it was impossible to pick out the tracks of any particular one.

2 B

The following morning my boys returned from the waggons, bringing with them my other horse. His lameness had been caused by a stump of wood sticking into the quick of the off hind hoof, and the place being not yet quite healed up, I extemporised a shoe, made from the outside skin of an elephant's ear, lacing it up to a piece of soft leather fastened loosely round the fetlock. This shoe put on wet overnight used to dry hard to the shape of the foot by morning, but I had to renew it every other day, as the horse's weight soon wore it through.

On the 20th we again found fresh spoor, in a thick grove of mahobo-hobo trees, and followed it a long way, but the elephants eventually got our wind, having doubled back parallel to their track, and when we found this out they had already got a long start, and although we galloped after them, we could not hold the spoor well, and at last lost it altogether.

The following day we got fresh spoor once more, and again lost it in much the same way. The elephants in this country are too clever by half; for instance, these last, as soon as they scented us, instead of running in a body, as any decent, sober-minded elephants would have done, in which case we might have galloped on their spoor, scattered in all directions, in ones, and twos, and threes. In trying to follow them we got separated, and Wood and I, after hallooing in vain for our friends, made for our camp on the Umsengaisi, thinking they would do the same.

We were riding along an old footpath, through a patch of leafless bush, when I saw some large black objects that I at first thought were buffaloes, but very soon made out to be elephants. We were about eighty yards from them when the foremost saw

us, and was breaking into a run when Wood pulled
in his horse, and with a bullet from his eight-to-the-
pound rifle bowled her over in her tracks. He
afterwards shot another, and I also killed two. There
were only eight of them—a tuskless cow, and seven
others not full grown. Elephants are, however, now
so scarce, that one cannot afford to leave even
smallish ones alone. Directly Wood fired, they all
scattered, and as the bush was rather thick, we could
not drive them together again. Just as the last fell
dead, Messrs. Clarkson and Cross came galloping up,
and our Kafirs followed soon after, all having heard
and been guided by our shots. Finding water in a
valley close to the dead beasts, and having our
blankets and other traps with us, we camped on the
spot, and spent the following day, Sunday, in idleness,
whilst our Kafirs were engaged in chopping out the
tusks.

CHAPTER XVIII

On Monday, September 23, we again turned our
faces to the north-east, and made for the Hanyane
river. On the following day, as we were riding
along, we spied an old eland bull, standing in the
shade of a tree. As we thought he would be fat,
and we were in want of this luxury, Wood, who had
the best horse, was deputed to shoot him, whilst we
held in our nags and watched events. The eland,
all unconscious of these designs upon him, stood
quietly swishing the flies from his sides, and it was
not until his enemy had approached to within 200
yards of him that he became aware of his proximity,
and trotted out into the open. Wood then let
"Wildfire" out, and a fast horse he was; but the
eland, heavy though he looked, broke into a springing
gallop, and held his own for the short distance that
the chase was within our view. Soon, however, we
heard a shot, and cantering up found Wood survey-

ing his victim, which stood, poor thing, on the farther side of a gully, looking ruefully with his soft brown eyes upon his destroyer. What a grand-looking beast an eland bull is, with his heavy though shapely body, low hanging dewlap, fine clean-cut limbs, and small game-looking head! He is one of those stately creatures that few reflecting men can slay without regret, and fewer still, I hope, would kill for sport alone, leaving the carcase to rot in the wilderness or fatten the wolves and vultures ; but at the same time, it is as necessary for the hunter, upon whose rifle, perhaps, a score of hungry savages are dependent for food from day to day, to shoot many beautiful and harmless animals, as it is for a butcher in a civilised land to poleaxe an ox.

We now drove him gently along to a hole of water, some distance down the gully before mentioned, when a bullet put a term to his misery. He had a very pretty, even pair of horns, with white tips, which measured 2 feet 4 inches in length.

The following day, September 24, we made an early start, still keeping a north-easterly course, and at about 10 A.M., within a few miles of the Hanyane river, crossed the fresh spoor of a troop of elephant bulls, which of course we followed, and as they were feeding quietly along, it was hardly noon when we sighted them. At the same moment they got our wind, and ran. There were, I think, nine altogether, five of which we shot, the other four, I am sorry to say, making good their escape. Those we shot were all old animals. Two carried tusks weighing 60 lbs. apiece, within a pound or two, and those of the other three were all over 40 lbs. each. There being water close by, we camped where we were. On the following day a lot of Mashunas came to our camp and asked permission to cut up the meat, which we granted.   They own allegiance to the petty Mashuna chief, Lo Magondi, whose kraals were situated amongst the hills, which we could see from our camp, and which were not more than ten miles distant.

On September 27 we rode down to have a look at the Hanyane river, as it is marked in Mr. Baines's last map.   By the Matabele this river is called "Hanyane," but by the Mashunas "Manyame," and near its confluence with the Zambesi, "Panyame." It is a fine running river, with long reaches of deep-blue water, neither few nor far between, along its course.   In many parts of it there are hippopotami, though about here the natives have persecuted them so much that they have gone in quest of fresh fields and pastures new.   At one place we found a large deep pool, fenced completely round, rude dams, as it were, having been built across the shallow water, both above and below it ; several stages, too, had been erected in the pool itself, surmounted by small platforms.   These preparations, the Mashunas told us, had been made to circumvent some hippopotami that were in the pool.   The fence was made to prevent their coming out to feed, and on the various platforms men were stationed with heavy spears, which they plunged into the backs of the amphibious monsters whenever they showed them-selves above water.   Altogether, the hippopotami must have had a rough time of it in that pool. Two, at any rate, must have met their death, for we saw their skulls lying there.   Just after leaving this pool we crossed the spoor of some elephants that had passed in the night, and, it being still early, followed them. We stuck to the spoor until about four o'clock in the afternoon, when we gave it up, as, from the appearance of the leaves that they had been eating, we were still as far behind them as when we started. They had described a regular circle round our camp, so that although we had ridden many miles we were still at no great distance from it, and managed to get home just before dark. The following day we rode out again in the direction of Lo Magondi's town, which lies amongst the hills to the north of our camp ; we saw no elephant spoor, but whilst returning home came across a fine old eland bull, which we shot for the sake of the meat and fat.

During the next three days we rode out regularly both up and down, and on the farther side of the Hanyane river, but saw no more fresh elephant spoor, though the country about here must have been full of these animals only eight days before, when we shot the five bulls. Our firing seemed to have frightened them all away, so shy are elephants at the present day. What may perhaps have had something to do with their disappearance, too, was the presence of bands of Mashunas all over the country, engaged in netting game, parties of whom we came across constantly. These nets are neatly made of cord manufactured from the inner bark of the machabel tree. Each individual net is from fifteen to twenty yards in length, and six or seven feet in breadth, and when set for game a great number of them are arranged upon poles in a row, so as to form a continuous line of netting, several hundred yards in length. Into these nets antelopes of all kinds are driven and entangled, and as they are very elastic, and give to their weight, it is only the very largest animals that can break through them ; indeed the Mashunas assured us that they would hold anything running, with the exception of the elephant and rhinoceros.

On the evening of October 1, my driver Jantje came to our camp from the waggons at the Umbila river, bringing rather alarming news, for he informed us that upon the day of his arrival there, the cattle-herd had caught three tsetse flies in the kraal, and that he himself had seen " fly " not a mile from the waggons. Being a Hottentot blessed with more " nous " than the generality of his tribe, whose rule is always to let things slide, he had at once inspanned the waggons and trekked over to the Umsengaisi river, and then came on to our camp to tell us what he had done. Of course we thought that all our oxen and the two horses we had left at the waggons were " fly-stuck," and cursed our luck accordingly ; but we were eventually very agreeably disappointed, for we did not lose a single ox, though two of mine and one of Wood's showed evident signs of having been bitten, becoming very thin, and running at the eyes. They were all young animals, however, and at last pulled through, though one of mine did not commence to make flesh again for more than a year. These facts convinced me that it takes more than one fly-bite to kill an ox or any other animal, and that recovery from tsetse bite is possible when the blood has not been too strongly impregnated with the poison. Jantje had shot a fine old elephant bull, whose tusks weighed 56 lbs. and 57 lbs. apiece, and two cows, besides two hippopotami which he came across in the Umniati river.

The following day, October 2, my horse being again very lame, I left my friends, and walked over to the waggons at Umsengaisi, with the intention of

going into the "fly" on foot, for ten days or so.
I reached the river just at dark, and thinking I was
below the waggons, followed its course for a long
way in the night.   When day broke, however, I saw
by some hills that I was wrong, and so had to retrace
my steps, and did not reach the encampment until
mid-day.   Here I found Goulden, who had come
over from our big camp on the Umfule to look
us up.

During the following night four elephant bulls
passed close by the waggons, so near indeed that
the dogs ran out and barked at them, and the next
morning we took their spoor.   However, the dogs
must have given them a fright, for they walked on
in single file, mile after mile, without ever stopping
to feed, so that we never gained upon them in the
least, and eventually left the spoor, reaching the
waggons late.   That day I saw two bush pigs, which
I think are rare in this part of the country, as they
are the only ones I have seen.   They were of a
reddish colour, with long hair down their backs, their
heads and snouts being like those of a domestic pig.
When they ran their tails hung down, whereas a
wart hog, the common wild pig of the country,
always carries his tail held straight in the air.   I had
only twice seen these animals before, and that was in
the thick bush to the west of, and not far from, the
river Gwai.

The following day, just before sundown, Messrs.
Clarkson, Cross, and Wood rode in from the Hanyane,
having seen no more elephant spoor since I had left
them.   Next day being Sunday, we took things easy,
and had a day's rest.   About mid-day two Boer
hunters—Cornelius Engelbreght and Karl Weyand
—rode up to our camp, having followed on our

waggon spoor from Umfule to try and get some
powder, coffee, etc., from us. They had shot a few
elephants near the sources of the Umfule, and had
also seen fresh spoor on this side of our main camp.
When we showed them the ten fine tusks of the bulls
we had shot at the Hanyane, Cornelius exclaimed
enviously, " Alle-mächtig, yella Engelesche is geluc-
kach gewes "—*i.e.* By the Almighty, you English
have been lucky.

It was now arranged that Cross, Goulden, and
Wood should return to our big camp with the Boers
on the following day, and hunt the country between
the Umfule and Zweswe rivers, whilst Clarkson and
I remained behind for a short time to hunt the
mahobo-hobo forests in the neighbourhood of our
present camp. On the 8th of October Clarkson
went out on foot to look for a pig down the river,
whilst I, having hurt my foot the day before,
remained at the waggons alone. About ten o'clock
the cattle-herd came running up, saying there were
some elephants amongst the oxen. Of course I got
up the horses, and taking one of Clarkson's, rode
with the boy to where he had seen the elephants, which
had now decamped. I soon got the spoor, and as
they had run off in single file, was able to gallop
along at a good pace. Now and then, however, they
had separated, and I had then to go slowly, and take
the spoor carefully. At last, after I had been riding
for about an hour, I sighted their dusky forms, and
was soon alongside of them. Never was an expectant
hunter more disappointed. There were about a
dozen elephants, three large, tuskless cows, and the
rest little bits of things, not one amongst them worth
shooting. I rode twice round them, and was very
nearly turning back without firing a shot, but

thinking that the meat, at any rate, would come in handy, I shot the largest amongst them, a heifer with tusks about 5 lbs. in weight.   I then left them and rode back to the waggons, intensely disgusted at the bad luck I had met with, for the veldt was very open, and had the elephants only been worth shooting, I might have had a good and remunerative day's sport with them.

The next day we rode across to the Umbila river to look for elephant spoor, but saw none.   Whilst on our way back I shot a sable antelope cow, with a very fine pair of horns.

On the 11th, as we were getting no fresh elephant spoor about the Umsengaisi, we inspanned the waggon and started back for the Umfule.   We had just outspanned late in the afternoon, and were getting things square for the night, when the cattle-herd ran up to tell us that two rhinoceroses were coming down to water a few hundred yards up the valley.   We seized our rifles, and ran down to try and get a shot at them, and soon espied two black rhinoceroses just emerging from the bush on their way to the water. The bush was very open, and the sharp-scented though short-sighted beasts seemed suspicious of danger ; however, taking advantage of the cover afforded by a very small bush, I managed to approach within seventy yards of the cow, which was then standing broadside to me.   I was just raising my rifle to fire when she must have made me out, for she wheeled round and faced towards me.   Seeing that there was no time to be lost, I gave her a shot between the neck and the shoulder, which brought her to her knees, but she recovered herself at once, and wheeling round, was just starting off when Clarkson gave her another shot in the ribs that again knocked her down.   She was up again in an instant, however, and galloped off after the other as if unhurt. They both of them soon settled into a trot, but a rhinoceros trots as fast as an eland, and although we ran as hard as we could, we did not get near them. The dogs having heard the shots, now came rushing past, and were soon barking and jumping up at the ears of the rhinoceroses.   However, they pursued the even tenor of their way, never stopping to fight with the dogs, and having crossed the open valley, were soon lost to our sight in the bush beyond.

Early the following morning we again inspanned and trekked on, but as I thought that there was a chance of finding the rhinoceros cow we had wounded the previous evening, I saddled up my horse and rode on her spoor, but after following her for several miles, and finding she had never once stopped, I gave it up and returned to the waggons, which I found outspanned.   I will take this opportunity of remarking that I have found it, as a rule, of very little use following either elephants or rhinoceroses, however desperately they may have been wounded, unless, indeed, one of their legs has been injured ; for these beasts, unlike other animals, do not go and stand, but walk on and on until they drop. This, I say, I have found, after considerable experience, to be the rule, though, of course, it is not an invariable one.   On reaching the waggon I found that Clarkson had just shot an eland bull which he had seen as he was trekking.

Early on October 15 we reached our camp on the Umfule, and found that our friends Cross, Goulden, and Wood were still away hunting near Intaba Insimbi, between the Umfule and Zweswe rivers.

On the 16th, taking with us provisions and corn

for the horses sufficient to last ten days, Clarkson and I again left camp, and following the waggon-track, rode towards Zweswe, intending to hunt for a few days amongst the Machabi hills, through which that river runs. That day we only got as far as the Griqua encampment, and on the way Clarkson shot a sable antelope. The Griquas, we found, had shot no elephants during the last month. The following day we rode on again, still keeping the waggon-track, and crossing the Zweswe river, reached Gwāzān early in the afternoon. Here we set to work to make a rude sort of hut that would protect us from the weather, as we intended to remain where we were for several days, and a heavy thunderstorm was brewing, which, indeed, burst upon us before our hut was completed. Early the following day we were again in the saddle, and leaving all our baggage at the skerm, in charge of a couple of boys, took a round through the hills to the south of the waggon-road. These hills are clothed for the most part with forests of the machabel tree, the favourite food of the elephant ; but, though several herds of these animals had been about during the last month, we did not find any very fresh spoor. At last we emerged from the hills, and rode out upon the open treeless downs which lie between this range and Intaba Insimbi. Here we came across a black rhinoceros cow, right in the open plain, and, as we wanted meat for ourselves and our boys, shot her, though not without a hard gallop, for these unwieldy-looking beasts run at a pace that, with their short legs and heavy bodies, one would not believe them capable of. She was in excellent condition for a black one, and we got some very good meat from her ribs, which was probably due to the fact that she was within a few days of calving.

Two days later we were again riding amongst the hills, and had just entered a large opening, when I espied two elands, a bull and a cow, standing in the shade of a small tree about 400 yards distant. Clarkson at once went for the bull, and as he was much better mounted than I, I just followed at a canter, not caring to distress my horse needlessly. The elands stood watching my friend's approach until he was within 200 yards of them, then, his real character seeming all at once to strike them, they wheeled suddenly round, and made off at a hard trot. This, however, availed them but little, for soon the pursuing steed, now urged to his utmost speed, dashed up to within fifty yards of them. Then, indeed, they broke into a gallop, each one taking his own course, and my friend followed the bull. I had a fine view of the chase, for, as the eland ran in a semicircle, I was never very far distant. The bull ran hard for his life, as most elands in this part of Africa do, when not overburdened with fat. For quite a mile, I think, he never broke from his gallop, and as long as he galloped my friend could not pass him, but just kept about twenty or thirty yards behind him. Then, however, his race was run, for directly he broke into a trot, the longer-winded horse dashed past him. Clarkson did not at once shoot him, but brought him back at a hard trot—the foam flying in long silver threads from his mouth, as he turned his head alternately from side to side—to where I was standing, near the steep bank of a deep gully, in which there were several pools of water ; then cantering past him, and pulling in his horse, he fired from the saddle as the eland trotted broadside past him ; but the horse must have moved slightly as he fired, for the bullet, instead of inflicting a mortal

wound, struck the animal too high up just in front
of the loins, and must have just grazed the backbone,
for he fell to the shot as if struck by lightning.

As we had but very few cartridges left, and
feared to run short in case of meeting with elephants,
and as the eland appeared unable to rise, we did not
at once despatch him, but waited for the Kafirs to
come up and administer the *coup de grâce* with their
assegais. In the meantime, we led the horses down
to the nearest pool of water, about 100 yards distant,
and after off-saddling, knee-haltered them. The
Kafirs were now close up, so calling to them
to come on quickly, Clarkson and I walked back
to the eland. As we neared him he made another
violent and almost successful effort to rise, so I
turned again and shouted to the Kafirs to bring an
assegai. Three of them ran up, but not having
heard what I said, and seeing the eland lying flat
on the ground, apparently dead, they had only
brought knives to cut up the meat. As they rushed
up, the eland made another tremendous effort, and
this time gained his feet. For an instant he stood
still, then staggered forwards, gaining strength at
every step, till he was soon going off at a trot that
a footman stood no chance of keeping up with.
Having neither rifle nor assegai, we were unable to
hinder his escape in any way. Clarkson and the
boys ran after him, shouting to the other Kafirs to
bring a rifle ; whilst I, thinking they would never
get up to him on foot, ran back to the water, hastily
caught and saddled up Clarkson's horse, and then
seizing my rifle, galloped at full speed in the direction
taken by the eland, that was now out of sight in a
patch of scattered bush. At length I caught sight
of him, and galloping in front, endeavoured to turn

him back again to the water, but do what I might
he would not swerve from his course, so I jumped
off and gave him a shot through the heart, as he
trotted past me. That day several of our Kafirs
having lagged behind, missed our spoor, our blanket-
carriers amongst them, and as they did not come up
by nightfall, we had to sleep upon the bare ground,
which, however, as it was fine, did not inconvenience
us much.

On the 21st we rode back to our waggons at
Umfule to see if our friends had returned. They
had not arrived, but we heard from a boy they had
sent on, that they would be in camp on the following
day. We this day witnessed a very pretty sight,
as we were riding across a wide, open down between
the Zweswe and Umfule rivers. We had a short
time previously noticed a solitary old sable antelope
bull feeding on the edge of a small strip of bush
that intersected the plain. Suddenly this antelope,
which was 600 or 700 yards distant, came running
out into the flat straight towards us, on perceiving
which we reined in our horses, and looked
around for the cause of its alarm. This was soon
apparent, for before long we saw that an animal
was running on its tracks, and though still distant,
overhauling it fast, for the sable antelope not
being pressed was not yet doing its best, so that
when it was about 200 yards from us, its
pursuer, which we now saw was a wild dog, was not
more than fifty yards behind it. The noble-looking
antelope must just then have seen us, for it halted,
looked towards us, and then turning its head, glanced
at its insignificant pursuer. That glance, however,
at the open-mouthed dog thirsting for its life-blood
must have called up unpleasant reminiscences, for

To face page 384.   SABLE ANTELOPE PURSUED BY WILD DOG; MASHUNA LAND, OCTOBER 21, 1878.

instead of showing fight, as I should have expected it to have done, it threw out its limbs convulsively, and came dashing past us at its utmost speed. It was, however, to no purpose, for the wild dog lying flat to the ground as a greyhound, its bushy tail stretched straight behind it, covered two yards to its one, and came up to it in no time. It just gave it one bite in the flank, and letting go its hold instantly, fell a few yards behind ; at the bite the sable antelope swerved towards us, and upon receiving a second, in exactly the same place, turned still more, so that, taking the point on which we stood for a centre, both pursuer and pursued had described about a half - circle round us, always within 200 yards, since the sable antelope had first halted. As the wild dog was just going up the third time it got our wind, and instead of again inflicting a bite, stopped dead and looked towards us, whilst about 100 yards from it the sable antelope also came to a stand. The baffled hound then turned round, and, pursued by Clarkson, made off one way, whilst the sable antelope, delivered from its tormentor, cantered off in another. This is the only time I have ever heard of a wild dog pursuing an animal by itself, especially such a formidable antagonist as a sable antelope bull, which can use its horns with wonderful dexterity. The wild dog, I fancy, must have been well aware of this fact, and, if so, that would account for its only inflicting a bite, and at once letting go its hold, for if, like a tame dog, it were to have held on, it would have been infallibly transfixed. Whether in time it would have succeeded in tearing the sable antelope's flank open, and then pulling its entrails out piecemeal, which was its evident intention, I cannot say ; but I think it a

2 c

curious fact, and one well worth noticing, that an African hunting dog is capable of overtaking and attacking single-handed such a powerful animal as a male sable antelope.

On the following day, Cross, Goulden, and Wood came into camp just before sundown. They had shot two white rhinoceroses not more than three miles from the waggons, and that same morning had ridden out and shot a solitary old buffalo cow, the only buffalo seen by any of our party this season. They had also been more fortunate with elephants than Clarkson and myself, for one afternoon as they were sitting in their camp, near the river Zweswe, their Kafirs sighted a herd of these animals coming towards them. They rode after them at once, and the country being very open, and favourable for working with horses, they killed the entire troop, consisting of twenty-one elephants, with the exception of two tuskless ones, which they allowed to escape.

The next day we sent all the Kafirs and two pack oxen to bring in the meat of the two white rhinoceroses. I myself took a round to look for oribi antelope, but though I saw several, they were very wild, and I could not manage to bag one. These graceful little antelopes are common about here, and become more numerous towards the north-east ; but to the south-west, in the direction of the Matabele country, I have never seen any after crossing the river Zweswe. They stand higher on their legs than steinbucks, and can be at once distinguished from them by their black tails and ringed horns. They are, I think, specifically identical with the oribi of the Cape Colony. Besides on the higher portions of the Mashuna country, I

have met with the oribi on the open plateau of the
Manica country, to the north of the Zambesi, at
Gazuma vley, about thirty miles to the south-west
of the Victoria Falls (but nowhere else in the
surrounding country), and on the marshy flats in
the neighbourhood of Linyanti, on the northern
bank of the river Chobe. All over this part of the
country the remarkable standard-winged nightjar
(*Cosmetornis vexillarius*) is very common ; indeed,
one can scarcely ride ten miles through the veldt
without putting one up. The males had now
assumed their long wing-feathers, which, if I am not
mistaken, they only retain during the breeding
season ; at least I have observed that one does not
see any nightjars with long feathers in their wings
before September, or after December, and it is in
the former month that the females usually lay.
Like all other nightjars, these birds lie very close
during the daytime, and when disturbed only fly
twenty or thirty yards, and again alight and lie close
to the ground. The females when sitting will
almost allow one to tread upon them before they
move ; indeed, I have seen one sit still whilst four
horsemen and about thirty Kafirs walked past within
a yard of her in single file. Like its European
congener, the African standard-winged nightjar lays
two eggs upon the bare ground, the only difference
being that the marblings are pinky-brown instead of
grey. There is another species of nightjar, the
Caprimulgus mozambicus, also very common in this
part of the country, whose nesting habits and the
colour of whose eggs are very similar to those of
C. vexillarius, from which species, however, it may
be at once distinguished by being of a greyer colour,
and wanting the six bars across the wings which

mark the female of the latter species. The cock birds are easily recognised, *C. mozambicus* having no long feathers in the wings.

As we had now very little corn left, it was arranged that Clarkson and I should take one waggon and trek down to Lo Magondi's, near where we had shot the five elephant bulls a month previously, and endeavour to buy a load; so on the afternoon of the 25th we inspanned and started, taking our old road again as far as the Umsengaisi. After crossing this river, however, we had to make a road all the way to Hanyane, and, as in some places the mahobo-hobo forests grew very thickly, we had a good deal of chopping to do. Nothing worth relating happened during the trip. On our way to the Hanyane we one day came upon five white rhinoceroses as we were trekking with the waggon, but before we could get a shot at them, the dogs drove them away. On another occasion we came upon two bull elands, and mounting our horses pursued and shot them both, and loaded up all the meat to buy corn with from the Mashunas. Upon reaching our destination, we bought all the corn we required in two days. In the mountains about here, extensive excavations have been made, but whether for gold or iron we could not learn. Whilst we were buying corn, I shot three more elands, but they were all in very low condition. There did not appear to have been any elephants about at all since we were here before, but during our return to Umfule, and when near the Umsengaisi river, we very nearly came up to two fine bulls. Having started the waggon, Clarkson and I rode out to look for game, and before long crossed the fresh spoor of the two bulls that were feeding and sauntering slowly along, unfortunately in the direction of our track, which they must have crossed just a little in front of the waggon. Shortly afterwards they must have heard the whip, or the talking of the Kafirs, and, of course, at once decamped. When we reached the place where they had got the alarm, they could not have been gone more than a quarter of an hour. We followed them up at once at a trot, and were very near them a second time in a thick mahobo-hobo forest; but, by a sudden turn, they got our wind, and again made off, this time in real earnest. We tried to gallop on the spoor, but the ground was hard in many places, and we could not hold it well, and at last gave it up in despair and rode back to the waggon. Whilst we were following these two elephants, we came upon a black rhinoceros, that did not see us until we were within fifty yards of him, when he turned and trotted off.

On November 3rd, we again reached our camp at Umfule, having neither seen nor shot anything but a few sable antelopes and tsessebes. One of my dogs also caught a large wild pig and held it fast single-handed until the Kafirs assegaied it. During this trip we lost three good dogs in the Umsengaisi river, all of which were caught by crocodiles. One of them was an old favourite of mine, that six years previously I had rescued from the jaws of a crocodile in the river Gwenia, whose teeth, however, had left some indelible scars upon his hind-quarters. Since that time he had faithfully followed his master's wandering footsteps over many hundreds of miles of wilderness, and had ever done his duty at pulling down wounded game, or catching wild pigs, and could show at least a dozen honourable scars, chiefly administered by the tusks of these latter animals, and now in his old age he had found a damp and dismal grave in the maw of another of these voracious monsters. Poor old Bill ! it was terribly hard luck.

When we reached the Umfule again, we found that during our absence our friends had been equally unsuccessful with ourselves in coming across elephants ; so, as it seemed that there were no more of them about, and the rainy season was coming on apace, we resolved to finally break up our camp, and trek slowly out to the Matabele country, taking a road more to the south than that by which we had come in to the hunting veldt.

Accordingly, on November 5th, we made a move, and trekked about twelve miles to the south-west, all along the bank of a beautifully clear stream, a tributary of the Umfule. On the way I shot a zebra, and an eland bull with a fine even pair of horns 2 feet 5 inches in length. That night the rains came down with a vengeance, and we were detained for a week in the same spot by constantly recurring storms.

One morning Wood and myself, taking advantage of a few hours of clear weather, rode out to look for game, and after shooting a roan antelope bull, were returning home, when, in a small patch of bush, we rode right on to a black rhinoceros, that we at once saluted with two bullets. As the wounded animal galloped off, we saw for the first time that it was followed by a small calf, which could not have been more than a day or two old, for it seemed unable to keep up with its mother, and upon our approach ran under the legs of Wood's horse, who, calling to me to go on and kill the cow, pulled in, in order to secure it. With another bullet I despatched the cow accordingly, and returning to my friend, found him sitting under a shady tree, and the little rhinoceros

standing close beside his horse, which did not mani-
fest the slightest alarm at the near proximity of the
uncouth-looking and, no doubt to him, strangely-
smelling little beast.   The young rhinoceros, too,
that was scarcely larger than a half-grown pig, did
not seem at all frightened when either Wood or
myself, or any of the Kafirs approached it, but stood
quite still when we went up to it and passed our
hands down its back.   It was, of course, too young
to have any sign of horns, but two round patches on
the nose showed where they would in time have grown ;
in other respects, with its prehensile lip, large ears,
and little twinkling eyes, it was a perfect miniature
of an adult black rhinoceros.   One circumstance, I
remember, that struck me at the time was that it
sweated most profusely all over the back, which I
never remember to have seen an adult animal do.
As we found that it followed Wood's horse as closely
as if it had been its own mother, we determined to
try and get it to the waggons, which were about six
miles distant, and endeavour to rear it on thin gruel,
for, unfortunately, we had no milch cows with us ;
so, leaving the Kafirs to cut up the old cow, we rode
home, the little rhinoceros following us like a dog
the whole way.   The heat of the sun seemed to give
it great inconvenience, for it halted and remained
behind beneath every shady tree ; but, as soon as the
horse was about twenty yards ahead, it would twist
up its little tail, give a squeal, and come trotting up
alongside of it again.   At last we reached the waggons,
when of a sudden the nature of the hitherto quiet
little beast seemed changed ; whether it was the sight
of the dogs, that came barking round it, or of the
waggons, or the *tout ensemble* of sights and smells
with which its eyes and nostrils were assailed, I know

not, but it was now transformed into a perfect little demon, charging people, dogs, and even the waggon wheel, with great fury. I now passed an ox-rein round its neck, and behind one shoulder, when it rushed alternately to the length of its tether, springing from the ground in its fury, and then back again at me, when it would inflict several bumps on my knees with its nose. Its *modus operandi* was to lower its head between its legs, and then, by throwing it up perpendicularly, strike several blows in quick succession with its nose. Small and weak as the poor little creature was, it still battered my knees with considerable violence. After being secured to the waggon-wheel it presently became quieter, though it still charged out to the full length of its tether at any dog or person that approached it. It, however, as I feared, obstinately refused all food, though I have no doubt it would have drunk milk had we had a cow with us ; so, knowing that to let it run loose would be merely to condemn it to a lingering death from starvation, or an equally painful one by the fangs of lions or hyænas, I judged it most merciful to put a bullet through its head, which I did, though not without regret, for I should much have liked to rear it.

The rains having now fairly set in, and the ground being thoroughly soaked, we made but slow progress with the waggons, and did not reach the river Gwenia —which, as far as shooting is concerned, may be considered as the southern boundary of the Mashuna hunting country — until the 11th of December. During all this time we saw no signs of elephants, though we found other game fairly plentiful, and shot a few rhinoceroses, elands, sable, roan, and tsessebe antelopes, etc. Twice Cross, Wood, and I

made short trips on foot into the " fly," hoping to
find elephants along the Umniati, Sebakwe, and
Se-whoi-whoi rivers, but here too we were disappointed, and never even saw a fresh spoor.　At
Gwenia I was fortunate enough to bag a lioness.
One Saturday evening Cross and I walked over from
the river Se-whoi-whoi to old Jan Viljoen's waggons
at Gwenia, hoping to hear some news from the
Matabele.　Mr. Viljoen, we found, was still away
hunting with his son and sons-in-law on the other
side of Intaba Insimbi, but we were most hospitably
received by his wife and nieces, who regaled us *ad
lib.* upon bread and butter, and buttermilk, an
indescribable treat to us who had been so long
strangers to such luxuries.　The old lady informed us
that they had been much troubled by lions during
her husband's protracted absence, they having twice
attacked the cattle in broad daylight, killing two
cows and two young oxen ; she told us, too, that
one had been prowling about the kraal for several
nights past, and had caught two of the best dogs.
Of course, we hoped we might have a chance of
coming to conclusions with the marauder, but scarcely
looked for such luck.　That evening a calf was
missing, and though we searched both up and down
the river we neither saw nor heard anything of it.
The following day was Sunday, and it must have
been about ten o'clock in the morning, when, as
Cross and I were sitting in the hut, talking to
Mrs. Viljoen, we suddenly heard loud screaming and
shouting, and one of my Matabele boys came running
up with the gun of my waggon-driver (a Griqua
named Jantje, who was with us), calling out, " Isilouān,
isilouān ! lions, lions !—the lions have caught a
woman ! " Luckily my gun and cartridges were in

the hut, but Cross had to go down to our camp to
get his, and so lost his chance of a shot, for under
the circumstances I could not well wait for him, but
ran with Jantje to where I could now hear the dogs
barking. As we neared the spot, we could distinguish
the low murmuring growls of the lion mingling with
the sharp yelping of about twenty dogs. We were
just getting nicely up to the brute, that was lying
flat on the ground, at the foot of a small mopani
tree, holding the remains of the missing calf between
its fore paws, when a Kafir of Mrs. Viljoen, who
carried a musket, fired from behind me, and immediately afterwards Jantje also fired. They both missed
the lioness, however, and with a growl she jumped
up and cantered off, hotly pursued by the whole
pack of dogs. With a curse both loud and deep,
I followed at my best pace, and as she only ran
about 300 yards before the dogs brought her to
bay again, I was soon up with her once more. She
stood with her tail held straight in the air, growling
savagely at the dogs, that were barking all round
her, and occasionally making a grab at one of them
with her paw. I now ran up behind a small bush
to within forty yards of her, and waiting till she
turned broadside to me, gave her a bullet through
the two shoulders, which at once put her *hors de
combat.* Just as she fell, Cross, who had lost no time,
rushed up. She was an average-sized lioness, in low
condition, and with a mangy coat—one of those old
beasts that, being past their full strength, and unable
any longer to catch game with certainty, take to prowling about the habitations of men, catching goats, dogs,
and, when pressed by hunger, women and children.
Such lions are far more dangerous to human beings
than younger and more vigorous animals. At length,

towards the end of the month, we once more reached
Inyati, where we spent the merriest of Christmases
beneath the hospitable roof of the Rev. W. Elliott
and his charming wife, and thus brought to a close
the hunting season of 1878.

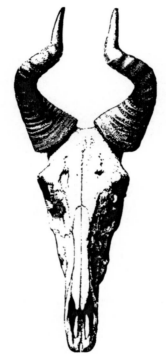

SKULL AND HORNS OF THE KONZE ANTELOPE (*Alcelaphus Lichtensteinii*) ♂
Now in the Collection of the British Museum.

CHAPTER XIX

In January 1879, after having seen the Inxwāla dance, I left the Matabele country and trekked southwards as far as Klerksdorp in the Transvaal, from whence, after laying in a fresh supply of stores, ammunition, etc., I at once started on another hunting expedition to the interior, which I reckoned would have extended over two or three years, had not a most deplorable occurrence, which I will relate farther on, obliged me to again travel southwards as far as the Diamond Fields early the following year.

On April 14 I again reached Bamangwato, and having obtained permission from "Khama," the chief, to travel through his country to the Mābābe river, on condition that I would leave my waggons there, and hunt farther north on the Chobe and Sunta rivers, I made a start on the 17th. On this expedition Miller again accompanied me, as well as another young colonist, Mr. Sell, a German by birth, and a very hard-working, trustworthy young fellow. They were both shooting on the halves for me, according to the usual conditions. I also had an old fellow with me, sent by Khama to look after my waggons whilst I went away hunting. His name was Ai-eetsee-upee (Knows nothing). He was a very grumpy, disagreeable old fellow, but looked well after my property when I was away from the waggons. A nephew of "the man who knew nothing," my two waggon - drivers, and an old Damara named Jacob, with his son Marman, completed our party.

After passing the "Liclutse" river and the pits of Klabala, we reached a small shallow vley called Maha-kabe, about 10 P.M. on April 22nd. There is never any water in this little pan, except after recent rains. The whole road about here was strewn with articles —ploughshares, hencoops, boxes, etc., thrown from the waggons of the emigrant Boers when on their way to Damaraland last year—melancholy relics of their disastrous journey through this dreadful waterless desert.

On April 23 we went out under the guidance of two Bushmen to look for elands. In the course of the forenoon we saw a great deal of spoor, one, two, and three days old, but none fresh enough to follow. About mid-day I shot a steinbuck, and shortly afterwards we crossed the spoor of a herd of elands that had passed during the night. This we followed, and about 2 P.M. came up with them, a troop of about a dozen cows and a lot of last year's calves. After driving them on for two or three miles in the direction of the waggons, I shot one, and then turning another out, drove her to the road, where I shot her too. She was in splendid condition, and the fat on her rump was over an inch thick.

On April 26th, having been travelling hard since the previous afternoon, we reached Inkōuāne (a large chalk-pan, in one corner of which we found a little rain water) just at daylight. In the middle of this pan there were three waggons, left here last year by the emigrant Boers, the oxen that pulled them having died of thirst, besides ploughshares, a mill-stone, and other articles.

April 27th.—Still at Inkōuāne. A little before mid-day some Bushmen came to the waggons saying that a troop of elands had passed the pan early in the morning, and asking us to take the spoor and shoot them some meat. So Miller and I saddled up the horses, and following the spoor came up with the elands about 2 P.M. There were a few full-grown cows and a great many young animals, but there was not a bull amongst them. I soon galloped alongside of one and shot her, as the wind being from the wrong quarter she would not drive towards the waggons. Finding she was very poor, I rode after Miller and the troop again, and eventually ran down the best-looking cow amongst them, after a hard burst, for in this heavy sand a horse cannot gallop at any great pace, the extra weight of its rider sinking it much deeper in the yielding soil than the unburdened eland. This cow proved to be nice and fat. Miller also shot two elands, so that the Bushmen got lots of meat.

Early on the morning of May 1 we reached Tlakāne, a valley with several pits of water in it, having trekked about eleven hours from Touāne pits during the night. We found that three waggons had left here the previous evening, taking the direct road to Inkōuāne, so that we just missed one another. About mid-day another waggon arrived from the north, which proved to belong to Mr. Shelton, the well-known trader at Lake Ngami, and was in charge of a Mr. Saunders.   He told us that two of the waggons that had left Tlakāne the previous day belonged to Mr. Swithin Wood, another trader, and the third to a trek Boer, who was returning to the Transvaal from Ovampo Land in a destitute condition.   We learned from Mr. Saunders that the country on ahead was very dry, and the water in the Botletlie river very low.

On May 4, having got a little very brackish water half-way in a pit, on the edge of the large salt-pan of Chukutsa, we at last reached the Botletlie or Lake river.   Here we found living a lot of Makalakas and Bushmen.   These people are subject to Khama. This is one of the most abominable spots I have yet visited ; one small mud-hole from which a little filthy water was all we could get for ourselves or the oxen, and yet on the map this river looks like a young Mississippi.   At certain seasons it is doubtless full, but just now it is a horrible parody upon a river.   Hearing on all sides that there is no water on ahead between here and the kari-kari or great salt-pan, and that the deep mud in the pan itself renders it impassable, I determined to trek along the eastern bank of the Botletlie, until well north of the kari-kari, and then strike eastwards to the Mabābe road.

On May 5, therefore, we crossed the river at a very good drift, the river being quite dry, and travelling westwards along its bank, reached, the following day, a fine hole of water, where our oxen and we ourselves had a good drink of clean water, the first we had had for many days.

At daylight on the morning of May 8, we reached a small encampment of Bushmen, but there being

insufficient water for the oxen, had to trek on again.
However, as the Bushmen said there were giraffes in
the bush near at hand, and two of them offered to go
with us and look for some, Miller and I saddled up
the horses, and sending the waggons on in charge of
Sell, went out with our two dusky guides.   We had
ridden for a little more than an hour, straight away
from the river, when we espied a single old giraffe bull
and at once gave chase.   As I was very much better
mounted than Miller, I was soon alone with the bull,
the bush being very thorny and awkward to ride
through.   I gave the giraffe four shots, and then,
seeing that he was done for, galloped round him,
upon which he stood reeling under a tree, and I was
just pulling my horse in, when a lion, a lioness, and
two half-grown cubs jumped out of the bushes just
in front of me and trotted slowly away.   Just at this
moment, too, I saw four stately giraffe cows walk
out of the bush in single file about 500 yards ahead.
The lion, after trotting a few paces, turned round,
and stood, broadside on, looking at me, offering a
splendid shot.   I was on the ground in a moment,
and gave him a bullet just behind the shoulder.
With a growl he galloped away for about 100
yards, and then rolled over on his side, stone dead.
I just rode up to assure myself of the fact, and then
galloped on after the giraffe cows, for I had good
hopes that they would be fat, whereas I knew that
the meat of the old stink-bull would only be good
for the Bushmen.   I soon shot two of the cows and
then waited until Miller came up, when we proceeded
to cut them up.   One of them was in splendid condition, and kept us in fat for a month to come.
Miller had ridden right on to the lioness and cubs,
but his horse would not let him fire.   After a bit the

Bushmen came up. They had found the dead lion and covered him up with bushes and grass to prevent the vultures from getting at him. After cutting the best meat off the fat giraffe we went back to the lion and skinned him, and then Miller and I, leaving the Bushmen behind, rode back to where we had left the waggons in the morning, and gave the thirsty horses a good drink of water, of which they as well as we ourselves were much in need. We then again saddled up, and, following the track, reached the waggons about an hour after dark, having had a pretty hard day. The skin of this lion when pegged out measured 10 feet 6 inches, but he had a very small mane.

On May 10 we again proceeded on our journey. During the first trek I shot a young impala ram. In the afternoon, whilst walking in front of the waggons, carrying my little Martini carbine, I shot an enormous bustard, which was excessively fat and heavy. Unfortunately I had no scales with which to weigh it, but I do not think it could have been less than 40 lbs. before it was cleaned. The fat on its back was nearly an inch thick. Just before sundown I saw two gemsbuck, the antelope of all others of which I longed to shoot a fine specimen. With a good deal of trouble I managed to creep to within shot of them, and took, as I thought, a very careful aim. I certainly hit the one I fired at, but it was with the little rifle, and game will often go a long way after receiving apparently a mortal wound from such a small fast-travelling bullet, which lets out but little blood and gives no shock to the system. Directly I fired, one of the dogs came up from behind, and, running on the spoor, caught up to the wounded gemsbuck. Hearing the dog baying I ran on, and soon

saw the beautiful antelope standing at bay behind a
bush facing the dog.   I now made sure he was mine
and ran towards him, but before I could get a clear
shot he saw me, and, breaking away again, went off at
a great pace, making for some thick bush on ahead.
Thinking that the dog would bring him to bay again,
I ran to the waggons, which I now saw approaching,
and saddled up my horse.   It was all to no purpose,
however, for the dog had left him, and after following his spoor till dark I had to give him up.   At
daylight the following morning, after having inspanned and started the waggons, I saddled up my
favourite horse, " Bob," and rode out by myself in
search of gemsbuck, having had proof positive that
there were some of these animals about.

Soon after leaving the waggons I came across a
hartebeest and a tsessebe antelope, two old bulls that,
I think, had struck up an acquaintance.   Shortly
afterwards I sighted a small herd of gemsbuck, whose
long, straight horns, heavy though symmetrical
bodies, and long bushy tails, there was no mistaking.
There were eight of them altogether, though only
three of them seemed to be full-grown animals.
After a sharp burst I put a bullet into the best cow,
and then galloping past her, turned her away from
the others, and drove her for several miles towards
the course taken by the waggons.   Before cutting
the spoor, however, she came to a halt and would
not go any farther, and I had to shoot her.   Though
full-grown in point of size she was still a young cow,
and her horns, which measured 3 feet 1 inch, would
have grown longer.   However, she was my first
gemsbuck, and it was with a feeling of intense
satisfaction that I cut off her beautifully marked head
and thick bushy tail, which are amongst the most

valued of my hunting trophies. Having off-saddled Bob for a short time, I again set off, and, carrying the gemsbuck's head before me on the saddle, at last reached the waggons about 2 P.M. The meat and skin I was forced to leave to the vultures, for which I was the more sorry as the animal was in fine condition ; but as I had not a single Kafir with me I could not do otherwise, for, not knowing when we should again get water, and my horse having had none since noon the previous day, I could not load him up too heavily. In the evening, just at sundown, we again reached the river. At the place where we struck it, it was very narrow, with steep banks and not many reeds in it.

At this place we found living a family of three-quarters-starved Bushmen. It is a marvel how these poor wretches managed to keep body and soul together. They had been living for a long time past, they said, on nothing but a few small berries and an odd tortoise, and were in such a fearful state of emaciation that it made one shudder to look at them. Their hollow shrunken faces looked like skulls with dried skins stretched tightly over them. All the flesh on their limbs seemed to have atrophied, the knee and elbow joints and the bones of the pelvis standing out in unsightly knobs, whilst (owing to their having to eat a great quantity of very innutritious food to sustain life at all) their stomachs were enormously distended ; altogether they were as pitiful-looking objects as it is possible to imagine. I gave them some meat and a little corn, and told them that on the following day if they would go with me and show me game, I would shoot them a good supply of meat. This they willingly agreed to do, though the old gray-headed father of the family said that game was very scarce about here, and that, unless God helped us, we should not find anything.

According to agreement, I was up at daylight the following morning, and after having a cup of strong coffee took the field under the guidance of the old Bushman and his son in search of game. We were out nearly the whole day, but never saw a living thing, nor the spoor of any large game such as giraffes or elands fresh enough to follow. Wretched objects though the Bushmen looked, they stepped along briskly the entire time in front of my horse with a dogged perseverance that an unkind fate did not reward. The following day, May 13, I started the waggons at sunrise and then rode out again in search of game. The young Bushman was knocked up with his exertions of the previous day, but the old gray-headed sportsman again accompanied me. Once more we were unsuccessful, seeing nothing larger than a steinbuck. It seemed hard that Providence did not throw an eland or a giraffe in my way to kill for these miserable children of the desert, who seemed to be starving to death by inches. This day we trekked through frightfully thick thorn bush. It was dreadful work for the oxen, as there was no road, the sand was very heavy, the sun hot, and they got scratched to pieces by the wait-a-bit thorns. Whilst trekking along close to the bank of the river the following morning, we met some Makalakas, who asked me to stop a bit and hunt; as they said there were a good many gemsbuck about, I decided to do so.

May 15th.—Rode out and came across a small herd of gemsbuck, eight altogether, all cows and calves. After a sharp chase in heavy sandy ground, and through innumerable small thorn bushes, I shot the finest cow. I could have shot more, but I did not care to gallop my horse any farther through the heavy sand and sharp thorns, for he is the only animal I have to depend upon to keep the waggons in meat. The cow I shot had a very fine pair of horns measuring 3 feet $6\frac{1}{2}$ inches in length. They were not straight, but had a very appreciable curve backwards. The following morning I again rode out with the Makalakas, and came across a giraffe cow with a half-grown calf. After giving the cow a shot I headed her, and then drove her right down to the path along the river, a little in front of the waggons. Here I shot her, and in the afternoon trekked on to where she lay, and we slept close alongside of the carcase.

In the evening of the following day, having been unsuccessful in finding game in the morning, I trekked on to a little Makalaka village, where I bought some Kafir corn. Early the next morning after starting the waggons I took a round under the guidance of some Bushmen and Makalakas, and coming across a single eland cow, drove her right down to the river, through the Makalaka corn-fields, killing her within twenty yards of the village, to the great joy of the inhabitants. This eland was striped like the elands in the Mashuna country, but not so distinctly as some I have seen to the north of the Zambesi. In the evening we trekked on, following the edge of a steep bank which overlooks the river. As we were trekking Miller and I walked on in front of the waggons. We saw a great many hideous crocodiles, and a large herd of at least fifty blue wildebeests drinking in the river.

On May 20, having passed two or three more small Makalaka villages, we left the river, and striking north-north-east under the guidance of two Bushmen, reached a fountain just before sunset. This fountain is called "Nwongwe." On the way from the river to this place I shot an eland cow. In the evening of the following day we made another trek to the north-east.

On May 22 we inspanned early and trekked across some immense open flats, devoid of bush, and full of small brack-pans, reaching three small pools of water about mid-day. The latter of these is called Cum-Karekoo by the Masaras, and Renāka Cocone (wildebeest's horn) by the Bamangwatos. Soon after we had started I saw from the waggons two giraffe cows, each with a last year's calf, walking across the open flat, so, saddling up Bob, I went and shot one of them, bringing her right up to the waggons, on which we outspanned, cut off a good supply of meat, and then trekked on again to the pan. On the way Miller shot a springbuck and a wild cat. I also wounded a springbuck, but lost it. In a dry pan close to where we outspanned, we saw a large herd of blue wildebeests and zebras, and innumerable springbucks.

In the afternoon we again trekked on, and a little before sunset reached a pit with a good deal of water in it, where we found a lot of Bushmen living. This water had a most foul and disgusting smell and taste, which boiling did not modify, as tea made from it was undrinkable. During the trek we saw a troop of ostriches from the waggons, so Miller and I saddled up the horses and went after them. We found there were nine ostriches, four cocks amongst them—and an old blue wildebeest bull. We had a good spin after them, but without success. The short thorny bush through which they led us was very awkward

for the horses.   Besides this, my small rifle being out
of order, I carried a heavy 10-bore rifle, which is not
at all the gun for ostrich-shooting.   Miller, though
he had an excellent rifle, and is a rattling good shot,
was very badly mounted.

On May 25, soon after sunrise, we reached the
pan of Cum-Kerees, which is a permanent spring
that never dries up, having passed the dry pan
of Kama-Kama about mid-day the previous day.
Cum-Kerees is only a few miles from Sode-Garra, a
permanent water on the hunting-road to the Mābābe.

May 26th.—Rode out and shot three eland cows,
all of which were slightly striped.   On the following
day we remained at Cum-Kerees and got in all the
eland meat.

May 28th.—Inspanned at daybreak, and trekking
about eight miles eastwards, reached the fountain of
Sode-Garra, where we again rejoined the main hunting-
road to the Mābābe.   Though it is three weeks since
we left this road at the first Makalaka kraal on the
Botletlie, it is only five days' journey to that place
by the direct route across the great salt-pan.

The Bushmen at this place all declared that the
country between here and the Mābābe river was
impassable, as no rain having fallen the previous
summer, there was not a drop of water along the
road.   Never having known the untutored savage
to tell the truth, however, before, I thought these
Bushmen were lying, wishing to frighten me out of
prosecuting my journey.   Ai-eetsee-upee also said
that he had never heard of the large pans between
Sode-Garra and the Mābābe being dry at this season
of the year ; so, as no one likes to be thwarted in
any enterprise upon which he may once have entered,
I resolved to risk it, and trek on, but at the same

time act as if there really was no water near, and trek day and night until I got some.

On May 29, about mid-day, we inspanned, having first taken the precaution to fill every available cask, pot, and calabash with water to drink along the road, as my party had now been augmented by four Makalakas that I had engaged on the Lake river. Well, all that day we trekked on, all the night, all the next day, and all the next night, without coming to any water ; we passed pan after pan, but they were all as dry as dust, and it began to look as if the Bushmen for once in their lives had told the truth, when they said there was no water on ahead.   As no waggon had travelled along this track for two years, we found it very much overgrown and full of little thorn-bushes that scratched the poor oxen to pieces. Luckily, it was just about full moon, or we should never have been able to hold the road through the mopani forests.   On the morning of the third day the poor oxen that had been in the yoke, pulling day and night almost without intermission ever since leaving Sode-Garra, and had been without water all that time, began to show signs of distress.   They were now too thirsty to feed, and when outspanned for a short period to rest, stood round the waggons, lowing and licking the tires of the wheels.

On the morning of May 31, Miller, Sell, and I walked on ahead, and were presently rejoiced to see some hyæna and jackal spoor in the road, which we thought betokened that there was water somewhere near.   About mid-day we came to a small hollow in which there had evidently been a little water very lately, and round which the grass was green.   On the edge of this little pan grew three enormous baobab trees, to the top of one of which I climbed to survey

the surrounding country. From my exalted position
I could see a hollow about 300 yards away in the
midst of some thick bush, to which I directed my
companions, from whom a loud hurrah a few minutes
later informed me that, as I had hoped might be the
case, they had found a little water. It was not
much to boast of, being just the dregs of a large
shallow pan, that in another few days would have
been quite dry. Nevertheless, these few gallons of
muddy water were of inestimable value to us, and
averted what might have been a great disaster.
After letting the horses drink their fill first, we then
brought the oxen down three at a time, for if they
had been allowed to go down in a body, they would
have trampled the water into mud, and none of
them got any at all. The poor, thirsty beasts drank
the little pan quite dry, and though they did not
even then get enough to satisfy them, they at any
rate washed a little of the dust out of their parched
throats, and were able to feed a bit, and put a little
strength into their worn-out limbs. I then let them
feed on the green grass round the first little pan for
about three hours, and late in the afternoon again
inspanned. Early in the night, we passed the
numerous splendid deep pans, known collectively
under the name of Scio, in which Ai-eetsee-upee
had held out strong hopes of our finding water.
They were, however, all dry. Matters now began
to look desperate, for the nearest place where we
could hope to get water was in one of the large
deep pans close to the upper end of the Mābābe
Flat, and many a weary mile of heavy sand lay
between Scio and the nearest of these pans.

All through this night we journeyed on, and all
the next day. The poor oxen were now wellnigh

spent, and it was painful to look at them as they toiled along with hollow sides and tongues protruding from their mouths, but shadows of the sleek-looking beasts they had been but four days before. The continuous and unceasing toil, too, through day and night, was telling upon the drivers, leaders, and Kafirs. Whenever we outspanned they all threw themselves down on the sand, worn out with fatigue, and instantly fell asleep. Of course we whites took good care not to follow their example ; otherwise, we should all be lying between Sode-Garra and the Mābābe now. Up to this time I had never been on the waggon, but had walked day and night in front with Ai-eetsee-upee and old Jacob the Damara, a very tough old specimen of humanity, who knew the road, having been in the Mābābe before. Just at sundown on this the fourth day of our journey, we reached the first of the broad heavily-timbered sand-belts which lie to the south of the Mābābe Flat. After the next trek, leaving Sell to bring on the waggons, no light duty under the circumstances, Miller and I saddled up the horses and rode on to the large pans I have spoken of before, to see if there was any water in them.

About 2 A.M., having ridden along by the light of a glorious full moon for about five hours, we came to them—splendid deep pans, that one would not believe could ever dry up. Yet dry they all were ; and our hearts sank as we rode into the largest of all, and found that, although there was still a little mud in it, there was not a drop of water. It was at these pans that two years previously the noted old Dutch elephant-hunter Martinus Swart and ten members of his family died of fever, only six surviving out of a party of seventeen whites.

In the mopani forests a little beyond these pans the road became untraceable, so we returned to the last pan and waited for daylight.

By the light of day, however, there was no more sign of a road than by moonlight. However, we found some buffalo spoor, not many days old, and knowing that these animals are never found many miles away from water, we searched all the morning for the life-sustaining element, but in vain. Though we found many pans, they were all quite dry, so we gave it up at last, and retraced our steps to the waggons, which we met only a few miles short of the large pan where we had passed a portion of the night.

The oxen were now quite told out, and stood all in a heap under a cluster of mopani trees, trying to escape the fierce rays of the sun.

I now questioned Ai-eetsee-upee and old Jacob as to how far we still were from the Mābābe river, and learned from the latter that, if we struck through the mopani forests to our left, we should very soon cut into the upper part of the flat, and might reach the river before midnight. He said, however, that he was afraid that where we got water we should find the tsetse fly. This was, however, a secondary consideration : our first care was to reach the water. So, five minutes later, we abandoned the waggons, and following old Jacob, who stepped out briskly in front, started with bullocks, horses, dogs, and Kafirs, in search of the river.

Just before sundown, we emerged upon the great open plain known as the Mābābe Flat, and old Jacob at once pointed out to me the smoke of some grass fires which were burning at a distance of about twelve miles. " Those fires are burning in the reeds of the

Māb̄abe river," said the old man.   I looked at my poor, hollow-sided, jaded cattle, and then again at the distant smoke, and wondered whether they would all be good for the journey.   We now saw a great many zebras about the flat, and I said to old Jacob that I felt sure that there must be water nearer than the river, or otherwise how could the presence of so many zebras and the buffalo spoor be accounted for. The old fellow said there were some pans just within the edge of the mopani, close to us, but that as the large vleys we had passed were dry, he did not think it likely these little ones would still hold water. However, we went to look, and five minutes later found a long shallow vley full of water.   I could have hugged the dirty old man with delight.   What a sight it was to see the poor thirsty oxen come trotting down to the pan, as soon as they smelt the longed-for water, and rush knee-deep into it !   What a sudden relief the sight of that pool of muddy water was, too, and what a weight of fear and anxiety it lifted from our hearts !   Only an hour before it had seemed that I was doomed to lose all my live stock —nearly everything I possessed in the world—from thirst ; and now the danger was past, and not a single ox had given in.

The following morning I sent the drivers back with the cattle to bring the waggons down to the vley.   They arrived in the evening.

In the course of my various hunting expeditions, I have had several experiences of this kind whilst travelling through the inhospitable deserts of South-Western Africa, and I will therefore give my experience as to the capabilities of oxen for standing thirst.

It must be remembered that when I talk of travelling through the " thirst," I mean trekking day and

night, only outspanning for very short periods and at
long intervals ; so that in the twenty-four hours the
bullocks are from eighteen to twenty hours in the
yoke.   Wherever, too, in the interior of South Africa,
large tracts have to be traversed without water, the
soil is invariably for the most part fine, deep sand,
into which the waggon wheels sink over the felloes,
which in itself is terribly trying to the oxen, which, in
addition to what they suffer from the heat of the
tropical sun, are half choked by the clouds of burning
dust that rise from the heated sand.   Under these
circumstances, good sturdy oxen, not too fat, but in
good hard-working order, will not pull a waggon
without water for more than three days and four
nights in the winter time, when the nights are long
and cold, and the days not intensely hot.   In the
summer, when the days are long, and the air in these
desert wastes becomes heated to the temperature of a
furnace, whilst the nights are short and warm, bullocks
will not pull a loaded waggon for more than two days
and two nights.   However, even after they have
become incapable of moving a waggon, they will still
walk, when unyoked, many miles farther to the water,
especially during the night.   One often hears of oxen
trekking for from five days and nights to nine without water.   My experience of the capabilities of these
enduring animals is as I have stated above.   The
oxen that stand thirst the best are the breed possessed
by the Bechuana tribes along the borders of the
desert, which are all legs and horns to look at.

On June 3, whilst the drivers were away fetching
the waggons, I went with old Jacob to another pan
that he knew of at a distance of a few miles along the
edge of the mopani.   In this pan, which was deep and
circular, we found a good supply of fairly clear water.

June 4th.—Sent the waggons to the pan we found yesterday, and then, saddling up Bob, took two young Makalaka boys with me, and rode across the flat to look for game. I had been riding for about a couple of hours, and was near the farther side, when I heard a lot of hyænas making a tremendous noise. Thinking they were feeding on some carrion, I galloped in the direction from whence the sounds proceeded, and presently sighted a whole troop of hyænas trotting away towards the belt of thorns which skirts the upper end of the flat. On in front of the hyænas I saw three animals that seemed larger than they, and, hoping they might be lions, I put the spurs into Bob, and galloped as hard as he could go, in order to catch up to them before they reached the thorn-bush. As I galloped, I passed and counted fifteen hyænas, trotting along like dogs, most of which stood and looked at me as I rode within 100 yards of them. I now saw that the three larger animals were lionesses. They were trotting quietly along, and in front of them again were several more hyænas, so that there must have been more than twenty of these animals altogether. Just as the lionesses reached the edge of the thorn-bush, I was close behind them, and pulling in Bob, jumped to the ground. The hindmost of the three as I did so stopped, and, wheeling broadside to me, turned her head to look at me. Before I could fire, however, she sprang away with a loud purr and a whisk of her tail, and went off after her comrades at a canter. As she ran, I gave her a shot from behind, which knocked her over. After rolling about growling for a few moments, she regained her legs, and rejoined her friends that were trotting slowly along. She soon, however, left them, and lay down in a patch of bush, where, having marked her well, I rode on after the others. The bush now commenced to get thick, and the lionesses separated, so I followed the larger. She soon turned round in a patch of bush and faced me, growling savagely and swishing her tail. I was within fifty yards, so, pulling in, jumped off at once. As I raised my rifle, she turned and stood directly facing me, with her head held low. At the same time I saw her tail raised straight in the air like a bar of steel. She was standing amongst some grass and weeds that grew as high as her back, which made it difficult to see her ; but I knew there was not a moment to lose, and fired for her mouth. Without a growl, she at once sank to the ground. I now walked up to her, and found she had fallen all of a heap, stone-dead, the bullet having struck her full in the face, just below the eye, and passing right through her skull and all down her neck, lodged under the skin behind her shoulder.

I now rode back to the one I had first wounded, which I found still lying in the little patch of bush where I had left her. On seeing me approach, she stood up, standing broadside to me, with her head turned towards me, snarling and growling, when I gave her a shot right through the lungs, which settled her. These were both old lionesses, and must have had cubs, as they were in milk. Their skins only measured 8 feet 10 inches each when pegged out, and though both were in perfect hair, they differed much in colour.

When my two young Makalakas came up, we skinned the one lioness, but only took the entrails out of the other, and then, splitting it open, packed it entire on to the horse, together with the skin of the other. I then walked back to the waggons, leading Bob by the bridle.

This will show how little instinctive fear this horse had of lions; and my experience is that, speaking generally, animals that are entirely unacquainted with these carnivora have no instinctive fear of them. I have seen many instances of both horses and oxen not evincing the slightest concern at the near proximity of lions, although the latter were above the wind. Once, however, let a horse or an ox either be mauled by a lion, or witness the death of a comrade by the teeth and claws of one, and he will become demoralised, and ever afterwards evince great terror at the near proximity of these animals. I think, too, that a few terror-stricken oxen will communicate their fears to a whole herd, and the distances that cattle frightened by lions will sometimes travel before stopping to feed are very great.

June 6th.—Rode across the flat again with my two young Makalakas to where I shot the lionesses. I then rode into the thick thorn-bush and shot a fine large crested bustard, knocking a large hole through him with my heavy single 10. After getting through the belt of thorns, I came out upon a large open tract of turf, walking across which, but at a great distance, I saw two giraffes. Directing my boys not to leave the horse's spoor, I took my rifle and cantered quietly towards them. The ground was one mass of holes and deep cracks, all overgrown with short grass, so that, going even at a slow canter, I found it difficult to keep my horse on his legs. I had worked my way to within about a quarter of a mile of the giraffes, which all this time had been walking quietly along towards some thorn trees on the farther side of the turf flat, when I saw something move in the grass beneath a solitary little thorn-bush, about a hundred yards ahead of me, which, on approaching a little

AN UNEXPECTED MEETING, WITH TWO LIONS; MĀBĀBE PLAIN, JUNE 6, 1879.

nearer, I saw was a lion, or rather I saw two lions, for there was another on the other side of the bush. I now pulled in, and walked my horse towards the bush, and when within sixty yards of it, a splendid old lion with a fine mane jumped up and cantered into the open, the other lying flat under the bush. The one that jumped up only ran about twenty yards, and then turning, stood broadside and looked at me. I was already on the ground, and the next instant fired. With a growl he acknowledged the shot, and again made a few bounds forwards, then turning round, he stood facing me, holding his head down between his shoulders, growling hoarsely, and looking the very picture of rage. He held his tail straight in the air, and I made sure he was coming at me, for, not having heard the bullet strike, I did not know whether I had hit him. Glancing quickly to my left, I saw too that the other lion was now lying with its head crouched on its outstretched paws, eyeing me intently. Owing to the condition of the ground there was no chance of escape from a charge through the speed of the horse, so pushing in another cartridge, I stood ready for the worst. After a few growls, however, the black-maned lion sank down, and then rolled over on his side, when I knew that his spirit had fled, and all his power to harm me gone. My bullet, as I afterwards found, had passed through both his lungs high up, the very best shot one can give a lion.

I now turned my attention to the second lion. As, owing to the grass, I could not see him clearly, I mounted my horse and gave him a shot from the saddle, as he lay half facing me, gazing towards me with anything but a pleasant expression of countenance. Whether he realised the misfortune which had befallen his comrade or not I cannot say, but he certainly had

2 E

an angry, put-out sort of look.   As I fired, a loud
roar announced that the bullet had struck him, and I
could see that he was hard hit.   He now sat on his
haunches like a dog, holding his head low, and
growling savagely.   In this position he exposed his
chest, so hastily pushing in another cartridge, I jumped
to the ground before he could make up his mind what
to do, and firing quickly, struck him in the centre of
the breast, just under the chin.   This rolled him over,
and riding up, I saw that he was in his last agonies,
so left him, and took a look at the first I had shot, a
magnificent old lion with a fine black mane, and a skin
in beautiful condition, and of a very dark colour all
over.   All this, which has taken so long to relate,
must have occupied less than a minute of time, and
the lions being both dead, I again turned my attention
to the giraffes.   The shots had startled them and
caused them to stop, so that whilst I was shooting the
lions, they had been standing still, and were now just
starting away at a slow canter.   They, however, soon
pulled up, and stood looking back as I rode towards
them, picking my way through the treacherous turf.
At last I got up to them and gave the cow (they
were a cow and bull) three shots.   I then galloped
past her, and rolling off as she came by, gave her a
fourth, broadside.   This, however, did not stop her,
though she was now almost done for, and only went
on at a slow canter.

I now wanted to turn her towards the dead lions,
and was just galloping round her when my horse
trod into a deep grass-covered hole, and came down
with me.   I went over his head, and the rimpy
which I always have attached to my belt from the
bridle, broke.   On regaining his legs Bob trotted off,
and would not let me catch him for a long time.   At

last, however, I got hold of him again, and once more took up the chase of the wounded giraffe, which all this time had been walking and cantering alternately, and was now nearly a mile away, and hard by the thick thorn-bush. Just, however, as she reached the bush I was up with her once more, and despatched her with another bullet. As she fell, I saw the bull in front of her, that I suppose had been waiting for her within the shelter of the thorn thicket, and as we wanted meat at the waggons, I killed him too. Then after having cut out the tongues, and left my saddle-cloth suspended on a stake to keep the vultures away from the cow, which was nice and fat, I rode back into the turf flat to look after my boys and the lions. I thought that by this time they would have nearly skinned them, and was much disgusted, when at last I found them, to hear that they had not seen the lions at all. However, knowing pretty well where they were, I rode straight to them, and we then set to work and skinned them. By this time the sun was almost down, and as it had been very hot, and neither myself, my Kafirs, nor my horse had drunk anything since daylight, we were all very thirsty; so packing the two reeking lion-skins on Bob, with the great heads and paws intact, I led him back to the waggons, which we did not reach till some time after dark, resolving to fetch the meat of the giraffes on the following day. The skins of these two lions measured 10 feet 9 inches and 10 feet 10 inches respectively. They were in beautiful condition, and very massive and heavy.

A few days later than this I had a sharp attack of fever, from which I was recovering, when, early one morning, I heard some of my Kafirs say, "There's a white man," and looking up, was much surprised to see my old friend Mr. H. C. Collison ride up. This gentleman I had met previously, first on the Diamond Fields, and later on in the Zambesi country, where he was hunting for several months during 1877. I had heard, too, that he had returned to the colony, and was going to make a second hunting trip into the interior, in company with my old friends Messrs. Clarkson and French ; but having heard nothing further of their plans prior to leaving Bamangwato, I thought that they had either given up the idea or else gone to the Mashuna country. I now found that Messrs. Collison and French (of Mr. Clarkson I will speak later on) had reached Bamangwato about a fortnight after our departure, and had been doing their best to catch us up ever since. Having started from Sode-Garra a few days previously, they had got on without water to just this side of Scio. Their oxen were then quite done up, so Mr. Collison had brought them on with the horses to the water, having reached the shallow pan where we had first found some, late the preceding night. All the drivers and Kafirs belonging to the waggons had also come on, Mr. French having alone remained in charge of everything, having with him a supply of water sufficient to last him, with economy, ten days. Several of my friends' oxen (ten, I think) had died of thirst before reaching the pan, and the survivors were in a dreadful state from the effects of the hardships they had endured. My oxen, however, which were all young animals, had by this time pretty well recovered from their hardships, so that same evening I sent them off under charge of my own drivers, who rode on horseback, and four Kafirs, all carrying water, to bring in my friends' waggons. It took them over thirty hours' continuous travelling to reach the place where Mr. French was keeping guard over them. The oxen, however, having walked along unencumbered, were still pretty fresh, and being inspanned at once brought them, on the third day (having been all this time without water), to the hard ground on the Mābābe side of the great sand-belt, and not more than twelve miles distant from the pan where my waggons were standing. They were then sent on to the water, and my friend's own oxen went and brought the waggons down to the pan. All things considered, I think we had good reason to congratulate ourselves upon having safely traversed the immense waterless tract of country, which now lay between us and Sode-Garra, with the loss to my friends of only a few oxen.

A fortnight later, after we had started to hunt in the " fly " country, some of Khama's waggons arrived from Bamangwato, in charge of several of his headmen, who had come in in charge of hunting parties, and to collect tribute from the Bushmen. They lost fourteen oxen from thirst, though their waggons were absolutely empty, and their bullocks fresh and fat when they left Bamangwato, whilst our waggons were all heavily laden, which makes a very great difference in a heavy sandy road. Messrs. Collison and French had started from the Diamond Fields in company with my old friend and former hunting-companion, Mr. Matthew Clarkson. He, poor fellow, was, however, struck by lightning near Klerksdorp, in the Transvaal, at the very outset of the journey. Mr. Collison was inside the waggon, and within a few feet of him when poor Matt was struck, and was himself stunned by the shock. The fire of heaven, that could scarcely have lighted on a better fellow, struck him right on the head, and boring a clean round hole through his hat, then passed out at his side above the hip and ran down the iron rung of the waggon into the earth.   The horses broke loose at the flash, and were not caught until the following day.   There was not a man in the interior, white or black, who did not grieve to hear of poor Clarkson's untimely death.   A better fellow never stepped. Short of stature, but very strong and active, he was, like most colonists, a capital shot and first-rate rough-rider, qualities that could hardly fail to make him a successful hunter.   Morally speaking, too, he was upright and honourable in his dealings with his fellow-men, cool in danger, and as plucky as a bull-dog.   May his spirit find a good hunting-country in the next world !

My friends had received permission from Khama to hunt on horseback in the Mababe country ; as, however, owing probably to the severe drought, there were few or no elephants about, they decided to go with me on foot, and hunt in the fly-infested country farther north. . So, a few days later, we trekked down to the head of the reed-bed into which the Mababe river pours itself, and there formed a permanent camp for the season.

CHAPTER XX

On June 18 we left the waggons, and crossing the
Mababe river at the Masubia towns, about nine
miles below our waggons, made a start northwards,
accompanied by over fifty Makuba and Masubia
Kafirs, whom we had hired between us.

At first we followed the course of the Machabe
river, but finding that our party was so large as to
make it difficult to keep all our Kafirs in meat, we
separated, French and Miller crossing the sand-belts
to the Sunta river, whilst Collison, Sell, and I held
on up the Machabe. Two or three days later, however, as we found that there were many Kafir hunters
from Lake Ngami in front of us, and as we saw no
elephant spoor, Collison and I left Sell and struck
over to the Chobe, where a few days later we rejoined

Miller and French. We then held along the river north-west as far as Mai-ini's town, but finding no elephant spoor, and the Kafirs refusing to take us through the river, we turned back, and shortly afterwards again met Sell. Collison, French, and Sell then went back to the waggons, whilst Miller and I crossed the Sunta, and again striking the Chobe, followed it down to nearly opposite Linyanti, where we made a camp and hunted for some time. We here shot four elephants and many buffaloes, and other animals, amongst them five of the beautiful little spotted bushbucks peculiar to the Chobe. I here tried very hard to shoot a specimen of the situtunga antelope (*Tragelaphus Spekii*), hunting for them almost daily in a canoe at early dawn and just after sunset, amongst the vast reed-beds through which the Chobe here runs. Searching for these retiring animals amongst such immense beds of reeds and papyrus is, however, almost tantamount to looking for needles in a haystack. I only saw one female just at dusk one evening, standing up to her belly in water, amongst the reeds, but did not get a shot at her. Early on the morning of the 5th of August, I had the good fortune to find a dead situtunga ram, that had been killed, apparently by a rival, during the night. At any rate he had received a deep wound in the side, just behind the ribs. He was lying quite in the open, in a piece of boggy ground, where the reeds had been burnt off. On examining him I found that he was a fine old ram, very thick-set and heavy, with an immense neck. He was as nearly as possible the same size as a lechwe ram. I took his skin, and preserved his head and feet very carefully. Shortly after this French and Collison again joined us, Sell having gone higher up the Chobe towards Mai-ini's town by himself.

On August the 23rd I crossed the Chobe, and paid a visit to old Mamele, the headman of this part of the Chobe, whom I had known in 1877. The object of my visit was to obtain permission from him to hunt elephants between the Chobe and the Zambesi. This I at last obtained, after a palaver that lasted for two entire days. Before entering upon this trip, it was, however, requisite for me to return to the waggons and get a fresh supply of ammunition, a little tea and rice, and some goods to pay Mamele for the right to hunt in his country. So, recrossing the Chobe—it took about five hours to paddle through the different channels that intersect the marsh, and connect the two main branches of the river—I forthwith started. Collison accompanied me, intending to remain and hunt on horseback near the waggons. Between Gat-Garra, a permanent water in a limestone basin, and the Mababe, a distance which it took us eleven and a quarter hours to walk, there was no water, so we walked the greater part of the distance by night, as the sun was getting very hot, and the soil was deep soft sand.

On September 2, I again started back for the Chobe, and on the 5th rejoined French and Miller at our old skerm near Tcharo's town.

On the 8th we crossed the southern branch of the Chobe, and striking north towards the site of Sebituane's old town, slept on the Salubanda, a small stream near the northern channel.

The following day we crossed this branch of the river, and then proceeded eastwards to Mamele's town, passing the site of Linyanti (Sekeletu's old town) on the way. Here we found several tires of

wheels and nave bands lying about, that had once
belonged to the waggons of the ill-fated Makololo
mission party, sent by Dr. Livingstone's advice to
Sekeletu, nearly twenty years previously. The
country now about here is quite uninhabited, and
herds of buffaloes roam undisturbed over the pastures,
where whilom grazed the flocks and herds of the
once all-powerful Makololo. With the buffalo, too,
has come the deadly tsetse fly, which now swarms all
along the river's edge. Early on the morning of
the 14th we reached Mamele's town, where we
remained for two days, arranging preliminaries for
the hunt. On the way we came across four lionesses,
one of which, a very dark-skinned animal, I shot,
making the tenth of these beasts that had fallen to
my rifle. Miller and French also wounded two of
the others, but lost them in the long grass.

On the 16th, having left one of my waggon-
drivers in charge of a hut containing a supply of
provisions, ammunition, etc., we again left Mamele's
town, and started upon a journey that I would fain
pass over in silence, but that I feel it to be my duty
to give some account of it.

Upon setting out from Mamele's village we were
accompanied by more than a hundred natives, who
went with us in the hope of getting some meat ; for,
as the crops had failed this season, the Makubas all
along this part of the Chobe were at the time of our
visit reduced to great straits for want of food—a fact
which the emaciated limbs and protruding stomachs
of all but the upper classes brought vividly to one's.
mind.

On the afternoon of the 17th we reached the site
of the Makololo town of Linyanti. In the evening,
the headmen who were accompanying us took some

beads and meat, and laying them upon Sekeletu's grave, prayed to the spirit of the departed chieftain for good luck with the elephants.

Soon after leaving camp the following morning, we passed the best part of the skeleton of a man, who had been killed and eaten by a lion a few days before our arrival. His head and feet were missing, otherwise the skeleton was perfect. Three fine new assegais lay beside his bones, which none of the Kafirs with us would touch ; indeed, they expressed great horror when Miller picked them up to examine them. A little farther on we came upon an immense herd of buffaloes feeding quietly along the river's edge. One of these I shot to please the Kafirs, and a little later Miller shot a hippopotamus cow that we found alone in a small lagoon. This animal was dreadfully poor, and all covered with scars of wounds, half an inch deep, inflicted, the Kafirs said, by other hippopotami. We found an old bullet in her head, and no doubt it was on account of this wound that her comrades had treated her so roughly. Here we remained all day, whilst our headman sent Kafirs to see if there were any elephants on a large island which he says is a favourite resort of theirs.

September 19th.—Shot a buffalo cow shortly after starting. We then went on a little farther, and halted whilst our guide sent messengers to a small Makuba town to get news of elephants. About an hour later one of these Kafirs returned, saying he had crossed fresh elephant spoor, so we at once packed up and went to see about it. We soon came upon the spoor of a large herd of cows, coming down from the sand-belt to drink in the river, and followed it first to the water, and then along a broad footpath that eventually led us to a small Makuba town, the inhabitants of which informed us that the elephants had passed their village during the night. As it was already about 2 P.M., we thought it too late to follow the spoor farther, especially as the Makubas assured us that the elephants would be sure to drink near here again the following night, so we waded across the marsh to an island, and camped a good way from where we thought the wary brutes were likely to drink.

The Makubas along this part of the Chobe are a very primitive-looking people, not many degrees in the social scale above the Bushmen. Their huts are simply a few grass mats stretched over a framework of light poles. They had no domestic animals, but a few half-starved jackal-looking dogs, and seemed to be living entirely upon the roots of an aquatic plant which they called " seeta," a few fish, and an odd head of game, which they either catch themselves in a pitfall, or else take from the lions. These animals, they say, are here very numerous and daring, and the fact that the little villages we saw were surrounded by palisades of poles, all slanting outwards at an angle of 45°, and sharpened at the points as if intended to prevent these beasts from springing over them, seemed to indicate that such was the fact.

September 22nd.—As yet we had seen nothing more of the elephants, notwithstanding that we had paid a visit to the grave of Sebituane, the renowned warrior who founded the Makololo kingdom, taking with us the carcase of a reedbuck entire, with which to propitiate his ghost, and going through all sorts of mystic incantations, which included having our rifles and cartridges spat upon by a professor of demonology. The Kafirs swore that they had never known Sebituane to be so perverse before, and could not make it out at all ; no more could we, so we determined to leave the river and make for a pit they knew of, away in the sand-belts. This we reached about mid-day on the 23rd. On the march French shot two tsessebe antelopes and two zebras ; in the evening I also killed a fat zebra mare. We had to dig, or rather the Kafirs had, for about two hours before we got any water in the pit.

September 24th.—Reached a pool of water after about a four hours' walk in the bed of what was evidently once a river. Our headmen told us that when Sebituane was alive, this river was full of water, so that they could travel up it in their canoes, from Linyanti on the Chobe to Sesheke on the Zambesi. I find on referring to " Livingstone's Missionary Travels " that this was actually the case when he first visited Linyanti. There can be no doubt that year by year the overflow of the Chobe, which occurs during the dry season, independently of the rains, and simultaneously with that of the Botletlie, Okavango, Machabe, Tamalakan, and Mababe rivers—a phenomenon of which no satisfactory solution has ever been offered—is becoming gradually less and less. Finding that four big elephant bulls had drunk at this pool during the preceding night, we camped near it, but well below the wind, in the hope that they would return again that night. A troop of lions had also killed and eaten a tsessebe very shortly before our arrival ; the whole place stank of them. The weather is now intensely hot, both day and night.

The following day, as the bulls we were expecting had not drunk again during the night, we took a turn in the bush to look for spoor, and had not proceeded far when we heard an elephant call at no great distance, and shortly afterwards a tree was broken down with a loud crash. We soon cut their spoor, and a few minutes later came up with the animals themselves, a poor lot of cows, with one young bull amongst them. After a very severe run Miller and I killed the young bull, four large cows, and a heifer ; two more good cows getting away very badly wounded. These I should have bagged, I have little doubt, but the Kafir who carried my spare cartridges did not keep up with us, so that I only had thirteen shots—twelve in the belt and one in the rifle—all of which I fired away. French, who was not much of a runner, shot one cow before they started, but did not follow up the herd. When we all met again, he told us that he had also pursued a wounded one for some distance, and given it a shot in the rump, and that he intended following it up. I urged him strongly not to do so, not because any thought of the dreadful issue ever crossed my mind, but simply because I knew from experience that in nineteen cases out of twenty it is useless to follow a wounded elephant on foot.

Unfortunately, my ill-fated friend thought otherwise, and calling two of his Kafirs (his gun and water carriers) started on the spoor, saying, however, that he would not follow it very far. This is the last time I ever saw him alive. Miller and I then went back to our camp, which was not more than three miles distant. We were scarcely there when we heard two heavy shots fired in quick succession, and at once concluded, that, contrary to our expectations, French had come up with the wounded elephant, and that as he had overtaken her so quickly he would soon be with us again in camp. But as

hour after hour passed and he did not arrive, we
thought the elephant must have escaped him a
second time, and that he was still on her spoor. A
little before sunset, thinking that he must then at
any rate have abandoned the pursuit, and would be
making for camp, the exact whereabouts of which he
perhaps did not know, I went out and fired two
shots with my heavy elephant rifle to guide him.
Later on I fired again, but heard no answering
reports.

It must have been about eight o'clock when we
all heard a very distant shot right away in the
direction of the river, which I at once answered.
Shortly afterwards we saw a grass fire burn up in
the direction from whence the shot had sounded.
Thinking that this fire had possibly been lighted by
French, either accidentally or as a signal, I called up
three of his Kafirs, and taking with me my large
rifle, walked towards its light. After walking about
an hour, and when still a long way from the fire, I
fired two shots, but got no answer. I then went
on until I got right up to where the fire was burning,
when I again fired, but heard nothing in reply. I
now felt convinced that French had struck for the
river, and so returned to camp, which I did not
reach till long after midnight. I had been so far
away that neither Miller nor any of the Kafirs had
heard my last two shots.

We did not feel at all uneasy about French, as
we felt sure that he had made for the river—which
ran round us in a semicircle at a distance of not
more than fifteen miles, and thought he would sleep
there, and then follow up the broad footpath we had
made, the following day. Many things concurred to
make us think he had taken this step. In the first

place, we argued that after firing the shot we all
heard, which sounded far away towards the river,
and a long way off, he must have again walked on
in the same direction, right away from the camp,
and gone so far that when I reached the grass fire
near where he must have discharged the shot we
had heard, he was so far in front of me—still in the
direction of the river—that he did not hear my shot,
and we therefore concluded that he was striking
straight for the water.   What misled us as much as
anything was some remarks French had made a day
or two previously, when we were at the other pit
of water, to the effect that now we had left the river
it might be difficult to find our way back to camp if
we got belated, in which case the safest plan would
be to make for the river at once during the cool
hours of night.   It was, too, a fine moonlight night.
There was one other step we thought he might have
taken, which was to make straight for the path along
which we had come from the river; for as the
Kafirs accompanying us numbered over a hundred
altogether, and had all walked in single file, they
had made a track that must have been plainly visible,
even by moonlight.   Of the two Kafirs who were
with French, one was a Bamangwato boy, whom I
knew to have been in the habit of going in hunting
every year to the Mababe, and whom I always found
very good at finding his way about, taking game
spoor, or anything else of that nature required of a
Kafir in the bush.   Besides this, French had his
compass with him, knew the course of the river, and
the moon and Southern Cross were both shining
brightly.   Unfortunately, he was a very self-willed,
obstinate man, and there is little doubt that he lost
his life through disregarding the Kafirs' advice, and

continually trying to make his way back to our camp, until he became exhausted by the heat and from want of water, and then felt too weak ever to reach the river.

Early the next day, September 26, Miller and I took some of the best spooring Kafirs and tried to follow up the tracks of the elephant French had pursued the preceding day. The ground, however, was very difficult to spoor in, as it was covered for the most part with tufts of short curly grass, on which neither the elephant nor its pursuers had left much impression. No one but a Bushman could have followed a spoor well in such ground. In the afternoon, whilst we were returning to camp, we saw vultures settling not far off, and going to the place, found the remains of a giraffe. Amongst the contents of the paunch of this animal we found a bullet that had been fired unmistakably from French's 8-bore rifle, and we at once felt sure that the two shots we had heard shortly after reaching camp the preceding day must have been fired by him at this giraffe. Though we searched carefully, we could not find any traces of footprints about the carcase. Upon returning to camp and hearing that French had not arrived, we thought that after reaching the river he had probably gone back to Mamele's, where we had left a supply of stores, ammunition, etc., in charge of one of my waggon-drivers ; so I went to the headman amongst the Kafirs who were with us and got him to give me two boys to go direct with a letter through the bush to Mamele's, telling French that we would return to the river on the next day but one, and would meet him at Sasinkoro's town. At the same time I sent him his small rifle and his blankets.

2 F

On the 29th we accordingly made a start for the
river about 8 A.M. and struck it near Sasinkoro's
town about 2 P.M., having twice rested on the way,
as all the Kafirs were heavily laden with elephant's
meat.

The Kafirs at Sasinkoro's reported a herd of
elephants amongst the islands, so I sent another
messenger to Mamele's to inform French of the fact,
and telling him that we would await his arrival before
attacking them.

On October 1, I had a slight attack of fever, but
went out in the evening and shot two zebras.
Although I have not referred to it before, I may
here say that all this season, ever since reaching the
Māb̄abe in the previous June, I had been troubled
by attacks of fever more or less severe, which had
made me rather thin and weak.   This night we were
camped right out in the marsh, and surrounded on
all sides by lagoons of shallow water.   It must have
wanted about an hour to daylight when we were
roused by the headman and informed that a Kafir
had just arrived who said there was a large elephant
bull not far off, which we must go and shoot instantly.
It appeared that the messenger was one of a small
party who had cut up the two zebras I had shot the
preceding evening, and hung up the meat to dry just
on the water's edge, about a couple of miles from
our camp.   This man told us that as they were sitting
round their fire, making a night of it, they heard
an elephant drinking not far off, and presently saw
one come walking across the open ground straight
towards their camp, which they had made just on the
side of an ant-hill.   When the elephant got quite
close up, and still came walking on, they thought he
was going to attack them, and, jumping up, ran

behind the ant-heap, and then down to the water's edge. After waiting some time, and neither seeing nor hearing the elephant, our informant crept back and found the monster still standing close to their fire, apparently smelling the strips of zebra meat. Here he had left him, and come straight to us with the news. He said he could see that the elephant had very large tusks. It did not take us many minutes to prepare ourselves and start back with our guide, hoping we might still find the creature investigating the Kafir encampment. The moon, a little past the full, was shining splendidly, making it almost as light as day. We had to wade across several broad lagoons, one of which took us up to our arm-pits, before reaching our destination. It had been a hot sultry night, and the water felt cool and refreshing. Day was just breaking when we reached the ant-heap where our guide had left his companions. Here we found, sure enough, traces of the footsteps of a mighty bull elephant. The inquisitive animal had advanced to within six paces of the fire, and evidently stood some time on this spot ; at length, however, he had gone off at a quick walk towards the sand-belt. Filling the calabashes with water, as we anticipated a long chase, we at once took up his spoor. Before following it far we found that it joined the spoors of three other bulls and a little calf. The smell of the Kafirs and the zebra meat had evidently aroused their suspicions, as, instead of feeding, they had walked on, after joining, in single file, and at a quick pace. We could not have been half an hour behind, as the dung was quite hot, but we did not gain on them in the least. Hour after hour we trudged on, and at last, to make a long story short, they got our

wind, just as we were approaching them, and at once
decamped, of course, without our ever having seen
them.

I had been feeling very ill for some time, but
the excitement and the expectation of sighting the
elephants every instant had kept off the attack of
fever that I knew was coming on.   When I found
they had got our wind and run, I at once turned
back, and underwent a sharp attack of ague on the
way to the river.   In the afternoon I went through
the hot dry stage, and towards evening broke into a
perspiration, and at once felt better.   Just at sunset
I was sitting just outside our skerm, feeling very
weak and ill, when I saw a long string of Kafirs
approaching from Mamele's.   When they came close
I recognised " Boy," French's gun-carrier, walking
in front.   He was still carrying his heavy rifle.   When
he came close up my heart misgave me, for I saw by
his eyes that something untoward had happened.
" Where is the white man, your master ? " I said.
" He is dead," he answered ; " the sun killed him."

It now but remains for me to give Boy's narrative
of this terrible occurrence, which I took down from
his own lips a few days later.   It is as follows :—

" After leaving you, my master, with myself and
Nangora (the Makuba carrying water), followed the
spoor of the wounded elephant for some distance,
but at length lost it.   We then made for camp, and
whilst on our way there, came across a giraffe, which
my master shot.   He then told Nangora to cut
some fat meat off the giraffe and follow us to camp,
he and I going on at once.   My master now walked
in front, but did not hold what I thought was the
right direction to reach camp, though when I told
him so he would not listen to me, but only said,

'Asi molato hahaho' (That's not your business) ; so
I followed him in silence. When it got dark my
master fired two shots, but hearing nothing in reply,
again went on. Shortly afterwards, hearing some
one shouting, we answered, and Nangora came up
carrying the water and some giraffe meat. He had
also lost himself, but hearing the shots had come in
the direction of the sound. My master now took a
drink from the calabash, and gave me some too.
He then told me to go in front and make for camp.
I told him that I did not now know whereabouts the
camp lay, as we had held such a zigzag course all
the afternoon, and urged him to go to the river
during the cool of night. However, he would not
do so ; and after looking at his compass, again took
the lead. After a time we sat down and fired two
more shots, and my master then told me to set fire
to the grass, which I did. He then said he would
sleep there, but soon changed his mind ; so we got
up and went on again. We now walked on till late
at night, often through thick patches of bush, my
master always holding a very uncertain course. I
now advised him to make for where the moon was
setting, in order to cut the path by which we had
come from the river. However, he would not, so
we lit a fire and then lay down to wait for daylight.
We here drank all the water that remained in the
calabash. At daylight the next morning my master
again told me to go in front and make for the camp
near where we had shot the elephants. I told him
I did not know where the camp lay, and again
advised him to strike for the river, whose course I
knew. He only swore at me, and told Nangora to
go in front. After a time my master said we were
going wrong, and again took the lead himself. In

this way we went on all day, not holding a good line, but always going more or less towards sunrise. In the afternoon my master commenced to cough and spit a great deal of blood (māre hela), resting at very short intervals, but always getting up and going on again until late at night. He then lay down, and spat a great deal of blood. Presently he called me to him and said, 'Boy, I am dying ; light some grass and hold it near me that I may write.' He then wrote on his rifle, and on his belt. He then said, 'Take this rifle to Selous, and tell him to look after my waggon and other property.' He did not speak again, and shortly afterwards died. When I thought he was dead, I opened his shirt and put my hand over his heart, but as it did not beat I knew he was no more. As soon as Nangora and I knew that this was the case, we broke a few branches and put over the body, and then taking the rifle and belt started for the river. We walked all the remainder of the night, and early the next morning reached the river, just at the site of the town of Linyanti. We then went to Mamele's, and as soon as my master's boys came there saying you were going to Sasinkoro's town, I started with them at once to meet you. This is all."

I now examined the rifle. On the inside of the small piece of wood that fits under the barrel in front of the trigger-guard, these sad words were very illegibly written : "I cannot go any farther ; when I die, peace with all." The writing inside the leather belt we could not decipher.

What my feelings were, upon the receipt of this horrible and unexpected news, I will not endeavour to describe. The mental anguish, however, which I suffered, just at a time, too, when I was far from well in body, brought on a succession of attacks of fever that very nearly ended my troubles. For several nights I never slept, as the vision of my lost friend (for we had always hit it off very well together), wandering about and dying by inches, continually haunted me.

According to Boy, French had died on the night of September 27, and it was not until October 2 that the news reached me, and we were then nearly thirty miles from where he had struck the river at Linyanti after leaving the body, which I felt it to be my first duty to try and recover. I asked Boy if when we reached Linyanti he would be able to find his way back to where his master had died. He replied that it was in the night when he had left him, and that as the whole country was covered with thick level forests without any landmark to guide him, he would never be able to find the spot, unless we could follow his spoor. As this was already five days old, I knew it would be impossible to do so, but determined to try. Accordingly, the following morning, October 3, we made a start along the river. I was very weak from the effects of fever, but determined to reach Linyanti before nightfall.

It was a long tramp—nearly thirty miles, I should think ; wading a great part of the way, too, through innumerable lagoons. At last, however, we reached the site of the old town. I was thoroughly exhausted, and, it only having been the sustained exertion that kept off the fever, soon became very ill. The next day I was worse, and utterly incapable of doing anything ; Miller, however, went out with Boy and searched for the spoor, but unsuccessfully. In the evening I called up the headman, and tried to get him to send all the Kafirs with him into the bush to

search for poor French's remains. He, however,
replied that, according to the time it took Boy to
reach the river after leaving his body, he must have
died so far away from the river, that they would
have to carry water and sleep in the bush, and search
for the body on the second day ; and that, as they
had not many of them got calabashes, this, in the
present state of the weather, would be impossible.
He added, too, that as the whole country was covered
with dense forests, and Boy did not in the least know
the direction in which the remains lay, it was almost
useless searching for them.   I knew that what he
said was just, yet still, had I been well enough, I
would have searched the country for several days
to the best of my ability.   As it was, the headman
promised that as soon as the rains fell he would send
all his people out in search of my friend's remains,
and I promised a large reward should they ever be
brought, with the watch and compass that were on
his person when he died, either to myself or to Mr.
Westbeech at Pandamatenka.   Up to the end of last
year no discovery had been made.   Thus died poor
French, adding one more to the long list of Englishmen whose unburied bones lie bleaching in the
wilderness far from their native land.   He was as
fine and manly a fellow as ever stepped, but terribly
obstinate when he took anything into his head, and
it is to this unfortunate trait in his character that I
feel sure the loss of his life is due, for had he listened
to the Kafir's advice and struck for the river the first
night, he would be alive now ; as Boy said to me,
" Had it been any other white man but my master,
he would have taken my advice and gone to the
river, whose course we knew well, instead of trying
to find his way to a single point in the bush."

Some people have expressed surprise at poor French dying so quickly, but it must be remembered that at this time of year, just before the rains fall, the heat is something terrific in this part of the country. In 1879, three Kafirs hunting with Mr. Sell near the junction of the Chobe and Zambesi, died of thirst within twenty-four hours of the time they left the last water. Let me now, however, dismiss this sad theme. I have given as straightforward an account of it as I could, and I do not care to discuss it any further.

During the next few days, as I have said before, I was very ill with repeated attacks of fever—so ill that Miller made a stretcher on which to have me carried, as he did not think I would be able to walk. However, as my mind recovered from the shock it had received, my body gained strength too, and, as neither of us cared to hunt any longer in this part of the country, we recrossed the river and started for the waggons, which we reached on October 11.

Here we found Collison and Sell, the latter lying dangerously ill with fever. He had, however, beaten us all with the elephants, having killed three bulls and a cow, one of the former with very fine tusks, weighing nearly 70 lbs. apiece. A few days later, when Sell commenced to mend a little, Miller was struck down in turn with a sharp attack, from which, however, he began to recover in a few days.

During the remainder of October I stayed at the waggons with Collison, in the hope that the rains would speedily fall and allow us to make our escape out of this wretched, waterless country ; for as there were absolutely no elephants to be found, there was not the slightest inducement for us to remain any longer where we were. However, as long as the drought continued we were prisoners, for the long stretch of waterless desert that lay between the Mababe river and Sode-Garra was now utterly impassable, as the weather was intensely hot, both day and night.

By the end of the month, being tired of shooting the zebras, blue wildebeests, and tsessebe antelopes, which, owing to the drought, had assembled in large herds from an enormous area of country to drink in the Mababe river, and hundreds of which might be seen at any moment from the waggons, I determined to make another journey on foot, in search of elephants, to the Chobe.

Accordingly, on the 26th, I started, taking only five Kafirs with me. I was in rather a weak state of health, and had two or three slight attacks of fever during my trip. The weather was most intensely hot both day and night, and very sultry and oppressive, as it always is just before the rains fall. This time I went as far as Mai-ini's town again, but finding no traces of elephants, and as the rain was threatening, I then retraced my steps. In the evenings it was quite a sight to see the herds of game coming down to drink. In cooler weather these animals would most of them have waited for the protecting cover of the night before venturing down to the river, but the intense heat made them forget their usual caution. Every evening, from about five o'clock till dusk, I was seldom out of sight of game of some kind — buffaloes, impalas, koodoos, lechwes, reedbucks, blue wildebeests, tsessebes, and wild pigs, being the commonest varieties ; whilst sable and roan antelopes, zebras, and an occasional giraffe or eland, were also to be seen. The day before I reached Mai-ini's the natives had managed to harpoon a fat hippopotamus, and from my camp I could hear them singing and dancing as they feasted the whole night through. During this journey I shot one elephant, a young bull, that I found standing by himself in a bed of reeds, and wounded another. This latter was one of a herd that I heard screaming and drinking in the river about two miles from my camp. As it was a tolerably clear moonlight night, I resolved to have a shot at one, for in my weak state I knew that I stood but little chance of coming up with them the following day. On my way towards the elephants I came across a herd of giraffes ; they allowed me to approach quite close to them in the moonlight before they became alarmed. I also saw three animals trot away from me, that were either lions or hyænas. At last I got up to the elephants, having had to wade through two deep lagoons before doing so. The animals were then feeding in a small patch of bush, crashing down small trees and breaking off branches in all directions. I got close up to one that was feeding just outside the bush, and fired for behind her shoulder with my large single rifle. Although there was a very good moon, I could not see the sights at all, but, as I was so near, felt certain I should kill her. I did not do so, however, nor could I find any traces of blood when I came back the following morning. One night, as I was returning to the waggons, we slept at the last hole of water in the bed of the Sunta, which we did not reach until just dusk. We were all of us fagged out, having made a long march in the intense heat, so my Kafirs made no skerm, and, it being so hot, collected very little firewood. Soon after dark I heard a troop of lions roar in the distance ;

presently they roared again, evidently nearer ; then again and again, but always getting nearer, till there was no doubt that they were coming down to drink at the water, close to which we were encamped. The night was intensely dark, as the sky was overcast and the moon did not rise till late. At length the lions reached the water just beneath us, having roared grandly at intervals of ten minutes or so, ever since we first heard them. The noise they made was truly appalling, for as our camp was just on the top of a steep bank underneath which was the pool of water, we could not have been more than fifteen yards from them. We had scarcely any fire, and being surrounded by bush, what we had threw no light over the water, so that I do not think the lions had any idea of our near proximity. When they were drinking we could hear them lapping the water quite plainly. They roared three times just beneath us, before taking their departure. One would commence, then a second join in, then a third, and at the time when they were all roaring at once, the effect was most grand, not to say awful. I think there must have been four of them. Upon several previous occasions I have heard lions roar very close to me, but never quite so close as upon this occasion. Surely nothing can be more unjust and misleading than to compare the voice of the lion to the sound emitted by the ostrich, as Dr. Livingstone does in his very one-sided description of the former animal. The booming noise made by the cock ostrich during the breeding season sounds, at a distance of fifty yards, very like the roar of a lion heard at a distance of three miles ; but, *ceteris paribus*, the two notes are as different the one from the other as those emitted by a concertina and a cathedral organ. As I have remarked elsewhere, I think, in this book, there is no sound in nature more grand, and at the same time more awe-inspiring, than the roaring of several lions in unison, if heard, be it understood, at close quarters.

By the middle of November I again reached the waggons, and a few days later, to our great joy, the long-wished-for rain at length fell. It was not, however, until the 4th of December that we were able to make a start southwards with the waggons. As far as the Botletlie river we got along easily enough, as, the rain having fallen copiously, every vley was full of water. Between that river, however, and Bamangwato, we again very nearly lost all our oxen from thirst, and, indeed, after trekking as far as they would go without water, had to drive them to the river Luali, on the road from Bamangwato to the Zambesi, to obtain a supply of that essential element. At last, however, after spending a very miserable Christmas without food or water, we once more reached Bamangwato, where we met with true Kafirland hospitality from our friends and countrymen, the traders stationed at that distant outpost of civilisation.

A few days later, as it was necessary that I should hand over poor French's property to his executors on the Diamond Fields, and make an affidavit concerning his death, I made a start southwards, and trekking down as far as Klerksdorp in the Transvaal with my waggons, took the passenger waggon from there to the Fields. The cold climate of these regions, in comparison with the warmer air of the interior, brought out the fever that was still lurking in my system, and I suffered first from a series of attacks of ague, and latterly, when on the Fields, from a sort of low fever very prevalent there, that reduced me to a very low ebb, from which nothing but the unremitting attention and careful nursing which I received at the hands of those kindest of women, my old and very dear friends Mrs. Frederick Barber and her daughter Mrs. Alexander Bailie, at length rescued me. To these two ladies I owe a debt of gratitude which, if life is worth living, I can never repay.

By the end of March I had sufficiently recovered to enable me to return to my waggons at Klerksdorp, and a week later I once more started upon my eighth and last hunting trip to the far interior.

END OF 1879.

CHAPTER XXI

Hippopotamus Paths—Rhinoceros—Bad Rifle—Waterbucks—Difficult Country — Sable Antelope — Native Villages — Bargaining — Lo Magondi—Native Weaving—Trip with Lo Magondi—The Lory —Pool of Hippos—Sea-Cow shooting—Matabele—Superstition— Beaconsfield Cataracts—Shooting Buffalo—Lion at night.

It had been my intention this year to have crossed the Zambesi and endeavoured to pass through the Mashukulumbwe country to the upper Kafukwe, and thence penetrate, if possible, as far north as Lake Bengweolo. However, these ambitious projects were rudely frustrated by Sir Owen Lanyon, the Administrator of the Transvaal, refusing to grant me "any arms or ammunition whatsoever"— to quote his own words in reply to my letter ; for to have started on an expedition that would in all probability have extended over two years without a good supply of ammunition, would have been madness. As it was, however, necessary for me to visit the interior and look after some property I had left there, before leaving the country, I determined to join my friends Messrs. Collison, Jameson, and Dr. Crook in a hunting trip to the Mashuna country.

Reaching the Matabele country in the latter end of May, I found them all still at the king's kraal, though impatient to get amongst the game. A few days later we all trekked away together *en route* for

the hunting veldt.   As the greater part of the
country through which we hunted during this season
was familiar to me, and as I have given some account
of it in other parts of this work, I will confine
myself to giving a narrative of a journey made by
Mr. Jameson and myself on foot to the junction of
the Umfule and Umniati rivers, a point never
previously visited by a European, an abstract of
which appeared in the *Proceedings of the Royal Geographical Society* for June 1881.

On the 24th of July 1880, Mr. J. S. Jameson
and myself left our waggons, which were standing
on the banks of the Umfule river (not far from
the spot marked Constitution Hill on Mr. Baines's
map), and started on foot on a trip into the " fly "
country to our north.   Our party consisted of
ourselves, a little Griqua boy named " Bokkie,"
who looked after the cooking and made himself
generally useful, and thirteen Matabele and Makalaka
Kafirs, who carried our ammunition, guns, and
provisions.   Mr. Jameson's battery consisted of a
double 10 and a double 500 " Express," both by
Rigby, and both most excellent weapons ; my own
of a single 10 (Whitworth rifling) and a single 450
" Express "—the latter by Gibbs of Bristol.

It was already late in the day when we made a
start, and so, as the sun was getting low in the
heavens when we reached a fine clear stream—a
tributary of the Umfule, running beneath a hill
known to the Kafirs as " Intaba-go-umbundwan,"
and about three hours' hard walk from our waggons
—we decided to camp upon its banks, the more so
as we did not know exactly how far we were from
the next stream, or from the main river.   As we
were without meat for dinner, we each of us took

our gun-carriers, and, leaving the remainder of the
Kafirs to make a camp, went in different directions
in search of game. About sundown I returned
with an oribi ram, and found Jameson there before
me with a reedbuck, whose kidneys and undercut
were already, under the care of Bokkie, frying to
the tune of a most appetising sizzle, in our little
frying-pan.

At the above-mentioned hill the " fly " commences, and extends to the north and the north-west
without a break, right up to the banks of the Zambesi.
On the eastern side of the Umfule there is still a
large area of country free from fly, extending as far
as Lo Magondi's mountains to the north-east.

Early on the following day we struck the main
river, and followed its course until sundown. On
our way we saw many waterbucks, and the tracks of
several rhinoceroses, but as they only come down
to the river at night to drink, and remain during
the heat of the day in the forests and thickets at
a considerable distance from the water, one stands
little chance of seeing any, unless by following them
up. We also met some Matabele hunters who had
just shot a waterbuck ; they were all loaded up with
the skins (cut into long strips and dried for sjamboks)
of two hippopotami, which they had shot, they said,
about a day's walk farther down the river. They
told us that we should find the country very mountainous farther on.

July 26th.—As the Kafirs had foretold, we got
into a very rough hilly country, through which the
river had forced its way in a succession of foaming
rapids, rushing over great boulders of rock, interspersed here and there with great, deep, still pools
of dark-blue water.

2 G

These pools must have harboured many herds of hippopotami at no very distant date, for the broad, well-beaten, double footpaths made by these bulky beasts (the hippopotamus always forms a double footpath with a little ridge in the centre, as it moves its feet along in parallel lines), and leading from one pool to another, sometimes up and down very steep and rocky hillsides, were to be met with all along the river. The hippopotami had, however, disappeared from the scene, and betaken themselves to more secure retreats farther down the stream. This day we made a sad mess with a black rhinoceros, which, at some distance from the river, as we were going down a sloping hillside, I descried about 100 yards in advance of us, slowly making his way through some short scrub. We soon crept down to within fifty yards of him, and then waited till he came past us. When almost opposite he stood with his shoulder just behind a tree about a foot in diameter ; here he remained for some seconds, then took another step, and stood again, evidently listening. I was afraid that he suspected something, and might wheel round at any moment, so, as he had enough of his shoulder beyond the tree, to allow a bullet to reach his heart, I nudged Jameson, and fired, and, sad to tell, instead of putting my bullet into his shoulder, I struck the tree. I hurried my friend's shot too, so that he only hit the brute too far back as it sprang forward, and in fact we lost the rhinoceros. What we said and the oaths we swore are fortunately not written in any book of Chronicles.

This disgracefully bad shot, I have reason to believe, was not my fault, for, after making a few more failures for which I could not account, I fired at a mark, and found that the bullets fell all over the place ; and at last I had to lay the rifle on one side, and take again to an old one which I had discarded in its favour, having only just got it out from England—this, indeed, being its first trial.

Soon after this little incident we again struck the river, and whilst picking our way over the great boulders through which it ran, came suddenly upon a small herd of waterbucks, making their way across a ledge of rocks towards a bushy island that lay just in front of us.   Here was another chance for dinner ; we both fired, and I tumbled my buck off a stone into the water ; but in a few moments he recovered himself and plunged through the river and into the thicket after the others.   Jameson, however, struck his in the right place, the expanding bullet smashing its shoulder and blowing its heart to pieces ; however, it did not fall at once, but rushed madly forwards for about fifty yards, and had almost gained the shelter of the bush before succumbing.   We crossed over to the island where it lay, and then followed mine by the blood spoor, but as it took us out of the way, and as we had meat enough, we left it, maybe to recover from its wound, though I am afraid that the chances are the poor animal fell a prey to hyænas.

The following day we crossed to the eastern bank of the river, and from daylight till dark toiled through a series of the most exasperating stony hills that it is possible to imagine.   Sometimes we kept away from the stream to avoid those that sloped precipitously to the water's edge, and whose sides were too steep to afford a footing.   During the whole day, however, we never saw a single head of game ; indeed, the country was too rough for anything but waterbucks or an odd black rhinoceros, which both delight in rugged hills ; and even in the river, although we saw recent traces of hippopotami, we came across none of the animals themselves.

Towards evening reaching a large range of hills running east and west, and, cutting the Umfule at right angles, we got into a perfect labyrinth of rocky ravines and gorges, through which we toiled till sundown, eventually camping on the bank of a small stream at some distance from the main river.

That evening we discussed the situation. We appeared to be getting into a country which became day by day more impracticable and toilsome, and the farther we advanced the scarcer game seemed to become, which was the most important consideration of all, for our Kafirs were entirely dependent upon our guns for their daily food, and we ourselves had but a very small supply of rice and flour.

We knew nothing of the country, nor did our Kafirs, so that one direction was as good as another, always excepting the way we had come ; for having said when we left the waggons that we should be away at least a month, we could not, for very shame, go back at the end of a week and say we had been driven out of the wilderness, through inability to obtain food,—we who for so many years had always lived by our rifles, and seldom gone hungry.

We finally determined to strike to the eastward, along the range of hills already mentioned, and eventually, if possible, reach the Hanyane, and follow it down to the Portuguese town of Zumbo on the Zambesi. After walking steadily for about three hours we at length descried a small herd of sable antelopes feeding down towards a stream of water that ran through a grassy glade just in front of us. With a little care we managed to get into the bed of the stream unobserved, from whence a

careful crawl soon brought us within range of the
still unsuspicious herd. Jameson then fired, and
knocked over a fine cow. Once more all gloomy
thoughts of possible starvation ahead were banished,
and, having wood, water, and meat, we at once proceeded to make a hearty meal, after which we again
struck away to the east.

All that day we passed through great quantities
of elephant spoor, but all, alas! too old to be of any
use to us. One herd, that must have been there
less than a month before us, had literally strewn the
ground with broken branches over many acres, and
peeled the bark from every second machabel tree
(the bark and leaves of this tree are the favourite
food of the elephant in this part of the country). A
little before sunset we struck a fine stream of beautifully clear water babbling over a rocky bed, and
followed it into a deep gorge through the hills. As
we were picking our road along the steep side of
this gorge, a waterbuck bull rushed out of the reeds
below us, and took up the hill on the opposite side
of the ravine. I fired at and missed him with my
first shot, but knocked him over with a second.
Here we camped for the night in order to make the
most of the meat, for game still appeared to be very
scarce. During the night a light drizzling rain fell.

July 29*th.*—We made our way through the gorge
into an open marshy valley between two ranges of
hills, and, after a struggle through an immense vley
of long wet grass, struck a Kafir footpath, which we
resolved to follow, as we thought it would be pretty
sure to bring us to a kraal, where the people would
be able to give us some information about the
country on ahead. As we had surmised, a three
hours' steady tramp brought us to some old mealie

gardens and deserted Kafir huts, and just over the
next ridge, we came upon a small kraal, which we
found to be one of Lo Magondi's outlying villages,
that august personage being a petty Mashuna chief,
holding his life and property at the caprice of the
Matabele king, Lobengula.

Finding that our Kafirs had meat which they
were willing to sell for meal, ground-nuts, etc., the
villagers soon came trooping down to our camp,
intent upon barter.   As they were tired of a continuous vegetable diet, and our boys were equally
tired of meat, the exchange was very brisk.

The women usually brought the produce of their
gardens down themselves in very small baskets or
wooden plates, and then, sitting at a little distance
from us, gave them to some male friend to sell for
them, keeping, however, a sharp eye on the whole
transaction, and assisting or hindering the barter
with a never-flagging tongue.

Altogether, it was a noisy and amusing scene ;
the fashion of the huts and corn-bins, the tame
pigeons flying in and out of the public dovecot
(obtained from the Portuguese and found in every
kraal along the Zambesi) ; the arms and dress of the
men, and the wonderful way in which some of them
had frizzed and got up their hair, all recalled to my
mind a Banyai kraal on the banks of the Zambesi,
to which tribe, indeed, I have no doubt that these
people belong.

At last the noise and bustle were over ; our boys
had sold all their meat, and obtained a fair supply of
meal and mealies ; still they were not satisfied, but
were now trying to blarney the girls into making
them presents of something more in the eating line.
As far as I could see, however, these daughters of

Eve were proof against all flattery, however delicately
or thickly it might have been laid on, for, according
to my experience, all Kafirs are alike in one thing,
however much they may differ in other particulars
—they will give nothing for nothing, and as little as
possible for sixpence.

We now got a boy to show us the way to the
chief's kraal ; the path to it took us through another
village, and across a large extent of cultivated ground.
The people seemed to be very industrious, cultivating
great quantities of Kafir corn, mealies, ground-nuts,
and a few sweet potatoes ; they had any amount of
vegetable food and lots of beer, and what they
seemed to wish for most was a good blow-out of
meat, fat if possible ; but meat in any shape—fat,
lean, fresh, or stinking—was evidently to them a
most coveted luxury.

We found old Lo Magondi living in a small
village occupied apparently only by his own wives
and a few intimates, and perched upon the summit
of a very steep hill.

When we reached the top, the old fellow, with
some of his sons and a councillor or two, was seated
on a bark mat with a huge pot of beer in front of
him ; two years previously, in 1878, having paid a
visit to one of his other towns, and he himself having
also brought some ivory to our waggons at Umfule
to sell, he soon remembered me, and at once offered
us beer and ground-nuts and made himself very
friendly. He was very much disappointed to find
that we had no trading goods with us, and begged
hard for a shirt, in order, as he put it, to show that
white men had visited him.

At this little kraal we noticed a man weaving a
blanket on a native hand-loom and out of native

cotton ; it seemed very slow work, and, judging
from the progress he made whilst we were there,
it must have taken him at least a month to finish ;
we also saw that they had planted a few cotton
bushes near the huts and enclosed them with a
hedge.

Later on, when we were down the Umniati, I
noticed that at every Banyai kraal we visited the
people had planted and enclosed a few cotton bushes
near their villages. On being questioned, old Lo
Magondi gave us the following information : That
there were now no Portuguese at Zumbo, or
Mandombi as the natives call it ; that we should
get no game down Hanyane, as there were a great
many Kafirs living along its banks between his kraals
and the Zambesi ; and finally, that, if we would go
with him to the lower part of the Umfule, he would
show us lots of hippopotami, and consult his god to
find out where the elephants were. He also stated
positively that the Umfule ran into the Umniati,
not many days' journey below where we were to find
the sea-cows. This last statement decided us to
give up the Hanyane and follow down the Umfule
to its junction with the Umniati, so as to establish
the fact ; for in all maps of South Africa hitherto
published the Umfule is marked running into the
Zambesi, about half-way between the Umniati and
the Hanyane rivers.

That evening Lo Magondi sent us a plate of
"pogo," porridge, and a strip of sea-cow fat about
two inches thick, which, he said, was to show how
fat his cattle were. It was, however, stinking, and
useless to us, though our boys ate it with great relish.
The next morning, although on the previous evening
the old fellow had promised to make an early start,

we found great difficulty in getting him to move ; at last, however, he stepped out all ready for the journey. He wore a broad-brimmed straw hat, and a gaily-coloured Portuguese cloth bound round his loins and hanging to the ground all round him like a skirt ; over his left shoulder he carried a strong 10-bore muzzle-loading rifle, a present, as he told me, from Lobengula, and in his right hand a battle-axe, made, handle and blade, entirely of native Mashuna iron.

This day we had a short but rather tedious journey through a very rough hilly country, crossing one very high and steep range ; we always kept a general course of north-west, and followed a well-beaten footpath leading to another of Lo Magondi's villages, which we reached about four in the afternoon. That night the people of the village gave a dance, in honour of their chief's visit, and the feast they anticipated, if we were successful amongst the hippopotami.

The infernal and monotonous tom-toming (which, when I was on the other side of the Zambesi, elicited enough bad language from myself alone in the course of six months to endanger the souls of at least fifty men) was kept up with the usual accompaniment of discordant yelling, and clapping of hands, until far into the night. In all these performances that I have seen, the men alone dance, the women and girls standing round clapping their hands and singing. Our boys, of course, all went and joined in the fun.

The following day we might easily have pushed on and reached the pools in which our guide expected we should find the hippopotami, but he preferred to sleep a few miles on this side, just where a tributary stream ran into the Umfule, so that we might have the whole

day before us.   Since leaving Lo Magondi's we
had seen very little game—nothing, in fact, but a
few waterbucks.   In the morning I had knocked
over a fine bull, but lost him, although I followed a
long way on his blood spoor.   A little later on,
however, Jameson had bowled over a cow of the
same species, so that we had meat, though the
waterbuck is the least-esteemed antelope, from a
culinary point of view, to be found in the country.

July 31*st*.—We started down the bank of the
river in high hopes of soon falling in with hippopotami, for on the preceding evening we had already
seen abundant signs of their having been about
very recently.   In the course of an hour we passed
some magnificent pools several hundred yards long,
broad and seemingly very deep, for the water looked
dark blue, and from the fresh tracks and dung on the
broad footpath which the hippos had made all along
the river's edge, we expected to see or hear some every
instant.   Here for the first time I saw the beautiful
Lory or plantain-eater (*Corythaix porphyreolophus*).
These birds, with their bright scarlet wings, dark
purple-green body, crested heads, and loud cry of
Glock, glock, glock, must, wherever met with, at once
attract attention ; beautiful green pigeons, too (*Treron
delalandii*), flew in flocks from tree to tree as we
advanced.

At length, about nine o'clock, we reached the pool
in which were the unsuspecting hippos.   We came
upon them suddenly, as they were all lying lazily on
the top of the water, and not more than thirty yards
from the bank.   When we approached they seemed
utterly unsuspicious of danger, only pricking their
little ears and raising their heads higher in the water.
Jameson opened the ball by striking a large cow

right in front of the head with a 10-bore bullet. In an instant every head had disappeared, and in a few moments the bubbling waters had subsided, and every ripple on the surface of the pool was gone. However, we knew they must come up again, and so prepared to receive them ; Jameson guarded the top of the pool, and I ran down to the lower end, and whenever a head appeared one or other of us saluted it with a bullet. For some time the fun was fast and furious, and before very long it became evident that there were very few sea-cows left to shoot at. The herd had originally consisted of seven—a large bull, four cows, and two half-grown calves. Now, however, the bull and three of the cows were dead, the fourth was wounded, and the two calves alone remained unscathed to tell of the dire destruction that had been worked upon their family. About mid-day the two first killed floated to the top of the water, and a little later on the other two also came to the surface. I may here say that a hippopotamus when killed sinks to the bottom and the carcase does not rise to the surface before from three to six hours have elapsed : in cold weather, and if the animal be in poor condition, he will often remain at the bottom for a much longer period. The old bull was in very poor condition, but the cows were excessively fat ; indeed, when the skin was stripped off in large squares, their whole bodies were covered with a layer of white fat from shoulder to rump, from half an inch to two inches in thickness. The old cow that was still alive was now excessively shy, and only offered very bad chances for a shot, as she stopped from five to ten minutes under water at a time, and when she came up to blow, only exposed a small portion

of the head for just a couple of seconds or so, giving
no time for a deliberate aim.   If she had been
unwounded we would have let her alone, but we
could see when she rose two white bullet-marks on
her, one through her nose and the other a little
behind her ear.   By this time the dead sea-cows
had floated down to the tail of the pool, and all our
boys and Lo Magondi's followers were hard at work
cutting up the meat.   Towards evening I crossed
the river where it ran in several channels through
the rocks and boulders at the bottom of the pool,
in order to try and circumvent the still surviving
cow.   Waiting till she went down, I ran forwards
and took up a position as near as possible to the
place where she had last appeared ; I then watched
her for a time, and finding that she rose again and
again nearly in the same spot, I covered the place
with my rifle and when she next rose got the sight
just under her ear, and pulled the trigger as quickly
as possible.   I heard the bullet strike, and saw that
I had killed her, for after raising her head once or
twice at short intervals and evidently with great
difficulty, she at last only just managed to throw
her nozzle above water, and then sank to rest for
good.   This hippopotamus was a large cow, and,
like the others, very fat.   I shot her with a single
450 Express by George Gibbs of Bristol, using an
ordinary Express bullet, the hollow plugged with a
peg of soft wood, and only backed by $3\frac{1}{2}$ drachms
of powder.   We found on examination that I had
struck her just under and at the root of the ear, and
the solid end of the bullet had either penetrated to,
or driven splinters of bone into, her brain.   I think
this a wonderful performance for a 450 Express
rifle ; with a solid bullet it would have been nothing,

but I used the ordinary small hollow bullet.   No
praise can be too high for Mr. Gibbs's admirable
little Metford Express rifle ; with the same little
weapon about which I am now speaking, I had
killed in the preceding June two black rhinoceroses,
each with a single hollow bullet, and three large full-
grown lions with four bullets.

Sea-cow shooting is a sport that I care very little
about.   In the first place, it is usually so difficult
to know the result of one's shot, and if you do
kill your animal, you have to wait several hours
before you can secure it.   In a large river like the
Zambesi, where you have to shoot out of a canoe,
and the sea-cows can take clean away up or down
the river, or, as they sometimes do, attack the boat,
this sport needs excessive skill and quickness in
shooting, and is sometimes attended with a certain
amount of danger.   In a small river like the Umfule,
however, where the poor animals are in a comparatively narrow pool, from which there is no
escape for them until night hides their movements,
and where the requirements of nature force them
constantly to expose themselves as they raise their
heads to breathe, one feels that they are too heavily
handicapped, and after the excitement of the first
few shots wears off, the sport soon palls.

In this case, however, I must confess that both
Jameson and myself enjoyed the fun whilst it lasted.
When, after having disposed of three, we asked Lo
Magondi if we had not killed enough meat, he gave
us to understand that he had people enough to eat
twenty hippopotami, and begged us to kill the rest,
so that at any rate there was no fear of the meat
being allowed to go to waste, and we had the
satisfaction of knowing that the slaughter of these

creatures would bring more joy to the hearts of
these poor but voracious heathen, than all the tracts
and Bibles ever published for their benefit. The
following day we devoted to cutting up and drying
the meat.   Lo Magondi sent messengers to his
towns to call the people to come and assist, and
bring meal, ground-nuts, etc., with them. I gave
him three of the sea-cows entire, and besides this,
his people bought all the leaner portions of the other
two from our boys, for meal and ground-nuts.   We
now revelled in comparative luxury ; the fresh sea-
cow meat was really most delicious, very rich in
flavour and withal tender and juicy, and the amount
of it that we got outside of was really astonishing.
We were also enabled to melt out two large calabashes
full of soft white lard, which kept us in fat cookies
(unleavened cakes of meal and water baked in fat)
until we got back to the waggons.   Whilst I was
attending to the distribution of the meat, Jameson
took a stroll up the river, and I soon afterwards
heard him fire.

When he returned he told me he had found a
huge old hippopotamus bull lying high and dry on
an island in the middle of the river, and as he
wanted a fine pair of teeth had fired at him ; upon
which the brute had plunged into the river and got
round to the other side of the island, where he
remained out of sight. He had also shot a large
crocodile, which had tumbled into the water,
apparently writhing about in its death-agony.

However, I advised him not to inquire further
into the matter, as the Matabele are very superstitious
about this animal, believing that any one possessed
of its liver is able to bewitch other people, and play
the devil generally ; and it was as likely as not that

if the king heard that our party had killed one he might give our boys some trouble by accusing them of having preserved the liver for occult purposes.

Although Lo Magondi's people must have known better, they all declared that the Umniati river was three hard days' journey on foot to the west of where we now were. I did not believe them; and as it was advisable that we should keep our main camp in the same place for a few days yet, in order to thoroughly dry a good supply of fat meat, I proposed to Jameson that we should each make a tour of inspection in different directions in order to spy out the land, taking each our own boys, and leaving some behind to guard the camp. This plan we adopted; so, on the 2nd of August, taking four days' provisions with us, we bade adieu for a short time, and each took a different course; my friend making for a stream Lo Magondi had told him of to the S.W., where he would be likely to fall in with buffalo; and I striking pretty well due west, having determined to reach the Umniati, if possible, before turning back. I first followed the river's bank, intending to cross at a place Lo Magondi had told me of, where there was a waterfall. At a pool about two miles below our camp I came upon the two young hippos, the survivors of the herd we had so nearly annihilated, and which, I forgot to mention, had made good their escape the same day, as soon as darkness fell. I did not molest them, but went on until I reached the falls. The river here runs over and amongst huge boulders of granite rock in three channels, altogether quite 300 yards broad, and when swollen by heavy rains these streams must all be united into one broad expanse of seething cataract, foaming over a bed of solid rock, and at such times could not fail to present a grand and awesome sight.   There are three small falls, which are, however, insignificant, the highest being that on the eastern side, which falls into a deep hole the water has worn in the rock.   These falls Jameson afterwards christened the Beaconsfield Cataracts, not that their appearance entitled them to the distinction of being named after so distinguished a man, but just to show his appreciation of that able statesman's genius.

After crossing the river I became involved amongst a series of steep, stony hills, but holding steadily to the west gradually got into a less broken country. During the day I had seen much old buffalo spoor, and just before sunset came upon the tracks of a herd that I thought fresh, but soon found they had passed the evening before.   Being in want of water before camping, I followed the spoor to a rather muddy hole in the bed of a deep gully, and there I camped.   Next morning I was up early, and still kept to the west, crossing much buffalo spoor only a day or two old, and also the tracks of several black rhinoceroses (there are no white ones in this part of the country).   About nine o'clock, from the point of a ridge of hills, I saw the Umniati river running just below me, and a native kraal perched on the summit of a hill beyond.   So much for native information ; instead of being three days' journey from our camp, the Umniati, after all, was barely five-and-twenty miles as the crow flies.

Whilst making this reflection, I saw three old buffalo bulls below me on the edge of the short thick bush with which the hillside was covered ; they had, unfortunately, heard us talking, and dashed away into the thicket.   With April, my gun-carrier, in close attendance, I ran after them, but could not get

a shot ; so, having noticed the fresh spoors of a large
herd while running, I went back to these, judging it
would be better to follow them than the three old
bulls, which, already alarmed, had all their wits about
them. I first made a cup of tea and ate a strip of
broiled sea-cow meat, and then took up the spoor ;
but although it looked as fresh as paint, we found
the buffaloes had passed here the preceding afternoon on their way to the water, and so we had first
to follow all their peregrinations down to a little
tributary of the Umniati before getting into their
fresh tracks, and though we kept at it hard, it was
very nearly sunset before we at last sighted the
herd. They had already risen from the place where
they had been lying during the heat of the day, and
were slowly feeding along in a straggling line through
the bush ; there must have been fifty or sixty of
them. Taking the precaution to keep well below
the wind, I got, after a good deal of stooping and
crawling, level with the foremost animals, and then,
dropping on my knees, crept close up to the still
unconscious herd. The nearest buffalo to me was
a bull with rather a fine head, so, as he was facing
nearly straight away from me, I put a ball from my
10-bore just behind his ribs, aiming obliquely forwards, so that the bullet might pierce both lungs.
Like lightning the herd wheeled round, and rushed
off in mad affright. I followed at my best pace,
both gun-carriers well up.

After running about 400 yards my bull fell dead.
Then the herd turned and looked towards me, and I
struck a cow right in the chest with my Express,
and got another shot into a bull with the 10. He
at once turned out, and soon settled to a trot. I
followed, and hearing me running behind him, he

2 H

suddenly stopped short, and wheeling broadside on, stood looking towards us with upraised head and glaring eyes.   Seizing the 10, I fired for his shoulder —I thought with a steady aim ; but whether the run had unsteadied me, or my gun, in which I now placed but little faith, played me false, I do not know ; anyhow, instead of giving the buffalo a dead shot, as I ought to have done, I apparently did him no harm, and, indeed, do not know whether I hit him at all, for when I fired, he went off again at a gallop.   I followed him till the sun was well down, but never saw him again, and returned to the bull I had first killed, very ill satisfied, for I had wounded and lost two animals, and only secured one.

That night we slept without water alongside the carcase, and early the next morning cut up the meat and went to the native kraal we had seen the day before.   These people informed me that from here to the junction of the Umfule and Umniati rivers it was only a short two days' walk, but over very rough country.   After asking two or three different men about it, and comparing their statements, I came to the conclusion that they were really endeavouring to speak the truth, which is as much as can be expected from a Kafir ; so I determined to get back to our encampment, and return here with Jameson as soon as possible, that we might solve the problem for ourselves.

As soon as my boys had finished buying meal and ground-nuts with their buffalo meat, I once more made a start, and slept at a small stream not far from the Umfule.   Both on this night and the preceding, lions roared not far from my camp.   About mid-day on the following day I got back to our big camp, and found that Jameson had arrived just before me. He had found no buffaloes, but had shot two black rhinoceroses, besides some smaller game. Old Lo Magondi was still here with half his tribe, women and children, all of whom were trying to get outside of as much sea-cow meat as possible. Poles had been cut and raised upon uprights in every direction, all of which were red or white, with festoons of meat and fat. Some of the meat smelt very high, for Lo Magondi's people had let one sea-cow go bad before they cut it up ; I do really think that they like half-putrid meat better than fresh. The trees that surrounded the pool were covered one and all with the griffon and little black vultures, and here and there sat a couple of the carrion-eating marabout storks, eyeing the bones and ribs of the five sea-cows, now well picked, which strewed the rocks at the lower end of the pool. As soon as darkness set in, hyænas began to approach from every direction, and laughed and screamed and howled over the remains of the feast in a manner that must be heard to be appreciated.

In the middle of the night, when the fires were burning low, old Lo Magondi, who always slept at our skerm amongst our Kafirs, suddenly jumped up and called to our boys to make up the fires, as there was a lion close to us. Though I was awake I had heard nothing ; but soon after the boys had rekindled the fires, a low, deep growl, of disappointment, I suppose, broke the silence of the night—such a growl as can only issue from the throat of a lion ; the deep sullen sound was twice repeated, seemingly within fifty yards of where we lay, and then all again was still, nor were we further disturbed that night. The brute must have been sneaking about trying to steal some meat, for the old man said he had heard him just behind his head, walking over the dead leaves. Small game is very scarce about here, and that lion was doubtless hungry ; so that the man who had gone out into the darkness behind our skerm just before he growled would have had, I fancy, a bad time of it.

HORNS OF WHITE RHINOCEROS (*Rhinoceros simus*) ♂
Shot in the Mashuna Country, between the Umzweswe and Umniati rivers, July 1880.   Scale 1 inch to the foot.

CHAPTER XXII

Ancient track of Hippopotami—Starving Hippos to death—Elephant-
hunt—Mountainous Country—Buffaloes—Rhinoceros—Paddling
a dead Hippo—Nasty Accident—Lionesses.

EARLY the next morning we packed up our traps,
divided the sea-cow meat, now pretty well dry,
amongst our Kafirs, and bidding good-bye to Lo
Magondi, whom we voted to be a very decent old
fellow if it were not for his begging propensities,
made a start for the Banyai village on the Umniati,
where I had already been, and from whence we had
determined to make a trip to its junction with the
Umfule. We crossed again at the Beaconsfield
Cataracts, and early the following day reached the
Umniati, crossing a good deal of buffalo spoor on
the way ; then, leaving some of the boys to make
a camp, we took the rest and went out to look for
fresh meat. Jameson went up the river and knocked
over two fine old waterbuck bulls with a right and
left shot from his 500 Express. I also shot one at
a little distance from the river.

The following day we were up betimes, and
leaving Bokkie and three boys to look after the
bulk of our traps, started with the rest for the
junction of the rivers, taking our blankets, some
ammunition, and provisions for a week. We first

went to the kraal—about a mile down the river—
where, by the offer of ten loaded cartridges, we got
a man to go with us as guide, it being at the
same time understood that we were, if possible, to
shoot him a buffalo or sea-cow, in which expectation he took with him three young fellows to help
carry the meat.   At this kraal the people had a
large canoe with which they cross the river when it
is flooded in the rainy season.   After half an hour's
delay, we again made a start, and for about three
hours kept along a well-beaten Kafir footpath, running in a north-easterly direction parallel with and
not far from the Umniati.   We then left the path,
which our guide told us led to another kraal on the
banks of the river, and about eleven o'clock reached
a large hole of water in the bed of a dry stream.
At this place it was evident from the spoors that
several black rhinoceroses were in the habit of
drinking nightly.   Here we made a cup of tea and
fried some meat, and then pushed on again ; the
country had not been very level all the morning,
but we now got into a mass of hills of a very rough,
broken character ; we saw no small game, but a
good many black rhinoceros spoors.   Whenever we
topped a higher hill than usual, the prospect that
met our eyes was always the same—an unbroken
succession of wooded hills, that stretched as far as
the eye could reach towards the north, north-west,
and north-east.

Upon reaching another deep gully with a pool of
water in its bed about three in the afternoon, our
guide told us that we must sleep here, as the next
water was a long way ahead.   Here, as at the last
pool, there was a good deal of rhinoceros spoor, so,
leaving all the Kafirs but our gun-carriers to make

a camp, Jameson and I went for a ramble, taking
different directions in order to cover more ground ;
neither of us, however, saw anything. A four hours'
walk through a hilly country brought us the following morning to the banks of the Umfule. At the
point where we struck the river we found a large
pool enclosed on all sides by a thick hedge, and on
the beach the remains of a lot of huts and poles for
drying meat showed where a large number of people
had made temporary homes. Here, our guide
informed us, his people had last year starved to
death and slaughtered a herd of seven hippopotami.

As a few days later we had an opportunity of observing this process of starving a herd of these animals
to death in a large pool in the Umniati, about which
I shall in due course give some account, I will here
say nothing more concerning this cruel and ex-
terminating practice. Close to this place I wounded
a waterbuck, and whilst following its spoor, came
upon another herd, one of which Jameson shot ; he
had hardly put a fresh cartridge into his rifle, when
two wild pigs (wart hogs) rushed past him, one of
which he bowled over in fine style, as it dashed at
full speed down the hill. About here the river runs
through a succession of rocky gorges, dashing over
huge boulders of basaltic rock. Through these
ravines hippopotami must have wandered for count-
less ages, for in one place where a ledge of rock ran
along the bank of the river, they had worn a path
for about twenty yards across it, at least four inches
deep into the hard stone. This path worn into the
solid rock was the very facsimile of those recently
made in soft ground, having the slight ridge all
along the centre which I have before described.

Now, from the nature of the river, and the sparse-

ness of vegetation along its banks, I do not think
that hippopotami could ever have been much more
plentiful about here than they are at the present
day ; so that as they do not every night make use
of the same path, the time required by them to
wear a track four inches deep with their soft feet
in this excessively hard rock, seems almost beyond
calculation.

Late in the afternoon of this same day, as we
were approaching a small stream, an old buffalo bull
jumped out of the long grass in front of us, and
rushing down the bank climbed out on the farther
side ; upon reaching the top he turned to take a
look at us, standing broadside on.   I only had my
little Express in my hands, and Jameson was some
distance behind, so I aimed for his lungs, high up
behind the shoulder, as I was afraid that the hollow
bullet would not penetrate the thick flesh and
shoulder-blade that would have to be pierced before
a bullet could reach his heart.   On receiving the
shot he galloped away at full speed, and we heard
him clattering over the stony ridge beyond ; we
were, however, soon on his spoor, which, from the
quantity of blood he evidently threw out from his
mouth and nostrils, was easy enough to follow ; we
had not very far to go, as we came upon him lying
dead, about 300 yards from where I had fired at
him.   Upon cutting him up we found that the
little bullet had gone through the centre of both
lungs.   That night we slept alongside of the carcase,
after being informed by our guide that we should
reach the junction of the rivers early on the following day.

August 11*th*.—Up at daylight, and after a two
hours' scramble over the great masses of rock through

which the Umfule here runs, at last reached its junction with the Umniati. Although there are large deep pools of water, the home of the hippopotamus, more than a hundred miles nearer the sources of the former river, it only pours a narrow stream of water three or four yards wide and knee-deep into the Umniati at this season of the year. The Umniati itself is narrow and rocky just at this point, but a little below the junction it opens out into a sandy bed, fully 400 yards broad, through which two or three narrow channels of water find their way.

Just below where the waters of the two rivers met, there was a fine deep-blue pool, in which a herd of about ten hippopotami were disporting themselves. They evidently did not know anything of firearms, and appeared to be as unconcerned at our presence, and as unsuspicious of danger, as the hippopotami are when inspected by visitors at the Zoological Gardens. For some time we sat on the rocks at the edge of the pool, and the uncouth-looking beasts kept coming to the surface not more than thirty yards from us, staring at us in a stolid, lazy sort of way, and then again sinking to the bottom. Our guide now clamoured loudly for us to shoot one for him, and as our boys and we ourselves also wanted some more fat meat, Jameson killed a fat cow. As the pool was very narrow, we might easily have shot them all, but, with the exception of this one, we did not molest them in any way.

During the heat of the day we occupied ourselves in superintending the cutting up of the meat, and in jotting down the directions of the two rivers by compass.

The Umniati here runs to the north-east, and the Umfule enters it almost at right angles. About

four miles below the junction, however, the united
Umniati runs right against a chain of hills, and then
taking a sudden turn flows along their base towards
the north-west, which is the general course it must
hold until it finally empties itself into the Zambesi,
just at the entrance of the Kariba Gorge.

The following day we remained where we were
in order to partially dry the meat, and on the 13th
started on our return journey, following the course
of the Umniati all the way. Of this journey there
is but one circumstance to record, and that is our
coming upon a party of Kafirs engaged in starving a
herd of hippopotami to death. The pool in which the
poor brutes were enclosed was a large one, over two
hundred yards broad and about four hundred in
length. On the farther side, where the bank was
low, a thick hedge had been made all along the water's
edge, behind which several temporary huts had been
erected ; above and below the pool, where the river
ran in several streams amongst little bushy islands
and rocks, strong dams had also been made and
more huts erected. On our side of the river the
bank was about twelve feet high and very steep, so
that egress from the fatal pool was impossible for
the poor prisoners, unless indeed they could muster
up courage to make a rush and burst their way
through one of the barriers, and this, even when in
the last extremity of hunger, they do not appear
ever to attempt. When we came to the pool there
were still ten living hippopotami in it ; eight of
these seemed to be standing on a bank in the middle
of the water, as more than half their bodies were exposed ; the poor brutes were all huddled up in a
mass, each with his upraised head resting on another's
body. It was a very pitiful sight ; two more were

swimming about, each with a very heavily-shafted
assegai sticking in his back ; these assegais are
plunged into them at night when the starving beasts
come near the fences seeking for a means of exit
from their horrible prison.   Besides these ten living
hippopotami, two dead ones were being cut up in a
corner of the pool, and many more must have already
succumbed to hunger and assegai wounds, for all
round the pool festoons of meat were hanging upon
poles to dry, and besides this, there were at least a
hundred natives, men, women, and children, encamped
round about, all of whom were living upon nothing
but hippopotamus meat.

As far as I could make out, these poor animals
had been enclosed for about three weeks, and it was
self-evident that the survivors were all but played out,
for it must be remembered that as the Umniati here
runs over either sand or stone, there is no vegetation
whatever in the bed of the river, and therefore, as
the natives remarked, the poor brutes had nothing
but water with which to sustain life.   Judging by
the amount of meat we saw drying, I calculated
that when the remaining ten hippopotami had died
or been killed, not less than twenty of these animals
would have been destroyed at one fell swoop.
Although this mode of circumventing and killing
game must be most revolting to all men with any
humane or sportsmanlike feeling about them, yet,
after all, the natives can scarcely be blamed for
employing the only means in their power of obtaining
a supply of animal food ; for they have no firearms,
and trust entirely to pitfalls, and traps of the above
description, for killing large game ; at any rate,
when they do kill anything, nothing is wasted, and
is it not too much to say that out of these twenty

hippopotami not a pound of meat, and but very little of the hides, was allowed to rot. I do not think that these natives often succeed in enclosing such a large herd, and I fancy that usually the greater part of the animals manage to get out at nights before the dams are completed ; otherwise hippopotami could not be so numerous as they are, both on this river and the Umfule.

The following day, the 16th, we again reached our camp, and found Bokkie and the three Kafirs we had left there in a great state of excitement, and busy packing up the things, with the intention, in case we did not return, of sleeping at the native village down the river, because the night before a lion had paid them a visit and frightened them considerably. It appeared that in the middle of the night one of the Kafirs had awakened, and sitting up, saw a large male lion standing in the moonlight not ten yards in front of him ; he gave a yell of fear, and sprang to his feet, upon which the lion at once bolted ; they had then kept up the fires and sat up talking till morning, fearing that their unwelcome visitor might return, which they felt sure he would do to-night. At first I thought the fellow was rather drawing upon his imagination when he said the lion had been so near, but upon asking him to show me the spoor, he pointed out the footprints of a large lion, plainly enough discernible in the sandy ground ; the brute had walked slowly up to within ten paces of the fire, and then turned round and gone off at a run, frightened, I suppose, by the shouting of the Kafir. Upon further examination, I found he had come along a footpath running near the bank of the river, and that evening I set a gun across the path, hoping that he would return, but he did not.

The following morning we again struck camp and started homewards, intending to follow the course of the Umniati, and, later on, its tributary the Umzweswe, from which river we could strike across to our camp on the Umfule. In order to avoid the hills, at whose base the river ran, we kept away at some distance from its banks, and had been walking for about three hours through leafless, dreary-looking mopani forests and patches of dense scrub, when we emerged upon a large open valley, where we saw feeding several herds of zebras and a large troop of impala antelopes.

We at once guessed there was water not far off, and soon afterwards found a beautiful vley covered with water-lilies,[1] and surrounded by some fine wide-spreading thorns, amongst them a huge old wild fig-tree, whose thick dark-green foliage offered a splendid shade. On the surface of the vley several of the large black-and-white spur-winged geese were slowly swimming to and fro, not to mention a large flock of wild duck or teal. There was, too, a good deal of black rhinoceros, buffalo, and other game spoor about, that showed it to be a favourite drinking-place ; indeed, whilst we were breakfasting, a herd of koodoos came down the opposite slope, walking slowly and warily towards the water ; upon seeing us, however, they bounded away again, and soon regained the shelter of the bush.

Our meal over, we filled our calabashes with water, and struck away to the south-west, intending to curve down towards the river in the afternoon. We had been walking in this direction for maybe two hours, and had just emerged from a large patch

---

[1] Rather smaller than our own, but of a pale beautiful forget-me-not blue.

of very thick bush, a splendid cover for either elephants or buffaloes, upon a tract of open forest, devoid of underwood ; here every blade of grass had been burnt off by a recent fire, and the stunted trees, denuded of leaves, had their trunks scorched black by the flames, the whole landscape presenting a picture of dreary desolation. My gun-carrier, April, was leading, I being just behind him, and Jameson behind me. Suddenly I heard Jameson say excitedly, " Look, man ! look ! elephants, by God ! " and upon looking where he pointed, straight ahead, I saw two elephant bulls coming towards us at a quick walk. Hastily throwing up a little sand to see that the wind was right, we knelt down and prepared to receive them. Unfortunately, the Kafir who carried Jameson's heavy rifle was right behind, so that he had to trust to his Express, which, though a splendid weapon of its kind, is not the sort of rifle one would choose for elephant-shooting. However, there was nothing else to be done ; the two mighty beasts were fast approaching, one behind the other, at a quick pace, bringing their huge ears forward with a twitch at every step. We had a splendid view of them : the sight was nothing new to me, but yet my heart beat fast with excitement, and what my friend's feelings must have been—for it was the first wild elephant his eyes had ever beheld wandering free and unfettered in its native wilds—I leave to any lover of the wilder sports to imagine.

The elephants were now almost abreast of us, and about sixty yards off. The first was a big full-grown bull, but the tusk on our side, which was all we could see, was broken short off, not far beyond the lip ; the other was a younger and smaller animal,

but showed two long, even, white tusks, projecting
far beyond the lip. "Wait till they get square and
then shoot the second one," I said to my friend ;
"I will take the one in front." In another moment
they were broadside to us, and not over fifty yards
off. "Now then!" I whispered, and we fired almost
simultaneously. I ought to have shot my bull right
through the heart, but my rifle was a most execrable
weapon (the one before mentioned), upon which no
dependence whatever could be placed ; so that I
never knew whether to attribute the loss of an
animal to my own bad shooting or to the fault of
my rifle. Like lightning the great brutes swung
themselves round on their hind-legs, and went off
at top speed, we following at our best pace. Jameson's elephant was probably but little the worse for
the two expanding Express bullets that he carried
in his ribs, and mine appeared to be equally lively.
As my friend waited, shouting and cursing, for the
Kafir to come up with his big rifle, I got on ahead,
and soon found myself alone with my gun-carrier
April, a strong active Makalaka, and a Matabele
boy named Jonas. After a severe run of half a
mile or so, the elephants settled to a steadier pace,
and we, going at a smart trot, began again to over-
haul them. Soon I was not more than eighty yards
astern of them, April in close attendance, and Jonas,
who had run a little wide, ranging up level with
them. "Tiba, tiba, Jonas !" I shouted, upon which
he, a Kafir who understands elephant-shooting, made
a spurt, and, when level with the foremost, shouted
as loud as he could yell ; at the first shout the
elephants wheeled quickly away from the sound,
giving me, who had run a little wide of them on
the opposite side in expectation of this move, a

splendid broadside shot at about sixty yards' distance. Taking a hasty aim I fired ; to my disgust the cap did not explode, but on cocking again, and taking a second aim, it went off.   I had fired at my own elephant, and soon saw that the shot had taken effect, for he slackened his speed at once, and his companion, with a generosity which did him credit, but cost him dear, did the same.   They now walked side by side at a good swinging pace, with which, however, I could keep up without any great exertion.

I now gave Jameson's elephant a shot just at the root of the tail, upon which he at once stopped, and wheeling to the right, stood broadside to me.   My elephant also stopped, standing just in front of him. Pushing in another cartridge I gave him a second ball about the shoulder, when he wheeled towards us and came on with head raised and ears outspread at a half run.   I think there is little doubt that he wanted to charge, and was trying to make us out. I stood perfectly still with my rifle at full cock, April crouched behind me.   This is the best thing to do in such cases, as, so long as you are motionless and the wind does not betray you, an elephant seems to think that you are a tree or something inanimate, and will stand quite close to you without appearing to make you out ; but if you only move, he knows at once what you are.   My friend was now coming unpleasantly near — indeed, he was within twenty yards, so, just as he passed a tree, I put a bullet fair into his chest, upon which he reeled backwards and swerved off to one side, where Jameson, who had come up with his big rifle, saluted him with a couple more balls.   My elephant now moved on again, so I went after him, leaving Jameson to finish his.   I killed mine about a mile farther on, in the centre of the patch of thick bush through which we had come in the morning.

He was evidently a very old animal, not having any hair left on his tail. Unfortunately he had only one tusk, and that was broken off a few inches beyond the lip. This tusk, when weighed at the waggon, turned the scale at 32 lbs.; on the following day we measured him carefully, taking a straight line between two assegais placed parallel, one at his shoulder, the other at the sole of his foot. Thus measured, he must have stood 9 feet 11 inches in vertical height at the shoulder;[1] of course the top of his back would have been some inches higher.

We were just leaving my elephant when Jameson came up with the rest of the Kafirs. He had despatched his also, and we went back to where it lay in the open burnt forest. It was comparatively a young bull, but carried fine tusks for its size, long and very white; they weighed 32 lbs. and 34 lbs. respectively. We slept that night beside the dead elephant, without water, or grass to make a camp with—Jameson upon one of the huge ears, and I upon a square flap of skin. At the first streak of dawn we sent some boys back to the vley we had left the preceding day to get water, and upon their return made a capital breakfast off elephant's heart, roasted upon a forked stick before the fire, and then set to work to chop out the tusks.

When the boys I had sent to my elephant returned to us with its single tusk, they reported that they had seen fresh elephant spoor. It was then

[1] Two more old bull elephants, subsequently shot by Mr. Jameson and myself, and carefully measured in a similar manner, must have stood 10 feet and 10 feet 4 inches at the shoulder respectively. The tusks of the smaller of these two elephants weighed 50 lbs. apiece.

too late to do anything, but we thought our best plan would be to go back again to the vley we had left, and hunt about for a few days. This we did, and making a comfortable camp, remained there eight days, hunting the country round about, and returning every evening to our vley. We were unfortunate with elephants, for twice we got close to some of them in the thick bush, but they must have detected our tread upon the dead leaves, for we only heard them crashing through the branches, and never even saw them.

These thickets we found to be full of buffaloes, which drank in the river, passing the noontide heat in the shade of the thick bush. Almost every day we saw large herds of them, and might have killed several, but we only shot two cows for food.

The open valley in front of the vley of which 1 have before spoken was a great resort of zebras, sometimes as many as a hundred of these beautiful animals standing round us in troops of from ten to thirty, as we crossed it on our way to or from camp. There were also great numbers of the graceful little oribi antelopes always to be seen in twos and threes in this valley.

One day we did not get back to camp from our day's hunting till about ten o'clock at night ; we had had a hard day of it, and a most toilsome walk home in the dark through the thick thorny bush. When we reached the valley on the other side of which, at a distance of about two miles, our camp was situated, the moon was well up, and cast a soft, subdued light over the long dry grass. We were stepping along the edge of the valley in single file, following a game path, when the leading Kafir stopped, and pointing across the vley, said, " Ini loco " (What's

that ?) adding, " There's a rhinoceros " ; and looking
in the direction he pointed, we saw something dark
looming in the moonlight ; it was coming towards
us and we soon saw plainly that it was a black
rhinoceros.   When he was about thirty yards from,
and half facing us, we both fired, dropping him on
his knees ; however, he was up again in an instant,
and wheeling round, went off at a gallop, snorting
loudly, across the open valley.   We followed the
path, plainly perceptible in the moonlight, that he
had made through the long thick grass ; by sweeping
our hands along it we could feel that it was wet
with blood, and we returned to camp, determined
to take up the spoor again on the morrow.

Thus, at an early hour the following day, we
were once more upon his blood-stained tracks.   For
about a mile he had never stopped galloping, and all
the time had been throwing blood in jets from
his nostrils in astonishing quantities, so that we
knew he had been struck in the lungs, and expected
to find him dead at every instant.   After a time,
however, the blood almost ceased flowing, and he
seemed to have settled down to a very slow walk,
as we had great difficulty in following his spoor ; but
one of my Makalakas, with a patience and sagacity
which would have done credit to a Bushman, got it
away into some softer ground, and we then went
along briskly for several miles till we came to a place
where the animal had lain down and rolled in the
sand ; here there was a pool of blood.   A little
farther on we found a second place where he had
been lying, and we then thought he was about done
for, but we were greatly mistaken ; he seemed to have
once more arisen, like a giant refreshed, and led us
for many a mile, always holding one course towards

a large patch of thick bush which we knew of. At last, still sticking to his spoor, we entered the bush, and I felt sure that we should find him dead or alive within that sombre thicket. A quarter of an hour later we found a place from which he had only just risen ; he had evidently heard us. I was peering about in front of me when I suddenly saw him standing, half-facing us, perfectly still and motionless ; the next instant we both fired. For a short distance he crashed through the dense scrub, and then pulled up, when another bullet from my friend's rifle finished him.

He must have heard us approaching as we trod upon the thickly-strewn leaves, and in such dense bush had a splendid opportunity for a charge, yet he never attempted it. Upon cutting him up we found that only one of us had hit him on the preceding evening, and that the bullet had raked one lung, which accounted for the quantity of blood he had thrown from his nostrils. This lung was quite white-looking and empty of blood, except that portion discoloured by the bullet wound.

Upon returning to camp we found some natives who had come to cut up the elephant left in the thick bush, and which, except that his tusks had been chopped out, and his trunk cut off, had not been disturbed by us. This carcase we had passed almost daily during the last week, and on the preceding evening the hyænas must have torn it open for the first time, as the stench was sickening, at a distance of at least half a mile below the wind ; and now these men were going to cut up and eat the putrid, stinking meat, which had lain eight days and nights festering beneath the fierce rays of a tropical sun ! Truly some tribes of Kafirs and Bushmen are fouler

To face page 485.

HIPPOPOTAMI AT HOME; LOWER UMNIATI RIVER, AUGUST 23, 1880.

feeders than either vultures or hyænas.   This is not
an isolated case, as they are constantly in the habit of
eating putrid meat, and there is little doubt that they
like it just as well as, if not better than, good, sweet
flesh ; curiously, too, it does not seem to do them
any harm.

It was on the second day after we had turned our
faces homewards, as we were following the course
of the river, that we heard a hippopotamus blow in
the pool below us, from which we were separated by
a narrow strip of bush.   Making our way through
this and climbing down the steep bank, we beheld a
scene interesting at once both to the sportsman and
to the naturalist.

Upon a spit of white sand which jutted into the
pool from the opposite bank, stood, high and dry, a
herd of at least twenty hippopotami, their huge,
bulky carcases looking, as they all stood huddled
together, like so many great black rocks.   Exactly
opposite to us, motionless as a statue, with ears
pricked and gaze fixed intently upon us, stood a
noble old waterbuck bull, poised upon a ledge of
rock overhanging the water.   From just below ou
feet a skein of about a dozen of the handsome
Egyptian geese winged their way across the deep-blue
pool, whilst a pair of the large white-headed fish
eagles wheeled in rapid circles above the whole scene.
The waterbuck soon made up his mind tnat we were
dangerous neighbours, and climbing the steep bank
above him quickly disappeared amongst the bushes.
The hippopotami, however, though we were in full
view and only about 250 yards from them, did not seem
to notice us, but stood quite motionless and apparently
asleep, except that now and then one would move
his enormous head slowly to the one side or the

other. We might have crept down to the edge of
the water and fired upon them, as they stood from
within a hundred yards, but both Jameson and myself
felt it would not be quite the thing to do so, and
preferred to let them get into the river, where, as
the pool a little below them was both broad and long,
they would have a fair chance for life. At length
they heard us talking, and commenced, one after the
other, to walk into the river. When their bodies
were half immersed they let themselves down with a
splash, and either swam into deep water with just
the tips of their heads out, or dived out of sight at
once ; I suppose there must have been a ledge beside
which the water deepened suddenly. There were
some quite small calves amongst them, and these
little beasts all ran into the water with a splash, whilst
the full-grown animals stepped in slowly and sedately.
As we only wished to kill two, which would furnish
us with a sufficient supply of fat meat to last us on
our way back to the waggons, and were anxious not
to wound any more, we were a long time before firing
a shot. At length, however, finding themselves undisturbed, they gained more confidence and kept their
heads longer above water, so that a little before sundown we each struck a large cow fair in the head.
Jameson caught his under the ear, whilst I shot mine
from behind, right between the ears. They sank
at once, and though we thought we had killed them
we were not absolutely sure, and as the carcases
would not rise for several hours the question could
not be settled before the morrow.

At daylight the next morning we were at the
water's edge, and at once saw that two dead hippopotami had floated to the top during the night ; all
the rest of the herd had taken advantage of the

darkness to beat a retreat to some other part of the river. One of the dead hippos was already in the shallow water at the tail of the pool, but the other had been taken by the wind to the other side and was now stationary against the bank exactly opposite us. This was very awkward, as it necessitated our carrying the meat nearly three-quarters of a mile round the pool although the carcase was only the breadth of the river (about 250 yards) from our camp. Under these circumstances I determined to go round and paddle the now inflated and buoyant carcase to our side ; this I accomplished with the aid of a thick stick for a paddle. It was rather difficult to keep one's balance, as the body rolled most alarmingly from side to side, and when I was just in the middle of the river, aided by a strong breeze, the slippery carcase heeled over so much, that I could not maintain my seat astride of it, but fell off into the water. The pool was full of crocodiles, or at any rate I thought it was, so I lost no time in regaining my position, for the thought that my naked legs might attract the attention of one of these voracious monsters added tenfold to the strength of my exertions ; I then paddled quietly to the bank just below our camp, and by sundown our boys had cut up every scrap of the two hippos. I may here mention that I shot my animal with a hollow 450 Express bullet. At dusk when I went down to the remains of the carcase I found a lot of large barbers [1] tugging away at the shreds of meat that still adhered to the bones.

The two following days we remained where we were, drying the meat ; on the second day

[1] A species of siluroid fish, common, I believe, to most African rivers, and called barbers by the Cape colonists.

I went out for a stroll, and whilst running down a steep, stony hill, rifle in hand, in pursuit of a black rhinoceros which I had wounded, fell heavily, and jamming my hand between my rifle and a stone, tore the nail of my middle finger clean out ; however, although it looked a nasty place, it gave me no trouble, but healed up right away by first intention. There is nothing, I should fancy, like elephant-hunting on foot to keep the blood in good order.

In the afternoon we were visited by a small party of Matabele hunters ; they told us what we already knew—that elephants were very scarce this year, and that they themselves had only killed a calf. Just after they left our camp we heard a shot, and soon one of them came running back to say that he had killed an "imbabala," and asking if I would buy the skin. This I was very glad to do, and for a few cartridges I obtained the skin, horns, and skull of a fine spotted bushbuck ram ; it proved, too, a very interesting specimen, being an intermediate type between the dark-coloured, slightly spotted bushbuck of the Cape Colony, and the beautifully striped and spotted bushbuck found to the north-west, on the banks of the Chobe. The next morning we again continued our journey, following the course of the river ; during the forenoon the walking was pretty good, but by mid-day we again got amongst a lot of stony hills, up and down which we clambered during the rest of the day. Just as the sun was sinking we reached the junction of the Umzweswe river with the Umniati, and here we camped for the night. The next morning we followed the course of the Umzweswe, which we found ran over a rocky bed full of immense boulders, between a series of high and precipitous hills. First we tried following the

river's bed, a task of no small difficulty, owing to
the great boulders over which we had continually to
climb.   It was not so bad for us who had only our
rifles to carry, but some of our Kafirs had loads of
from 30 to 40 lbs., and these poor fellows had a very
rough time of it.   We then tried keeping away from
the river among the hills, but here we found the
ravines so steep and frequent, that we took to the
river again.   At last about twelve o'clock, we emerged
from the hills, and during the rest of the day travelled
over a comparatively level country, always following
the course of the stream.   During the day, besides
waterbucks and klipspringers, we saw three magnificent old koodoo bulls ; and when night came, we
slept on a little island in the river.

The following morning we continued our journey,
always keeping along the river's bank, until about
mid-day, when we reached a chain of hills at a little
distance from the river.   My boy Jonas now knew
the country, and as he said it would be our best plan
to leave the Zweswe here, and strike across due east
to the Umfule, we determined to follow his advice.
During the whole morning we had seen troop after
troop of waterbucks and impala antelopes, and in a
valley which we reached just after leaving the river
we found an immense mixed herd of these animals
quietly feeding, besides a lot of wild pigs.   It was
not long after this, that, as we were walking along
in single file, Jonas leading, I saw, just from the corner
of my eye, and during just a second of time, a lioness
enter a patch of grass away to our left.   However,
though the vision was so momentary, I was quite
certain that it was no delusion.   Here was another
chance for Jameson to get what he so much coveted
—a lion ; for although he had wounded one before,

it managed to make its escape. The long grass I
have spoken of was a little patch about ten yards
square, which had somehow escaped the grass fire
that shortly before had swept over the whole country.
On one side it was separated by scarcely twenty
yards from a patch of forest and scrub, and it was
from this side that I had seen the lioness enter it.
On the other side lay an open valley as bare of cover
as a billiard-table.   Close to the farther side of the
patch of grass stood a single mopani tree.   Jameson
and I now advanced with our rifles on full cock, my
friend being ready to take the first shot.   We had
got right up to the grass without seeing anything,
and I had just said, " Well, I know she went in here ;
go round that side," when, with a startled sort of
purr, a lioness followed by a cub sprang through the
grass, and gained the shelter of the bush without
giving either of us a chance of a shot.   She had come
from the foot of the mopani tree, and as our eyes
were again turned there, another lioness, that must
have been asleep, stood up, and with her hind-quarters
turned towards us, stood looking fixedly right away
from where we were : at the same time I saw that a
half-grown cub was still lying at the foot of the tree,
watching us intently.   At that instant Jameson fired,
dropping the lioness in her tracks, and then let go
the second barrel at the cub as it made for the bush.
The lioness was dead, my friend's bullet having
caught her in the neck just behind the head.   We
found that these lions had killed an eland cow
just within the edge of the forest, and the one I so
opportunely saw must just have been coming from
a luncheon off the carcase, to join the other under
the mopani tree.

The next day we had a very long walk, as we

stuck at it, with few and short intervals of rest, until sundown, when we camped beside a stream running beneath a hill which we had taken to be our old friend "Intaba-go-Umbundwan."

On the morrow, however (August 30), making an early start, we did reach the hill in question by nine o'clock, and by two P.M. the same afternoon once more got home again to our waggons, after an absence of nearly six weeks.

From this date until the rains commenced to fall, I continued hunting on horseback, sometimes alone, at others in company with Mr. Jameson ; but as no very stirring incidents happened during that time, and as the country through which I hunted, and the game I encountered, was for the most part similar to that met with in 1878, I think the reader will agree with me, that any detailed account of my proceedings would be superfluous.

In November we left the hunting-grounds of the Mashuna country, and trekked out to Gubulawayo, where we spent a few pleasant days with Mr. James Fairbairn, the well-known Matabele trader. This gentleman's name I have, I think, mentioned more than once in the course of these pages ; but let me here assure him, on the chance that these lines may some day meet his eye, that the many acts of kindness I have received at his hands, and the many pleasant days—and nights—I have spent from time to time, during my visits to the Matabele country, beneath the homely but hospitable roof of "New Valhalla" will ever live green in my memory.

In December we bade adieu to Lobengula, and again started southwards, and journeying slowly along, enjoying a little shooting here and there, reached Bamangwato towards the end of the month, where we spent a very merry Christmas with Mr. John Bennion and some of the other resident traders and their wives.

The outbreak of the war in the Transvaal, just at this juncture, prevented our travelling through that state, as had been our intention, so we journeyed along the borders of the Kalahari desert to Griqualand, and ultimately reached the Diamond Fields on 15th February 1881, after having been much delayed on the road by heavy rains.

I here disposed of my waggon, oxen, and horses, and went down by passenger-cart to Port Elizabeth, where I soon afterwards took ship for England, which I reached, after a very fine and quick passage, early the following April.

My work is now over, and should my pages have afforded either amusement or instruction to any sportsman-naturalist, or supplied definite information to any roving spirit, whose inclinations bid him bend his steps towards the splendid hunting-grounds which still exist in the far interior of South Africa, I shall feel amply compensated for the time and trouble that the compilation of this volume has cost me.

List of Game Shot during the Year 1879

Jan. 25. Two tsessebe antelopes (Impaqui river).
    30. One Burchell's zebra (Macloutsie river).
Feb. 3. One blue wildebeest (Serule river).

Feb. 13. Two hartebeests (Boatlanarma).
    28. Three blesbucks (Transvaal flats).

Notuane River

April 5. One steinbuck.
    6. Three impala antelopes.
One serval (tiger-cat).

April 7. One licluse jackal.
One steinbuck.

Mahakabe Vley

April 22. One Burchell's zebra.
    23. One steinbuck.
Two elands.

April 25. Two blue wildebeests.
    27. Two elands (Inkouäne vley).

Botletlie River

May 8. Three giraffes.
One lion.
    10. One impala antelope.
One great-crested bustard.

May 11. One gemsbuck cow.
    15. One gemsbuck cow.
    16. One giraffe cow.
    18. One eland cow.

Between the Botletlie and Sode-Garra

May 20. One eland cow.
    22. One giraffe.

May 26. Three elands.

Mãbãbe River

June 4. Two lionesses.
    6. One great-crested bustard.
Two lions.

June 6. Two giraffes.
    12. Two elands.
    15. Three buffaloes.

Machabe River

June 19. One wildebeest bull.
Two impala antelopes
One reedbuck ram.
One reedbuck.

June 20. One lechwe ram.
    21. One blue wildebeest.
    22. Three buffaloes.

Sunta Outlet

June 28. Two lechwe rams.
One reedbuck ram.

June 30. One lechwe ram.
One wart hog.

Chobe River, near Mai-ini's Town

July 2. One hippopotamus.
5. One black rhinoceros.

July 5. Three buffaloes.
11. Three impala rams.

Sunta Outlet

July 12. One lechwe ram.
13. One lechwe ram.
14. One tsessebe bull.
15. One wart hog.

July 15. One koodoo bull.
One sable antelope bull.
Two buffaloes.
20. One waterbuck bull.

Chobe River, near Linyanti

July 22. Three buffaloes.
24. Two lechwe rams.
26. Two spotted bushbucks.
27. One spotted bushbuck.
28. Three elephants.
30. One koodoo cow.
Aug. 2. One buffalo cow.
6. One buffalo bull.
One sable antelope bull.
8. Two buffaloes.
9. One wart hog.
10. Two Burchell's zebras.

Aug. 12. Three buffaloes.
14. One impala ram.
17. One koodoo.
18. Two buffaloes.
20. Six buffalo bulls.
21. One wildebeest bull.
22. One koodoo bull.
25. One impala antelope.
27. One koodoo.
30. One impala antelope.
Sept. 2. Three wildebeests (Mababe Flat).

Chobe River

Sept. 4. One sable antelope.
5. One buffalo cow.

Sept. 7. One buffalo cow.

Near Linyanti, between the Chobe and Zambesi

Sept. 8. One lechwe ram.
9. One Burchell's zebra.
10. One Burchell's zebra.
12. Two buffaloes.
13. One lioness.
16. One blue wildebeest.
Two buffaloes.

Sept. 18. One buffalo cow.
19. One buffalo cow.
20. Two buffaloes.
23. One Burchell's zebra.
25. Five elephants.
29. Two Burchell's zebras.
30. One reedbuck.

Chobe River, Southern Side

Oct. 4. One impala antelope.

Oct. 5. One impala antelope.

Mābābe Flat

Oct. 11. One blue wildebeest.
12. Three blue wildebeests.
14. Two blue wildebeests.
One tsessebe antelope.
17. One blue wildebeest.
One tsessebe antelope.
20. One lioness and a cub.
21. One roan antelope bull.

Oct. 21. Two Burchell's zebras.
22. One blue wildebeest.
24. Three blue wildebeests.
Two tsessebe antelopes.
26. One blue wildebeest.
Two Burchell's zebras.
27. One tsessebe bull (Gat-Garra).

Sunta Outlet

Oct. 28. One impala antelope.
One waterbuck bull.
29. One buffalo cow.
30. One elephant.
One reedbuck ram.
31. One reedbuck.
Nov. 1. Two reedbucks.
2. One reedbuck ram.

Nov. 3. One koodoo bull.
4. One wart hog.
5. One koodoo bull.
One reedbuck ram.
One buffalo cow.
6. One reedbuck ram.
7. One buffalo bull.
8. One impala antelope.

Mābābe River

Nov. 12. Three tsessebe antelopes.
14. Two tsessebe antelopes.
16. Two buffaloes.
21. Three tsessebe antelopes.

Nov. 23. Four buffaloes.
25. One steinbuck.
28. Two buffaloes.

Mābābe Flat

Nov. 30. One Burchell's zebra.
One ostrich.

Dec. 1. One ostrich.

Between the Mābābe and Botletlie Rivers

Dec. 3. One Burchell's zebra.
6. Nine zebras.
Two eland bulls.
8. One gemsbuck bull.
10. Two eland bulls.

Dec. 12. One gemsbuck bull.
16. One blue wildebeest.
20. One steinbuck ram.

TOTAL—229 head.

LIST OF GAME SHOT DURING THE YEAR 1880

In North-Eastern Mashuna Land

May 5. One koodoo antelope.
10. One zebra.
15. One koodoo antelope.

June 14. One waterbuck.
18. One sable antelope.
One zebra.

June 20. One koodoo.
    23. One tsessebe antelope.
    24. One lion.
    25. One waterbuck.
       Two tsessebe antelopes.
    26. Two zebras.
    27 One spotted hyæna.
    30. One tsessebe antelope.
       Two black rhinoceroses.
July   1. One python.
    2. One waterbuck.
    7. One lioness.
    8. One waterbuck.
    10. One tsessebe antelope.
       One roan antelope.
       One eland.
    13. One sable antelope.
    14. Two sable antelopes.
    15. One eland.
    16. One tsessebe antelope.
       Three lions.
    19. One reedbuck.
    20. One oribi antelope.
       One spotted hyæna
       One wart hog.
    23. Two zebras.
       One waterbuck.
    24. One oribi antelope.
    28. One waterbuck.
    31. Two hippopotami.
Aug.   3. One buffalo bull.
    8. One waterbuck.
    10. One buffalo bull.
    15. One elephant bull.
    18. One buffalo cow.
    19. One black rhinoceros.
    23. One hippopotamus.
    26. One klipspringer.
    28. One duiker.
Sept.   1. Two koodoo bulls.
    2. One oribi antelope.
       One cock ostrich.
    4. Two sable antelopes.
    5. One sable antelope.
    7. One zebra.
    8. One eland bull.

Sept. 10. One elephant bull.
    12. One sable antelope.
    14. One sable antelope.
    15. One sable antelope.
    17. One waterbuck.
    19. One roan antelope.
    22. One tsessebe.
       One sable antelope.
    23. One wart hog.
    24. One tsessebe antelope.
    26. One eland.
       One wart hog.
    28. One reedbuck.
    29. One reedbuck.
       One impala antelope.
Oct.   1. One reedbuck.
       One waterbuck.
       One koodoo.
    4. Two eland bulls.
    5. One eland bull.
    13. One sable antelope.
    16. One sable antelope.
    19. One koodoo bull.
       One black rhinoceros.
    22. Two tsessebe antelopes
    24. One steinbuck.
       Two tsessebe antelopes.
    26. One eland bull.
       One sable antelope.
Nov. 27. One koodoo bull.
       One steinbuck.
    28. One wart hog.
Dec.   2. One reedbuck.
       One steinbuck.
    4. One giraffe bull.
    5. One giraffe bull.
       One great-crested bustard.
    6. One steinbuck.
    9. Two steinbuck rams.
       One impala ram.
    14. One zebra.
    28. One hartebeest bull.
    29. Two springbucks.
    30. One impala ram.

TOTAL—112 head.

List of Game Shot between the 1st of January 1877 and the 31st of December 1880

Elephant	20	Zebra (Burchell's)	48
White rhinoceros	2	Wart hog	17
Black rhinoceros	10	Ostrich	3
Hippopotamus	4	Crested bustard	6
Giraffe	18	Lion	13
Buffalo	100	Spotted hyæna	3

Antelopes

Eland	39	Flat-horned hartebeest	3
Sable antelope	33	Tsessebe	42
Roan antelope	12	Blesbuck	3
Gemsbuck	4	Springbuck	3
Koodoo	19	Impala	29
Spotted bushbuck	5	Duiker	5
Waterbuck	19	Oribi	4
Lechwe	16	Steinbuck	16
Pookoo	5	Klipspringer	2
Reedbuck	19		
Blue wildebeest	23		548
Hartebeest	3		

2 K

INDEX

Lightning Source UK Ltd.
Milton Keynes UK
UKOW05f1852290813

216212UK00001B/339/A